HUMOR IN
IRISH LITERATURE

HUMOR IN IRISH LITERATURE

A Reference Guide

Don L. F. Nilsen

GREENWOOD PRESS
Westport, Connecticut • London

Library of Congress Cataloging-in-Publication Data

Nilsen, Don Lee Fred.
    Humor in Irish literature : a reference guide / Don L. F. Nilsen.
      p. cm.
    Includes bibliographical references and index.
    ISBN 0–313–29551–4 (alk. paper)
    1. English literature—Irish authors—History and criticism—
Bibliography. 2. Humorous stories, English—Irish authors—History
and criticism—Bibliography. 3. Humorous poetry, English—Irish
authors—History and criticism—Bibliography. 4. Irish wit and
humor—History and criticism—Bibliography. 5. Irish literature—
History and criticism—Bibliography. 6. Ireland—In literature—
Bibliography.   I. Title.
Z2039.W57N55   1996
[PR8815]
016.8209′9415—dc20   95–39489

British Library Cataloguing in Publication Data is available.

Library of Congress Catalog Card Number: 95–39489
ISBN: 0–313–29551–4

First published in 1996

Greenwood Press, 88 Post Road West, Westport, CT 06881
An imprint of Greenwood Publishing Group, Inc.

Printed in the United States of America

The paper used in this book complies with the
Permanent Paper Standard issued by the National
Information Standards Organization (Z39.48–1984).

10 9 8 7 6 5 4 3 2

Copyright Acknowledgments

The editor and publisher gratefully acknowledge permission to reprint excerpts from the following copyright material:

Lionel Abel. "Wrong and Right: The Art of Comedy" from *Salmagundi*, vol. 28 (1975). Reprinted by permission of *Salmagundi*.

Mark S. Auburn. *Sheridan's Comedies: Their Contexts and Achievements* (1977). Permission granted by the University of Nebraska Press.

Samuel Beckett. *Watt* and *Murphy*. The author and publisher thank the Samuel Beckett Estate and the Calder Educational Trust, London, for permission to quote from the prose works of Samuel Beckett: *Watt* copyright © Samuel Beckett 1953, 1963, 1970, 1976; *Murphy* copyright © Samuel Beckett 1938, 1963, 1977, and copyright © The Samuel Beckett Estate 1993 and by permission of Grove Atlantic Press.

From Robert H. Bell: *Jocoserious Joyce: The Fate of Folly in "Ulysses."* Copyright © 1991 by Cornell University. Used by permission of the publisher, Cornell University Press.

Robert H. Bell. "Sterne's Etristamology" from *Thalia*, vol. 4.1 (1982). Reprinted by permission of *Thalia* and Robert H. Bell.

Zack R. Bowen. *Ulysses as a Comic Novel* (1989). Permission to reprint granted by Syracuse University Press and Zack R. Bowen.

John M. Bullitt. *Jonathan Swift and the Anatomy of Satiric Technique* (1953). Reprinted by permission of Harvard University Press.

John M. Bullitt. "Swift's *Rules of Raillery*" in *Veins of Humor*. Edited by Harry Levin. *Harvard English Studies*, vol. 3 (1972). Used with permission of Harvard University, Department of English and American Literature and Language.

James M. Cahalan. " 'Humor with a Gender': Somerville and Ross and *The Irish R. M.*" from *Eire–Ireland*, a Journal of Irish Studies, vol. 28.3 (1993). Published by The Irish American Cultural Institute of St. Paul, Minnesota. Reprinted with permission.

Ruby Cohn. "A Comic Complex and a Complex Comic" in *Samuel Beckett: The Comic Gamut*, Copyright © 1962 by Rutgers, The State University. Reprinted by permission of Rutgers University Press.

Gladys Crane. "Shaw's *Misalliance*: The Comic Journey from Rebellious Daughter to Conventional Womanhood" from *Educational Theatre Journal*, vol. 25 (1973). Reprinted by permission of *Educational Theatre Journal* and Gladys Crane.

Seamus Deane. *Celtic Revivals: Essays in Modern Irish Literature—Joyce, Yeats, O'Casey, Kinsella, Montague, Friel, Mahon, Heany, Beckett, Synge* (1985). Wake Forest University Press and Faber and Faber, Ltd., publishers. Used by permission.

Anthony Esolen. "Spenserian Allegory and the Clash of Narrative Worlds" from *Thalia*, vol. 11.1 (1989). Reprinted by permission of *Thalia*.

C. S. Faulk. "John Millington Synge and the Rebirth of Comedy" from *Southern Humanities Review*, vol. 8 (1974). Reprinted by permission of *Southern Humanities Review*.

Katharine Haynes Gatch. "The Last Plays of Bernard Shaw: Dialectic and Despair" from ENGLISH INSTITUTE ESSAYS by the English Institute. Copyright © 1954 by Columbia University Press. Reprinted with permission of the publisher.

A. M. Gibbs. "Comedy and Philosophy in *Man and Superman*" from *Modern Drama*, vol. 19 (1976). Reprinted by permission of *Modern Drama*.

Roger B. Henkle. "Wilde and Beerbohm: the Wit of the Avant-Garde, The Charm of Failure" in *Comedy and Culture—England—1820–1900*. Reprinted by permission of Princeton University Press.

Earl G. Ingersoll. "Irish Jokes: A Lacanian Reading of Short Stories by James Joyce, Flann O'Brien, and Bryan MacMahon" from *Studies in Short Fiction*, vol. 2 (1990). Reprinted by permission of Earl G. Ingersoll.

Eugene Nelson James. *The Development of George Farquhar as a Comic Dramatist* (1972). Permission granted by Mouton de Gruyter, A Division of Walter de Gruyter & Co., publishers.

Quotations from James Joyce. Permission granted by The Estate of James Joyce.

A. N. Kaul. *The Action of English Comedy: Studies in the Encounter of Abstraction and Experience from Shakespeare to Shaw*. Published by Yale University Press (1970). © 1970 by Yale University.

Mary Nesta Skrine (Molly) Keane. Quoted material from the Keane chapter of Ann Owens Weekes's *Irish Women Writers*. Reprinted by permission of Mary Nesta Skrine (Molly) Keane.

Shirley Strum Kenny. "Richard Steele and the 'Pattern of Genteel Comedy' " in *Modern Philology*, vol. 70 (1972). Published by The University of Chicago Press. Permission granted by the University of Chicago Press and Shirley Strum Kenny.

Michael A. Klug. "The Comic Structure of Joyce's *Ulysses* from *Eire–Ireland*, a Journal of Irish Studies, vol. 11.1 (1976). Published by the Irish American Cultural Institute of St. Paul, Minnesota. Reprinted with permission.

Robert Langenfeld. "*Memoirs of My Dead Life*: George Moore's Comic Autobiography" from *Eire–Ireland*, a Journal of Irish Studies, vol. 11 (1986). Published by The Irish American Cultural Institute of St. Paul, Minnesota. Reprinted with permission.

Charles G. Masinton. *J. P. Donleavy: The Style of His Sadness and Humor*. Reprinted by permission of Bowling Green University Popular Press (1975) and James Patrick Donleavy.

John A. Mills. *Language and Laughter: Comic Diction in the Plays of Bernard Shaw* (1969). Permission granted by The University of Arizona Press.

Sean O'Casey play excerpts. Reprinted with permission of MacNaughton Lowe Representation Ltd. All rights for balance of Sean O'Casey plays are handled by M.L.R. Ltd., 200 Fulham Road, London SW10 9PN.

James C. Pierce. "Synge's Widow Quin: Touchstone to the *Playboy*'s Irony" from *Eire–Ireland*, a Journal of Irish Studies, vol. 16.2 (1981). Published by The Irish American Cultural Institute of St. Paul, Minnesota. Reprinted with permission.

Robert M. Polhemus. *Comic Faith: The Great Tradition from Austen to Joyce*. Published by The University of Chicago Press (1980) and Robert M. Polhemus. © 1980 by The University of Chicago.

Alice Rayner. *Comic Persuasion: Moral Structure in British Comedy from Shakespeare to Stoppard*. Published by The University of California Press (1987). Copyright © 1987 by The Regents of The University of California. Permission granted by The Regents of The University of California and Alice Rayner.

Marian Robinson. "Funny Funereels: Single Combat in *Finnegan's Wake* and *Táin Bó Cuilnge*" from *Eire-Ireland*, a Journal of Irish Studies, vol. 26.3 (1981). Published by The Irish American Cultural Institute of St. Paul, Minnesota. Reprinted with permission.

Charles Ross. "The Grim Humor of Spenser's *Faerie Queene*: Women and Laughter in a Renaissance Epic" in *Humor: International Journal of Humor Research*, vol. 2.2 (1989). Permission granted by Mouton de Gruyter, a division of Walter de Gruyter & Co., publishers.

H. Grant Sampson. "Comic Patterns in Goldsmith's Plays" from *English Studies in Canada*, vol. 10 (1984). Reprinted with permission of *English Studies in Canada* and H. Grant Sampson.

Quotations from the prose and plays of Bernard Shaw. Permission granted by The Society of Authors on behalf of The Bernard Shaw Estate.

B. L. Smith. "O'Casey's Satiric Vision" (1978). Published by Kent State University Press. Reprinted by permission of Kent State University and B. L. Smith.

John M. Stedmond. *The Comic Art of Laurence Sterne: Convention and Innovation in Tristam Shandy and A Sentimental Journey*. Published by The University of Toronto Press (1967). Reprinted by permission of the publisher.

Peter Steele. *Jonathan Swift: Preacher and Jester* (1978). Used by permission of Oxford University Press and Peter Steele.

Valerie Topsfield. *The Humour of Samuel Beckett* (1988). Copyright © Valerie Topsfield, 1988. Reprinted with permission of St. Martin's Press, Incorporated, and Macmillan Press Ltd.

Maureen Waters. *The Comic Irishman*. Reprinted from *The Comic Irishman* by Maureen Waters by permission of The State University of New York Press. © 1984 State University of New York.

Barbara Bellow Watson. "The New Woman and the New Comedy" in *Fabian Feminist: Bernard Shaw and Women*. University Park: the Pennsylvania State University Press, 1977, 114–119. Copyright 1977 by The Pennsylvania State University Press. Reproduced by permission of The Pennsylvania State University Press.

Ann Owens Weekes. *Irish Women Writers*. Reprinted from Ann Owens Weekes, *Irish Women Writers*, copyright © 1990 by The University Press of Kentucky, by permission of the publisher and Ann Owens Weekes.

George Woodcock. *The Paradox of Oscar Wilde*. Reprinted by permission of T. V. Boardman & Co., Ltd., 1973.

Every reasonable effort has been made to trace the owners of copyright materials in this book, but in some instances this has proven impossible. The author and publisher will be glad to receive information leading to more complete acknowledgments in subsequent printings of the book and in the meantime extend their apologies for any omissions.

"There is a sense in which every Irishman and Irishwoman is a comedian who from time to time takes time off to be serious."
—Desmond MacHale

Contents

Preface

In searching for humor materials on the reference shelves of a number of different libraries, I was struck by the fact that there were virtually no reference books on the subject of Irish humor. Because I had been researching the subject of humor in British literature, this was especially ironic because humor in Irish literature not only held its own, but frequently surpassed humor in the rest of British literature. It was at that point that I decided to publish this reference guide on humor in Irish literature.

Since Irish humor developed out of the oral tradition (the telling of jokes and stories in Irish pubs), it is very epiphenal in nature. Like Jewish humor, Irish humor developed out of pain and tragedy that resulted in a diaspora. Irish humor, like Jewish humor, contains much wordplay, and like Jewish humor, much of Irish wordplay is bilingual and/or bicultural, relating to both the Gaelic/Celtic and to the English language and culture. There are many Irish people around the world who are trying to reestablish their roots, and it is the humor in Irish written and oral literature that is helping them to do so. There are Irish-studies programs throughout the United States and around the world, and there are large quantities of excellent humor in Irish literature; however, there are not as many critical and secondary materials as there should be, and these critical/secondary sources need to be adequately referenced.

This book is designed to show the range of humor in Irish literature, but more importantly, it is designed to show the common features in Irish humor, the features that can be found in most or all of Irish literature, and which are rare in other literatures. The book is also designed to investigate those aspects of Irish history and culture which impact on the humor. This book is not concerned with vernacular (oral) humor, except when it is written down and published, and only then if it is important enough to have stimulated critical commentary, for this book is not about the humor itself, but is about how various critics have reacted to the humor.

This book is arranged chronologically according to the birth year of the author being discussed. Note that for ease of reference, the birth and death dates of the various authors are given both in the text and in the index. The main body of the book is divided into three centuries, eighteenth, nineteenth, and twentieth; however, there is also a "foregrounding" chapter on sixteenth century Irish humor, and the section on twentieth-century Irish humor has been divided into three separate chapters. What this shows is that Irish literary humor started late and started slowly because the Irish were more concerned with survival than with written literature. But it also shows that once Irish literary humor started, it expanded rapidly to become the most distinctive and perhaps the most significant humor in all of the British Isles. An extensive Index is provided so that authors and subjects can be accessed alphabetically. The length of a particular entry is not determined by the importance of the author, but is rather determined by the amount of critical reaction to that author's humorous devices (caricature, comedy, epiphany, irony, paradox, parody, puns, satire, tragi-comedy, wit, etc.).

Acknowledgments

I would like to express my appreciation to members of the Arizona State University Humanities Computing Facility--James Allen, Dan Brink, James Dybdahl, Lorna Hughes, Kurt Johnson, Peter Lafford, and Gary Walker--for managing the facility in such a way as to make it convenient to provide high quality camera ready copy to the publisher. I would also like to express my appreciation to Karen Adams, Dawn Bates, Susan Braidi, Willis Buckingham, Lee Croft, Nancy Gutierrez, Barbara Lafford, Roy Major, Jim Ney, and Wendy Wilkins, for their encouragement and support of scholarly research. Special thanks goes to my wife, Alleen, who has seen or heard the manuscript in many forms and has offered much constructive criticism. Special thanks also goes to Gregory Castle, our A.S.U. expert in Irish literature, for reading a draft of the manuscript and offering important suggestions for revision and expansion. I would also like to thank Nicolette (Nilsen) Wickman, George Butler, and Barbara Zamat for reading the manuscript and suggesting a number of important editorial revisions.

HUMOR IN
IRISH LITERATURE

CHAPTER 1

Overview: The Humor of Ireland and of Irish Literature

In a country where "Irishness" is hotly contested, it is important first of all to establish what it means to be Irish. For the purposes of this book I am including those who are Anglo-Irish, those who are Gaelic-Irish, those from the Irish Republic, both the North and the South, and those who were born in Ireland, both the ones who stayed in Ireland and those who for one reason or another exiled themselves from Ireland; I also include those first-generation Irish expatriots who were born in England, or America. In short, I am suggesting a broad and heterogeneous definition of Irish humor. But all of these writers have three things in common. 1. They are all very conscious of Irish issues; 2. they are all very conscious of religious issues, especially issues related to Irish Catholicism; and 3. they all developed out of the story-telling tradition, and whatever genre they now write in, there are still traces of this storytelling tradition.

"Ireland has generated an inordinately large number of story tellers, in pubs and in print." Furthermore, Irish short stories bear striking resemblances to Irish jokes. The stories in Irish literature have the same narrative structure as the stories that are told and retold in pubs. These stories can be considered to be "elaborated jokes," since they have "scrupulously engineered structure of expectations and their inevitable punchline" (Ingersoll 237). Irish stories, like Irish jokes, and like other jokes as well, tend to have special joke-related qualities. Irish stories tend to be embellishments of stories, legends, and jokes previously told, and part of the public domain. The audiences of Irish stories tend to listen especially carefully so that they can later recount these same stories as their own. And these Irish stories are often told from a male perspective, and with a female as the target. Extending insights earlier developed by Sigmund Freud with his concept of "tendentious humor," Jacques Lacan with his concept of "purloined punchline," and Jerry Aline Flieger with his concept of "Joke as Textual Paradigm," Earl Ingersoll makes these points in an article entitled "Irish Jokes: A Lacanian Reading of Short Stories by James Joyce, Flann O'Brien, and Bryan MacMahon." Ingersoll supports his contention by telling one typical joke-story from James Joyce ("Two Gallants"), one from Flann O'Brien ("The Martyr's Crown"), and one from Bryan MacMahon ("Exile's Return") (Ingersoll 237-245).

All three of these stories begin with two friends walking down an Irish street. In James Joyce's "Two Gallants" (from The Dubliners) the two friends are named Corley and Lenehan. Corley tells how he has found a "slavey," who pays him for sex with tram fare and with fine cigars. His friend Lenehan has little money for tram fare, let alone fine cigars or sex. From a distance Lenehan observes his friend with the "slavey," and then he goes over to him to see if he has been successful. Corley opens his hand, for Lenehan, and "a small gold coin shone in the palm." Lenehan's response to Corley's punchline is considered by Ingersoll to be "a marvelous parody of pseudosophistication"--"That takes the solitary, unique, and, if I may so call it, recherché biscuit!" (Ingersoll 239).

Analogous to Joyce's "Two Gallants" is Flann O'Brien's "The Martyr's Crown." This is again a joke elaborated into an Irish short story, and again told from the masculine point of view that illustrates Freud's, Lacan's, and Flieger's sense of "tendentious humor," in which a woman is the target of the joke. O'Brien's "two gallants" are known as Mr. Toole, and Mr. O'Hickey. Like Corley and Lenehan the story begins with their walking down the street in the midst of friendly conversation. As they are walking down the street, Mr. Toole has the habit of saluting total strangers--but only strangers who are well dressed and have an air of importance. Finally, Mr. O'Hickey asks, "Who was that?" And of course the answer is the expected story. Mr. Toole says that he knows this person's mother very well, and that she is a saint, and then he begins his story. It was in 1921, and Mr. Toole and five of his friends ambushed two lorries full of British soldiers and hid out in the house of the Widow Clougherty.

> One day the inevitable happened: Toole looked out of the window to find the street full of two lorries of soldiers whose officer is at the door. Toole focuses attention upon the Widow's "big silver sateen blouse," which she immediately begins unbuttoning as she moves downstairs toward the Brit. The speed with which she moves into the role of victim-seductress, complete with the "guttiest voice" Toole has ever heard, is telling. In response to the officer's question, as to whether there are any men in the house, she replies: "sairtinly not at this hour of the night; I wish to God there was. Sure, how could the poor unfortunate women get on without them, officer?" (qtd. in Ingersoll 242).

The Widow is said to wear the "martyr's crown" because she chose a fate worse than death in supporting the Irish cause. And the young stranger is the "inverted quintessential Irish hero, for unlike others content to die for the Poor Old Woman, he was born the bastard issue of the Brit's rape of Mother Ireland" (Ingersoll 242).

The second analogue to Joyce's "The Gallants" is Bryan MacMahon's "Exile's Return." Again there are two friends walking down the Irish street engaged in conversation. This time their names are Timothy Hannigan and Paddy Kinsella. Kinsella is returning after six years in Birmingham, where he had gone to work in order to support his family. They go into a pub, where Hannigan tells everyone there that Kinsella, the exile, has returned because he had become a father several years after he had gone into exile. Hannigan asks Kinsella what he's going to do about it, and Kinsella responds that he's going to drink his pint. "Then, as likely as not, I'll swing for her!" After Hannigan and Kinsella leave the pub they hear a hearty roar of laughter coming from where they had just been. MacMahon, as a good story teller, gives a number of hints, but never lets us know for sure, that while Kinsella has been away, Hannigan has been taking his place in his wife's bed. Thus it is especially ironic when Hannigan reassures Kinsella that his betrayal was a "chance fall," "One night only it was. . . . 'Twould mebbe never again happen in a million years" (385). Later at night Paddy Kinsella is at home with his wife, and the little girl, Mag, who was born after he left, hears him making a noise and calls out, "You're in the kitchen, Timothy Hannigan. I know your snuffle." Ingersoll adds, "It is a wise child who knows her own father!" (Ingersoll 244).

In a book entitled, The Humour of Ireland, David James O'Donoghue says that Irish humor is "more imaginative" than any other type of humor. Furthermore, it is "probably less ill-natured than that of any other nation," though O'Donoghue admits that the Irish also have a special ability to say things that can hurt. O'Donoghue says that the most illiterate of Irish peasants can put more scorn into a retort than the most highly educated professionals of another country (O'Donoghue xii). O'Donoghue indicates that humor is an important aspect of almost every incident and detail of Irish life. "It overflows in the discussions of the local boards, is bandied about by carmen, comes down from the theatre galleries, is rife in the law courts, and chronic in the clubs, at the bar-dinners, and wherever there is dulness to be exorcised." He concludes that in Ireland, jokes are as plentiful as blackberries (O'Donoghue xiv). The most important subjects for joking are courting, drinking, and fighting. The Irish tend to drink long, and deeply, with a smile on their faces, and O'Donoghue suggests that "there can be no question of Ireland's supremacy in the literature devoted to Bacchus" (O'Donoghue xv).

The Irish enjoy playing games with words; they have a sense of the grotesque or the macabre, a playful irreverence, and a darkly humorous attitude (Topsfield 28). Vivian Mercier says, "No aspect of life is too sacred to escape the mockery of Irish laughter" (Mercier 248). Sean O'Tuama talks about the "dramatic, astringent, and sometimes openly humorous nature of the best of the Irish Bardic Poems" (1000-1200), and indicates that these qualities distinguish the Irish Bardic Poems from other medieval love poetry (O'Tuama 221). Mac Con Glinne's Vision, written in the thirteenth century, is "one of the most brilliantly written satires against the church and pomp ever produced in Ireland." O'Tuama goes on to discuss such Irish Hero Tales as Táin Bó Cúalnge (The Cattle Raid of Cooley) as the centerpiece of the hero tales known as the Ulster cycle. In this story, Cú Chulain is depicted as the most renowned and greatest of the Ulster warriors, and he singlehandedly repulses an army of cattle-raiding Conmacht men who invade his province. The other Ulster heroes, known as the Red Branch Knights remain uninvolved in the battle because they have been struck down by a nine-day sickness (O'Tuama 220).

The Book of the Dun Cow was a manuscript written sometime before 1100, and the narrator tells stories that are filled with Irish wit. One tale is about a young hero who challenges all warriors of an enemy stronghold. The enemy leader sends out an army of bare chested women, because at this time it was taboo to look at a woman's bare chest, so the young hero had to cover his eyes and he was easily defeated because he had neither the use of his eyes or his hands in the battle (Mercier 13). Another early set of Irish hero legends involves Finn MacCool. He is a hunter who was an important part of Irish oral literature from the thirteenth to the fifteenth century. Furthermore, he is still an important personage in Irish folk narrative (O'Tuama 220).

In 1366 the Statues of Kilkenny were signed. These statutes were designed

> to keep the English settlers in Ireland from adopting Irish ways of life: from intermarrying, from concubinage or from the fostering of children, from using the Irish language, from dressing, wearing their hair and riding horses in the Irish fashion, and from maintaining or entertaining Irish minstrels, poets or storytellers (Jeffares 7).

This show of blatant racism angered the Irish and exemplified the English oppression of the Irish, the oppression that the Northern Irish continue to fight and that is the source of much Irish humor (Jeffares 7).

By the seventeenth century, a small number of English and Scottish landlords had settled Ireland, and the government of England and Ireland had established the Settlement of Ireland Acts designed to assimilate the Gaelic people. In order to augment the assimilation process, the government imposed severe penalties against the practice of the Roman Catholic religion, the speaking of Gaelic, and the serving of Gaelic chieftains. Ironically, it was the impoverishing and disenfranchising of the Irish people, and the increase in the ignorance of the Gaelic-Irish people that made visible the previously invisible religious difference. Thus, the Acts ultimately did more to buttress differences than to promote assimilation (Weekes 10). Ireland was emasculated, and came to be often viewed as a woman of one sort or another. In one poem, Seamus Heaney speaks of

Ireland as a woman. Here, Ireland is seen as a "stretchmarked" female body; England is seen as the "imperial male;" and the "Acts of Union" are seen as a rape. In this position, Ireland has three choices: 1. to cajole, 2. to humor or tease, or 3. to ignore the intruder (Weekes 14).

> Centuries before Heaney, poets writing in both Gaelic and English could only picture their enslaved country as female, "the old hag of Beare," "the Sean Bhean Bhoct" (poor old woman), "Dark Rosaleen"; later disillusioned writers would depict the country as "harridan" and "crone" or, in James Joyce's characteristic terminology, "the old sow who eats her farrow." The convention of seeing Ireland as a wronged woman was by the eighteenth century so popular that whole schools of poets wrote Aislingi, or dream-visions, poems that foretold the Stuart protector's freeing of the beautiful woman. (Weekes 14)

The Parliament of Clan Tomas, written about 1650 was an early sample of Irish satire. According to Sean O'Tuama, this is savage satire which targets various peasant attitudes (O'Tuama 222).

Seamus Deane notes that there are recurrent themes in the writings of Irish and Anglo-Irish authors, and many of these themes relate to the difficulties of living in Ireland:

> For almost three hundred years, Ireland has experienced a series of serious social and political breakdowns. Constitutionally, the failures are legion. Among the most obvious are the Whig Revolution Settlement of 1688-90; the Irish Parliament of 1782-1800; the Act of Union, 1800-1922; Home Rule; and the Anglo-Irish Treaty of 1922, the effects of which still resonate in Northern Ireland. (Deane 11)

Deane continues,

> Along with that catalogue of political failure there is a long history of rebellions and of agrarian disturbance. The insurrection groups which plotted these--the United Irishmen, the Fenians, the Irish Republican Brotherhood, the Citizens Army, the Irish Republican Army--represented the alternative, and more violent, tradition which culminated in the successes of the 1916-22 period. (Deane 11-12)

Other subjects often discussed in Irish literature are the great battle of the Boyne in 1690, which had the effect of inaugurating the triumph of the Protestant Ascendancy in Ireland and the decline of the Catholic Gaelic civilization, the Irish Famine of 1848, the Gaelic League, which was founded in 1893 by Douglas Hyde, Sinn Fein's great electoral triumph in 1918, and the 1921 founding of the Irish Free State (Deane 12).

There have been two Celtic Revivals, one beginning in the late eighteenth century, and the other in the late nineteenth century. But even though many of these events are tragic, and even though the Irish have seldom been totally successful in dealing with these tragic events, Irish writing is nevertheless filled with wit and humor. And here again there are recurring Irish themes--the language, the land, and the song. The Irish are sad that their own language has been virtually destroyed and that the hateful language of their repressors has replaced it; but they nevertheless use their English skills, their Gaelic skills, and their bilingual skills to make their writing more lively and effective. The Irish are also sad that their land has been confiscated. The Land League was formed by Michael Davitt to assert the rights of the tenantry against the landlords. Parnell, a member of the Land League, became a hero in Ireland by using this organization as a tool of insurrection. Place names and other Gaelic terms, such as Cathleen ni Houlihan, Eireann, Eire, Saorstat Eireann, the Republic, Shan Von Vocht, the Six Counties, Ulster, Northern Ireland, and Derry, often carry a strong political charge (Deane 13). Irish music, and especially the Irish ballad, is also filled with an emotional tie to Ireland:

> The ballad has a noteworthy position in modern Irish politics because it popularized sentiments that otherwise might have remained safely preserved in literature. Although this was essentially a nineteenth-century phenomenon, it keeps a vestigial existence up to the present day. Its association with the Gaelic tradition is sustained by two factors. First, the melodies are often based upon old Gaelic airs. Second, its iconography-- harp, wolfhound, tower, old hag transformed into young queen, and so on-- draws heavily on some traditional motifs of the Gaelic poetry translated in the nineteenth century by Sir Samuel Ferguson and others. (Deane 14)

Deane notes that although much of Irish writing and singing is political, Irish nationalism is not a "political ideology" so much as it is a "moral passion" (Deane 14-15).

Being Irish means different things to different people Louis MacNeice was proud of being a member of the "Middle Nation," and said that he liked being Irish partly because it was so difficult for the English to figure out the thinkings of a person who had been "baptized with fairy water." This is an enigmatic statement to someone like The Duke of Wellington, however, an Anglo-Irishman who didn't like to be reminded of his Hibernian origins. Wellington used to say, "Damn me, sir, if a man is born in a stable that doesn't make him a horse" (Reid 84). The Anglo-Irish emigré writers "made the field of English comedy peculiarly their own. Their rich line, continuing into the 20th century, included William Congreve, George Farquhar, Oliver Goldsmith, Richard Brinsley Sheridan, Laurence Sterne, Oscar Wilde, and George Bernard Shaw" (Greene 420).

Because of their hardships, the Irish, and the Anglo-Irish have developed a remarkable double vision. They are able to see things not only as they are, but also how they ought to be, and it is the discrepancy between these two visions which produces the laughter (Reid 85). John Synge and Samuel Beckett both had this double vision. In both of these authors, "the double vision of the comic writer goes hand in hand with the tragic poet's demand for our emotional involvement." Beckett goes so far as to speak openly of mankind's predicament as a "cosmic joke" (Reid 90). The Irish are not humorous; they are witty. Irish humor is not about an ambassador in a tuxedo and top hat slipping on a banana skin as he walks down the embassy steps. It is Oscar Wilde's "work is the curse of the drinking classes." Ann Saddlemyer notes the large number of Irish playwrights who deal with comedy based on wit. English playwrights, in contrast, do not write witty comedies; they write farces. Their humor plays primarily on the emotions rather than on the intellect (Reid 85). Such Anglo-Irish writers as Jonathan Swift and Samuel Beckett like to push things to the limit, a trait which is utterly un-English. Irish writers also tend to have a glorious double vision. The keening in the Irish wake, for example, is followed by singing, dancing, and drinking. There is "a simultaneous recognition of life and death, and a practical assertion that one can have no meaning without the other" (Reid 86).

The Irish critic Seamus Deane suggests that Irish English is a political language. The accents, the pronunciation, the place names of Irish English all carry a political charge. In the British public mind, Irish English represents the language of the IRA bomber, the RUC reservist, the Noraid propagandist, or such Irish patriots as Gerry Adams, MP, or the Reverend Ian Paisley. Paradoxically, however, Irish-English is also the best-loved of regional accents (McCrum 179). Terry Wogan is a newscaster on the BBC who broadcasts in Irish English. Anthony Clare, one of his fellow broadcasters, explains why Terry Wogan's Irish accent is not only acceptable, but even superior:

> He is the classic Irish talker--mocking, self-deprecating, playing with words, attacking his betters, getting the boot in, but doing it in a way which would be thought aggressive from an English person. . . . You could accuse him of really saying very little, which again is very Irish. "Mind you, now, I've said nothing." That's a phrase you hear all the time in Dublin. (McCrum

179).

The Irish have the "gift of gab," "the gift of eloquence," or expressed in a more flippant expression, "a touch of the blarney." The term "blarney" originated during the reign of Queen Elizabeth I. At this time Blarney Castle in Cork was occupied by Cormac MacCarthymore, a local chieftain, and a man noted for his gift of talk and prevarication. Queen Elizabeth considered his loyalty to the English throne to be questionable, and she called on him to surrender his castle:

> MacCarthymore replied, via Elizabeth's favourite the Earl of Essex, with speeches of great flattery that he was, of course, just about to do as his queen desired. But nothing happened. Elizabeth repeated her demand, and received the same response: he would when he could, but there were one or two matters of great urgency he had to attend to first. Eventually, after many such exchanges, the frustrated queen is said to have exclaimed, "It's all Blarney--he says he will do it, but he never means to do what he says." (McCrum 150)

Some say that Ireland's harsh weather is responsible for the Irish sense of humor. It was the harsh climate which forced the Irish into their pubs, and it was in the pubs that they used their skills in telling humorous stories to develop into close social groups. George Bernard Shaw suggested that the role of humor in Ireland was due to the Irish climate, "as if wit or a sense of humor were a disease like rheumatism or tuberculosis, both of which are often blamed on the prevailing dampness in Ireland" (Mercier vii).

The English imposed the English language and culture on Ireland. Although English is not the native language of Ireland, the English act as if it were. And ironically, such Irish writers as Spenser, Congreve, Swift, Sheridan, Wilde, Yeats, Synge, Shaw, Joyce, Beckett, and Heaney have written some of the best works to be found in English literature (McCrum 149). This is partly because the Irish are such excellent storytellers. They are admired for the lyrical quality of their expression. Their daily talk and teasing is filled with "Irish logic." There is a story told about the railway station at Ballyhough. It had two clocks, but the clocks did not tell the same time. When an irate traveller asked a porter what was the use of having two clocks if they didn't tell the same time, the porter is said to have replied, "And what would we be wanting with two clocks if they told the same time?" (McCrum 149).

Ireland is famous for its "Irish Bulls." There is an old saying in Ireland that the difference between an "Irish bull" and any other bull is that an Irish Bull is pregnant (Colum 33). Sir Boyle Roche, an Irish member of Parliament in the last quarter of the eighteenth century was famous for his Irish Bulls. It was Roche who said:

> "My love for England and Ireland is so great, I would have the two sisters embrace like one brother."
>
> "I stand prostrate at the feet of my Sovereign."
>
> "The cup of Ireland's misfortunes has been overflowing for centuries, and it is not full yet."
>
> "The profligacy of the times is such that little children, who can neither walk nor talk, may be seen running about the streets cursing their maker."
>
> "Single misfortunes never come alone, and the greatest of all possible misfortunes is generally followed by a much greater." (Bartel 37-38)

Bayne Bernard, the biographer of Samuel Lover described the Irish sense of humor as follows: "An air of burlesque romance runs through half of this people's history. They seem to turn life into a carnival in which the only occupation is the concoction of a good joke or the pursuit of a mad adventure. Even misfortune does not sadden them" (Waters 174). The Irish face death or disaster with a heightened sense of comic tension. "Laughter is provoked by the intensity of the comic performance, the deliberate heightening of illusion by one who consciously resists defeat" (Waters 174). According to Maureen Waters, the appeal of the comic Irishman rests on his ability to laugh at death or disaster, not because he is indifferent, but because this is the only defense available to him. "Like the druid he is a shape changer" (Waters 174). William Carleton's Denis O'Shaughnessy, John Synge's Christy Mahon, and Patrick Kavanagh's Tarry Flynn have the power to ennoble themselves and their communities by sheer imaginative force. This is in contrast to Samuel Beckett's Murphy, whose inflexibility causes him to be doomed to extinction (Waters 175).

> The fact that Irish comedy is so concerned with anti-heroes or clowns is probably related to the unhappy course of history. From the sixteenth through the nineteenth century there was little opportunity for the peasant intricacies of romance, which provide the traditional pattern of comedy. Irish heroes were tragic figures who gave their lives for Cathleen ni Houlihan. (Waters 176)

The perspective of the comic Irishman is complicated by the fact that in Irish iconography, death is often represented as a beautiful woman; and therefore death has a certain seductive appeal. Thus macabre humor is an important aspect in the writings of John Synge, James Joyce, Sean O'Casey, Brendan Behan, Sean O'Brien, and Samuel Beckett. Irish characters have a certain amount of bravado, as they aggressively tease and grapple with fate thinking that somehow they might be able to overthrow the specter of death (Waters 176-177). In Irish folklore, and in Irish literature, the hangman and the devil both appear as clowns. In her book entitled The Comic Irishman, Maureen Waters discusses the Irish "tribal man of letters" during the middle ages. He was often employed to satirize the enemies of a patron-king, but if he was not adequately compensated for his writing, he might turn his satire on his patron, "raising boils on his neck or demeaning him forever with an invidious nickname or verse" (Waters 85). During this period, it was believed that satire had the power to cause injury and death, and some poets were therefore banished from Ireland. In addition, specific admonitions against the misuse of their powers were codified in Irish law. There were seven kinds of satire that could require an "honor-price." 1. a nickname that stuck, 2. recitation of a satire or insults in a person's absence, 3. satiric distortion of the face, or laughing toward the side, 4. sneering at a person's form, 5. magnifying a person's blemish, 6. satire written by a bard who is far away, and 7. satire which is recited in person. Here there is no clear distinction between magical incantation and mockery or invective; in the Irish language the same words (commonly aer and its derivatives) are employed. During this period, there were even divisions of satirists in the royal armies, which one Gaelic king could send to destroy another Gaelic king (Lyon and Moore 106). In the middle ages satire took on a sophisticated literary form, which employed a sustained narrative and an elaborate system of parody. It reveals a delight in mockery and wit and an emphasis on "word play" rather than "word magic" (Waters 86). According to Waters, the modern equivalent of the comic Irishman is "morose, impulsive, fiery, loquacious, literary, and, of course, thirsty" (Waters 91).

The comic Irishman springs from a culture that was "under sentence of death for hundreds of years." He played the role which was created for him in order to survive, but he gradually changed this role by the force of his own temperament. In Gaelic Ireland there were three indications of dignity, 1. a fine figure, 2. a free bearing, and 3. verbal eloquence. Therefore the archetypal hero had great verbal as well as military skills. An Irish proverb says, "It is conversation that keeps away death," and in Ireland there were three kinds of people who prized good conversation, the country people, the poets, and the story tellers:

> The first two engaged in extemporaneous battles of wit in which their powers of rhetoric and composition were publicly displayed and publicly

judged. Storytelling was a performance in itself, structured by simple but specific rituals. A session began and ended with a traditional formula, but details were improvised and so could last for two hours, punctuated by verbal response which might take the form of encouragement or a brief commentary or jest. (Waters 173)

Padraic Colum says that most of Irish humor is somehow connected with words. When Arland Ussher visited Ireland, he said that the Irish race "tired the sun with talking." The Irish language is filled with "quips, hyperboles, cajoleries, endearments, lamentation, blessings, curses, tirades--and all very often in the same breath" (Colum xiv).

During much of their history, the Irish have lived dreary lives that were bound by poverty, custom, and religious restraints. Death for the Irish was often the only means of escape from the trials of this world. In a life with little social contact, and few joys, the wake became a central ritual in Ireland. Wakes were purely social affairs, which many times were orchestrated by the deceased on their death beds (Waters 70). The macabre humor of the wake functioned to provide an "edge against despair and a defense against the maudlin or the sentimental" (Waters 99). The Irish wake was an antidote to grief, and there was performance and gaiety of every kind, including courtship rites, music, mime, dance, and story telling. Linda Harrington suggests that the use of macabre humor provided group therapy at these Irish wakes (Harrington 4):

When a relative of the deceased arrived, the lament for the dead (keena) would be sounded and everyone in attendance would begin to cry. Once the newcomer blended into the crowd, the gaiety would resume. Any time another relative arrived, the pattern was repeated with all the merrymakers crying until their eyes were "as red as a ferret's." With this round of mourning completed, they settled back into diversions such as songs, jokes, and games just as if nothing had happened. The newcomer would then shake hands with the friends of the corpse, get a glass or two and a pipe, then in a few minutes would be as merry as the rest of them. (Colum 410)

In Ireland during the nineteenth century wakes were held not only for the dead, but also for many of the young Irish people who left Ireland in search of a better life--often they moved to America. Realizing that people who left Ireland would probably not return to their homeland, the sorrowful Irish families would hold wakes for the emigrants. The wakes consisted of music, song, good-natured humor, gossip, and boisterous flirtation (Colum 471). Mock marriages were often performed during wakes, and such games as Making the Ship and The Bull and the Cow have a strong phallic element, and in fact suggest that the wake originally included fertility rites (Waters 174).

During the nineteenth century, there were a number of entertainers who traditionally attended Irish wakes. The "Seanchai" or "story teller" was one of these entertainers, and these "Seanchai" linger in isolated parts of Ireland even today (Weekes 1). One story that the Seanchai often told is that faeries surrounded the house of the dead, and that the people inside must not cry. If they did cry, the sound of the crying would encourage the faeries to break in and steal the soul of the dead person (Uris 5). The "Seanchai" provided much entertainment and humor at the wake, but there was also a mock priest who attended the wakes to officiate at the "Frannsa," or the mock wedding. The mock wedding dates back to pagan times and, probably was some sort of a fertility ceremony. The mock priest dressed up in straw vestments and wore a string of potatoes around his neck symbolizing a string of rosary beads. He would choose a couple at the wake to "marry," and then he would pronounce a blessing on the couple. During this part of the ceremony there was a great deal of Irish wit exhibited through the creativity, the genius, and the humor of the mock priest (Murphy 110).

Folklore offers innumerable accounts of tricks played with a corpse which is being waked. In a typical example the ropes binding the rigid limbs are cut so that the corpse suddenly appears to sit up. In other tales someone pretends to be dead or is led to believe he has died, a trick which worked its way in to Handy Andy, The Shaughraun, The Shadow and the Glen, and The Tailor and Antsy. (Waters 177)

This idea of mirthful death appealed to James Joyce when he began to chronicle the adventures of Tim Finnegan, and it is humorously parodied by Samuel Beckett in Murphy. (Waters 174). The irony of mirth during an Irish wake is also exhibited in a wide variety of other Irish writers, including Samuel Lover, William Carleton, Dion Boucicault, John Synge, and Sean O'Casey (Waters 174).

In a book entitled The Irish Comic Tradition, Vivian Mercier notes that Gaelic satire contains many lampoons framed as alliterative epithets aimed at specific individuals rather than at folly or vice in general. There is a great deal of word play in which the large number of synonyms and nonce-words creates special problems for editors and translators. The Irish also delight in the absurdity of a tale and they are inclined toward the fantastic and the macabre (Waters 89).

In The Comic Irishman, Waters also discusses the four comic archetypes that are most prevalent in Irish literature, the Rustic Clown or Fool, the Rogue, the Stage Irishman, and the Comic Hero. As examples of the Rustic Clown or Fool, she lists Samuel Lover's Andy Rooney in Handy Andy, and Major Yeates, the Resident Magistrate in Somerville and Ross's Irish R.M. Stories, and Michael Miskell and Mike McInerney in Lady Gregory's The Workhouse Ward. Waters makes the following statement about the Rustic Clown archetype:

> The Irish clown was primarily the creation of Anglo-Irish and English writers. Although the clown shares some of the features of the folk fool, the humor which he generates is largely based on cultural differences. In the early nineteenth century he is a blundering, often hot tempered but benevolent buffoon, ignorant of the modern world and incapable of speaking English properly. (Waters 27)

A second Irish archetype which Waters considers is the "comical rogue." This is the archetype represented by the playboy in John Synge's Playboy and the Western World and the paycocks in Sean O'Casey's Juno and the Paycock (Waters 32). It is the archetype represented by Finn MacCool in James Joyce's Finnegans Wake (Waters 33). It is also the archetype of characters who appear in the plays of Samuel Lover, and Dion Boucicault. These characters tend to be articulate and flamboyant, but they are outsiders, and they live by their wits in order to avoid the drudgery of other men. They flourish because they break through conventional boundaries and ordinary domestic relationships. These rogues are entertaining and high spirited, and they diffuse violence with their use of humor. Although they are flirtatious, they seldom form any lasting alliances with women (Waters 40).

A third Irish archetype which Waters treats is the "stage Irishman" as represented by John O'Keefe's Thady MacBrogue, the vigorous servant in The She-Gallant, and Felix, the devil-may-care wanderer in Wicklow Gold Mines (Waters 42). About this archetype, Maurice Bourgeois says,

> The Stage Irishman habitually bears the general name of Pat, or Paddy or Teague. He has an atrocious Irish brogue, perpetual jokes, blunders and bulls in speaking and never fails to utter, by way of Hibernian seasoning some wild screech or oath of Gaelic origin at every third word; he has an unsurpassable gift of blarney and cadges for tips and free drinks. His hair is of the fiery red; he is rosy-cheeked, massive, and whiskey loving. His face is one of simian bestiality with an expression of diabolical archness. .

. . In his right hand he brandishes a stout blackthorn, or a sprig of shillelagh, and threatens to belabour therewith the daring person who will tread on the tails of his coat. (Bourgeois 109-110).

The fourth Irish archetype which Waters considers is the "comic hero." This is Denis O'Shaughnessy in William Carleton's "Denis O'Shaughnessy Going to Maynooth." It's also Christy Mahon in John Synge's Playboy of the Western World. Maureen Waters points out that whether these are farcical characters, like the inhabitants of Lady Gregory's little village of Cloon or the more clever and engaging heroes of William Carleton, Dion Boucicault, or John Synge, the Irish comic hero reveals a real gift for language. He may blunder, or misinterpret events, but he usually exhibits a boldness, an invention, and a flair for the narrative. Waters is paraphrasing Mathew Arnold when she says:

By the latter part of the nineteenth century the brogue came to be regarded as something of an asset, associated with "blarney" rather than "blundering" and with the ability to perform and improvise. . . . The Irishman's fault lay in an excess of imagination, a tendency to prefer sound over sense, to resist the "despotism of fact." The importance of speaking well was rooted in an oral tradition in which poet and storyteller played central roles, stimulating the minds of the people despite the severe hardships they endured. As Lady Gregory pointed out, in the isolated rural communities where there was little commerce and few books, good conversation was highly prized. (Waters 80)

Here we are concerned not only with the Irish writer, but with the Anglo-Irish writer as well. Alec Reid says that there are five important qualities for the Anglo-Irish writer, and that most Anglo-Irish writers have at least four of these qualities. First, the writer must have been born, or at least educated, in Ireland. Second, if the writer has any religious faith, it is not Roman Catholicism. Third, if he or she has a university education it should have been acquired at Trinity College, Dublin. Fourth, he or she should have spent a considerable time outside of Ireland. And fifth, he or she has a natural irreverence, and a tendency to push ideas and/or language much further than an English writer would push them (Reid 84-85).

To force people to focus their attention on the situation in Ireland, Jonathan Swift often used irony and satire in describing the plight of the Irish people. Swift notes that every day the Irish people are "dying, and rotting, by cold, and famine, and filth, and vermin, as fast as can be reasonably expected." John Bullitt says that this statement shows "the pressure of an outraged conviction subdued and controlled by sustained artistic intention" (Bullitt 191).

Concerning writings of Oliver Goldsmith, a writer who is sometimes English and sometimes Irish in his attitudes and writing style, Leigh Hunt indicated that Goldsmith's writing about truth was richly colored, and overflowing with animal spirits. Then he went on to say the English have no dramatists to compare in this respect with the Irish. Farquhar, Goldsmith, and Sheridan surpass them all; and O'Keefe, as a farce-writer, stands alone (Hunt 316).

David Greene says that there are basically four literary strands in the tradition of Irish literature: 1. Irish Pre-Christian Mythology, 2. Gaelic Poetry, 3. Anglo-Irish Literature, and 4. Irish Literature in English. One of the heroes of Irish Literature is Oisin, and in the Ossianic tales Ossin meets St. Patrick on his return from the land of Youth.

In the story, fantasticality and grotesque become a new thing--satire, the beginning of the Irish mockery that fills much of the Gaelic poetry of the 17th and 18th centuries and the Anglo-Irish literature of the 20th. The story is also significant in that it has the Swiftian form of a voyage. Both Irish satire and Irish pathos are usually about wandering. It is appropriate that the great Irish epic of the 20th century should be called Ulysses. (Greene 420)

Much of Irish literature is presented from the male point of view; however there is some very important Irish literature that is presented from the female point of view, much of it mentioned in Ann Owens Weekes's Irish Women Writers: An Uncharted Tradition. Weekes says, "Although exaggerated, the picture Maria Edgeworth presented in her novel Castle Rackrent (1800) and that E. O. E. Somerville and Violet Martin presented in Some Experiences of an Irish R.M. (1889) of the jovial, drinking, Anglo-Irish sportsman may be closer to the actual than is the received picture of the Anglo-Irish man." (Weekes 18)

It should be noted here that Mary Lavin, Julia O'Faolain, and Jennifer Johnston don't view themselves as feminists, because their politics and actions are often in disagreement with those of other feminists. Ann Weekes notes the following irony: "Jennifer Johnston . . . suggests that while Irish feminists have a real injustice to combat, their actions, like those of the Provisional Irish Republican Army who seek to overthrow an unjust system in the north of Ireland, alienate rather than gain them support" (Weekes 30).

The Humor of Ireland and Irish Literature Bibliography

Baily, Karen. Irish Proverbs. San Francisco, CA: Chronicle Books, 1986.

Bartel, Roland. Metaphors and Symbols: Forays into Language. Urbana, IL: National Council of Teachers of English, 1983.

Bourgeois, Maurice. John Millington Synge and the Irish Theatre. London, England: Constable, 1913.

Birmingham, George A. Now You Tell One: Stories of Irish Wit and Humour. London, England: Valentine and Sons, 1972.

Bullitt, John M. Jonathan Swift and the Anatomy of Satire: A Study of Satiric Technique. Cambridge, MA: Harvard Univ Press, 1953.

Colum, Padraic. A Treasury of Irish Folklore. New York, NY: Crown, 1954.

Davies, Christie. "The Irish Joke as a Social Phenomenon." Laughing Matters: A Serious Look at Humour. Eds. John Durant and Jonathan Miller. New York, NY: Longman, 1988, 44-65.

Deane, Seamus. Celtic Revivals: Essays in Modern Irish Literature--Joyce, Yeats, O'Casey, Kinsella, Montague, Friel, Mahon, Heaney, Beckett, Synge. Winston-Salem, NC: Wake Forest University Press, 1985.

Escarbelt, Bernard. "Sheridan's Debt to Ireland." Aspects of the Irish Theatre. Eds. Patrick Rafroidi, Raymonde Popot, and William Parker. Paris, France: Eds. Universitaires, 1972, 25-37.

Flieger, Jerry Aline. "The Purloined Punchline: Joke as Textual Paradigm." Lacan and Narration: The Psychoanalytic Difference in Narrative Theory. Ed. Robert Con Davis. Baltimore, MD: Johns Hopkins University Press, 1983 941-967.

Freud, Sigmund. Jokes and their Relation to the Unconscious. New York, NY: Penguin, 1976.

Greene, David H. "IRELAND: Literature." The Encyclopedia Americana: International Edition. Danbury, CT: Americana Corporation, 1978, 420-423.

Harrington, Linda. "Death in Nineteenth Century Ireland: Healing the Heartaches with Humor." Unpublished Paper. Tempe, AZ: Arizona State University, 1992.

Healy, James N. Comic Irish Recitations. Cork, Ireland: Mercier, 1981.

Healy, James N. Jokes from the Pubs of Ireland. Cork, Ireland: Mercier, 1977.

Hunt, Leigh. Wit and Humour. New York, NY: Folcroft Library Editions, 1972.

Ingersoll, Earl G. "Irish Jokes: A Lacanian Reading of Short Stories by James Joyce, Flann O'Brien, and Bryan MacMahon." Studies in Short Fiction 2 (Spring, 1990): 237-245.

Jeffares, Norman A. Anglo-Irish Literature. New York, NY: Schocken, 1982.

Kelleher, John V. "Humor in the Ulster Saga." Veins of Humor. Cambridge, MA: Harvard University Press, 1972, 35-56.

Krause, David. The Profane Book of Irish Comedy. Ithaca, NY: Cornell Univ Press, 1982.

Lamont-Brown, Raymond. Irish Grave Humour. Dublin, Ireland: The O'Brien Press, 1987.

Lyon, David, and George Moore. "Satirists and Enchanters in Early Irish Literature." Studies in the History of Religions. Eds. David Lyon and George Moore. New York, NY: Macmillan, 1912, 98-106.

McCarthy, John, ed. The Best of Irish Wit and Wisdom. New York, NY: Continuum, 1987.

McCrum, Robert, William Cran, and Robert MacNeil. The Story of English. New York, NY: Penguin/Viking, 1992.

Magrath, Myler. The Book of Irish Limericks. Cork, Ireland: Mercier, 1985.

Mercier, Vivian. The Irish Comic Tradition. Oxford, England: Clarendon, 1962.

Murphy, Frank. The Bog Irish: Who They Were and How They Lived. Victoria, Australia: Penguin, 1987.

O'Donoghue, David James, ed. The Humour of Ireland. London, England: Walter Scott, 1894; New York, NY: AMS Press, 1978.

O'Tuama, Sean. "Gaelic Literature." The Encyclopedia Americana: International Edition. Danbury, CT: Americana Corporation, 1978, 220-222.

Pepper, John. John Pepper's Illustrated Encyclopedia of Ulster Knowledge. New York, NY: Appletree, 1983.

Pepper, John. John Pepper's Ulster Phrasebook. New York, NY: Appletree, 1982.

Rafroidi, Patrick, Raymonde Popot, and William Parker, eds. "Aspects of Irish Comedy." Aspects of the Irish Theatre. Paris, France: Eds. Universitaires, 1972, 17-63.

Reid, Alec. "Comedy in Synge and Beckett." Yeats Studies 2 (1972): 80-90.

Roach, Hal. His Greatest Collection of Irish Humor and Wit. Garden City, NY: Rego, n.d.

Robinson, Fred Norris. "Satirists and Enchanters in Early Irish Literature." Studies in the History of Religions Presented to Crawford Howell Toy. Eds. David Lyon and George Moore. New York, NY: Macmillan, 1912, 95-130.

Sharp, William. "Getting Married: New Dramaturgy in Comedy." Educational Theatre Journal 11 (1959): 103-109.

Sheedy, John J. "The Comic Apocalypse of King Hamm." Modern Drama 9 (1966): 310-318.

Solomon, Susan. The Comic Effect of Playboy of the Western World. Bangor, ME: Signalman, 1962.

Sorell, Walter. "Irish Humor and Eloquence." Facets of Comedy. New York, NY: Grosset and Dunlap, 1972, 114-125.

Topsfield, Valerie. The Humour of Samuel Beckett. New York, NY: St. Martin's Press, 1988.

Uris, Leon. Trinity. New York, NY: Doubleday, 1976.

Waters, Maureen. The Comic Irishman. Albany, NY: State Univ of New York Press, 1984.

Weekes, Ann Owens. Irish Women Writers: An Uncharted Tradition. Lexington, KY: University Press of Kentucky, 1990.

Whittock, Trevor. "Major Barbara: Comic Masterpiece." Theoria 51 (1978): 1-14.

CHAPTER 2

Humor in 16th Century Irish Literature

Edmund Spenser (c1554-1599) IRELAND

Edmund Spenser claimed kinship with the Spencer family in Althorp, Ireland, and he won that claim. Spenser showed a strong bias against the relentless subjugation of Ireland in his View of the Present State of Ireland (1596). Spenser received a grant from Kilcolman Castle, near Cork, Ireland, as part of the forfeited estates of the Earl of Desmond, and in 1598 Spenser became the sheriff of Cork. During this same year, Kilcolman castle was burned by the Irish insurrectionists, and Spenser lost his youngest child in the fire. He also might have lost some additional books of the Faerie Queene. His wife and other children were barely saved. He died on a mission to London, and was buried in Westminster Abbey near Chaucer (Neilson 1391).

Anthony Esolen considers the allegorical form of Spenser's Faerie Queene to be witty and at times even funny, because this form delights the entire palette of the reader's interpretive powers, including our sense of "tone, balance, decorum, comedy, irony, and, most urgently, humor" (Esolen 3). Allegory is filled with a galaxy of "messages and pretended messages," of "congruities and incongruities," of "ironies and half-ironies," and of "nudges and winks" (Esolen 7).

Spenser delights in giving the reader both congruities and incongruities at the same time in his allegories. Very often he will descend from high allegory to homely naturalism without warning. In the battle between Redcross and the dragon, for instance, every motif seems to assume theological significance. On the first day, the knight sleeps safely after he has fallen into the Well of Life. On the second day the knight is covered by the Tree of Balm. On the third day, the knight arises and slays the dragon. According to Anthony Esolen this represents Christ's death and resurrection, and Spenser even identifies the dragon with the Serpent of the Bible (I.xi.47). The killing of the dragon is the getting rid of evil incarnate. But Spenser realizes that the world is not easily cleansed from evil, and as the onlookers regard the dead dragon,

> One that would wiser seeme, than all the rest,
> Warned him not touch, for yet perhaps remaynd
> Some lingring life within his hollow brest,
> Of many Dragonets, his fruitfull seed;
> Another said, that in his eyes did rest
> Yet sparkling fire, and bad thereof take heed;
> Another said, he sawe him moue his eyes indeed. (xii.10.11)

Spenser is saying that a Christian should trust in God, don the armor of righteousness, and participate in that victory, but he is also saying that although evil has been destroyed by Christ, the destruction is unambiguous only from the vantage point of eternity. From the viewpoint of the Redcross, the onlookers, and the readers, evil still remains in the world (Esolen 9). The allegory form, which is intended to teach the difference between good and evil, is ambivalent and inconsistent. For Esolen, this is not a problem, if we discard the criterion of consistency. "Or better, if we overrule it with a criterion of humor or playfulness--the scene becomes a delightful set piece, allegorically effective because it suddenly relaxes the allegorical grid" (Esolen 9).

Esolen suggests that Spenser has tongue in cheek as he encourages us to think of his Faery Land as a magical place where the magic is a little bit out of control. "Allegory thrives on motivational confusion. It not only embraces many sorts of motifs, some allegorical and some not, but it pretends to present one sort of motif as another sort, creating new classes of motifs dependent upon the transparency, irony, humor, or mendacity of the pretense" (Esolen 12). The Faerie Queene needs to be read within the larger context of Tudor cultural mythmaking. In this way, the poem becomes a fearful commentary on the artistic subterfuges through which power legitimizes itself. Much of the humor of The Faerie Queene results from the absurdity of using knights and elves to allegorize religious and political truths. What makes The Faerie Queene work is that allegory allows conflicting opinions to rub against each other. It works because it plays with concepts and violates its own rules of consistency. When Charissa meets the Redcross knight, "her necke and breasts were euer open bare" (I.x.30). Esolen explains that this is because Charissa is the allegorical figure representing charity and love. The reader is surprised by her appearance because it is both congruent and incongruent with her allegorical significance (Esolen 12).

Scatology and crudeness are appropriate aspects of the allegory as long as they are used to depict the negative allegorical figures. Thus, it is appropriate that during her battle with Redcross, the monster Errour does something that would not be appropriate in the world of romance, but is perfectly appropriate in its allegorical significance. She vomits, and

> Her vomit full of bookes and papers was,
> With loathly frogs and toades, which eyes did lacke
> And creeping sought way in the weedy gras:
> Her filthy parbreake all the place defiled has. (I.i.20)

There is an "interesting congruity between those who publish heretical treatises, or the readers who digest them, and Errour's spawn" (Esolen 5). It is less appropriate, however, for the positive allegorical figures to act as Errour acted. It is inappropriate for the reader to see Amoret living her daily mundane life and having to relieve herself in the forest-- "The whiles faire Amoret, of nought affeard, / Walkt through the wood, for pleasure, or for need" (IV.vii.4). The reader is allowed to intrude into the private--even privy--life of Amoret and is shocked that an allegorical figure of Amoret's sensibilities is behaving so indecorously, and what we may have here is not allegory, but mock allegory. Henri Bergson says that "we laugh whenever a human being appears as a thing: a man slips on a banana skin, and in an instant he falls from rational enveloper of the universe to a sack of mass and acceleration" (Esolen 10).

We laugh when a human becomes a thing, and we also laugh when a thing becomes a human, as Alma's castle is mock-allegorically described as an intestinal tract where the noyous traveled along winding secret passage ways, and until it came to the back door where it was finally "auoided quite, and throwne out privily" (Esolen 6).

In an article entitled "The Grim Humor of Spenser's Faerie Queene: Women and Laughter in a Renaissance Epic," Charles Ross suggests that Spenser uses laughter as a way of signaling an absence of power (Ross 153). In medieval literature, laughter and mockery occurred when someone was about to be smitten by love (as in Chaucer's Troilus and Creseda for example). For Spenser, laughter is a danger signal; it is linked to sexual identity, and this can clearly be seen in Spenser's depiction of a giggling nymphomaniac named Phaedria in book II. It is Phaedria's job to ferry Guyon, the night of Temperance, across the lake of idleness, and on the journey to Acrasia's Bower of Bliss, Guyon passes an attractive dainty damsel who laughs loudly. Guyon would like very much to stay with the two naked laughing nymphs in a fountain, but forces himself not to. According to Ross, "Laughter is sexual, although sex is not necessarily humorous in The Faerie Queene" (Ross 156-157).

Throughout The Faerie Queene, the laughing male knights seem to exemplify the sudden glory from the derision of others that is so much a part of Thomas Hobbes's model of humor interpretation (Ross 159). Nevertheless, laughter in The Faerie Queene is often the first indicator of weakness as well. In the "Mutability" cantos at the end of The Faerie Queene, Faunus laughs when he sees the goddess Diana naked. Diana interprets this laughter to be incontinence, and she ponders about whether she should castrate him, drown him, or set her hounds on him as punishment (Ross 160).

The Squire of Dames laughs heartily in the third book of The Faerie Queene. The Squire loves Columbell, who sends him out to "do service unto gentle Dames." Columbell is referring to "service" in the non-sexual sense, and her sentence is a punishment to the Squire who had serviced, in a sexual sense, three hundred women. The Squire is thus sent back out into the world until he is able to find an equal number who would refuse his advances. But after three years, the knight had been able to find only three women who denied his advances. One of the three was a professional courtesan who wanted payment. Another was a nun who was already being well taken care of by her priest, and the third was a virtuous country girl of low degree. This last girl was the only person who denied him on principle (Ross 158).

According to Charles Ross, the longest running joke of The Faerie Queene relates to Britomart, the knight of Chastity, who is a woman disguised as a man. In contrast to Britomart there is the paranoid nymphet Amoret, probably the most desirable woman in The Faerie Queene. Amoret's name means love, and she was raised by Venus, the goddess of love. She is destined to become the wife of a knight named Scudamor, whose name means "Shield of Love." But Scudamor becomes jealous of a rival night named Britomart, who is actually a woman disguised as a man, when Ate stirs up Scudamor's jealousy by telling him that she has seen Amoret kissing another knight. Even though he is a wimp, Scudamor must defend his honor, and he teams up with Artegall to do battle with Britomart. During the fight, Britomart's helmet is knocked off and her long hair falls out (Ross 162-163).

In an ironic bit of role reversal, Spenser humorously valorizes women when the lady warrior Britomart knocks both Sir Scudomor and his horse to the ground. Sir Scudomor is so shaken by the event that he ends up talking to his horse. Spenser is using humor and irony and satire to target the doddering old-timers of the Roman Catholic Church during Spenser's times, and to satirize women, but his characters are clearly distortions and caricatures. Furthermore, Spenser is not mocking age or women, but is rather targeting pride, wantonness and vanity. Spenser's targets are not the people, but the vices of the people (Ross 161).

J. E. Shen describes Spenser's Merlin from The Faerie Queene as a traditional sixteenth-century magician, associated with mythical forces and spirits. When Glauce approaches him to request that he use his magical powers to free Britomart of her gloom, Merlin responds first with smiles and then with a "bursting forth in laughter" almost as if he is the victim of overpowering mental forces (Shen 153). Glauce, who has used her own herbal remedies to try to release Britomart from her gloom, is aware of Merlin's awesome powers, and therefore approaches him with extreme caution. There is a disparity between Glauce's small powers and domestic concerns and Merlin's strong powers and national concerns, and the coming together of these dissimilar magicians provides a comic frame of reference.

In The Shepherd's Calendar, Spenser writes twelve poems, one for each month. These poems, according to E. K.'s gloss, divide into three categories, plaintive, recreative, and moral, with the plaintive and recreative poems being funny only to the extent that the reader laughs at the misery and pains of love. The moral tales, however, are satirical, and are clearly meant to provoke mirth. In "Februarie," for example, the old shepherd Thenot tells the young Cuddie a sad story about how a young briar bush was so proud of its berries and its greenery that it had a woodman chop down a neighboring old tall oak, of which the bush was envious. It was only then that the bush learned that the oak tree had been its shelter from the wind and rain (Ross 154-155). In "Maye" a shepherd named Palimode says that there are four things that are hard to live with: "women who've had sex and want more, anger that calls for vengeance, thirst, and a fool's talk" (Ross 155). Spenser's "September" is an attack on Popish prelates, and by "October" Spenser's shepherds "appear to be the butts of a vast celestial joke that requires poets to live in poverty and go unrecognized" (Ross 155). According to Ross, the life of the shepherd poet in "December" is as bleak as is the month which forms the title for the poem. Spenser's humor is so sophisticated, complex, and ironic that at least one critic (Thenot) has attributed it to Chaucer. Part of the ironic effect of the poems comes from the discrepancy in the poems between the sad messages told in the stories, and the exuberant language that is used to tell the stories. The reader is convinced that despite the tragic mode, life is nevertheless ultimately uplifting. These poems are comic in Dante's religious sense of a fortunate ending (Ross 155).

Frances McNeely Leonard suggests that until recently few Spenser critics have found humor in Spenser's writings, and when they have found it they usually shrugged it off with a comment like "This seems to be one of Spenser's few consciously humorous passages" (Leonard 133). However, recently many Spenser critics have been reading Spenser's works with a new eye for humor, and those critics who speak of Spenser's comedy tend to hold it in high praise. In The Poetry of The Faerie Queene, Paul Alpers says, for example, that Book 3 is "one of the great comic poems in English, and . . . to find its equal we must go to Chaucer and Shakespeare." Leonard concurs:

> Like Chaucer, Spenser is a comic poet; like Chaucer, too, he is an allegorist; he is, in fact, the last significant maker of allegories to trace his lineage back to Chaucer, and his achievement in blending comedy with allegory thus concludes a tradition that endured in English poetry for more than two hundred years. (Leonard 134)

Edmund Spenser Bibliography

Alden, Raymond MacDonald. "Edmund Spenser." The Rise of Formal Satire in England under Classical Influence. New York, NY: Archon, 1961, 74-75.

Cazamian, Louis. "Spenser." The Development of English Humor. Durham, NC: Duke University Press, 1952, 358-362.

Esolen, Anthony. "Spenserian Allegory and the Clash of Narrative Worlds." Thalia: Studies in Literary Humor 11.1 (1989): 3-13.

Hall, John M. "Braggadocchio and Spenser's Golden World Concept: The Function of Unregenerative Comedy." Journal of English Literary History 37 (1970): 315-324.

Holleran, James V. "A View of Comedy in The Faerie Queene." Essays in Honor of

Esmond Linworth Marilla. Eds. Thomas Austin Kirby and William John Olive. Baton Rouge, LA: Louisiana State Univ Press, 1970, 101-114.

Leonard, Frances McNeely. "The Comedy of The Faerie Queene." Laughter in the Courts of Love: Comedy in Allegory, from Chaucer to Spenser. Norman, OK: Pilgrim, 1981, 133-167.

Neilson, William Allan. Webster's Biographical Dictionary. Springfield, MA: G. and C. Merriam, 1971.

Ross, Charles. "The Grim Humor of Spenser's Faerie Queene: Women and Laughter in a Renaissance Epic." HUMOR: International Journal of Humor Research 2.2 (1989): 153-164.

Shen, J. E. "The Comic Merlin in Spenser." WHIMSY 1 (1983): 153-155.

Wade, Clyde G. "Comedy in Book VI of The Faerie Queene." Arlington Quarterly 2.4 (1970): 90-104.

Watkins, W. B. C. "Spenser's High Comedy." Shakespeare and Spenser. Princeton, NJ: Princeton Univ Press, 1950, 293-304.

CHAPTER 3

Humor in 17th Century Irish Literature

Cyril Tourneur (c1575-1626) IRELAND

Cyril Tourneur was a dramatist who served in the Low Countries. After this service he was put ashore among the sick in Ireland, and it was in Ireland that he died. Tourneur's first publication was The Transformed Metamorphosis, and it appeared in 1600. Some critics include this work in the category of formal satires of this period (Alden 161).

The greater power of Tourneur's The Revenger's Tragedy allows for a greater density of ironic suggestion. The flashes of humor in this play can be said to be "sardonic" in tone (Cazamian 341). In the last act of The Revenger's Tragedy, there are sets of masquers intent on killing the same victims, and there is much irony when the second set stab the bodies that have already been killed by the first set. "It can be very eerie, and grotesquely funny as well" (Brooke 6). The themes of lechery, unchastity, and materialism appear in the imagery and content of Tourneur's The Revenger's Tragedy. These three themes plus the theme of death are developed with a tone of cynicism and horror (Peter 256-257). Unlike The Revenger's Tragedy, The Atheist's Tragedy contains quite a bit of double entendre. The message is determined by the placement of dialogue in the mouths of sympathetic or unsympathetic characters. "Actually only Levidulcia, Sebastian, Cataplasma, Fresco, and Snuffe are allowed to speak suggestively, and it is plain that Tourneur has deliberately allowed them this license in order to represent them as sensual and contemptible" (Peter 284).

Louis Cazamian writes about the comic themes in Tourneur's The Atheist's Tragedy, such as Act 2, Scene 5, in particular, and the development of the character Snuffe, the Puritan, in general. Cazamian feels that the comic themes of The Atheist's Tragedy are discrete and reserved. There is much obscenity in The Atheist's Tragedy, but this is not obscenity for its own sake. Rather, it is used as part of the development of the main plot. John Peter feels that Snuffe is given a mild punishment for his deeds, while Cataplasma, Soquette, and Fresco are given more severe punishments, and he feels that by doing this, Tourneur is saying that "even hypocritical Puritanism was preferable to downright looseness" (Peter 284). Peter feels that both Tourneur and Shakespeare were Christians, and he feels that they had similar if not identical beliefs on the subject of Christianity. He feels that the difference between Tourneur and Shakespeare in this regard is that Shakespeare invites the audience to explore rather than wanting it just to acquiesce. Shakespeare's writing presents us not with formulas and conclusions already fixed, but with "the mass and aggregate of life from which we see such conclusions, or similar ones, in process of arising." Peter continues.

> In Tourneur's case we have to take his conclusions more or less on trust, while in Shakespeare's we ponder the problems equally with the dramatist, and come to our conclusions (though they are his) as if of our own accord. It is because he invites this creative participation from his audience or reader that, in this sense, Shakespeare is profound, and it is this that allows us to call him a universal genius. (Peter 286)

While Shakespeare was looking to the future, Tourneur was looking to the past, for he was exploring the common ground that existed between the tradition of the Complaint and the type of tragedy that had evolved out of the Morality play, and he was reincarnating these traditions in his own works (Peter 287).

Cyril Tourneur Bibliography

Alden, Raymond MacDonald. "Cyril Tourneur." The Rise of Formal Satire in England under Classical Influence. New York, NY: Archon, 1961, 161-162.

Brooke, Nicholas. Horrid Laughter in Jacobean Tragedy. New York, NY: Harper and Row, 1979.

Cazamian, Louis. "Tourneur." The Development of English Humor. Durham, NC: Duke University Press, 1952, 341-342.

Oates, Joyce Carol. "The Comedy of Metamorphosis in The Revenger's Tragedy." Bucknell Review 11.1 (1962): 38-52.

Peter, John. "Tourneur's Tragedies." Complaint and Satire in Early English Literature. Oxford, England: Clarendon Press, 1956, 255-287.

CHAPTER 4

Humor in 18th Century Irish Literature

Jonathan Swift (1667-1745) IRELAND

As a satirist, Jonathan Swift is a true craftsman. Swift described the Earl of Wharton as "a Presbyterian in politics, and an atheist in religion; but he chooses at present to whore with a Papist." Irvin Ehrenpreis feels that "There is nothing accidental about the order of these phrases, the parallels and paradoxes, the rhythmic balance or the savagely ironic tone," and he concludes that "a gifted satirist composed the sentence" (Ehrenpreis 215). When Swift became Dean of St. Patrick's in Dublin a poem was posted on the door:

> This place he got by wit and rhyme,
> And many ways most odd,
> And might a bishop be in time,
> Did he believe in God. (O'Donoghue xvii)

Swift takes many liberties in writing his satires. "He invents outrageous spokesmen for religious and political positions he despises, and exotic countries which crazily reflect vices at home; he plays fast and loose with logic and arithmetic; he wins arguments by splendid perversions of truth" (DePorte 53). Many of Swift's readers, both those contemporary with Swift and those ever since, have interpreted his satires as "underlining with savage laughter man's fundamental viciousness" (Ingram 39). John Bullitt indicates that Swift's satiric devices evolve organically out of the disparity between reality and expectation, and it is this which provokes the comic spirit. But Bullitt feels that Swift scholars have devoted too much attention to Swift's environment, and to his attitudes, and not enough attention to his satire as an art form, thereby confusing the means with the ends (Bullitt Anatomy vii). It was Swift's view of life as a "ridiculous tragedy" that enabled him to become one of the great comic writers. Swift viewed satire as "the unillusioned perception of man as he actually is, and the ideal perception, or vision, of man as he ought to be." Bullitt feels that satire can become a vital force in literature only if there is a rather widespread agreement about what man ought to be, and because most people in the late seventeenth and early eighteenth century had this widespread agreement, the most successful flowering of satire in the history of literature took place during this time (Bullitt Anatomy 1).

In "Epistle to a Lady," Swift wrote the following poem:

> I may storm and rage in vain;
> It but stupefies your Brain.
> But with Raillery to nettle,

Set your Thoughts upon their Mettle:
Gives Imagination scope . . . (Topsfield 11).

Bullitt points out that during the eighteenth century there was an important distinction made between "raillery" and "ridicule." In his <u>Hints Towards an Essay on Conversation</u>, Swift devotes a paragraph to "raillery," which he calls "the finest part of conversation." Swift goes on to say that we got this word from the French, which gives it its special flavor. "Raillery was to say something that at first appeared a reproach or reflection, but, by some turn of wit unexpected and surprising, ended always in a compliment, and to the advantage of the person it was addressed to" (Bullitt "Swift's" 97). Swift goes on to prescribe what makes good conversation, part of which is determined by the humor, the raillery, and the wit of the language, combined with the ability of not making anyone feel uneasy (Bullitt "Swift's" 98). Swift was very sensitive to audience response, and he knew that raillery as a form of irony was susceptible to misinterpretation, and that its success depended as much upon the wit of the reader as that of the author (Bullitt "Swift's" 102). He therefore said:

> In conversation, as in letters, it behooves the ironist to choose his company well and avoid the error of those "men of wit and good understanding," Swift wrote in his <u>Hints on Good Manners</u>, who conceive a "better opinion of those with whom they converse than they ought to do. Thus I have often known the most innocent raillery, and even of the kind which was meant for praise, to be mistaken for abuse and reflection." (Bullitt "Swift's" 103)

Swift once faulted John Pope by saying that he has every quality and virtue that can make a man amiable or useful, but his back is bent. This is an example of raillery. While other types of understatement might "damn with faint praise," raillery does the opposite; it praises with faint damning (Bullitt "Swift's" 108).

Although Swift started out as a Whig, he ended up very decidedly as a Tory and a churchman, even though he often embarrassed both the Church and the Tory leadership. But even more than being a Tory or a Churchman, Swift was an Irishman, not only in the sense that he was born and died in Ireland, and was the Dean of St. Patrick's Cathedral in Dublin, but also because he was so deeply concerned with the Irish cause that he earned the name of "Hibernian Patriot" (Davis 2). Swift was also an English gentleman, and a close associate to Sir William Temple, Lord Sommers, the Earl of Oxford and the Viscount of Bolingbrook. In addition, Swift was a special friend of Alexander Pope, John Arbuthnot, and John Gay not to mention the fact that he was a cousin to John Dryden (Davis 2).

William Eddy points out that Swift's satires were received differently by different audiences. "The Swift who enlivened the company of Stella, Arbuthnot, Addison, Gay, and Pope is the Swift for modern readers, rather than the monster described by Thackeray, the bloodless rationalist depicted by Leslie Stephen, or the 'neurotic,' the exhumed 'skull,' and the 'tiger' of more recent biographies" (Eddy xi). Swift was known by his comrades as "the laughter-loving dean," "the merry yahoo," "Bickerstaff," and "martin Scriblerus," but he was known by other members of his audience as a "pathological misanthrope" (Eddy xi-xii). And part of the reason for this range of reactions to his writing is that Swift had a "unique talent for combining on the same page the fury of a moralist and the farce of a harlequin" (Eddy xiii). Even his greatest and most bitter satires were written in moments of diversion. The adventures of Gulliver were written into the <u>Memoirs of Scriblerus</u> as early as 1714, and Alexander Pope dedicated <u>The Dunciad</u> to Swift. It is interesting to note at this point that in "Thoughts on Various Subjects, Moral and Diverting," Swift said, "When a true genius appears in the world, you may know him by this sign, that the dunces are all in confederacy against him." It is from this statement that John Kennedy Toole got the title for his novel, <u>A Confederacy of Dunces</u> (Toole ii).

Swift also influenced other authors in his moments of diversion, and in fact suggested to John Gay that he write a Newgate pastoral. The result was Gay's Beggar's Opera. Eddy suggests that the effect of Swift's satires is not to have the victims appear as fools, but to have them appear as knaves, something which Eddy considers to be a more serious predicament. "One may be a knave with impunity in this world, where clever racketeers and captains of industry amass wealth and notoriety without damage to their reputations as supermen" (Eddy xxx). The major target in all of Swift's satire was man's vanity (Eddy xxxi).

All Swift critics, those during his lifetime and those afterwards, seem to agree on the effectiveness of Swift's satires; however, Edward Rosenheim laments that Swift's critics are divided, uncertain, or sometimes silent about the nature of his art as a satirist. For more than two centuries after Swift's death the hundreds of critics who have written about England's greatest satirist have had very little to say about satire itself, or about how Swift created it. Their studies detail Swift's life and times, the vexing problems of relating text to canon, the sources and consequences of Swift's ideas, and his stature as a clergyman, moralist, correspondent, historian, and pamphleteer. They address matters relating to Swift's personality and beliefs, and refer to his literary accomplishments as means of establishing his credibility.

> The only disturbing aspect of this preoccupation with Swift's personality is its implicit neglect of his art. Until the last ten or fifteen years, what seems most to have interested those who wrote about the great satirist is not his satire but rather his madness, his "marriage," his friends and enemies, habits and beliefs, and a dozen similar matters. (Rosenheim 4)

Part of the reason for the emphasis on Swift rather than on his writing is that a preacher-pamphleteer-satirist always works in the arena of public opinion (Rosenheim 237). His goal is to educate and/or to entertain. "In his appeal to the omnipresent audience he is prepared to be governed by its human desires, its capacity for shock, its cruelty . . . , and the limits of its intelligence" (Rosenheim 238).

In a book entitled Jonathan Swift: Preacher and Jester, Peter Steele indicates that "a reading of Swift which releases him from the bond of politics, religion, and history is likely to be misleading." Steele quotes Denis Donoghue as saying that in Swift's context, "satire, irony, and invective arose from a setting in which language, politics, religion and history were not separate activities, but one activity, taking these several forms" (Donoghue 24). Steele investigates the two antithetical and paradoxical aspects of Swift's personality and writing--preacher and jester--and suggests that it is the interplay between Swift as preacher, and Swift as jester which has led to much of the divergence of opinion of Swift's critics and biographers. Since Swift's work involves paradoxical descriptions, the critics are forced to arrive at paradoxical explanations of his work. But Peter Steele suggests that there is another latent irony here as well, that the work of an author who professed a plainness of style is actually filled with "Alexandrian complication." Steele proposes how Swift's writing should be evaluated: "If Swift is called to account, it is not by society at large, nor by any of the successive authorities with whom he had to do, nor by a specifically divine allegiance; but solely by his own powerfully held and powerfully willed sense of the true, the good, and the rational" (Steele 2). Swift is not an author prone to adjusting, to conceding, or to apologizing, though he may simulate all of these postures. In fact, Swift often appears to his audience to be wavering, but he is only feigning to be a waverer. "The ripple of apparent indecision that runs through many of his commanding works is like that in the flexure of a rapier: when the hand trembles, it does so deliberately." Swift's concessions are only tactical; indeed, they are not concessions at all. "When an air of understanding, or of what might be called magnanimity, insinuates itself, this is really a kind of Trojan Horse of the emotions. Companionable he may occasionally

seem, but he is rarely felt to be <u>essentially</u> a companionable writer." Steele feels that Swift
not only hates the sin; he hates the sinner as well (Steele 3-4).

Robert Polhemus discusses the ability which Swift has of uniting satire and religion:

> Swift uses his satirical humor as a deadly moral weapon to condemn the
> world.   His satire plays on the ugliness of the flesh and the moral
> repulsiveness of unredeemed human nature.   Much of his art of savage
> indignation and black humor comes out of the old <u>memento mori, danse
> macabre</u> Christian tradition, but his subtle, scathing irony is new and very
> important in the history of comic prose fiction. (13)

Most critics have concentrated on Swift as a preacher, and not so many critics have
concentrated on Swift as a jester; yet Swift was as much a jester as a preacher. Swift had
a good eye for the ungoverned copiousness of the world, what Steele calls "the soul of
Rabelais dwelling in a dry place." According to Steele, Swift had "much of Rabelais's
relish of the abundance, the near-sumptuousness, of some of the world's features. It is true
that, like many another satirical writer, Swift is most alert when the copiousness of life
takes the form of extravagance" (Steele 7).   Through this process of extravagance,
multitudes become hordes, generosity becomes prodigality, a ruler becomes a tyrant, and
a group becomes rabble. "If he is never quite the Lord of Misrule, there is a part of him
which is tempted to become so. It is as if the anger that kindles in him at the sight of
many abuses warms to fervour and imaginative enjoyment of multiplicity" (Steele 7). Swift
is often not of a single mind:

> There are the very many situations in which he savours, to the point of
> aesthetic relish, the things he is ostensibly denouncing. To say this is not
> to say that he is a hypocrite, or self-deceived. In the first instance, it is only
> to say that so firmly hewn a figure as he was may still be complex when in
> action. More teasingly, though, it is to imply that the interplay between the
> judicial or homiletic side of his mind, and the comic or sportive side, is both
> more subtle and more inevitable than one might have supposed. (Steele 8)

Therefore, Steele proposes that the comic elements which appear in Swift should not be
thought of as "intrusion, however memorable, into what is otherwise a process of definition,
but that they should themselves be regarded as crucial to the definition: and that in some
cases they have priority over the more overtly 'magisterial' moves in the work" (Steele 9).
Steele concludes his article by saying that "There are those who find Swift above all
complex, a trickster through and through; and those who, by contrast, take him to be
greatly skilled but essentially plain. But anybody who knows much about Swift knows that
there is usually a great deal going on in his work" (Steele 10-11).

William Eddy indicates that Swift's humor involves a wide range of genres. The
Brodbingnag piece represents farce; <u>Directions to Servants</u> represents grotesque
exaggeration; <u>Scriblerus</u> represents parody; <u>Genteel Conversation</u> represents overstatement
and comic juxtaposition of ideas; in addition, understatement and anti-climax are present
in a large number of Swift satires (Eddy xxx). Eddy divides Swift's satires into four
general types. 1. As examples of "ironical essays," Eddy lists <u>An Argument against
Abolishing Christianity</u>, <u>A Modest Proposal</u>, <u>A Letter of Advice to a Young Poet</u>, <u>A Letter
to a Young Lady on her Marriage</u>, <u>An Essay on Modern Education</u>, <u>A True and Faithful
Narrative of What Passed in London</u>, and <u>The Memoirs of Martinus Scriblerus</u>. 2. In his
division on "Satirical Diversions," Eddy lists <u>Memoirs of the Life of Scriblerus</u>, <u>A
Meditation upon a Broom-Stick</u>, <u>The Partridge-Bickerstaff Papers</u>, <u>A Compleat Collection
of Genteel, and Ingenious Conversation</u>, and <u>Directions to Servants in General</u>. 3. Most
of Swift's intimate and personal writings were to Stella, including <u>The Journal to Stella</u>,
and <u>Prayers for Stella</u> as well as a number of important letters and poems. But Swift also
wrote significant letters to L'Abbé des Fontaines, John Arbuthnot, Viscount Bolinbroke,

John Gay, Benjamin Motte, Alexander Pope, Thomas Swift, Esther Vanhomrigh, and Mrs. Whiteway. 4. Much of Swift's poetry was also ironic and satiric, such as "To a Lady (Who Desired the Author to Write Some Verses upon Her in the Heroic Style)," and "A Satirical Elegy on the Death of a Late Famous General," and "Verses Made for Fruit-Women," and "The Day of Judgment," and "On the Death of Dr. Swift" (Eddy vii-ix).

Herbert Davis divides Swift's satire into three general types. A Tale of a Tub represents what Davis calls "Literary Satire;" it was during this first period that Swift developed his artistic and aesthetic talents. The Examiner and M. B. Drapier represents "Political Satire"; it was during this second period that Swift developed his social and political awareness. Gulliver's Travels represents "Moral Satire"; it was during this last period that Swift developed his permanent moral and ethical values (Davis vi, 4).

A Tale of a Tub (1704) is a satire on the corruption of religion and education. It is also a satire against modernism and a defence of Christianity. Swift's persona in this piece, the Mad Modern, is an unsympathetic character who embraces the modern view. Through the Mad Modern's false wit and the absurdity and madness of his views, and through the fact that the Mad Modern has no sense of religion, Swift is establishing the correctness of all of the opposite positions (Palumbo 5). But Donald Palumbo believes that Swift is much more of a modern than Swift himself would have us believe. In an article entitled "Science Fiction as Allegorical Social Satire: William Burroughs and Jonathan Swift," Palumbo compares Swift's satire with that of William Burroughs:

> As Gulliver's Travels parodies travel literature and The Tale of a Tub the writing of tracts, Burroughs at times parodies the genres he employs, science fiction and the detective thriller. There is political satire in Burroughs's novels also, as there is in Gulliver. In Naked Lunch, the parties of Interzone--the Liquefactionists, Factualists, Senders, and Divisionists-- represent political attitudes, though not specific parties, that fall under Burroughs's fire. Pride, to Swift man's most offensive vice, is, in a Christian context, love of self above love of God. This glorying in the self is comparable to Burroughs's "addict" setting himself against nature, to his blind concern for not only his own needs and desires to the exclusion of any possibility of compassion or of any sense of responsibility to the external environment. The raw appetites of the Yahoos are man's addictions which (applying "the algebra of need") man must pervert his reason to satisfy, just as in Gulliver's Travels reason is seen as a tool tuned to the task of extending the range of man's corruption. Also, Swift's association of the Yahoos' stench with human corruption is like Burroughs's use of his montage technique. (Palumbo 6-7)

During the seventeenth century, philosophers and physicians, and Swift himself, acknowledged two kinds of madness. The first of these mental disorders was characterized by obsession, or by addiction, or by an idée fixe. The other type of mental disorder was marked by the loss of control over the orderly processes of thought whereby there was a confusion of fantasy with reality. Michael DePorte feels that Swift's Tale of a Tub is "an account by the member of one mad fraternity about members of the other" (DePorte 56). DePorte points out that Swift was also mentally disturbed in another way as the author of Tale of a Tub, in that he was criticizing something which he held dear:

> Swift could dismiss the charges of Wotton and others that the Tale was irreligious by saying that they failed to understand its irony. What Swift did not say, of course, is that his irony served also to enlarge the boundaries of covert discourse, that it gave him license to raise the sort of questions he publicly deplored as dangerous, but which he seemed privately to feel must be reckoned with. In the end, then, the disturbing power of Swift's satire

has perhaps less to do with saeva indignatio, which we can always deflect onto others, than with Swift's peculiar genius for discovering how to make the questions which threatened his peace of mind threaten ours as well. (DePorte 69)

The Battle of the Books (1704) is a travesty written in the form of Juvenalian satire on the controversy over ancient and modern learning. The satire of A Tale of a Tub (1704) like that of The Battle of the Books is Juvenalian. In A Tale of a Tub, Swift trod on the toes of theologians with his ironic treatment of various internal church bickerings. The satire, The Conduct of the Allies, was published in 1711. It was also around this time that Swift wrote his Journal to Stella, which contains intimate letters, most of them written in baby language. Drapiers Letters (1724) successfully urged the cancellation of William Wood's halfpence in Ireland.

Gulliver's Travels (1726) is Swift's most effective satire. It blends fiction, allegory, politics, adventure, ridicule in a philosophical view of man's darkest nature. It targets the cant and the sham of the courts, the parties, and the statesmen of eighteenth-century England. One of the reasons for the effectiveness of Gulliver's Travels is that it can be read on more than one level. For generations, it has been read not only as an excellent children's story, but as sophisticated satire as well:

> And within its satiric mode there appear to be discordant aims. Some critics have sought to reconcile these by more or less ingenious critical analysis. Ehrenpreis suggests that the search for a "careful intellectual structure" may be misdirected. The various paradoxes within the book may not be resolved; its ultimate brilliance and effectiveness must come from the stylistic control rather than from the moral integrity. (Browning 8)

Steele indicates that Swift was intrigued by the array of human stereotypes he saw around him. He also enjoyed playing with the most common human activities engaged in by these varying personalities; simple and common activities like eating, talking, traveling, and just existing and surviving were full enough of promise, menace, and curiosity to Swift to make him return again and again to these topics. And the relationships between the stereotypes in Swift's writings and the stereotypes in the real world are also not obvious and easy to establish. Hugh Kenner suggests that neither the Yahoo, nor Gulliver himself should be considered representative of man, for part of Swift's delight in writing came from his enjoyment of metamorphosis: "The reader is deceived by two counterfeits. The Yahoo is not human at all; Gulliver is not human enough. Gulliver, for whom the Fortran of the horses is the last word in explicit rationality, even becomes a two legged reasoning horse before our very eyes" (Kenner 142). Kenner goes on to say that Gulliver's Travels is "the only extensive work of English literature written by a horse" (Kenner 142).

Gulliver finds a peculiar and strange tribe of people whose style of writing is "neither from the left to the right, like the Europeans, nor from the right to left, like the Arabians, nor from up to down, like the Chinese, nor from down to up, like the Cascagians, but aslant from one corner of the paper to the other, like ladies in England" (Fromkin and Rodman 149). Gulliver also meets with people who cannot understand how it is possible to have lying or false representation. These people argue that the use of speech is to make people understand each other, and to receive information about the facts of the situation. "Now, if anyone said the thing which was not, these ends were defeated; because I cannot properly be said to understand him." Gulliver had great difficulty making these people understand the faculty of lying, "so perfectly well understood, and so universally practiced among human creatures" (Fromkin and Rodman 183).

In Book III of Gulliver's Travels, Swift devotes four chapters to the lives of theoretical scientists on the flying island of Laputa. Chris Worth notes that the flying island of Laputa is shaped like a metal button of the kind with which one would have fastened pants during Swift's time. This is a satirical reference to a man named "Button," the proprietor of a cafe at which various "high flying" scientific theories were discussed. According to Worth, here one can finally see a political-historical genesis to the Laputa episode. Furthermore, the Laputan's enjoyment of mathematics interspersed with music correlates to a similar interest in Swift's political nemesis, Mr. Steele. Worth says that the reason that it took this long to realize that these rather direct relationships might exist is that political winds were shifting so fast during the time of Swift's writing that by the time of publication of Gulliver's Travels, Button's cafe and at least one of its important patrons had ceased to be important figures (Worth 364). The scientists on Laputa are so far removed from the real world that they seem to have lost all of their humanity. Even their jargon, and their symbols are limited to mathematics and to music, as they praise the beauty of a woman in terms of rhombs, circles, parallelograms, ellipses, and other mathematical expressions. After they have finished their theoretical speculations these scientists are transferred to the Island of Lagado where they attempt to put their theories into application.

> Here we find them trying to extract sunshine from cucumbers, convert ice into gunpowder, build houses from the top down, teach the blind to mix colors for painters, soften marble into pillows and pin-cushions, develop a solution that will prevent sheep from producing wool, and so on. (Bartel 79).

It is in Lagado that the scientists in their desire to have a universal language have replaced words with things.

> Everyone carries a sackful of objects, and when people meet someone they want to talk to, they empty their sacks and point to the objects that replaced the words. Those who wish to conduct the most business carry the largest sacks. They walk down the streets doubled over into an animal posture, brutalized by the loss of language. The role of language in the creation of our humanity has been reversed. (Bartel 80)

There were many experiments being conducted in the School of Languages. Some professors were trying to shorten discourse by cutting polysyllabic words down to one syllable, and by leaving out the verbs and participles because in reality all things imaginable are nothing but nouns. There was another scheme for abolishing all words whatsoever, which would have advantages both in terms of health and brevity, because "every word we speak is in some degree a diminution of our lungs by corrosion" (Fromkin and Rodman 210).

> Swift was very aware of the power of words, and in fact said,
>
> The deepest account, and the most fairly digested of any I have yet met with, is this, that air being a heavy body, and therefore (according to the system of Epicurus) continually descending, must needs be more so, when laden and press'd down by words; which are also bodies of much weight and gravity, as it is manifest from those deep impressions they make and leave upon us; and therefore, must be delivered from a due altitude, or else they will neither carry a good aim, nor fall down with sufficient force. (Klamar 5)

A Modest Proposal (1729) is a bitter satire targeting the simple-minded attempts that have been proposed to resolve Ireland's shortage of food, shortage of money, and abundance of children. It also targets England's interference with Irish political affairs. The basic organization of A Modest Proposal is modeled on the traditional form of classical oration, which includes the exordium, the statement of facts, the digression, the proof, the refutation, and the peroration, in that order. It should be noted that the incongruity between the logic of the structure and the lack of logic of the proposal itself adds to the satire

(Thieme 14). That the language is very strong can be seen in the following excerpt: "A young healthy child, well nursed, is at a year old a most delicious, nourishing and wholesome food, whether stewed, roasted, baked, or boiled, and I make no doubt that it will equally serve in a fricassee, or a ragout" (Shibles 162).

George Mayhew wrote a doctoral dissertation at Harvard University on Jonathan Swift's "Games with Language." This material was later expanded and published as a book entitled Rage or Raillery: The Swift Manuscripts at the Huntington Library. Swift often engaged in language games, and the best example of this is a series of Anglo-Latin language games he played with his friend Dr. Thomas Sheridan between 1734 and 1736.

From 1738 on, Swift was haunted by the dread of going insane. His satire during this time became very dark, bitter, and trivial. It is during this period that he wrote such pieces as Directions to Servants, Polite Conversations, Hamilton's Bawn, Rhapsody on Poetry, and Verses on the Death of Swift. Much of Swift's satire was strong, and Peter Steele feels that this was an important feature of Swift's satire. He feels that if we were to take the sting and the savagery out of Swift's satire, all would be gone (Steele 3).

In Raillery and Rage: A Study of Eighteenth Century Satire, David Nokes concentrates on a Swiftian paradox. Although Swift was authoritarian in his personal pronouncements, he was almost anarchic in his satiric wit. Nokes demonstrates this apparent discrepancy with examples from Swift's The Directions to Servants, where Nokes examines Swift as having the attitudes of a master, but those of a servant as well. Nokes suggests that this ambivalence is similar to the opposite stances of the Houyhnhnms and the Yahoos in Gulliver's Travels (Nokes xii).

Leigh Hunt feels that "for the qualities of sheer wit and humour, Swift had no superior, ancient or modern." His wit was "a sheer meeting of the extremes of difference and likeness; and his knowledge of character was unbounded. He knew the humour of great and small, from the king down to the cook-maid." Much of his writing like that of his contemporaries was coarse, but the writings of Swift tended to be even more outrageously so (Hunt 287). Leigh Hunt compares Swift to Lucian, to Rabelais, and to Edmund Rostand, who wrote Cyrano de Bergerac. But an even more important influence on Swift was Samuel Butler whose rhymes he emulated. Nevertheless, nothing that Swift wrote was extensively derivative, and his long irregular prose verses with rhymes at the end are totally an invention of his own (Hunt 288).

Jonathan Swift explained the difficulty of defining "humor" in his famous couplet, "What Humor is, not all the Tribe / Of Logick-mongers can describe. /Here, onely Nature acts her Part, / Unhelpt by Practice, Books, or Art" (Levin 2). Although he was not able to define humor, Swift was nevertheless able to use it effectively, and David Nokes describes Swift's unique style as follows:

> Swift's real power is precisely that unease that his works continue to create as their shifting tones glide effortlessly from platitude to paradox or from axiom to absurdity without a syntactical tremor . . . . Swift refashions the enduring questions of human morality in ways which prohibit us from taking refuge in conventional formulas of belief. (Nokes 183)

An example of Swift's skill as a parodist is his Meditation upon a Broomstick, which was written as a mocking imitation of Robert Boyle. For Swift, much of the pleasure of parody lies in enjoying the confusion of the gullible ignoramuses who miss the joke. On one occasion, Lady Berkeley found a copy of Meditation, and not realizing it was a parody, she asked Swift if he would read it aloud, which he did (Browning 6):

> Lady Berkeley, not at all suspecting a trick . . . was every now and then . . . . expressing her admiration of this extraordinary man, who could draw such fine moral reflections from so contemptible a subject; with which, though Swift must have been inwardly not a little tickled, yet he preserved

> a most perfect composure of features, so that she had not the least room to
> suspect any deceit. (Browning 7)

Being aware of the jest, the elite in the room admired the poise with which Swift carried off the joke (Browning 7).

The central theme of all of Swift's satire is the idea that men's minds are so concentrated on the superficial aspects of life, and Swift felt that the secret to being happy was the same as the secret of being perpetually well deceived. A controlling metaphor in Swift's satire is the metaphor of the "anatomy." He refers to himself as a kind of "rational surgeon" (Bullitt Anatomy 2). In depicting the incompatibility between realism (the way things are) and idealism (the way things should be), Swift frequently used this anatomy metaphor. John Bullitt goes so far as to contend that "this analytical and dissecting tendency of Swift's realism, combined with the poignant idealistic desire to rid life of the disparity between what actually 'is' and what merely seems to be, provided the central impulse behind his satire" (Bullitt Anatomy 3). As an example, consider Swift's statement: "Last week I saw a woman flay'd, and you will hardly believe how much it altered her person for the worse" (Bullitt "Swift's" 191). Or consider the following surgical metaphor from The Tale of the Tub:

> I have . . . dissected the carcass of Humane Nature, and read many useful
> lectures upon the several parts, both containing and contained; till at last it
> smelt so strong, I could preserve it no longer. Upon which, I have been at
> a great expense to fit up all the bones with exact contexture, and in due
> symmetry; so that I am ready to shew a very compleat anatomy thereof.
> (Bullitt Anatomy 2)

Swift very much enjoyed his own satires. In a letter to his cousin Thomas, he tells of a "desperate weakness" he has for his own productions. "I have a sort of vanity, or Foibless, I do not know what to call it, and which I would fain know if you partake of it, it is (not to be cirmcumstantial) that I am overfond of my own writings, I would not have the world think so for a million, but it is so, and I find when I write what pleases me I am Cowley to myself and can read it a hundred times over" (DePorte 54-55).

Swift's satires were varied and complex, and they exhibit a wide range of emotions, anger being only one of them. The particular tension which distinguishes Swift's satires from those of all other satirists was once described by Swift himself as "a struggle between contempt and indignation." "The 'turn' of Swift's humour led him to see life sometimes as a comedy, sometimes as a lamentable tragedy, often as a source of angry frustration--and most frequently and effectively, perhaps, in such satires as A Modest Proposal or Gulliver's Travels, Swift reacted in all ways at once" (Bullitt Anatomy 5). John Bullitt considers Swift to be clearly England's greatest satirist, and suggests that he may be the greatest satirist of all time anywhere (Bullitt Anatomy 5). In a letter to Alexander Pope, Swift once wrote, "I never will have peace of mind till all honest men are of my opinion" (Bullitt Anatomy 4). Swift probably realized that with this condition, he would never have peace of mind on this earth; he therefore composed an epitaph for himself, as follows, "He has gone where fierce indignation can lacerate his soul no more!" (Palumbo 5).

Jonathan Swift Bibliography

Anselment, Raymond A. Betwixt Jest and Earnest: Marprelate, Milton, Marvell, Swift and the Decorum of Religious Ridicule. Toronto, Canada: Univ of Toronto Press, 1979.

Bartel, Roland. Metaphors and Symbols: Forays into Language. Urbana, IL: NCTE, 1983.

Beattie, Lester M. "The Lighter Side of Swift." Six Satirists. Ed. Austin Wright. Pittsburgh, PA: Carnegie Institute of Technology, 1965 35-50.

Brown, Norman O. "The Excremental Vision." Swift, A Collection of Critical Essays Ed.

Ernest Tuvison. Englewood Cliffs, NJ: Prentice-Hall, 1964 31-55.

Browning, J. D. ed. Satire in the 18th Century. New York, NY: Garland, 1983.

Bullitt, John M. Jonathan Swift and the Anatomy of Satire: A Study of Satiric Technique. Cambridge, MA: Harvard Univ Press, 1953.

Bullitt, John M. "Swift's Rules of Raillery." Veins of Humor. Ed. Harry Levin. Cambridge, MA: Harvard University Press 1972.

Davis, Herbert. The Satire of Jonathan Swift. New York, NY: Macmillan, 1947.

DePorte, Michael. "Swift and the License of Satire." Satire in the 18th Century. Ed. J. D. Browning. New York, NY: Garland, 1983 53-69.

Donoghue, Denis, ed. Jonathan Swift: A Critical Anthology. New York, NY: Harmondsworth, 1971.

Dyson, A. E. "Swift: Metamorphosis of Irony." The Writings of Jonathan Swift. Eds. Robert A. Greenberg and William B. Piper. New York, NY: W. W. Norton, 1973, 672-684.

Eddy, William Alfred. Satires and Personal Writings by Jonathan Swift. New York, NY: Oxford Univ Press, 1949.

Ehrenpreis, Irvin. "Swiftian Dilemmas." Satire in the 18th Century. Ed. J. D. Browning. New York, NY: Garland, 1983 214-231.

Evans, James E. "Irish Comic Literature." Comedy: An Annotated Bibliography of Theory and Criticism. Metuchen, NJ: Scarecrow Press, 1987, 177-182.

Fitzgerald, Robert P. "Swift's Immortals: The Satire Point." Studies in English Literature 24.3 (1984): 484-495.

Fromkin, Victoria, and Robert Rodman. An Introduction to Language. 3rd edition. New York, NY: Holt, Rinehart and Winston, 1983.

Gilmore, Thomas B., Jr. "The Comedy of Swift's Scatological Poems." Publication of the Modern Language Association 91 (1976): 33-43.

Guilhamet, Leon. "Swift." Satire and the Transformation of Genre. Philadelphia, PA: University of Pennsylvania Press, 1987, 125-163.

Horne, Colin J. "Swift's Comic Poetry." Augustan Worlds: New Essays in Eighteenth-Century Literature. Eds. J. C. Hilson, M. M. B. Jones, J. R. Watson. New York, NY: Barnes, 1978, 51-67.

Hunt, Leigh. Wit and Humour. New York, NY: Folcroft Library Editions, 1972.

Ingram, Allan. Intricate Laughter in the Satire of Swift and Pope. Hampshire, England: MacMillan, 1986.

Katz, Marjorie, and Jean Arbeiter. Pegs to Hang Ideas On. New York, NY: M. Evans, 1973.

Kaul, A. N. The Action of English Comedy: Studies in the Encounter of Abstraction and Experience from Shakespeare to Shaw. New Haven, CT: Yale Univ Press, 1970.

Kelling, Harold D. "Gulliver's Travels: A Comedy of Humours." University of Toronto Quarterly 21 (1952): 362-375.

Kenner, Hugh. The Counterfeiters: An Historical Comedy. Bloomington, IN: Indiana University Press, 1968.

Klamar, Zsolt. "The Fallacies of Language in Swift's Satires." Unpublished Paper. Tempe, AZ: Arizona State University, 1990.

L'Estrange, A. G. "Swift." History of English Humour. New York, NY: Burt Franklin, 1978, 44-61.

Levin, Harry, ed. Veins of Humor. Cambridge, MA: Harvard University Press, 1972.

Leyburn, Ellen Douglass. "Satiric Journeys I: Gulliver's Travels." Satiric Allegory: Mirror of Man. New Haven, CT: Yale University Press, 1956, 71-91.

Mayhew, George P. Rage or Raillery: The Swift Manuscripts at the Huntington Library. San Marino, CA: Huntington Library, 1987.

Nilsen, Don L. F. "Satirical Devices in Gulliver's Travels and A Modest Proposal." Nebraska Language Arts Bulletin 6.2 (1994): 17-20.

Nokes, David. Raillery and Rage: A Study of Eighteenth Century Satire. Sussex, England: Harvester Press, 1987.

O'Donoghue, David James, ed. The Humour of Ireland. London, England: Walter Scott, 1894; New York, NY: AMS Press, 1978.

O'Keefe, Daniel. The Book of Irish Wit and Humour. Cork, Ireland: Mercier, 1977.

Palumbo, Donald. "Science Fiction as Allegorical Social Satire: William Burroughs and Jonathan Swift." Studies in Contemporary Satire 9 (1982): 1-8.

Pearson, Hesketh. "Jonathan Swift." Lives of the Wits. New York, NY: Harper and Row, 1962, 1-51.

Peter, Laurence. The Peter Plan. New York, NY: Morrow, 1976.

Polhemus, Robert M. Comic Faith: The Great Tradition from Austen to Joyce. Chicago, IL: University of Chicago Press, 1980.

Price, Martin. "Swift in the Interpreter's House." Satire in the 18th Century. Ed. J. D. Browning. New York, NY: Garland, 1983 100-115.

Pullen, Charles. " 'The Greatest Art is to Hide Art': Satire and Style in Jonathan Swift." Satire in the 18th Century. Ed. J. D. Browning. New York, NY: Garland, 1983 53-69.

Robinson, Fred Norris. "Satirists and Enchanters in Early Irish Literature." Studies in the History of Religions: Presented to Crawford Howell Toy. Eds. David Lyon and George Moore. New York, NY: Macmillan, 1912, 95-130.

Rogers, Pat. Grub Street: Studies in a Subculture. London, England: Methuen, 1972.

Rogers, Pat. Hacks and Dunces: Pope, Swift, and Grub Street. New York, NY: Methuen, 1980.

Rogers, Pat. "Defoe as a Dunce." Grub Street: Studies in a Subculture. London, England: Methuen, 1972, 311-326.

Rosenheim, Edward W., Jr. Swift and the Satirist's Art. Chicago, IL: University of Chicago Press, 1963.

Ross, John F. "The Final Comedy of Lemual Gulliver." University of California Publications: English Studies. 8.2 (1941): 175-196.

Schmidt, Johann N. Satire: Swift and Pope. Berlin, Germany: Verlag W. Kohlhammer, 1977.

Shibles, Warren. Humor: A Critical Analysis for Young Children. Whitewater, WI: The Language Press, 1978.

Sitter, John. "Big Bodies and Little Bodies (Swift, Gay, Pope)." Arguments of Augustan Wit. New York, NY: Cambridge University Press, 1991, 101-113.

Sitter, John. "The 'Doctrine of Abstraction': Berkeley and Book III of Gulliver's Travels." Arguments of Augustan Wit. New York, NY: Cambridge University Press, 1991, 143-152.

Sitter, John. "Prose Character Progresses and the Novel: Swift and Fielding." Arguments of Augustan Wit. New York: Cambridge University Press, 1991, 39-44.

Sitter, John. "Swift's Progresses." Arguments of Augustan Wit. New York: Cambridge University Press, 1991, 11-21.

Snider, Rose. Satire in the Comedies of Congreve, Sheridan, Wilde, and Coward. New York: Phaeton, 1972.

Steele, Peter. Jonathan Swift: Preacher and Jester. Oxford, England: Clarendon Press, 1978.

Stone, Edward. "Swift and Horses: Misanthropy or Comedy?" Modern Language Quarterly 10 (1949): 367-376.

Thackeray, W. M. "Swift." The English Humorists: Charity and Humour: The Four Georges. New York, NY: Dutton, 1912, 3-46.

Thieme, Adelheid. "The Satiric Point in Swift's 'A Modest Proposal.' " Unpublished Paper. Tempe, AZ: Arizona State University, 1990.

Toole, John Kennedy. A Confederacy of Dunces. New Orleans, LA: Louisiana State University Press, 1980.

Topsfield, Valerie. The Humour of Samuel Beckett. New York, NY: St. Martin's Press, 1988.

Turner, F. McD. C. "Jonathan Swift." The Element of Irony in English Literature. Cambridge, England: University Press, 1926, 27-44.

Turner, F. McD. C. "Swift's Contemporaries." The Element of Irony in English Literature. Cambridge, England: University Press, 1926, 45-59.

Tuveson, Ernest. "Swift: The View from within the Satire." The Satirist's Art. Eds. Jensen, H. James, and Malvin R. Zirker, Jr. Bloomington, IN: Indiana University Press, 1972, 55-85.

Ulman, Craig. Satire and the Correspondence of Swift. Cambridge, MA: Harvard University Press, 1973.

Worth, Chris. "Swift's Flying Island: Buttons and Bomb Vessels." Review of English Studies 42 (1991): 343-360.

Zimmerman, Everett. Swift's Narrative Satires: Author and Authority. Ithaca, NY: Cornell Univ Press, 1983.

William Congreve (1670-1729) IRELAND

Dryden, Etherege, and Wycherley had written plays according to the conventions of Fletcher. What Congreve did was to take the Fletcher conventions and apply them to punitive comedy. The model which Congreve used had been proposed by John Dryden in An Essay of Dramatic Poesy, in which he advocated the position that "ideal stage comedy would combine the genius in characterization of Shakespeare, the correctness and strength in design of Jonson, the gaiety of Fletcher, and the elegance and grace in dialogue of Dryden's own age" (Gibbons 5).

The Old Bachelour (1693), Congreve's first play, is a typical Restoration comedy filled with dramatic stereotypes. The plot hinges on the dilemma of Heartwell, the "old bachelor," who can't stand the thought of marriage, but yet he must satisfy his desire for a particular wench, who stubbornly demands a husband (Wilcox 155). The Old Bachelour is a synthesis of earlier comic styles.

> Here are the old Restoration contempt for romantic love and the familiar preference for an unmoral and casual indulgence in the sex relation in which ties of affection have no place. Here the pursuit of women is the normal activity of a wit. Here the women gayly capitalize sex tantalization. Here marriage is assumed to be a black pall that threatens to come between a joyous past and a gloomy future. (Wilcox 156)

According to Brian Gibbons, The Old Bachelour is an excellent application of Dryden's proposed model (Gibbons 4). Gibbons goes further, to suggest that "Congreve's consistent and deliberate modification of the power and violence of Jonsonian comedy was a matter of choice as well as necessity," and that in fact this exploration of subtle comic blends was later to be further refined in the development of the genre of the novel (Gibbons 5).

Congreve's second play was entitled The Double-Dealer (1693). Sir Joseph Wittol is stupid, and Captain Bluffe is a braggart. They are both ridiculous on the level of physical fears and silly pretensions. Lord Froth is suited to the tone of high comedy, with his affected critical arrogance and condescension, and Sir Paul Plyant is dominated by the "humor" of forming blind judgments about his wife. Mellefont, Cynthia, and Careless are true-wits. These character types are frequently found in pre-Restoration comedy, and in early Restoration comedy, but they are not to be found in Molière's plays (Wilcox 158). Nevertheless, in The Double-Dealer, there is a clear resemblance between the intrigue of Congreve's Maskwell and that of Molière's Tartuffe. "Maskwell has Tartuffe's gift for securing blindly devoted friends. [Furthermore,] Lord Touchwood is like Orgon in his attachment to Maskwell" (Wilcox 159).

In The Double-Dealer, Lord Froth says, "There is nothing more unbecoming in a man of gravity than to laugh, to be pleased with what pleases the crowd. When I laugh, I always laugh alone." To this, Brisk replies, "I suppose that's because you laugh at your own jests" (L'Estrange 356). Macaulay says that Congreve's wit far outshines that of every other comic writer of his day except for Sheridan, whose fame has risen in the past two centuries (L'Estrange 358). The Double-Dealer is an enigma to critics, who have considered it everything from satiric comedy to tragedy. "Some critics have tried to show more than one operative norm; others have simply thrown up their hands in defeat" (Corman 357). Brian Corman suggests that the reason critics have had difficulty in pinning The Double-Dealer down to a single genre is that it is in fact a "mixed genre," which synthesizes the Jonsonian and the Fletcherian comic traditions. Congreve "turned to Jonson's plot form, punitive comedy, for overall structure and then reworked it in a distinctly Restoration way" (Corman 357-358). Dryden had attempted to develop a new type of mixed comedy that was based on both wit and humor, but Dryden had failed, for he was unable to achieve any balance, since his plays "preferred wit to humor." In The Double-Dealer, however, Congreve succeeded in achieving this balance, where Dryden had failed (Corman 356-358).

John Wilcox feels that in The Old Bachelour and The Double-Dealer, Congreve greatly advanced the genre we now call "comedy of wit," through his adept handling of epigrams, his felicity of comparisons, his boldness, and the aptness of his imagery. Congreve's writing was the climax and culmination of that style of Restoration wit which Etherege, Wycherley, Rochester, Sedley, Dryden, and Shadwell all helped to develop. John Wilcox asks us to contrast Congreve's with that of Molière. Molière's wit is "like a running brook, with innumerable fresh lights on it at every turn of the wood through which its business is to find a way." Molière's wit is "without effort, and with no dazzling flashes of achievement. It is full of healing, the wit of good breeding, the wit of wisdom." In contrast, Congreve's wit "is a Toledo blade, sharp, and wonderfully supple for steel. It is cast for duelling, [and is] restless in the scabbard, being so pretty when out of it. To shine, it must have an adversary" (Wilcox 157-158).

Congreve's third play is Love for Love (1695). In this play is to be found Valentine, Valentine's true-wit friend, three comically eager women, a clever valet, and a cuckolded astrologer (Wilcox 160). Here there is much excellent characterization. "The style regularly discloses the speaker, whether it be Angelica taunting Foresight for the infidelities of his wife, Scandal in his wild gallantries, Valentine making safety-valve speeches under the color of madness, or Sailor Ben with his fresh opinions and salty bluntness" (Wilcox 161). Like The Double-Dealer, Love for Love is a satire; however, it differs from the earlier play in that the ridicule is directed at social follies. Love for Love is a true comedy of manners, since it is "free from mere farce on the one hand, or heavy ethical freight on the other" (Wilcox 161).

The Way of the World (1700) like Congreve's earlier plays, is difficult for the categorizing critic to characterize, because of its blending of wit and humor (Gibbons 3). Philip Roberts feels that this play is the last word, dramatically in seventeenth-century comedy of manners (Roberts 41). The Way of the World is primarily concerned with the attempts of Mirabell and Millamant to liberate themselves from the excesses of their environment. Whereas the characters in earlier drama had been inextricably linked with their environment, Congreve's characters in The Way of the World openly flaunted their vices. In this play there are fops, mistresses, intrigues, the threat of scandal, and the clash between town and country values. There are also wits, and would-be wits. But none of this is what the play is about. It is about Mirabell and his affections for Millamant (Roberts 42).

During the "proviso scene," of Way of the Worlds Millament says that she will not be called names after marriage:

> Aye, as wife, spouse, my dear, joy, jewel, love, sweetheart and the rest of the nauseous cant, in which men and their wives are so fulsomely familiar . . . . Let us never visit together, nor go to a play together. But let's us be very strange and well-bred; let us be as strange as if we had been married a great while, and as well bred as if we were not married at all. (Bloom 67)

Mirabell accepts this condition and the other conditions as well, so an assumption can be made that he feels the same way (Bloom 67). As Millament and Mirabell battle each other in their duel of wits, he becomes more self-pitying while she becomes wittier. He grumbles about the impossibility of "winning a woman with plain dealing and sincerity," and she responds, "Sententious Mirabell! Prithee, don't look with that violent and inflexible wise face, like Solomon at the dividing of the child in an old tapestry hanging" (Lynch 422). Millament ignores Mirabell's plea "for one moment to be serious." She responds, "What, with that face? No, if you keep your countenance, 'tis impossible I should hold mine. Well, after all, there is something very moving in a love-sick face. Ha! ha! ha!--Well, I won't laugh, don't be peevish--Heighho! Now I'll be melancholy, as melancholy as a watch-light. Well Mirabell, if ever you will win me, woo me now. --Nay, if you are so tedious, fare you well" (Lynch 431). And she leaves him sputtering as she departs (Bloom 70). It has been generally acknowledged that the proviso scene brings Millament from girlhood to maturity; however, Donald Bloom suggests that this maturity happens to Mirabell as well, "for it is the rake's life that is the most thoroughly adolescent--with its antagonism to established morals, its slangy and obscene barracks wit, its preoccupation with girls as sexual objects, its endless drinking parties, brawls, and scrapes." Once Millament is sure that Mirabell has grown up, she then knows that she can put away her own coquetry, and the romance is complete (Bloom 72).

Many of Congreve's strongest female characters are based on Anne Bracegirdle, and the men who are controlled by these strong women represent Congreve himself:

> In his comedies . . . , man can be really powerless in the hands of the superior women he was fond of portraying. This is evident in The Way of the World, wherein Millamant has Mirabell twisted about her little finger. He is content if she will but confess she loves him. In Love for Love Valentine and Angelica are in a similar situation; Angelica has the upper hand and actually drives Valentine to feign madness in order to prove his love for her. Bellmour and Belinad present a somewhat weaker version of the same thing in The Old Bachelor, and in The Double-Dealer even Cynthia is represented as a more dominating character than Mellefont, her lover. (Snider 3)

Dryden feels that Congreve is an excellent author. He feels that Congreve is a better author than Thomas Southerne, and goes on to compare him favorably with Shakespeare (Gibbons 4). According to Rose Snider, the young Congreve was the first to perfect the comedy of manners, and after Congreve there was a decline of the genre until late in the eighteenth century, when it was revised by the young Sheridan (Snider ix). Congreve was able to write comedies of manners because he was raised in a distinguished family. His ambition to be a man of fashion conflicted with his ambition to be a great writer, and his comedies of manners allowed him to deal with both obsessions (Snider 1).

Alfred Gu L'Estrange feels that many of the subjects of Congreve's comedies might be objectionable to the modern audience. The humor in these comedies is not so much in the plot as in the general dialogue (L'Estrange 357). Nevertheless, Brian Morris suggests that Congreve wrote elegant and discriminating plays. Congreve was able to select the precise phrase, and the precise response to give the audience insights into human relationships. Congreve shows how relationships are "tentatively embarked on," but later become "deepened, enriched, cherished, and secured" (Morris xi). Brian Gibbons notes that Congreve's plays appeared during the final decade of the seventeenth century, and that they represent the "full expression of the accumulated experience of the Restoration comic writers" (Gibbons 3).

One of the things which most irritated Congreve about eighteenth-century England was the fact that society in general, and patrons in particular tended to feel superior to the poets of their day. Congreve was being ironic when he had Scandal say, "No, turn pimp, flatterer, quack, lawyer, parson, be chaplain to an atheist, or stallion to an old woman, anything but poet; a modern poet is worse, more servile, timorous and fawning, than any I have named" (Snider 39).

William Myers feels that Congreve's contribution to the history of comedy lay in his being a transitional writer, standing between the world of Etherege and that of Steele.

> Clearly in some significant ways he belongs more to Charles II's court than to William and Mary's London . . . . But more importantly he is traditionalist in his literary convictions as well as in his public stance . . . . It is his deep attachment above all to the Renaissance humanism, which asserted the relevance of wit to virtue, which explains Dryden's astonishing choice of him as his literary heir in that superb poem "To my Dear Friend Mr. Congreve." (Myers 77)

According to Dryden, Congreve's writing exhibited a balance of pride and humility, of careful discriminations and deliberate exaggerations. Dryden was convinced that Congreve would carry this balanced literary tradition well into the future (Myers 77).

William Congreve Bibliography

Bloom, Donald A. "Dwindling into Wifehood: The Romantic Power of the Witty Heroine in Shakespeare, Dryden, Congreve, and Austen." Look Who's Laughing: Gender and Comedy. Ed. Gail Finney. New York, NY: Gordon and Breach, 1994, 53-80.

Cazamian, Louis. "Congreve, Shaftesbury, Steele, and Addison." The Development of English Humor. Durham, NC: Duke University Press, 1952, 400-407.

Corman, Brian. " 'The Mixed Way of Comedy': Congreve's The Double Dealer." Modern Philology 71 (1974): 356-365.

Edgar, Irving I. "Restoration Comedy and William Congreve." Essays in English Literature and History. New York, NY: Philosophical Library, 1972, 52-70.

Foakes, R. A. "Wit and Convention in Congreve's Comedies." William Congreve. Ed. Brian Morris. London, England: Ernest Benn, 1972, 55-72; reprinted Totowa, NJ: Rowan and Littlefield, 1974.

Gibbons, Brian. "Congreve's The Old Bachelour and Jonsonian Comedy." William Congreve. Ed. Brian Morris. London, England: Ernest Benn, 1972, 1-20.

Holland, Norman N. The First Modern Comedies: The Significance of Etherege, Wycherley, and Congreve. Bloomington, IN: Indiana Univ Press, 1959.

L'Estrange, Alfred Gu. "Congreve--Lord Dorset." History of English Humour. New York, NY: Burt Franklin, 1978, 355-360.

Leech, Clifford. "Congreve and the Century's End." Philological Quarterly 41 (1962): 275-

293.

Loftis, John. Comedy and Society from Congreve to Fielding. Stanford, CA: Stanford Univ
    Press, 1959.

Lynch, Kathleen M., ed. Way of the World. Lincoln, NE: University of Nebraska Press,
    1965.

Morris, Brian, ed. William Congreve. London, England: Ernest Benn, 1972.

Muir, Kenneth. "The Comedies of William Congreve." Restoration Theatre. Eds. John
    Russell Brown, and Bernard Harris. New York, NY: St. Martin's, 1965, 221-237;
    Restoration Theatre Eds. John Russell Brown and Bernard Harris. New York, NY:
    Capricorn, 1967, 221-237.

Myers, William. "Plot and Meaning in Congreve's Comedies." William Congreve. Ed.
    Brian Morris. London, England: Ernest Benn, 1972 73-92.

Novak, Maximillian E. "Love, Scandal, and the Moral Milieu of Congreve's Comedies."
    Congreve Reconsider'd: Papers Read at a Clark Library Seminar, Dec. 5, 1970. Eds.
    Aubrey Novak and Maximillian Novak. Los Angeles, CA: Clark Library, 1971, 23-
    50.

Perry, Henry Ten Eyck. The Comic Spirit in Restoration Drama: Studies in the Comedy
    of Etherege, Wycherley, Congreve, Vanbrugh, and Farquhar. New Haven, CT: Yale
    Univ Press, 1925.

Roberts, Philip. "Mirabell and Restoration Comedy." William Congreve. Ed. Brian Morris.
    London, England: Ernest Benn, 1972 39-54; reprinted Totowa, NJ: Rowan and
    Littlefield, 1974.

Snider, Rose. Satire in the Comedies of Congreve, Sheridan, Wilde, and Coward. New
    York, NY: Phaeton Press, 1972.

Thackeray, W. M. "Congreve and Addison." The English Humorists: Charity and Humour:
    The Four Georges. New York, NY: Dutton, 1912, 47-87.

Turner, Darwin T. "The Servant in the Comedies of William Congreve." College Language
    Association Journal 1 (1958): 68-74.

Wilcox, John. "Congreve, Vanbrugh, and Farquhar." The Relation of Molière to Restoration
    Comedy. New York, NY: Columbia University Press, 1938, 154-126.

Sir Richard Steele (1672-1729) IRELAND

Like Addison, Steele was also fascinated by laughter. He devoted the entire
Guardian of April 14, 1714 to the subject of laughter (Ingram 4), where he said that a
"symphony of laughter" might just as properly be called a "chorus of conversation." In this
issue of the Guardian, Steele communicates serious reservations about laughter. The
laughter of "Men of Wit," for example, "is for the most part but a faint constrained kind
of Half-Laugh," while the fool's laugh is "the most honest, natural, open Laugh in the
World." "The horse-laugh, or the sardonic, is made use of with great success in all kinds
of disputation. The proficients in this kind, by a well-timed laugh, will baffle the most
solid argument" (Ingram 5). Steele continues by saying that the laugh is not really a sign
of unguarded honesty, but is rather adapted for a whole range of social stratagems and
disguises, and he describes the laughs of different types of characters:

> The grin is made use of to display a beautiful set of teeth; the effeminate
> Fop, who by the long exercise of this countenance at the glass, hath reduced
> it to an exact discipline will give spirit to his discourse and admire his own
> eloquence by a dimple; the Beau . . . practices the smile the better to
> sympathize with the Fair. He will sometimes join in a laugh to humour the
> spleen of a lady, or applaud a piece of wit on his own, but always takes care

to confine his mouth within the rules of good-breeding; and the Ionic Laugh is of universal use to Men of Power at their levées; and is esteemed by judicious Place-Hunters a more particular mark of distinction than the whisper. (Ingram 5)

For Steele, the laugh is not so much an expression of openness as it is a device for display (Ingram 5).

Steele's early plays were produced between 1701 and 1705. These early plays contained clever young couples and sallies of wit. There were derisible characters such as country boobies, fops, antiquated virgins, foolish parents, cuckolds, and husbands soon to be cuckolded, and much of the comedy of these early plays was in how these characters were duped in various ways. Furthermore, in the early plays there were bawdy lines, though they were more witty than titillating, and the wit was certainly not limited to the bawdry features of the plays (Kenny 22). In the early plays, Steele

> . . . fumbled his way toward a new kind of comedy; in his periodical papers, he developed his ideas about comedy and preached his theatrical morality; and, finally, in The Conscious Lovers, mounted about twenty years after the early plays, he worked, polished, reworked, and came up with the formula that was to influence generations of playwrights. (Kenny 22)

Shirley Kenny notes that of all of Steele's comedies, only his first one (The Funeral: or, Grief A-la-Mode [1701]) was not an adaptation based on a classical or a French model. The plot of The Funeral is a departure from the traditional Restoration "games and dupery." In this play, Lord Brumpton's faithful servant, Trusty, convinces him to let people think that he is dead so that he can test their loyalties. The ruse works, and Lady Brumpton is revealed to be not only a villainess but a bigamist as well, so that her hold on the Brumpton fortune is invalidated (Kenny 24).

Steele's second play is entitled The Lying Lover: Or, The Ladies Friendship (1703). This play was based on Pierre Corneille's Le Menteur (1642), which was based in turn on Juan Ruiz d'Alarcón's La Verdad Sospechosa. Dorante, the liar mentioned in the title, fabricates stories of absurd exploits, and succeeds for a time in fooling people, though he eventually gets caught in a web of his own lies. The Lying Lover is written in the "old" or Restoration style, in that the problem revolves around the wooing of a lady rather than the escape from some kind of tyranny. The play therefore had a comic plot rather than a tragic one. Most of the comedy arises from mistaken identity. In this play, the division between the comic and the sentimental materials is quite sharp. Ironically, Dorante's ability as a liar saves Dorante from public embarrassment in the last act of the play (Kenny 27). Kenny notes that this final act "throbs with pathos, but pathos that cannot be justified in terms of Acts I-IV." Furthermore, the basic characterization shifts abruptly in this last act (Kenny 28).

Steele's third play was written after he had failed at sentimental comedy. It was entitled The Tender Husband: Or, The Accomplish'd Fools (1705). Kenny describes this play as "laughing comedy," though a number of twentieth-century critics have described it as sentimental comedy. The Tender Husband is based on Moliére's Le Sicilien and also on his Les Précieuses Ridicules. The original aspects of the play are in the English stage tradition developed by Colley Cibber, William Burnaby, and other English playwrights. The "tender husband" mentioned in the title of the play is the Captain's older brother, Clerimont Senior, who sees that his wife's "innocent freedoms" are "bringing her to the brink of immorality." He decides to stop paying his wife's gambling debts, feeling that his wife may some day be forced to pay for her losses to a gentleman in "a different currency." To trick his wife into admitting to her problem, he encourages mistress Fainlove, to dress as a young man, gamble with his wife, woo her, and get caught in a compromising situation. The scheme works, as Clerimont Senior springs out of hiding and confronts his wife with her guilty behavior. The wife threatens Fainlove with a sword, but then she quickly repents. Until the time of her repentance, this scene is comic, as she resembles the fopposh wife frequently satirized in plays of the Restoration period (Kenny 29).

Steele's fourth play is entitled The Conscious Lovers, and was written in 1722, seventeen years after The Tender Husband. This play is very didactic, assuming that plays should encourage virtue, and should "strip vice of the gay habit in which it has too long appear'd, and cloath it in its native dress of shame, contempt, and dishonour" (Kenny 30). For Steele, plays should represent only "what is agreeable to the manners, laws, religion and policy of the place or nation in which they are exhibited" (Kenny 30). The Conscious Lovers is written in the comic mode, and is based on Terence's Andria, a source which is more compatible with sentimentality than his earlier borrowings from Corneille and Moliére, since Terence's plays tended to be quite "sententious and serious." In The Conscious Lovers, there are two kinds of dialogue--serious and comic--and these are divided between the main and subplots as sharply as are kinds of characterization. The Tom-Phillis scenes are entirely comic, and the scenes involving Mrs. Sealand and Cimberton are also entirely comic, but the Bevil-Indiana plot has two kinds of dialogue found in Steele's sentimental comedy, the "perceptual" and the "emotional." Every time that Bevil speaks, he comes up with an aphorism, or what Kenny calls a "sermon in small" (Kenny 36). In contrast, the most emotional words in the play are spoken by Indiana, the pathetic heroine, in the final scene of the play. Thus, the plot of the play consists of "devoted lovers, a melodramatic action, aphoristic speeches, and pathos," and the subplot of the play consists of "lively lovers, comic action, witty and humorous dialogue, and laughter" (Kenny 37).

Alice Rayner suggests that The Conscious Lovers is a prototypical example of eighteenth-century sentimental comedy, since it exhibits all of the features of this genre:

> The men and women of sentiment express only the noblest ideals and the most honest feelings; no excess of humors or obsessions moves the characters; no satire is directed against social institutions; marriage is a sacred estate, not a repressive confinement; and no Vice figure appears to mock the righteous. The audience at such a play should emerge edified and filled with examples of those positive virtues that will best govern their lives. (82)

The Conscious Lovers is also classified as "sentimental comedy" in that its language is something like that in a sermon (Rayner 83).

In all of his plays, Steele tried to develop his plot in a very structured way. Typically, the first four acts contain comic plot, comic characterization, and comic dialogue. This is followed by an Act filled with melodrama, but Steele's linear approach often failed. The Lying Lover played only six nights, and then disappeared for almost forty-three years at which time it was revived for another four nights in the spring of 1746, when it disappeared and was never heard from again. Nevertheless, Kenny feels that of all of the playwrights who wrote during the turn of the eighteenth century, Richard Steele affected the course of English drama more than any other. His characters were moral; his plots were serious, and the deep emotions of Steele's characters replaced the shallow emotions of the rakes, the light hearted love games, and the witty dialogue of the Restoration plays. During this period, "several playwrights consciously cleaned up their bawdry, but only Steele actively campaigned for a new kind of drama" (Kenny 22).

Richard Steele Bibliography

Cazamian, Louis. "Congreve, Shaftesbury, Steele, and Addison." The Development of English Humor. Durham, NC: Duke University Press, 1952, 400-407.

Green, Elvena M. "Three Aspects of Richard Steele's Theory of Comedy." Educational Theatre Journal 20 (1968): 141-146.

Ingram, Allan. Intricate Laughter in the Satire of Swift and Pope. New York, NY: MacMillan, 1986.

Kelsall, Malcolm. "Terence and Steele." Essays on the Eighteenth-Century English Stage. Eds. Kenneth Richards and Peter Thomson. New York, NY: Barnes, 1972, 11-27.

Kenny, Shirley Strum. "Richard Steele and the 'Pattern of Genteel Comedy.' " Modern Philology 70 (1972): 22-37.

L'Estrange, Alfred Gu. "Steele." History of English Humour. New York, NY: Burt Franklin, 1978, 62-76.

O'Donoghue, David James, ed. The Humour of Ireland. London, England: Walter Scott, 1894; New York, NY: AMS Press, 1978.

Rayner, Alice. "Cumberland and Steele's Aphorism: Use in Utopia." Comic Persuasion: Moral Structure in British Comedy from Shakespeare to Stoppard. Berkeley, CA: University of California Press, 1987, 81-103.

Thackeray, W. M. "Steele." The English Humorists: Charity and Humour: The Four Georges. New York, NY: Dutton, 1912, 88-132.

George Farquhar (1678-1707) IRELAND

Farquhar's first play was a burlesque entitled Love and a Bottle. Many critics have found this play to be coarse and unoriginal (James 69). In the play Farquhar demonstrated his assumption that the most important function of a comedy is to entertain. According to Farquhar every member in the audience, whether sitting in the Pit, the Box, or the Gallery ought to be moved to laughter, and Love and a Bottle was successful in this regard (James 300). In this play there is probably an overabundance of intrigue, since there are at least nine cases of disguise or mistaken identity. There are also many low-comedy characters in the play, and very many comic effects. James notes that "most likely this comedy succeeded mainly for its sheer quantity of comic effects rather than for the quality of its effects" (James 301).

Farquhar's second play was entitled The Constant Couple. This play contains intrigue in the form of Lurewell's tricks and Angelica's mistaken identity. It also contains a number of effective comic characters such as Vizard, Smuggler, Clincher, Clincher Junior, Dicky, and Tom Errand. The first scene in The Constant Couple is witty, and the lovers make a number of witty remarks throughout the play. James nevertheless considers it to be a comedy of bustling intrigue.

Farquhar's third play was entitled Sir Harry Wildair. In both Sir Harry Wildair, and Discourse upon Comedy, Farquhar expressed his contempt for rules by making the plays long, sprawling, and loosely connected. In the Prologue to Sir Harry Wildair, Farquhar is showing his disdain for the rules. In Sir Harry Wildair, Farquhar resolved the problem of unity by dispensing with the low comedy plot altogether, and by fusing the two love plots into a single action. In Sir Harry Wildair, the comic characters and the intrigues are cut to the bare bones in order to give unity to the plot, and also to give more of an opportunity for the characters to be witty (James 301). These characters exercise their wit on such subjects as love and marriage, war, men of honor, and women of quality. However, Farquhar had very strong feelings about these topics, and the wit therefore becomes a bit ponderous (James 302).

In his Discourse upon Comedy, Farquhar came to look on form as an important requisite to comedy (James 299). Farquhar had three basic rules that structured his comedies. He felt that comedy should entertain; it should instruct; and it should have form

(James 298-299). In his Discourse upon Comedy, Farquhar defined comedy as "a well-fram'd tale handsomely told, as an agreeable vehicle for counsel or reproof" (James 299).

Farquhar's fourth play was entitled The Inconstant. In The Inconstant, Farquhar dispensed with the low comedy plot, and separated the two love stories, minimizing the secondary love story of Bisarre and Duretete. In this play there is a balance between wit and humor. The Wild Goose is a hero who is capable of making witty remarks, and Oriana and Bisarre are two women who are both capable of matching his wit. Duretete and Old Mirabel are the two most comic characters in the play.

Farquhar's fifth play was entitled The Twin Rivals (1702); this was the play which introduced the bull-making Irishman to the stage (Waters 11). In this play, the comic effect was achieved mainly through the situations and the characterization.

> The intriguing of Mrs. Mandrake to get Elder Wou'dbee's fortune and fiancée for Young Wou'dbee and to engineer Richmore's amours and the efforts (or lack of effort) of Teague to foil her, form much of the humor of the play. Besides Teague and Mrs. Mandrake, other low comedy characters in the play are Subtleman, Balderdash, Clearaccount, and Mrs. Clearaccount. As for wit, the play is almost devoid of it, except for a few witty remarks of Aurelia and Richmore and a witty combat in Act II, Scene I, between Aurelia and Trueman. (James 302)

Farquhar's sixth play was entitled The Stage Coach. This is a play based on comic situation and comic character. Most of the humor comes from Squire Somebody's ignorance of the identity of Captain Basil, and on the mistakes taking place under cover of night in Act III. There is also humor provided by such characters as Micher, Macahone, Fetch, Dolly, and Jolt, though most of the wit occurs in only a few speeches (James 302).

Farquhar's seventh play was entitled The Recruiting Officer. In The Recruiting Officer, Farquhar unifies the play through the fusion of the comic plot (recruitment) with the main plot. This is a play which has been lengthened by the addition of comic characters and situations. The comedy of this play is mainly associated with such comic characters as Brazen, Kite, Bullock, Pearmain, Appletree, Pluck, Thomas, and Rosa. There are also intrigues, such as the recruitment, and the disguises of Silvia, Kite, and Lucy. There are also flashes of wit in The Recruiting Officer, though the characters are often too busy intriguing to be able to carry on very much witty talk (James 303).

Farquhar's eighth play was entitled The Beaux' Stratagem. In The Beaux' Stratagem, Farquhar uses both fusion and parallel structure by fusing the robbers' plot with the beaux' plot. In this final play, Farquhar is finally able to balance humor and wit. "Humorous situations are provided by the beaux' stratagem and the robbers' plot, and a great deal of humor is provided by such characters as Bellair, Sullen, Froigard, Gibbet, Hounslow, Bagshot, Bonaface, Scrub, and Lady Bountiful" (James 303). The wit is provided mainly by Archer, whom James considers to be the wittiest of all of Farquhar's heroes. The Beaux' Stratagem combines humor of character and humor of situation with a wit that achieves the balance that Farquhar had been seeking throughout his entire career as a playwright (James 303). Farquhar's reputation as an author comes mostly from his Beaux Stratagem, which, although it was not as humorous as was his Love and a Bottle, it had more bold action and sensational incidents (L'Estrange 353).

George Farquhar was quite fond of jesting about his various misfortunes (L'Estrange 351). Farquhar was a poor man, and although he produced a play nearly every year between 1703 and 1707, his expenses exceeded his royalties. His response to this situation was nevertheless gay, for he said, "I have very little estate, but what is under the circumference of my hat, and should I by perchance come to lose my head, I should not be worth a groat" (L'Estrange 350).

It is possible that Farquhar was the most popular of the Restoration dramatists over the centuries. James Lynch compares the popularity of various Restoration dramatists during Samuel Johnson's time:

> The most frequently revived author was Vanbrugh, whose The Mistake, The Confederacy, The False Friend, Aesop, The Provok'd Wife, and The Relapse were acted, the last two being among the most popular plays of the period. Five of Farquhar's comedies were revived--The Constant Couple, The Recruiting Officer, The Beaux' Stratagem, The Twin Rivals, and The Inconstant--and for a greater number of performances than even those of Vanbrugh. Indeed, so frequently acted were the plays of these two writers that 15 per cent of the evenings devoted to comedy were given over to one or another of these eleven plays, and together they account for almost one-twelfth of the entire theatrical repertory. (Lynch 41)

In the introduction to his work on Wycherley, Congreve, Vanbrugh, and Farquhar, Leigh Hunt suggests that Farquhar far surpassed all of the others in the number of editions. Farquhar is furthermore acted ten times more often on the stage than are the other playwrights (Hunt lxxix). Eighteenth-century critics also regarded Farquhar's plays highly, and they commended his subjects, his style, his wit, and his plots. Eugene James is not so complimentary, however. He feels that Farquhar's choice of subjects was "lucky" though his wit and style were "natural." James continues that "The only places where he exercised art were in plotting and inventing characters and incidents." James feels further that Farquhar's satire was weak, and that Farquhar was hasty in his writing. He also failed to follow his own rules (James 16). John Oldmixon agrees that Farquhar didn't follow his own rules, but he adds that "Mr. Farquhar had a genius for comedy, of which one may say, that he was above rules rather than below them" (James 17). But although Farquhar broke rules, and although he offended critics, he was nevertheless successful in the theatre (James 17).

It is clear that Farquhar marched to a different drummer. In his introduction to The Beaux' Stratagem, Bonamy Dobrée noted that Farquhar's comedy differed from that of the other Restoration writers, and it also differed from the later sentimental comedies. Dobrée, in fact, suggests (and so does Malcolm Elwin) that Farquhar's comedies are more comparable to Elizabethan comedies than they are to the comedies of his own times. Farquhar's comedies are Elizabethan in their swift movement, in their exuberance of word and phrase, and in their uninhibited desire to amuse (James 62). John Wilcox contrasts Farquhar's comedies with those of Vanbrugh, saying that Farquhar's comedies "seemed to be a more positive echo of long-forgotten Jacobean energy of action, and his gaiety was more intense and more dashing" (James 65). But Dobrée also noted modern resonances in Farquhar's comedies. "The most surprising thing about him is his extreme modernity . . . . He was two hundred years ahead of his time" (James 63).

Farquhar has the reputation of being the man who killed Restoration comedy. In The Thread of Laughter: Chapters on English Stage Comedy from Jonson to Maugham (1952), Louis Kronenberger states:

> It is his humor, not his wit, that distinguishes Farquhar from his predecessors. He is greater in germ, because richer in humanity and sheer creative fancy, than they are. But it is true that, as John Palmer says, he killed Restoration comedy as it had existed. And he killed it without creating anything better or even counter-balancing. (Kronenberger 174)

Both John Palmer and Louis Kronenberger concentrated on certain characters, certain scenes, and certain lines of The Constant Couple, The Twin-Rivals, and The Beaux' Stratagem to prove their thesis that "Farquhar killed the English comedy of manners brought to perfection by Congreve" (James 68), but Eugene James feels that these critics have the wrong focus. In The Development of George Farquhar as a Comic Dramatist,

James concentrates on Farquhar as an artist. James's book takes each of Farquhar's plays in order and judges it
> . . . according to the criteria that Farquhar himself set forth in his critical remarks in The Adventures of Covent Garden, Love and a Bottle, Preface to the Reader of The Constant Couple, A New Prologue to The Constant Couple, the Epilogue to The Constant Couple, the Prologue to Sir Harry Wildair, Discourse upon Comedy, and the Preface to The Twin Rivals. (James 68)

George Farquhar Bibliography

Hunt, Leigh, ed. The Dramatic Works of Wycherley, Congreve, Vanbrugh, and Farquhar. London, England: Folcroft, 1840.

James, Eugene Nelson. The Development of George Farquhar as a Comic Dramatist. The Hague, Netherlands: Mouton, 1972.

Kronenberger, Louis. The Thread of Laughter: Chapters on English Stage Comedy from Jonson to Maugham New York, NY: Arno, 1952.

L'Estrange, A. G. "Vanbrugh--Colley Cibber--Farquhar." History of English Humour. New York, NY: Burt Franklin, 1978, 340-354.

Lynch, James J. Box, Pit, and Gallery: Stage and Society in Johnson's London. Berkeley, CA: Univ of California, 1953.

O'Donoghue, David James, ed. The Humour of Ireland. London, England: Walter Scott, 1894; New York, NY: AMS Press, 1978.

Perry, Henry Ten Eyck. The Comic Spirit in Restoration Drama: Studies in the Comedy of Etherege, Wycherley, Congreve, Vanbrugh, and Farquhar. New Haven, CT: Yale Univ Press, 1925.

Waters, Maureen. The Comic Irishman. Albany, NY: State University of New York Press, 1984.

John Winstanley (1678-1750) IRELAND

John Winstanley was a Fellow of Trinity College in Dublin. His first humorous poems appeared in 1742, and his last poems appeared after his death in 1750. Winstanley's "Epigrams" are some of his most humorous writings (O'Donoghue 55-56, 432).

John Winstanley Bibliography

O'Donoghue, David James, ed. The Humour of Ireland. London, England: Walter Scott, 1894; New York, NY: AMS Press, 1978.

Arthur Dawson (c1700-1775) IRELAND

Irish humorist Arthur Dawson graduated from Dublin University and was appointed Baron of the Irish Court of Exchequer in 1742. Dawson's "Bumpers, Squire Jones" is one of his funniest pieces (O'Donoghue 70-73, 424).

Arthur Dawson Bibliography

O'Donoghue, David James, ed. The Humour of Ireland. London, England: Walter Scott,

1894; New York, NY: AMS Press, 1978.

Laurence Sterne (1713-1768) IRELAND

Laurence Sterne's life was not an easy one, but he used mirth and laughter to transcend his difficulties. Sterne writes, "I live in a constant endeavor to fence against the infirmities of ill health, and other evils of life, by mirth; being firmly persuaded that every time a man smiles--but much more so, when he laughs, that he adds something to his Fragment of Life" (Seidel 250). In his dedication of Tristram Shandy, Sterne says that he jests "in a constant endeavour to fence against the infinities of ill-health, and the evils of life, by mirth" (Topsfield 10-11). Sterne says that there is a difference between "bitterness" and "saltiness." Both can be expressions of wit; however, bitterness stresses the malignity, and saltiness stresses the festivity of wit. The first is "mere quickness of apprehension, void of humanity;" the second "willingly hurts no man but gives a new colour to absurdity" (Topsfield 11).

Jean-Jacques Mayoux says that Sterne is the first person to spread the humorous vision to the entire intellectual field--"all thinking, in a manner, has become humorous." Mayoux considers Sterne to be the "arch-humorist," because he has generalized the absurd. "This is the vast and glorious difference between Shandyism and Pantagruelism," and the formula of it is that "a man cannot dress, but his ideas get cloathe'd at the same time" (Tristram Shandy, Volume IX, Chapter xiii).

According to James A. Work, Sterne's satire is kindly, affectionate, and playful. The stricture that is contained in his satire is not so much a stricture of anything external as much as it is a stricture on the trivialities of Sterne's own mind (Stedmond 49). During Sterne's time, most books were dedicated to the patrons who supported the authors of the books financially, but Sterne's dedication in Tristram Shandy was different, since Sterne was looking for a different kind of patron or support, the reading public at large; he therefore dedicated the book to "Lord Public" (Stedmond 55). Sterne attempts to give the impression that he is genuinely in dialogue with the audience, and even leaves one page of the novel blank so that the readers can "draw their own picture of the 'concupiscible' Widow Wadman" (Stedmond 63-64).

> Throughout Tristram Shandy, Sterne obviously tries to give the impression that he is really carrying on what amounts to a lively conversation with his readers, allowing them, from time to time, opportunities to reply. But for all the apparent attempt to produce dialogue, the book is for the most part monologue. The "dear Madam," or "fair reader," or even "Sir Critick" addressed by Sterne is frequently a straw horse set up as part of the novel's devious rhetoric. Sterne's technique is close to that of the pedagogue, or the preacher: extended commentary on a text, dialogue with a book, which, like Sterne's reader, has its answers provided for it. (Stedmond 62-63)

Stuart Tave points out that Laurence Sterne was an enigmatic and controversial writer. He was beloved; he was despised; he was frequently disputed. In reviewing the last volume of Tristram Shandy, Gentleman's Magazine said, "In questions of taste, everyone must determine for himself; and what is humour is as much a question of taste, as what is beauty" (Tave vii). But Tave does not consider Sterne's controversial nature to be a negative, for he says that Sterne was the center of a great deal of "productive controversy that gave shape to freshly perceived possibilities of humor" (Tave vii). Robert Bell even devised a special term for Sterne's contribution--"etristramology" (Bell 9). This term is a blend of "Tristram" and "epistemology," and is defined as "Sterne's way of affirming that someone is actually there dazzling us with the artifice of art," for Sterne was fascinated by the relationship between reality and the author's representation of reality.

> Tristram violates artistic convention by shattering our willing suspension of disbelief; he delights in building and destroying his sand castle. He thumbs his nose at credibility and flaunts the process of composing a fiction, bombarding us with visual puns, such as blank, black, or marble pages; arbitrary and discontinuous chapters; a random dedication; diagrams of his wildly erratic "line" of plot; and so on. All this, and a complex of theatrical metaphors, insists on the created quality of the story. Tristram constantly refers to "this drama," "this scene," and directs himself to "drop the curtain, Shandy---I drop it." He mocks the very pretense of verisimilitude by inviting the reader to participate in the staging: "I beg the reader will assist me here, to wheel off my uncle Toby's ordnance behind the scenes, ---to remove his sentry-box, and clear the theatre, if possible" (Bell 8).

John Traugot considers Tristram's paradox to be that "reality can only be presented when one is forever conscious of the artificiality of representation" (Bell 8).

Robert Bell considers Tristram's point-of-view to be amusing, energetic, and appealing, but he agrees with Wayne Booth that it should not be accepted at face value. Booth says, "In some way the central subject holding together materials which, were it not for this scatter-brained presence, would never have seemed to be separated in the first place" (Booth 222). E. M. Forster feels that there is a deity hidden in Tristram Shandy, and he believes that the name of this deity is "Muddle" (Bell 4).

John Stedmond suggests that Tristram Shandy continues the tradition established by Erasmus in his Praise of Folly. Thus Tristram is seen as the "wise fool," but he also has the split personality of all characters in this tradition, such as Rabelais's Panurge and Pantagruel, and Cervantes's Don Quixote and Sancho Panza. "The main difficulty with Erasmian irony is in trying to assess its complex significance. It cannot simply be turned upside down--both of its polar meanings must be given full consideration. The implications of Sterne's irony, like Erasmus's, are not quite so obvious as some readers have assumed" (Stedmond 92).

Tristram Shandy is a comedy of humors in the pre-Jonsonian sense. "Toby would never hurt a fly; Walter is too much given to close reasoning upon the smallest matters, and Yorick loves a jest in his heart" (Bell 5), and Tristram's efforts are almost like a Rube Goldberg drawing as he "expends inordinate energy devising complex mechanisms to accomplish ordinary chores" (Bell 6-7).

Walter Shandy is Tristram's father. He is a perfect example of a person who possesses knowledge but not wisdom. "He is so lost in speculative philosophy that he has no thought of the genuine needs of those under his charge--his wife and sons" (Stedmond 59). Even though he is eloquent in his eccentric speculations, he has no real knowledge to communicate. "When Walter Shandy proclaims that the life of a family is nothing compared to an hypothesis which may bring one closer to truth, and that, in the forum of science, there is no such thing as murder, only death, Uncle Toby can but whistle 'Lillabullero' in answer" (Stedmond 59).

> Walter Shandy's eccentricities, especially his obsession with the notion that all humans are in jeopardy at the crucial moment of birth, and that in most cases the head of the infant is inevitably damaged by the pressures brought to bear upon it as it is thrust into the world, unless it is fortunate enough to be delivered feet first, or by Caesarean section . . . . Walter's comic flaw is his constant concern that so many things in this world are out of joint and his naïve belief that he had been born to set them right. Thus he "would see nothing in the light in which others placed it . . . would weigh nothing in common scales" (Stedmond 87).

Toby is Walter Shandy's brother, and Tristram's uncle. He has a tendency to treat human beings as things, and his dehumanized version of war is a dominant strand in the novel (Stedmond 60).

> Uncle Toby is the most Cervantic of all Sterne's characters, and our attitude to him, like our attitude to the Don himself, is not easy to assess. Toby is a figure of fun, and yet he is presented most sympathetically. Like Quixote he is at times a buffoon, and yet we cannot help developing an affection for him. His hobby-horse evolves out of his desire to speed his recovery from his wound. It has a therapeutic function. It stems also from his desire to communicate, to tell his story. (Stedmond 76)

In the war, Toby has been wounded in his groin, so he is now the comic fisher-king of this story; he is the maimed figure who is sacrificed to restore the fertility of the land (Stedmond 82).

John Stedmond considers the Parson Yorick to be an idealized portrait of Sterne himself, and in this satire, he is seen to be the "norm against which to test the clown-hero's world" (Stedmond 69). Yorick is modest, witty, unselfish, and thinks constantly of his parishioners, but he is not without his own special human foibles. He is indiscreetly frank in his denunciation of evil, and he is very naïve in many of his attitudes. Like Don Quixote, with whom he is often compared, he is also firmly attached to his horse (Stedmond 69). "Like Don Quixote, he [Yorick] must eventually succumb, disabused and disillusioned, though he will have at least one faithful friend by his side (Eugenius) and at least one chronicler who cares enough to tell his story" (Stedmond 70).

Corporal Trim must read a sermon originally prepared by Yorick (actually by Sterne himself in real life). According to John Stedmond,

> Trim is a puppet, moved by unseen strings, reading with all the arts of elocution, words he does not fully comprehend . . . . The sermon is a rather daring piece of foolery with sacred matters, particularly on the part of a clergyman author . . . . The meaning of this sermon as originally preached in York Minster is rather different from its meaning in the context of Tristram Shandy . . . . Like the play within the play, this sermon within the work of comic fiction must justify itself in terms of its relevance for that audience, both the fictional one and the actual one. The reader, coming upon the sermon as just one more in a whole series of digressions, is not inclined to take it very seriously. (84-85)

Sterne's constant digressions are part of his teasing temperament. Every digression is part of a fanciful pattern which he does both for his own amusement, and for ours. "Though meandering, Sterne is trying to achieve freedom from time, until he discovers that time carries him on inflexibly, digressing or not" (Mayoux 123).

Dr. Slop is a male-midwife and a papist as well. His arrival at the Shandy household is pure slapstick. His insistence on crossing himself just as he is colliding with Obadiah is largely responsible for his falling into a mud puddle. "Of all the alternative clown figures, Dr. Slop is given the roughest treatment. He makes his entrance 'unwiped, unappointed, unanealed, with all his stains and blotches on him,' and yet this is the man to whose fumbling hands Father Shandy is willing to entrust the coming of baby Tristram into the world" (Stedmond 80). When Dr. Slop feels that the situation is becoming too serious, he puns about "curtins and horn-works" thereby showing his "wit" and his "manliness," by his ability to jest about the serious business of sex (Stedmond 81). In reaction to the mention of "curtins" and "horn-works," the naïve and literal Toby solemnly and pedantically explains that " 'curtins' are not bed-curtains and that 'horn-works' have nothing to do with cuckoldom" (Stedmond 81).

Tristram Shandy, as the clown-narrator of the novel,

> draws attention to the very real obstacles which lie in the path of artistic accomplishment, emphasizes the human frailties of even the greatest author, and creates a critical awareness in the reader of some of the goals which authors have sought; in the process of all this he is perhaps calling into question the attainability of these goals, or even the desirability of attaining them. (Stedmond 68)

Tristram sees cause-effect relationships in a rather unorthodox way. In a chapter about "cock and bull stories," Tristram's circumcision is explained in terms of an infinite chain of causes and effects. He became circumcised because he "ventured to pee out of the window which fell because the sashweights were missing. Why? Because Uncle Toby and Trim confiscated them for backyard fortifications. Why? To reenact the Battle of Namur, at which Toby sustained his debilitating wound" (Bell 4). William Makepeace Thackeray said that Sterne was a great jester, but not a great humorist. Thackeray did, however, give him credit for having a dashing style, and the quick succession of ideas necessary for a successful author (L'Estrange 101). In 1768, the year of Laurence Sterne's death, he published a book entitled, A Sentimental Journey through France and Italy. To a large extent, this book was written in reaction to Tobias Smollett's book entitled Travels through France and Italy. In Sterne's book, Smollett is "portrayed in canker and spleen as the learned 'Smelfungus,' epitome of the worst kind of traveller, the man who can travel from Dan to Beersheba, and cry, 'Tis all barren' " (Sterne 115-116).

Laurence Sterne Bibliography

Bell, Robert H. "Sterne's Etristamology." Thalia: Studies in Literary Humor 4.2 (1982): 3-9.

Booth, Wayne C. The Rhetoric of Fiction. Chicago, IL: University of Chicago Press, 1961.

Dane, Joseph A. Parody: Critical Concepts Versus Literary Practices, Aristophanes to Sterne. Norman, OK: Univ of Oklahoma Press, 1988.

Farrell, William J. "Nature versus Art as a Comic Pattern in Tristram Shandy." Journal of English Literary History 30 (1963): 16-35.

Goodin, George. "The Comic as a Critique of Reason: Tristram Shandy." College English 29 (1967): 206, 211-223.

Howes, Alan B. "Laurence Sterne, Rabelais and Cervantes: The Two Kinds of Laughter in Tristram Shandy." Laurence Sterne: Riddles and Mysteries. Ed. Valerie Grosvenor Myer. Totowa, NJ: Barnes, 1984 39-56.

Jaén, Susana Onega. "Tecnica y Humor en Tristram Shandy." Literary and Linguistic Aspects of Humour. Barcelona, Spain: University of Barcelona English Department, 1984, 183-190.

Khazoum, Violet. "The Inverted Comedy of Tristram Shandy." Hebrew University Studies in Literature 7 (1979): 139-160.

L'Estrange, Alfred Gu. "Sterne, and Dr. Johnson." History of English Humour. New York, NY: Burt Franklin, 1978, 99-112.

Landow, George P. "Tristram Shandy and the Comedy of Context." Brigham Young University Studies 7 (1966): 208-224.

Mayoux, Jean-Jacques. "De Quincey: Humor and the Drugs." Veins of Humor. Ed. Harry Levin. Cambridge, MA: Harvard University Press, 1972 109-129.

Moglen, Helene. The Philosophical Irony of Laurence Sterne. Gainesville, FL: University Presses of Florida, 1975.

O'Donoghue, David James, ed. The Humour of Ireland. London, England: Walter Scott, 1894; New York, NY: AMS Press, 1978.

Seidel, Michael. Satiric Inheritance: Rabelais to Sterne. Princeton, NJ: Princeton Univ

Press, 1979.

Stedmond, John M. The Comic Art of Laurence Sterne: Convention and Innovation in Tristram Shandy and A Sentimental Journey. Toronto, Canada: Univ of Toronto Press, 1967.

Sterne, Laurence. Sentimental Journey in France and Italy. Ed. Gardner D. Stout, Jr., Berkeley, CA: Univ of California Press, 1967.

Stewart, Jack F. "Sterne's Absurd Comedy." University of Windsor Review 5.2 (1970): 81-95.

Stout, Gardner D., Jr. "Yorick's Sentimental Journey: A Comic 'Pilgrim's Progress' for the Man of Feeling." Journal of English Literary History 30 (1963): 395-412.

Tave, Stuart M. The Amiable Humorist. Chicago, IL: University of Chicago Press, 1960.

Thackeray, W. M. "Sterne and Goldsmith." The English Humorists: Charity and Humour: The Four Georges. New York, NY: Dutton, 1912, 222-266.

Topsfield, Valerie. The Humour of Samuel Beckett. New York, NY: St. Martin's Press, 1988.

Towers, A. R. "Sterne's Cock and Bull Story." Journal of English Literary History 24 (1957): 12-29.

Frances Chamberlaine Sheridan (1724-1766) IRELAND

David Garrick considered Frances Sheridan's first play, The Discovery, to be "the best comedy of the age." Frances Sheridan's second play is entitled The Dupe. Whenever Mrs. Friendly in this play has something important to say, her statement is so burdened with superfluous details that her hearers become totally exasperated. Robert Hogan and Jerry Beasley describe this character as an "engaging featherhead," and they further suggest that in both her character and her speech, she seems taken directly from real life. Some other characters in the play are nearly as well drawn. "The rakish, middle-aged curmudgeon Sir John Woodall, his unscrupulous mistress, Mrs. Etherdown, her disreputable accomplice Sharply, and the quick-tongued servant Rose--all are products of Mrs. Sheridan's genuine wit and real sensitivity to manners and language" (25).

Hogan and Beasley lament that the writings of Frances Chamberlaine Sheridan are scarcely known today. Her main reputation lies in the fact that she is the mother of playwright Richard Brinsley Sheridan, and in the fact that she created a character which was the inspiration of Richard Sheridan's famous Mrs. Malaprop. Frances Sheridan's character even had lines which Hogan and Beasley consider to be embryonic versions of Mrs. Malaprop's funniest lines.

Talking about Frances Sheridan's Sidney Biddulph, Hogan and Beasley say,

> The book does have its comic as well as its pathetic touches, and Richard Brinsley Sheridan seems to have used suggestions from it in both The Rivals (the characters of Faulkland and Julia Melville, for example), and The School for Scandal (Lady Teazle, Sir Oliver, and the two Surface brothers, Joseph the hypocrite and Charles the good-natured ne'er-do-well). (21)

Even though the characterizations in Frances Sheridan's earlier works were well depicted, Hogan and Beasley consider her A Journey to Bath to contain "the freshest, most diversified collection of characters that Frances had yet created." Here we can find a supercilious snob, a vulgar parvenu, a pompous politician, a sycophantic landlady, and Mrs. Tryfort, "a widow with such absurd pretensions to polite learning that she became the pattern for Dick Sheridan's immortal Mrs. Malaprop" (28).

Frances Chamberlaine Sheridan Bibliography

Auburn, Mark S. Sheridan's Comedies: Their Contexts and Achievements. Lincoln, NE:
    University of Nebraska Press, 1977.
Hogan, Robert, and Jerry C. Beasley, Eds. The Plays of Frances Sheridan. Newark, DE:
    University of Delaware Press, 1984.
Sheldon, Esther K. "Frances Sheridan's Comedies: Three Stages in the Development of Her
    Comic Art." Theatre Annual 26 (1970): 7-23.

Arthur Murphy (1727-1805) IRELAND

Robert Spector says that during Arthur Murphy's lifetime, his reputation as a comic playwright was equal to that of George Colman, Oliver Goldsmith, and Richard Brinsley Sheridan. Murphy specialized in writing "afterpieces," short plays designed to appease latecomers to the theatre who had either missed part of the main play, or who came late to take advantage of the half-price admission after the intermission (Spector 37). Between 1756 and 1765 Murphy wrote nine such afterpieces, and these afterpieces were mainly responsible for his reputation in the theatre. Murphy's The Apprentice, an afterpiece written in 1756 is typical of Murphy's comic style. This is a satire designed to ridicule amateur theatrical groups whose members were consumed by aspirations for fame on the stage. In the play, Dick is an apprentice to an apothecary named Gargle, but he neglects his duties in order to hone his skills as an actor.

In The Apprentice as well as in his other plays, Murphy uses "humour" characters because they effectively convey his ideas while at the same time giving him an opportunity for free play with satire and wit (Spector 60). Murphy's plays show a blend of Restoration comedy of manners and Augustan satire both in characterization and in plot development. Spector feels that The Apprentice "achieves the form of late-eighteenth-century humor commonly associated with Goldsmith and Sheridan" (61).

Murphy's Hamlet with Alternations, written in 1772, is in the Augustan Scriblerian tradition of burlesque and parody. "It is a sprightly and cunning attack on contemporary adaptations of Shakespeare's plays, but most particularly David Garrick's version of Hamlet, which was then in production." The scene of Murphy's play is in Garrick's theater, but after the audience has gone home. "Making three appearances, Shakespeare's ghost refuses to answer the questions of Garrick's underlings. They threaten him with calling the watch because he has paid no admission and warn that King David [Garrick] will not take kindly to such activities" (Spector 94). Murphy's play is a travesty written in anger at Garrick's manipulations.

> Garrick is depicted as a tyrant in his own theater, a man behaving with false
> regality. His parsimony and greed are matched only by his vanity. Murphy
> exploits Garrick's methods of expanding his reputation by packing the house
> with his friends, by playing up to his audience, and by puffing his
> performances in George Colman's periodical, the St. James's Chronicle. But
> most devastating is Murphy's praise of Spanger Barry, Garrick's foremost
> acting rival, whom Shakespeare's ghost describes as "my best Othello."
> (Spector 95)

In addition to his afterpieces, Murphy also wrote a number of significant full-length comedies, three of which have placed him in the company of Goldsmith and Sheridan as the three most important playwrights of their time. These three significant Murphy comedies are The Way to Keep Him, All in the Wrong, and Know Your Own Mind. Murphy's plays, like those of Goldsmith and Sheridan, should be classed as late-eighteenth-century rejuvenation of Restoration comedy of manners. Murphy, like Goldsmith and Sheridan, is revolting against the sentimental or weeping comedy prevalent in his day. This "weeping" comedy emphasized the pathetic rather than the humorous, the sensible rather than the satiric, emotions rather than reason (Spector 97).

In The Way to Keep Him, Lovemore is a philandering husband who treats his wife with casual disdain as he has an affair with Widow Bellmour. Mrs. Lovemore's servant, Muslin, discovers the affair and suggests to Mrs. Lovemore that she should repay her husband in kind, but she doesn't accept the advice. After a series of intrigues, adventures, and mistaken identities, all of the guilty characters are "properly chastized" and the ending, in typical comedy fashion has the future looking promising for all.

Murphy lightens his social commentary by using farce. This also keeps his tone from becoming too severe, and makes his instruction more palatable. "His plays depend greatly on mistaken interpretations, confusions in exchanges of letters, and maladroit intervention by meddling servants. The very action of The Way to Keep Him depends upon farcical misunderstandings" (Spector 101).

Arthur Murphy Bibliography

Caskey, J. Homer. "Arthur Murphy and the War on Sentimental Comedy." Journal of English and Germanic Philology 30 (1931): 563-577.
Spector, Robert Donald. Arthur Murphy. Boston, MA: Twayne, 1979.

Oliver Goldsmith (1728-1774) IRELAND

Oliver Goldsmith's favorite song was, "There was an old woman toss'd in a blanket, / Seventeen times as high as the moon." This was published in Mother Goose's Melody, which is supposed to be a collection of old didactic nursery rhymes containing droll maxims and ending with morals. Oliver Goldsmith himself collected the nursery rhymes, and furthermore, he himself wrote the humorous maxims. But then he pretended that he had taken them from such great authors as Plato, Pliny, and Puffendorff (Lear viii).

It was Oliver Goldsmith who coined the phrase "a nation of humourists" for England (Levin 6). Most researchers of British Literature specializing in the eighteenth century agree that Goldsmith and Sheridan rebelled against the dominant "sentimental comedies" of the period, and attempted to revive the "laughing" or satiric comedy of earlier times. This is a legitimate but ironic stance to take, because Goldsmith and Sheridan did satirize sentimental comedy, but they themselves were also infected by this prevailing sentimentalism (Hume 312).

A. G. L'Estrange considers Goldsmith's satire to be so general that it cannot inflict any wound. Goldsmith's writing affords amusement without animosity or indelicacy (131). Goldsmith's plays are filled with good wit and humor. "His comic writing is of the class which is perhaps as much preferred to that of a staider sort of people in general, as it is by the writer of these pages--comedy running into farce; that is to say, truth richly coloured and overflowing with animal spirits" (Hunt 316).

In an article entitled, "Comic Patterns in Goldsmith's Plays," H. Grant Sampson says that Goldsmith's plays adhere to six basic qualities that are in most good comedies. First, the action of the young lovers is interfered with by a "blocking character;" second, one or more characters in the play suddenly recognizes the truth about himself or herself; third, the young lovers are tested to determine or establish their moral worth; fourth, the action concludes with an exposure of the villain; fifth, one or more of the characters is obsessed, and the action of the play exposes the "humour" of such characters; and sixth, it is determined that society can no longer tolerate the pranks of one or more characters, and the action of the play somehow redeems such disruptive figures. According to Sampson, "these comic patterns share a common general formula; as Frye has put it, "the obstacles to the hero's desire, form the action of the comedy and the overcoming of them the comic resolution" (40).

The humor of Citizen of the World (1762) is the result of the Chinese perspective of a Chinese man living in England, writing to one of his friends in China. The manners and customs of England are thus viewed from a Chinese perspective. The Chinese man is surprised, for example, that when he goes to the English theatre, "the richest, in general, were placed in the lowest seats, and the poor rose above them in degrees proportionate to their poverty. The order of precedence seemed here inverted" (L'Estrange 132). The "Citizen of the World" also has difficulty understanding why there are so many old maids and bachelors in England. He finds bachelors especially contemptible, and he says that "mobs should be permitted to halloo after them; boys might play tricks on them with impunity; every well-bred company should laugh at them, and if one of them, when turned sixty offered to make love, his mistress might spit in his face" (L'Estrange 133). He feels that Old Maids should not be treated with this much severity, because their not being married is often not their fault. Nevertheless he tells about Sophronia, who loved Greek and hated men. "She rejected fine gentlemen because they were not pedants, and pedants because they were not fine gentlemen. She found a fault in every lover, until the wrinkles of old age overtook her, and now she talks incessantly of the beauties of the mind" (L'Estrange 133).

George Kitchin notes that even The Vicar of Wakefield (1766) can be read as humor, since it is a parody of the Book of Job in the Bible. The Good-Natur'd Man (1768) incorporates three aspects of the formula which has been traditionally associated with comedy. In the first place the hero proves his moral worth; in the second place he overcomes the "blocking characters" who obstruct young love; and in the third place the humours of a character whose posturing has led to serious complications are exposed (Sampson 41). Honeywood is the protagonist of The Good-Natur'd Man. He is a vehicle for the satirization of unintelligent and ultimately calamitous benevolence, for he is censured from beginning to end. "There is never any doubt that he is precisely one of those delineated in the essay on 'Sentimental Comedy' whose 'Faults and Foibles the Spectator is taught not only to pardon, but to applaud . . . in consideration of the goodness of their hearts' " (Rodway 67). However, Honeywood is an ambiguous character, since he demonstrates genuine wit in some of his verbal fencing with the acute Miss Richland. This genuine wit and verbal skill "implies more merit in Honeywood than is good for satire" (Rodway 68).

By the beginning of Act V, the action of The Good-Natur'd Man has reached total chaos. There has been deception, delusion, and confusion of identity, and tricks to keep truth and love from being recognized. H. Grant Sampson describes the denouement as follows:

> Honeywood recognizes that in spite of his good intentions his extravagance has led him to obstruct a path of the young lovers: "I now begin to grow contemptible, even to myself" (v). He expresses the action of the play in saying, "we have all been under a strange mistake here" (v). He recognizes the error of his ways; Olivia confesses who she really is; Croaker admits he has been a fool; Lofty is exposed as a fraud; and Miss Richland indicates her love for Honeywood. Following this self-recognition and clarification Sir William reveals himself. He has been the one person who, in the tradition of the figure of Providence, has not been enveloped in the deceptions. He set the testing scheme in operation and then witnessed its

unfolding. (42)

Following the formula of true comedies, the final part of the play brings about harmony and order: "Croaker accepts the love of Leontine and Olivia and joins their hands; Lofty is 'resolv'd upon reformation'; Miss Richland proposes to Honeywood. He takes his uncle's advice 'learn to respect yourself,' and the play concludes with a description of true good-naturedness.' " (Sampson 43). The play has moved from illusion to reality, from disorder to love, from ignorance to knowledge (43).

In the January 1st, 1773 issue of <u>Westminster Magazine,</u> Goldsmith published "An Essay on the Theatre; or, A Comparison Between Laughing and Sentimental Comedy," in which he discusses the "weeping sentimental comedy so much in fashion at present" (Sampson 36). Goldsmith contrasts weeping or sentimental comedy with "laughing, and even low comedy, which seems to have been last exhibited by Vanbrugh and Cibber" (36). And he suggests that the "principal question, therefore, is whether, in describing low or middle life, an exhibition of its follies be not preferable to a detail of its calamities?" (36). On the basis of this article, Oliver Goldsmith became linked with Richard Sheridan as "satirists of sentimentalism." However, H. Grant Sampson suggests that this struggle to reassert laughing against sentimental comedy is misleading, and suggests further that we need to be suspicious of the Goldsmith-Sheridan claim, because there is a distinct possibility that the article in <u>Westminster Magazine</u> "is essentially a puff to prepare the way for <u>She Stoops to Conquer,</u> first staged two months after the essay's appearance" (37).

In the prologue to <u>She Stoops to Conquer</u> (1773), Goldsmith laments the death of comedy. It is "Sentimentalism" who performs the murder.

> Pray would you know the reason why I'm crying?
> The Comic muse, long sick, is now a-dying!
> To <u>her</u> a mawkish drab of spurious breed,
> Who deals in <u>sentimentals</u> will succeed!

According to Allan Rodway, <u>She Stoops to Conquer</u> is "a farce pure and simple, and not comedy-manque, like <u>The Good-Natur'd Man</u> and as its humour characters are tenderly treated, it straightway inclines towards sentimentality" (69). <u>She Stoops to Conquer</u> is based on three comic patterns, each of them leading to the disclosure of the true identity of one or more characters. In the play there are the escapades of a "Lord of Misrule" (Tony Lumpkin). There is also the outwitting of the senex figure, the adult-blocking-figure, who wants to keep a fortune in the family. There is also the recognition by the young lover Marlowe of his true nature. In the play, Tony Lumpkin is described by his step-father as "a mere composition of tricks and mischief," is described by the landlord of his favorite alehouse as "a sweet, pleasant--damned mischievous son of a whore," and is described by his own cousin as "a good-natured creature at bottom." This Tony Lumpkin is drinking one evening at the local alehouse when he meets two strangers, Marlowe and Hastings, who have been invited by Hastings's girlfriend for a visit. Tony Lumpkin tells them that the house they are looking for is far away, but he also tells them that there is an Inn close by. In truth, however, the inn that he directs them to is actually the house which is their true destination. This prank leads to a series of misunderstandings which frustrate both lovers. By the end of Act IV the strangers have discovered Tony's prank, and they confront him. When Tony realizes the consequences of his actions he comes up with a scheme to make the situation right. This scheme is the famous coach ride

> which takes his mother, Mrs. Hardcastle, twenty-five miles through mud and rock and finally lodges her in her own backyard. This prank brings about the union of lovers and the redemption of Tony, who has recognized that his time as a Lord of Misrule is over. It is therefore appropriate that Hardcastle should disclose at the end of the play that Tony is actually of age: "While I thought concealing your age, boy, was likely to conduce to your

improvement, I concurred with your mother's desire to keep it secret. But since I find she turns it to wrong use, I must now declare, you have been of age this three months." (Sampson 45)

According to the formula for comedies, Tony has outgrown his role of "Lord of Misrule." He has earned his liberty and is now recognized as a responsible individual. He has indeed achieved maturity (45). Marlowe has also fulfilled one of the important rules of comedy. He has come to know himself. Earlier, Marlowe had not truly known himself. He was "painfully shy in the presence of a lady of quality, and joyfully forward in the presence of a bar-maid" (45). But Kate is two people--the lady of quality (whom Marlowe cannot look in the eye) and the bar-maid, with whom Marlowe has a perfectly free relationship (Sampson 45). "Kate, in stooping to seem to be a bar-maid [in a large house which Marlowe thinks is an inn] has conquered the shyness of the man she loves" (my underlining)(Sampson 46). The play concludes with a feast, at which Hardcastle remarks, "So now to supper; tomorrow we shall gather all the poor of the parish about us, and the Mistakes of the Night shall be crowned with a merry morning." This ends the play as a comedy should be ended, as it goes from the chaotic "mistakes of the night" to the harmonious "merry morning." As H. Grant Sampson notes, This is the action of not only this play, but of comedy in general (46).

Oliver Goldsmith Bibliography

Hume, Robert D. "Goldsmith and Sheridan and the Supposed Revolution of 'Laughing' against 'Sentimental' Comedy." The Rakish Stage: Studies in English Drama, 1660-1800. Carbondale, IL: Southern Illinois Univ Press, 1983, 312-355.

Hunt, Leigh. Wit and Humour. New York, NY: Folcroft Library Editions, 1972.

L'Estrange, A. G. "Cowper, and Goldsmith." History of English Humour. New York, NY: Burt Franklin, 1978, 127-140.

Lear, Edward. A Book of Nonsense. London, England: J. M. Dent, 1859.

Levin, Harry, ed. Veins of Humor. Cambridge, MA: Harvard Univ Press, 1972.

Loughlin, Richard L. "Laugh and Grow Wise with Oliver Goldsmith." Costerus 6 (1972): 59-92.

O'Donoghue, David James, ed. The Humour of Ireland. London, England: Walter Scott, 1894; New York, NY: AMS Press, 1978.

Rodway, Allan. "Goldsmith and Sheridan: Satirists of Sentiment." Renaissance and Modern Essays: Presented to Vivian de Sola Pinto in Celebration of his Seventieth Birthday. Ed. G. R. Hibbard. London, England: Routledge, 1966 65-81.

Sampson, H. Grant. "Comic Patterns in Goldsmith's Plays." English Studies in Canada 10 (1984): 36-49.

Styan, J. L. "Goldsmith's Comic Skills." Costerus 9 (1973): 195-217.

Thackeray, W. M. "Sterne and Goldsmith." The English Humorists: Charity and Humour: The Four Georges. New York, NY: Dutton, 1912, 222-266.

Tucker, Herbert F., Jr. "Goldsmith's Comic Monster." Studies in English Literature, 1500-1900 19 (1979): 493-499.

Sir Boyle Roche (c1740-1807) IRELAND

Sir Boyle Roche was born in the south of Ireland and distinguished himself in the American War. He became a member of Irish Parliament, and in 1782 became a baronet. He was noted for his very carefully prepared speech blunders. Roche's "Bulls" is one of his best humorous pieces (O'Donohugh 101-102, 431).

Sir Boyle Roche Bibliography

O'Donoghue, David James, ed. The Humour of Ireland. London, England: Walter Scott, 1894; New York, NY: AMS Press, 1978.

John O'Keefe (1747-1833) IRELAND

John O'Keefe was born in Dublin and worked as an artist before he finally became a popular actor and playwright. Most of the plays he wrote were operas and farces, and his play entitled Wild Oats was one of his best comedies. O'Keefe's "The Friar of Orders Grey," "The Tailor and the Undertaker," and "Tom Grog" are three of his most humorous pieces (O'Donoghue 93-101, 430). As to the characters in his plays, both Thady MacBrogue, the vigorous servant in The She-Gallant (1764), and Felix, the devil-may-care wanderer in Wicklow Gold Mines (1794), represent the "stage Irishman" (Waters 42).

John O'Keefe Bibliography

O'Donoghue, David James, ed. The Humour of Ireland. London, England: Walter Scott, 1894; New York, NY: AMS Press, 1978.
Waters, Maureen. The Comic Irishman. Albany, NY: State University of New York Press, 1984.

John Philpot Curran (1750-1817) IRELAND

John Curran was a noted orator and wit who was born in Cork. His eloquence and patriotic humor endeared him to his countrymen and caused his name to become widely familiar. Curran's "The Monks of the Screw," and "Ana" are two of his funniest pieces (O'Donoghue 102-105, 424).

John Philpot Curran Bibliography

O'Donoghue, David James, ed. The Humour of Ireland. London, England: Walter Scott, 1894; New York, NY: AMS Press, 1978.

Richard Brinsley Sheridan (1751-1816) IRELAND

Along with William Congreve, Oscar Wilde, and Noel Coward, Richard Sheridan is one of the masters of the comedy of manners. Rose Snider compares Sheridan to Congreve, saying that although Congreve was born in England and later moved to Ireland, while Sheridan was born in Ireland and later moved to England, both authors had acquired a "generous share of the irish comic spirit." Furthermore, Sheridan, like Congreve, was born into a rich and famous family (Snider 41).

Hesketh Pearson remarks that Sheridan was "the wittiest and most fascinating character of his age." He continues the tradition of his grandfather's light-heartedness, companionableness, and carelessness, and he also continues the tradition of his grandfather's ability to produce light verses and smart sallies, which had at times "lifted the darkness of Swift's mind" (70). Richard's elder brother was Charles, and it was Charles who was the father's favorite child. Charles was steady, prudent, docile, and had every quality needed to gain the approval of his seniors, such as being sanctimonious, self-seeking, and self-righteous. It was Charles who most contributed to the depiction of Richard Sheridan's character, "Joseph Surface" (Pearson 73).

One of Sheridan's special staging trademarks was his love for sudden surprises, often bordering on practical jokes. Such surprises were very successful when done on stage. "A screen is thrown down and Lady Teazle discovered behind it--a sword instead of a trinket drops out of Captain Absolute's coat--the old duenna puts on her mistress' dress" (L'Estrange 157).

Mark Auburn notes that after two centuries, three of Sheridan's plays, The Rivals, The Critic, and The School for Scandal, continue to play well on the stage. Auburn sums up Sheridan's contribution as follows: "Together these comedies represent a vital dramatic creation which surpasses in popular endurance in the repertory the output of any other English comic playwright between Shakespeare and Shaw" (3). Much of Sheridan's success can be accounted for by his effective use of dramatic irony, the technique of letting the audience in on the joke,

> rather than surprising them as Congreve does with Mirabel's deed at the conclusion of The Way of the World or as Colman and Garrick do with Lord Ogleby's unexpected support of Fanny at the conclusion of The Clandestine Marriage, for instance--[this] allows the audience the pleasures of both anticipation and expectation. Sheridan would work diligently with this technique in his farce St. Patrick's Day, his comic opera The Duenna, and his adaptation of A Trip to Scarborough until he achieved its greatest realization in The School for Scandal. (Auburn 59)

The Rivals (1773) is written by a master of comic technique, especially comedy of situation. The most effective scenes are those in which comic situations are steeped in dramatic irony--scenes in which truths are concealed from some of the characters but are known to other characters and also known to the audience (Auburn 58). The Rivals satirically attacks sentiment, but in a very muted way. There is, for example, the ridicule of Lydia Languish's misdirected notions of romantic love which come from her reading of popular "sentimental" novels. Lydia Languish is a lively and likeable character even though she illustrates to the extreme the eighteenth-century flair for sentimentality. "She has given her imagination free rein, and the result is a curious combination of sentiment, vanity, love, and sheer caprice" (Snider 45).

There is also Faulkland's "absurd delicacy of feeling." According to Allan Rodway, "sentimentality of a romantic kind is genuinely satirized in Lydia Languish and, of a moral kind, in Joseph Surface; both are ruthlessly and amusingly exposed" (68). According to Auburn the faults of these characters are handled "gently, with sympathy for the characters, and with little attempt to motivate self-realizations" (58). The characters in The Rivals are amiable humorists in their own right. They tend to be basically good-natured, and they tend not to represent identifiable personages in real life, so that the satire is broad rather than focused. The satire attacks typical human behavior rather than attacking particular humans.

Probably the most famous character in The Rivals is Mrs. Malaprop. Characters who confuse words the way she confuses words have become stock figures (archetypes) in many post-Sheridan plays. She says that Captain Absolute is the very "pine-apple of perfection," and she describes her daughter's considering marrying a penniless man as "hydrostatics." She does not require her daughter to be a "progeny of learning," but the daughter should have a "supercilious knowledge" of accounts, and she should also know about the "contagious countries" (L'Estrange 158). In this same play, Sir Anthony tells his son that the son must marry the woman which he (the father) selects for him even though she may have the "skin of a mummy, and beard of a Jew." When his son objects, he tells him not to be angry. "So you will fly out! Can't you be cool like me? What the devil good can a passion do? Passion is of no service, you impudent, violent, over-bearing reprobate!" (L'Estrange 158).

St. Patrick's Day; or, The Scheming Lieutenant (1775) is based on the formula of boy-gets-girl-in-spite-of-parents:

> Lieutenant O'Connor wants to wed Lauretta but Justice and Bridget Credulous object to the marriage. By disguising himself first as a bodyguard (the soldiers billeted in the area have been obstreperous of late) and then as a German physician, he tricks the mildly avaricious and cowardly Justice Credulous into giving him permission to marry. Talkative and pedantic Dr. Rosy is his confident and abettor in this design. (Auburn 62).

Isaac is the center of the comedy in The Duenna (1775), as every scene into which he enters he comes in a different disguise; Mark Auburn thus considers The Duenna to be a one-joke comedy, but then he adds that "so are many great comedies."

> Sheridan's brilliant stroke was to exploit this one joke to its fullest possible extent. And his favorite technique here--allowing Isaac multiple asides in which he praises himself and his cleverness, explains his intended actions, weighs his possible alternatives, and never recognizes the cleverness, action, or alternatives as precisely the things which guarantee his downfall-- intensifies the comic dramatic irony. (Auburn 79)

Auburn notes that there are a few additional comic effects which enhance the play in that some of Antonio's songs are very amusing in their witty cleverness, and some of Isaac's songs are "wonderfully whimsical for his ironic ignorance of himself" (79).

A Trip to Scarborough (1777) is a Sheridan adaptation of Sir John Vanbrugh's The Relapse. Mark Auburn says that he can find only one witty speech of any significance in A Trip to Scarborough that can be attributed to Sheridan, and it is "of the mildest sort" (102). Sheridan's adaptation was to simplify it as a "playing piece," typical of much comedy popular in his time, and to make the flavor more "genteel" (Auburn 103).

Sheridan's The School for Scandal (1777) is considered by Mark Auburn to be "the best playing comedy of manners in the English language" (104). Auburn says that what makes this comedy so entertaining is that merit is amiably rewarded and lack of merit is exposed. It is a carefully structured satiric attack on scandalmongering, and it contains one of the best exposure scenes in all of English comedy; this is the superb screen scene. According to Auburn, the play is not a morally serious comedy. Although scandalmongering is the object of satire, the decision not to attempt any reformation of Snake, Joseph, and Lady Sneerwell, shows Sheridan's awareness of the reality and perhaps the inevitability of evil (147). The characters are basically benevolent and good natured. Lady Sneerwell, Joseph, and Snake are merely exceptions in a world inhabited by crusty but benevolent Sir Peters, naive Lady Teazles, plain-dealing Charleses, and villains who are effectively neutralized by being expelled (Auburn 148).

In The Critic (1779), Phelim is portrayed as an aspiring Irish performer who wants Dangle, a theatrical amateur with influence on the new managers, to help him obtain a place in the Durry Lane company. Sneer is a cynic and critic, and Puff is a playwright and a theatrical hanger-on; Sneer and Puff discuss the state of the stage, and mock Sir Fretful Plagiary, who is a pretentious old deaf music critic. The play contains some comically bad music, and some genuinely good songs which intersperse some mildly dramatic criticism and some Eulogies of David Garrick (Auburn 151).

One of Sheridan's funniest characters in The Critic is Mr. Acres, a gentleman who "forsakes the familiar hunting-frock and leather breeches for the costume of the city fop; he undertakes to train his hair, since contemporary fashion had decreed the return of natural coiffures; he hires the services of a dancing-master to learn the then popular allemand and cotillion" (Snider 71). But Mr. Acres's funniest quality is his development of a new kind of profanity which he calls "sentimental swearing." Examples of this genteel method of imprecation include "odds frogs and tambours," "odds triggers and flints," "odds whips and wheels," and even "odds blushes and blooms" (Snider 71).

In his Letters and Journals, George Gordon, Lord Byron describes Sheridan's contribution to the stage as follows:

> He has written the best comedy (School for Scandal), the best drama (The Duenna) . . . , the best farce (The Critic) . . . , and the best Address (Monologue on Garrick), and, to crown it all, delivered the very best Oration (the famous Begum Speech) ever conceived or heard in this country. (Auburn 177)

Mark Auburn suggests that Sheridan's high achievement among writers of English comedy comes from his "complex, fast-moving, amiably comic plots peopled by probable yet theatrical characters; from a brilliance dependent not upon wit in the high Restoration comic sense but upon a full consonance of expression to character; and from a careful poise of expectation and surprise in situational comedy" (Auburn 181).

Richard Brinsley Sheridan Bibliography

Auburn, Mark S. Sheridan's Comedies: Their Contexts and Achievements. Lincoln, NE: Univ of Nebraska Press, 1977.

Auty, Susan G. The Comic Spirit of Eighteenth-Century Novels. Port Washington, NY: Kennikat, 1975.

Bowman, David. "Sheridan's Comedy of Rhetoric." Interpretations 6 (1974): 31-38.

Dixon, Campbell. "Sheridan." English Wits. Ed. Leonard Russell. London, England: Hutchinson, 1940 171-196.

Durant, Jack D. "The Sheridanesque: Sheridan and the Laughing Tradition." Southern Humanities Review 16 (1982): 287-301.

Hume, Robert D. "Goldsmith and Sheridan and the Supposed Revolution of 'Laughing' against 'Sentimental' Comedy." The Rakish Stage: Studies in English Drama, 1660-1800. Carbondale, IL: Southern Illinois Univ Press, 1983, 312-355.

Jackson, J. R. "The Importance of Witty Dialogue in The School for Scandal." Modern Language Notes 76 (1961): 601-607.

L'Estrange, Alfred Gu. "Sheridan et. al." History of English Humour. New York, NY: Burt Franklin, 1978, 150-163.

O'Donoghue, David James, ed. The Humour of Ireland. London, England: Walter Scott, 1894; New York, NY: AMS Press, 1978.

Pearson, Hesketh. "Richard Brinsley Sheridan." Lives of the Wits. New York, NY: Harper and Row, 1962, 70-123.

Rodway, Allan. "Goldsmith and Sheridan: Satirists of Sentiment." Renaissance and Modern Essays: Presented to Vivian de Sola Pinto in Celebration of his Seventieth Birthday. Ed. G. R. Hibbard. London, England: Routledge, 1966 65-81.

Sawyer, Newell W. The Comedy of Manners from Sheridan to Maugham. Philadelphia, PA: Univ of Pennsylvania Press, 1931.

Snider, Rose. "Richard B. Sheridan." Satire in the Comedies of Congreve, Sheridan, Wilde, and Coward. New York, NY: Phaeton Press, 1972, 41-73.

Brian Merriman (1757-1808) IRELAND

Merriman's <u>Midnight Court</u> (1926) is a long and rambunctious masterpiece (O'Tuama 222). It is furthermore filled with Rabelais-type language and images (Greene 420).

Brian Merriman Bibliography

Greene, David H. "Ireland: Literature." <u>The Encyclopedia Americana: International Edition</u>. Danbury, CT: Americana Corporation, 1978, 420-423.
O'Tuama, Sean. "Gaelic Literature." <u>The Encyclopedia Americana: International Edition</u>. Danbury, CT: Americana Corporation, 1978, 220-222.

Elizabeth Hamilton (1758-1816) IRELAND

Elizabeth Hamilton's <u>Translation of the Letters of a Hindoo Rajah</u> (1819) is a satire on British customs and the education of women.

Elizabeth Hamilton Bibliography

Hamilton, Elizabeth. <u>Translation of the Letters of a Hindoo Rajah</u>. Boston, MA: Wells and Lilly, 1819.

Edward Lysaght (1763-1810) IRELAND

Edward Lysaght was one of the most famous of Irish wits. He became a barrister; however, he was too much of a "bon vivant" to succeed well in that profession. He was not nearly as witty in his poetry as he was in person. Lysaght's "My Ambition" is one of his best humorous pieces (O'Donoghue 126-127, 428).

Edward Lysaght Bibliography

O'Donoghue, David James, ed. <u>The Humour of Ireland</u>. London, England: Walter Scott, 1894; New York, NY: AMS Press, 1978.

Henry Luttrell (c1766-1851) IRELAND

Mainly because of his powers of repartee, Henry Luttrell became one of the most popular men in London society. Born in Dublin, he became a member of the Irish Parliament. David O'Donoghue considers Luttrell's "Advice to Julia" and "Crockford House" to be good examples of clever satiric light verse. Luttrell's "Epigrams, Etc." is also a good piece of humorous writing (O'Donoghue 133-134, 428).

Henry Luttrell Bibliography

O'Donoghue, David James, ed. <u>The Humour of Ireland</u>. London, England: Walter Scott, 1894; New York, NY: AMS Press, 1978.

CHAPTER 5

Humor in 19th Century Irish Literature

Maria Edgeworth (1767-1849) IRELAND

Maria Edgeworth was an Anglo-Irish satirist in the tradition of Jonathan Swift, George Farquhar, Oliver Goldsmith, Laurence Sterne, and Richard Brimsley Sheridan, but she was an innovator as well. Her first novel, Castle Rackrent (1800) is a regional novel, set in Ireland. It is a subversive novel which not only questions the status of the Anglo-Irish landlord, but also looks askance at, and even ridicules, those who unquestioningly accept the absurd position of both Irish and English women (Weekes 19).

Edgeworth's second novel, Belinda: Oh What a Fine Confusion! (1801) is set in England and involves courtship. Maria Edgeworth's satirical perspective is that of an Anglo-Irish woman who dares to question traditional male-female relationships. Her satire deals with art styles, lifestyles, colonialism, feminism, and the nature of existence. She preserves moral boundaries but does so with a twinkle in her eye. In Northanger Abbey, Jane Austen railed against those who failed to recognize the depth of knowledge of human nature in Edgeworth's Belinda. Austen considered Edgeworth to have a happy tone, and a lively wit and humor (Lightfoot n.p.).

Maria Edgeworth Bibliography

Lightfoot, Marjorie. "A cornucopia of Satire: Edgeworth's Belinda." Éire-Ireland 29 (1994).

Waters, Maureen. The Comic Irishman. Albany, NY: State University of New York Press, 1984.

Weekes, Ann Owens. "Maria Edgeworth: Domestic Saga." Irish Women Writers: An Uncharted Tradition. Lexington, KY: University Press of Kentucky, 1990, 33-59.

George Canning (1770-1827) IRELAND

Although George Canning was born in London, both his father and his mother were Irish, and Canning therefore considered himself to be "an Irishman born out of Ireland." Canning was a brilliant member of Parliament, and became Prime Minister in 1827, but remained Prime Minister only for about three months. Canning's witty essays were written early in life, and were published in The Microcosm and in Anti-Jacobin. Canning's "A Warehouse for Wit," and his "Conjugal Affection" are both humorous pieces (O'Donoghue

127-130, 423).

George Canning Bibliography

O'Donoghue, David James, ed. The Humour of Ireland. London, England: Walter Scott, 1894; New York, NY: AMS Press, 1978.

Thomas Moore (1779-1852) IRELAND

Thomas Moore was the son of a Dublin grocer who graduated from Dublin University and studied law in London. His Irish Melodies (1806), was his first successful piece. An especially humorous piece of Moore's writing is his "Letter from Miss Betty Fudge" (O'Donoghue 134-137, 429).

Thomas Moore Bibliography

O'Donoghue, David James, ed. The Humour of Ireland. London, England: Walter Scott, 1894; New York, NY: AMS Press, 1978.

Sydney Owenson (Lady Morgan) (1783-1859) IRELAND

Sydney Owenson's father was Robert Owenson, a stage Irishman who went to Dublin, and who was so successful there that he was able to get his wife to join him in Ireland. The story goes that on December 25th, either on board a vessel en route to Ireland, or very shortly after landing, Mrs. Owenson gave birth to Sydney. Thus among Robert Owenson's fellow actors, the story went that Sydney had been born in the middle of the Irish Sea. This proved to be symbolic of Sydney Owenson, for "her merits and her faults, her struggles and her triumphs, all sprang from the fact that in hereditary traits, in religion, in politics, she existed continually in mid-channel" (Stevenson 3). In 1833, Sydney Owenson wrote in her diary that "the Irish destiny is between Bedlam and a jail" (Stevenson 289).

Sydney Owenson was famous for the parties she threw on Kildare Street. When Paganini visited Dublin, she won his heart by giving him an exact imitation of a Florentine dinner. Paganini told Owenson his life history, but she found him to be "a stupefied and almost idiotic creature." Owenson said that her famous dinners became very burdensome because of the thousand details that were necessary for setting up a "recherché" dinner, with only a few servants.

> When the British Association met in Dublin in 1835, Lady Morgan of course entertained in their honour. "My soirée very fine, learned, scientific, and tiresome! Fifty philosophers passed through my little salon last night." The event of the evening was a song, Fun and Philosophy, written and performed by Lady Clarke, and afterwards published in the Athenaeum. In the same week she had Moore to dinner, but he too, was growing garrulous. "Moore looks very old and bald, but still retains his cock-sparrow air." (Stevenson 291)

In her Italy, Sydney Owenson was critical of the Cardinal Archbishop of Westminster, saying that she doubted the authenticity of his having seen a particular sacred relic--St. Peter's chair. Owenson brought out a pamphlet in which she addressed this issue and said that the Cardinal had no more seen the chair than she had (Stevenson 310). Owenson also found fault with the Cardinal's literary style, and chided him for using a quotation from Horace, "more becoming to a Heathen satirist than a Christian Bishop." She concluded by advising him to go back to Ireland and learn from Father Mathew how to make himself useful to his countrymen. Of course the Press and the public were delighted with Sydney Owenson's pamphlet, which ran through five editions. In addition, Punch made this pamphlet the theme of a full-page cartoon, a poem, several puns, and a long dialogue between "Lady Fan and Cardinal Crozier," which "wittily summed up the whole dispute" (Stevenson 311).

Lionel Stevenson says that the two dominant traits of Sydney Owenson are her personal vanity and her dramatic imagination. It was Owenson's vanity that gave her the constant desire to knock ten years off from her age. "She suppressed all evidence of the true date of her birth, and insisted that the title of her first book had been Poems Written Between the Age of Twelve and Fourteen." Owenson's friends developed a game of trying to trap Owenson into an admission of her true age, but she evaded even the most ingenious of snares (Stevenson 313). In referring to Owenson's date of birth, the standard works disagree by as much as sixteen years. Lionel Stevenson says that of all of these years, he chose 1776, even though this was one of the few dates between 1770 and 1786 which no encyclopedia or biographical dictionary had selected. Stevenson's reason for selecting this date was that it was the "only date confirming with all the facts" (Stevenson v).

People had to smile at Owenson's vanity. On one occasion she said, "I know I am vain, but I have a right to be so. It is not put off and on, like my rouge; it is always with me; it sleeps with me, wakes with me, companions me in my solitude, and arrays itself for publicity whenever I go abroad." Owenson continues, "Did ever woman move in a brighter sphere than I do? My dear, I have three invitations to dinner to-day; one from a duchess, one from a countess, a third from a diplomat--I will not tell you who--a very naughty man, who, of course, keeps the best society in London" (Stevenson 314).

According to Ann Weekes, Sydney Owenson shared the early nineteenth-century spotlight with Maria Edgeworth. She celebrated Gaelic civilization, history, and aspirations, and made the first sympathetic presentation of Gaelic Ireland to reach a wide audience (Weekes 20). According to Gregory Castle, Sydney Owenson is an excellent teller of tales. Her story telling abilities are especially obvious in Wild Irish Girl: A National Tale (1807), and in Florence MacCarthy: An Irish Tale (1819). Lionel Stevenson considers Owenson's O'Donnel to be a novel filled with "satirical realism." In evaluating The Princess, or the Beguine, Stevenson quotes from a letter by Maria Edgeworth:

> We have been amusing ourselves with Lady Morgan's Princess, exceedingly amusing, both by its merits and its absurdities--that harlequin princess in her blouse is wonderfully clever and preposterous--a Belgian Corinna . . . . The hero is like one of the seven sleepers not quite awakened, or how could he avoid finding out who this woman is who pursues him in so many forms? But we must grant a romance writer a few impossibilities. (Stevenson 288)

Whenever Owenson was told that she was "looking so much better," she would reply, "perhaps I am better rouged than usual." The last time that she visited Sir Emerson Tennent, he congratulated her on her health, and she responded, "I believe that we might all live just as long as we liked; in fact, I look upon anyone that dies under a hundred as a suicide!" (Stevenson 314).

Sydney Owenson (Lady Morgan) Bibliography

Castle, Gregory. "Personal Conversation." Tempe, AZ: Arizona State University, August, 1994.
Stevenson, Lionel. The Wild Irish Girl: The Life of Sydney Owenson (Lady Morgan). London, England: Chapman and Hall, 1936.

Weekes, Ann Owens. Irish Women Writers: An Uncharted Tradition Lexington, KY: University Press of Kentucky, 1990.

Eaton Stannard Barrett (1786-1820) IRELAND

Eaton Stannard Barrett was a satirist and a poet, and one of the wittiest writers in Ireland. He was born in Cork, graduated from Trinity College, Dublin, and became a London barrister. Some of his satires, such as All the Talents, which targeted the ministry, were widely read. Barrett also wrote various burlesque novels, plays, and poems, but he was also able to write on serious subjects. Two of Barrett's most successful (but difficult to access) humorous pieces are "Montmorenci and Cherubina," and "Modern Medaevalism" (O'Donoghue 423). In The Heroine or The Adventures of Cherubina, Barrett is parodying the entire school of romantic writing, including that of Byron and Scott. The central theme of this novel plays on the relationship between the unromantic parent and the disdainful youth. In the tradition of Don Quixote, the errant damsel adventures into the country with her comic servant Jerry, representing Sancho Panza in the parody. The parody is broad, targeting almost every species of English fiction from Richardson's to Barrett's time; there are a variety of amusing caricatures (Kitchin 252).

Eaton Stannard Barrett Bibliography

Kitchin, George. Survey of Burlesque and Parody in English. Edinburgh, Scotland: Oliver and Boyd, 1981.
O'Donoghue, David James, ed. The Humour of Ireland. London, England: Walter Scott, 1894; New York, NY: AMS Press, 1978.

Thomas Ettingsall (c1790-1850) IRELAND

Thomas Ettingsall was a fishing-tackle manufacturer in Wood Quay, Dublin. He wrote humorous sketches and short stories for Dublin Penny Journal (1832), and for The Irish Penny Journal (1840). Ettingsall's "Darby Doyle's Voyage to Quebec" is a particularly humorous piece (O'Donoghue 148-160, 425).

Thomas Ettingsall Bibliography

O'Donoghue, David James, ed. The Humour of Ireland. London, England: Walter Scott, 1894; New York, NY: AMS Press, 1978.

Joseph O'Leary (c1790-c1850) IRELAND

Joseph O'Leary was the author of a collection of prose and verse entitled The Tribute. O'Leary was a contributor to the scurrilous Freeholder and to other Dublin papers. He went to London in 1834 and became a parliamentary reporter for the Morning Herald. O'Leary's humorous "Whisky, Drink Divine" first appeared in about 1820 in The Freeholder (O'Donoghue 130-132, 430).

Joseph O'Leary Bibliography

O'Donoghue, David James, ed. The Humour of Ireland. London, England: Walter Scott, 1894; New York, NY: AMS Press, 1978.

Jeremiah O'Ryan (c1790-1855) IRELAND

Jeremiah O'Ryan was born near Bansha in County Tipperary, and is generally known as "Darby Ryan of Bansha." Some of his songs were collected and published in Dublin in 1861. "The Peeler and the Goat" is a humorous O'Ryan piece (O'Donoghue 231-234, 430).

Jeremiah O'Ryan Bibliography

O'Donoghue, David James, ed. The Humour of Ireland. London, England: Walter Scott, 1894; New York, NY: AMS Press, 1978.

William Maginn (1793-1842) IRELAND

David O'Donoghue feels that William Maginn was an excellent parodist, and a great humorist in every way, in fact, probably one of the greatest scholars and humorists Cork has ever produced (O'Donoghue 428). O'Donoghue considers Maginn to have been the first writer who demonstrated a "genuine rollicking Irish humour" (O'Donoghue xviii). Maginn's most humorous pieces include "St. Patrick of Ireland, My Dear!" "The Last Lamp of the Alley," "Thoughts and Maxims," "The Gathering of the Mahonys," and "Daniel O'Rourke" (O'Donoghue 160-184, 428).

As early as 1819, Maginn was writing parodies and humorous Latin verse for Blackwood's Magazine. Maginn also adapted Lucian's Dialogues of the Dead into blank-verse comedies. George Kitchin notes that the parody style of Maginn's Whitehall, and his George IV (1827) is lively and effective. Whitehall is basically a parody of the school of "tushery," but there are other motifs as well. In order to communicate to his readers that he is writing parody, Maginn writes about contemporary persons who talk in exaggeratedly rude ways. This is contrasted with Smithers's romantic jargon. Maginn also parodied the language to be found in the society novels of his day (Kitchin 254).

During the 1840s Maginn supplied a number of parodies to Fraser's Magazine, the best of which are entitled, "Disraeli," and "Carlyle," published as part of the Maclise Portrait Gallery. "O reader dear! do pray look here, and you will spy the curly hair, and forehead fair, and nose so high, and gleaming eye, of Benjamin Disraeli, the wondrous boy who wrote Alroy in rhyme and prose, only to show how long ago Judah's lion-banner rose . . . ." Here Maginn is parodying Disraeli's sin of falling into regular verse in his ordinary prose. In parodying Carlyle's style, Maginn stressed the Germanic syntax, the Anglo-Saxon word craze, and the parenthetical entanglements (Kitchin 266).

William Maginn Bibliography

Kitchin, George. Survey of Burlesque and Parody in English London, England: Oliver and Boyd, 1931.
O'Donoghue, David James, ed. The Humour of Ireland. London, England: Walter Scott, 1894; New York, NY: AMS Press, 1978.

William Carleton (1794-1869) IRELAND

William Carleton's life was meager, with instruction that was often interrupted, and was provided by a variety of masters who usually met their students in barns or in roadside shelters, the so-called "hedge schools." In two of Carleton's stories, "The Poor Scholar," and "The Hedge School," he tells about the type of education available in Ireland during those days when the position of master was determined publicly through a battle of wits. It was the tradition of the day that the scholarly reputations of the school masters were open to challenge, and they could be ousted at any time by a more skillful debater (Waters Comic Irishman 63).

William Carleton's life seemed to be a training for his destiny as a comic writer. He said that he attended every wake, dance, fair, and merry event in the neighborhood, and became so celebrated for dancing jigs and reels and for blowing the hornpipes that he was soon without a rival in the parish. Maureen Waters notes that Carleton's wonderfully comic Denis O'Shaughnessy in "Denis O'Shaughnessy Going to Maynooth" is based on Carleton's memories of himself as a "local phenomenon" (Waters Comic Irishman 59). Denis is himself described as follows: "His nose was set upon his face in a kind of firm defiance against infidels, heretics, and excommunicated persons. His pompousness becomes even more outrageous once he has acquired a horse and a good suit of clothes. He begins to refer to himself as 'Dionysus,' a name which, he believes, carries more dignity than the common 'Denis.' " The satiric target of this story is the worldliness of certain priests, as Denis maneuvers to be selected as a candidate for the seminary at Maynooth. However, his family must first bribe the local priest and then even the bishop, before Denis can be accepted into the Priesthood (Waters Comic Irishman 64).

Traditionally, the plot of comedy has the hero overcoming the "senex figure," thus creating a dynamic renewal of the community. In" Denis O'Shaughnessy Going to Maynooth," however, there is no fundamental conflict between the "Senex" and the hero. "The son accepts the values of the father. And in choosing marriage instead of priesthood, Denis also confirms the tradition into which he was born" (Waters Comic Irishman 67). In a way, Denis is characteristic of the Irish comic character who uses language to dazzle and evade, "to create a mask which conceals his true nature" (Waters Comic Irishman 72).

Maureen Waters feels that "Denis O'Shaughnessy Going to Maynooth" is like "Phelim O'Toole's Courtship" in being "marred by narrative and structural defects;" however the defects are "far outweighed by the pleasure afforded through the wonderfully comic language" (Waters Comic Irishman 60).

> In this story much of the humor is in the talk; one is struck again and again by the Irish love of rhetoric and argument, even for rules of grammar and for obscure forms of knowledge. This was natural in an oral culture where the story teller was an important source of information and entertainment, and the ordinary means of education were unavailable to the mass of people. (Waters Comic Irishman 61)

Carleton noted that what the Irish lacked in material goods they compensated for by a richness of imagination. In "Denis O'Shaughnessy Going to Maynooth," as in many Irish tales there were dreadful puns, and playful rearrangements of history. The comedy of the piece is also based to some extent on the ignorance and superstitiousness of the country people (Waters Comic Irishman 63).

Carleton's dialogue tends to be "metaphorical, rich, peppery, and highly inflected." It expresses "the energy and wit of the Irish country people" (Waters Comic Irishman 60). It has a kind of wit and flair for the fantastic which is inherent to the Irish comic tradition (Mercier 11-46).

Irish humor frequently takes pleasure in distortion of bodily features which goes far beyond ordinary caricature, suggesting a link with the ancient practice of satire, often a form of intense ridicule aimed at specific parts of the body. Irish humor--and this is particularly true of Carleton--also makes use of extended figures of speech (or one figure capped by another) that are ironic or ambivalent in meaning. Thus the clause, "He must have a head like a bell," ostensibly suggests clarity, but there is a secondary implication of emptiness and noise, which is picked up (capped) in the last line and joined with a typical macabre joke: He'll "make a noise in conthroversy . . . if he lives." (Waters Comic Irishman 62).

Much of Carleton's humor is linguistic in nature. There is much humor based on blunders or malapropisms like "You blarnied and palavered me, you villain, till you gained my infections." With such humor, the reader is struck by "the energy and the wit of the Irish English idiom, by its taste for metaphor and alliteration, its pronounced rhythms and inflections." There is a teasing irony imbedded in the central metaphor in such expressions as "There won't be sich a lovin' husband, bedad, in Europe. It's I that'll wax you; an' butther you up like a new pair o' brogues." Here Phelim is addressing a woman who is "well seasoned"--that is, she is an older woman, and she has already been "butthered" up enough to have given Phelim her money. The comparison here between a woman and the shoes "is typical of the kind of ludicrous details yoked together in an Irish conceit" (Waters Comic Irishman 37).

Most of Carleton's stories are a blend of tragedy and comedy. His own theory was that no one ever possessed a "higher order of humor whose temperament was not naturally melancholy," and therefore, melancholy and mirth are frequently blended in Carleton's prose much in the manner of gallows humor (Waters Comic Irishman 59).

Phelim O'Toole is a comic rogue created by William Carleton (Waters Comic Irishman 5). Maureen Waters considers "Phelim O'Toole's Courtship" to be one of the best comic stories of the nineteenth century. The humor is prototypically Irish in nature. The wit in "Phelim O'Toole's Courtship" is sharply satiric. Phelim is an imposter, and a notorious liar, who is well known for his trickery and petty thievery. He is a man frequently called on to give false testimony for friends with legal problems (Waters Comic Irishman 35):

> Phelim's very appearance signifies his role as a witty rogue. As a result of small pox, one eye is closed in a perpetual wink, and his face resembles the "rough side of a cullender," or as he was often told in raillery, "You might grate potatoes on it." He is dressed in tatters and wears a cap of rabbit skin with the ears protruding over his forehead. (Waters Comic Irishman 36)

Maureen Waters notes that much of the visual description in "Phelim O'Toole's Courtship" is based on incongruity and fantasy. Rather than saying that Phelim has dirty legs, Carleton will say that the spots take on the character of Egyptian hieroglyphics. And Phelim's "state dress" is like a monarch's train sweeping to the ground at least two feet behind him. Using a typically ironic Irish conceit, Carleton indicates that Phelim is heir to a "snug estate of half an acre" (Waters Comic Irishman 38).

Billy Dawson is another comic rogue created by Carleton. In "The Three Wishes" Dawson is a lazy but clever ne'er-do-well, who repeatedly outwits the devil, who in turn supplies Billy with money, which he consumes as conspicuously as possible. Billy Dawson is a comical rogue who can be amusing and droll, especially in his contests with the devil.

> Like so many folk figures, he is able to outmaneuver a much more powerful antagonist by his cleverness and lack of scruples. He is quite willing to resort to cruelty in order to gain an advantage, whether it be against a neighbor or the devil himself. At one point he takes a pair of red-hot tongues and pulls on the devil's nose, which stretches like a "piece of warm

wax" until it extends through the chimney and five feet above the roof of the house. (Waters Comic Irishman 35)

Ironically, when Billy Dawson dies, he finds that both the gates of heaven and those of hell are closed against him. Defiantly, he puts his nose through the bars of hell and someone on the other side catches his nose by a pair of red-hot tongs. The nose burns fiercely because of all of the hard liquor that Dawson has drunk during his lifetime. Dawson ends up as a will-o'-the-wisp, haunting the bogs and quagmires in order to cool his nose (Waters Comic Irishman 35).

David Krause argues that the comic giant named Finn MacCool representing a deprecated father figure, dates back to the eighth century. In "A Legend of Knockmany," Finn is an evasive character who spins one yarn after another in order to conceal his fear of a rival giant:

> Despite his own great strength and the magical thumb from which he sucks wisdom and logic, he is saved primarily through the cleverness of his wife who disguises him as a child and then tricks Cucullin [the rival giant] into placing his own magical finger into the mouth of Finn. He immediately bites it off, destroying the source of Cucullin's strength and finally Cucullin, himself. (Waters Comic Irishman 33)

Maureen Waters considers Carleton's The Emigrants of Ahadarra (1848) to be comedy of politics and of economy, in which four families are threatened with personal or economic ruin. Jemmy Burke is a witty, genial, down to earth good man to work for (Waters "Comic Form" 87). Jemmy's voice has a vigorous, epigrammatic quality. As the story develops, Jemmy uses irony as a foil against his son, "pricking his vanity and leaving him increasingly confused about his father's intentions. The Burke household is an arena for verbal combat, much of it quirky and humorous" (Waters "Comic Form" 93).

Mrs. Burke's language is stilted and given to malapropisms, in her awkward attempts to sound "genteel." Mrs. Burke becomes comical by imitating the language and the manners of the gentry:

> She will have tea and no stirabout and must be driven in a horse and cart. Much of her behavior is harmless but, unfortunately, she has brought up her younger son, Hycy, to think of himself as a gentleman and to treat his father with contempt. What she doesn't realize is that the son is equally contemptuous of her and uses flattery to ensure her support of his extravagant life style. (Waters "Comic Form" 88)

Hycy is often playful and satiric in his choice of words. These words are sometimes interspersed with snatches of song. Hycy's satire is often aimed at his mother, whom he mocks by using "high English." His mother pretends to understand but doesn't really. The second family in The Emigrants to consider is the Cavanaghs. This is a family in transition. Although they still cling to some values which are outmoded and destructive, they are anxious to form an alliance with the wealthy Burkes, and they therefore encourage Hycy Burke as a suitor (Waters "Comic Form" 88).

The M'Mahon family is very patriarchal in its structure. The house and the land have both been inherited from the paternal line, and the paternal grandfather is a member of the family. The M'Mahon men are responsible for managing the property and for dealing with outside agents, while the M'Mahon women preside over the domestic chores. The M'Mahons live entirely in their small M'Mahon world. For them, Dublin is merely the residence of their landlord (Waters "Comic Form" 89). Problems begin for the M'Mahons when their new landlord fails to renew the lease granted by his father. It is mainly through their story that Carleton reinforces his argument in favor of tenant rights (Waters "Comic Form" 90).

Hogan is the name of the fourth family. The Hogans, who are tinkers, spend part of their time in the mountains distilling "poteen," and part of their time inhabiting the Cavanagh's kiln. Carleton's peasant upbringing gives him an unromantic view of the tinkers, and he presents them as an "ugly lot with no home or land of their own, [and] no well-ordered domestic routine" (Waters "Comic Form" 91). The antagonist in The Emigrants is Hycy Burke, a humorous pedant who invites the tinkers in to rob his father's house, thereby setting up a course of destruction that involves the Burkes, the Hogans, the M'Mahons, and the Cavanaghs as well (Waters "Comic Form" 92).

The Emigrants is like most Irish comedy, in being more interesting in what is being said than in what is being done. Carleton grew up in a bilingual and bicultural community, representing not only different, but in fact antithetical values.

> Throughout his fiction he experimented with the sound of language and with its effect on the listening audience. He brought to his writing the old Gaelic sense of language as power and pleasure. Unlike other nineteenth century writers who assigned a uniform "brogue" in varying degrees of accuracy to all peasants, Carleton tried to key the voice to the character; the result in The Emigrants is a wide range of memorable speaking voices. (Waters "Comic Form" 93)

In The Emigrants, the schoolmaster's name is Finigan.

> Finigan, serving up odd, disjointed bits of learning in a grandiloquent style, represents the ragged end of a classical tradition. He employs great "rocks" of English, weighty and original polysyllables, fused with incongruous bits of dialect and irregular Latin. His philomath's language is used to impress an illiterate audience as well as to support a towering self-importance. He is inclined to clothe his experience in luminous metaphor, vastly and comically out of proportion to actuality. (Waters "Comic Form" 95)

Still another character in The Emigrants is Teddy Phats, who appears to be slow witted and animal-like, but is, in truth, watchful and cunning and capable of savage and biting humor. Maureen Waters feels that Phats, Finigan, Hycy Burke, and to a lesser degree Jemmy Burke "all reflect Carleton's interest in the phenomenon of masking, an ancient device of comedy, but one with special significance to Irish society. Under a threatening foreign government, masking was a defense, a way not only of staying alive but of manipulating a powerful antagonist" (Waters "Comic Form" 97). Waters points out that much of the humor in The Emigrants as well as much Irish humor in general is like the humor of American blacks. Irishmen, like the blacks, appear amiable and entertaining and slow witted, but in fact are very much in control of the situation. "A striking feature of Irish adaptation was the use of the voice as mask. Turning the initial handicap of a foreign tongue to advantage, the Irishman pretended to understand a good deal less than he did" (Waters "Comic Form" 97).

The Emigrants is a love story, told in the comic mode, because it has a happy ending. In the end, the hero recovers his property and can afford to marry; at the same time, the heroine admits her affection for the hero, which she had been feeling the whole time (Waters "Comic Form" 98).

> The Emigrants concludes in the amiable tradition of comedy . . . : There is a great flurry of activity in which all problems are resolved and a new order is declared. Once the landlord has accepted his proper role in the community, Jemmy Burke asserts authority in his household, bringing back his older son, Edward, who had been studying for the priesthood, to inherit the farm. (Waters "Comic Form" 101)

A suitable match is found for Edward. Bryan and Kathleen exchange vows. The two candidates who battled over a seat in parliament even reach some sort of an agreement. "All the malefactors are soundly punished. The hot-headed priest who denounced Bryan is chastised for mixing in politics. Hycy is finally exposed, forced to leave his father's house, and eventually--we are told--dies in poverty. Teddy Phats breaks his rascally neck, and the Hogan men (Kate reforms) are transported, becoming 'the true emigrants of Ahadarra' " (Waters "Comic Form" 101).

In Carleton's "The Battle of the Factions" the narrator slyly tells the reader that the "bones of contention were numerous." This statement has literal as well as symbolic meaning. In this epic battle, numerous bones were secured from a graveyard and put to use by the fighters as they gleefully maimed and murdered each other (Waters Comic Irishman 177).

Maureen Waters says that Carleton's fiction "weaves back and forth between scenes of terror and degradation and scenes of wildly extravagant farce. His novels and short stories constitute the most compelling and vivid literature written in Ireland during this period" (Waters Comic Irishman 5).

William Carleton Bibliography

Mercier, Vivian. The Irish Comic Tradition London, England: Oxford University Press, 1969.

O'Donoghue, David James, ed. The Humour of Ireland. London, England: Walter Scott, 1894; New York, NY: AMS Press, 1978.

Waters, Maureen. "Comic Form and Historic Nightmare in Carleton's Emigrants of Ahadarra." Éire-Ireland 22 (1987): 86-101.

Waters, Maureen. The Comic Irishman Albany, NY: State University of New York Press, 1984.

Charles O'Flaherty (1794-1828) IRELAND

Charles O'Flaherty was first an apprentice to a Dublin bookseller and later a journalist on the staff of the Dublin Morning and Post, and still later he became the editor of the Wexford Evening Post. His humorous verse and songs enjoyed great popularity, especially "The Humours of Donnybrook Fair," which in 1813 was published in his Trifles in Poetry (O'Donoghue 184-187, 430).

Charles O'Flaherty Bibliography

O'Donoghue, David James, ed. The Humour of Ireland. London, England: Walter Scott, 1894; New York, NY: AMS Press, 1978.

Joseph Augustine Wade (1796-1845) IRELAND

Joseph Wade was an Irish genius whose humorous poetry and music were highly praised. Although his writings and music earned him large sums of money, he died in poverty. Joseph Wade's "The Turkey and the Goose" is an especially humorous piece (O'Donoghue 200-202, 432).

Joseph Augustine Wade Bibliography

O'Donoghue, David James, ed. The Humour of Ireland. London, England: Walter Scott, 1894; New York, NY: AMS Press, 1978.

Samuel Lover (1797-1868) IRELAND

Samuel Lover published a novel entitled Rory O'More in 1826. In 1838, Rory O'More reappeared as a play. Maureen Waters considers Rory O'More to be a new type of comic character--an Irish peasant who is a hero rather than a villain. He is as crafty, impudent, and witty as Billy Dawson or Phelim O'Toole, but he is a man of unswerving integrity (Waters 44). Rory is in the tradition of the rogue, and he is also in the tradition of the stage Irishman of the eighteenth century. He is an amorous Irishman who flatters women, and they find him difficult to resist. Rory is a rogue who has difficulty with the English language. He frequently uses the term "vagabones" for "vagabonds," and he also uses "portmantle" for "portmanteau." But he is nevertheless skillful with language, and he is fond of word play and punning in a farcical way. This play also contains several stories about drinking and about pigs; these are stock features of Irish comedy in the late eighteenth and the nineteenth centuries (Waters 45). In the tradition of the Comic Irishman, Rory was also an excellent entertainer, and a good teller of tales (Waters 46).

Andy Rooney in Samuel Lover's Handy Andy (1842), is the rustic clown, or what the Irish would call the "omadhawn," or "simpleton," in contrast to Rory O'More, who was more heroic, more playful, and more foxy. This figure is like the traditional Fool, who was considered lucky. He speaks with a comic brogue, and further amuses his audience with bulls and blunders. These were stock features of the stage Irishman of the nineteenth century. Maureen Waters distinguishes between the "blunder," and the "bull." "The blunder grows out of the confusion of the Gaelic speaker who doesn't fully grasp the meaning of English words." For example, inquiring about the sex of a new born infant, Andy wants to know if his friend, Dick Dawson, is now "an uncle or an aunt." The "bull" on the other hand, is "a metaphorical statement stressing apparent connections which are not real" (Waters 11).

Andy Rooney was a very popular character for English audiences because of the comic relief he provided them.

> He was the Step 'N Fetch It of his time, a foolish, amusing sort of fellow, quite harmless after all. He is untrustworthy, not because he is dishonest, but because he is not too bright. Fit only for the most menial kind of work, he readily accepts his role as a servant and, because he has a thick hide, he doesn't mind an occasional thrashing. (Waters 13)

Andy, however, is not a static character. He can develop into a comic hero. Sometimes the character of the "omadhawn" can make the melodramatic discovery that he is the long lost son of an eccentric aristocrat. "Thus the fool is redeemed, restored to his rightful heritage, and declared his own master" (Waters 13). Even though the "omadhawn" has "changed his motley clothes into the robes of an English peer, however, the servile foolish Andy is still there underneath his new dignities. Still the butt of humor, at dinner he manages to swallow the paper frill along with the main course" (Waters 14).

Waters compares the Irish "omadhawn" figure with the "schlemiel" of Yiddish folk culture. "Each is a born loser, a naïf, foolish in the ways of the world and easily duped by a faithless wife or cunning competitor. Each, because of an inexhaustible faith or optimism, manages to survive the vagaries of Fortune" (Waters 5). Andy Rooney is the butt, the blunderer, the inferior person who to the English symbolized Ireland. Andy's mistakes make the English feel superior, and they can laugh comfortably at his antics. Handy Andy was one of the first Irish comic novels, and also one of the first novels to employ folk materials. It is episodic in nature, and relies much on fantasy, farce, and romance. The tone ranges from the sentimental to the macabre, and the novel includes many delightful talks, like the legend of Tom Connor's cat who demanded shoes (Waters

9).

David O'Donoghue feels that it is from Lover that "we get the cream, and not the curds of Irish humour." He considers Lover to be "the Irish arch-humorist," adding that "it is difficult to exaggerate the excellence of his love-songs." Other pieces may be more classical, or more polished, or more subtle, but according to O'Donoghue, no writing is more irresistible (O'Donoghue xix). O'Donoghue feels that "Widow Machree," "Barney O'Hea," "Molly Carew," "Handy Andy and the Postmaster," and "The Little Weaver of Duleek Gate" are some of Lover's most humorous character sketches (O'Donoghue 202-228, 427).

Samuel Lover Bibliography

O'Donoghue, David James, ed. The Humour of Ireland. London, England: Walter Scott, 1894; New York, NY: AMS Press, 1978.
Waters, Maureen. The Comic Irishman. Albany, NY: State University of New York Press, 1984.

Rev. Thomas Hamblin Porter (c1800-c1890) IRELAND

Reverend Thomas Porter graduated from Dublin University in 1836. His humorous "The Nightcap" appeared in a Dublin magazine in about 1820 (O'Donoghue 187-188, 431).

Rev. Thomas Hamblin Porter Bibliography

O'Donoghue, David James, ed. The Humour of Ireland. London, England: Walter Scott, 1894; New York, NY: AMS Press, 1978.

John Baldwin Buckstone (1802-1879)

John Buckstone is English, but in his The Green Bushes (1845) there is a good example of the stereotypical stage Irishman. Wild Murtogh is a comical villain who appears on stage in rough dress flourishing a shillelagh and threatening to do violence to anyone "who'll tread on the tail of his coat." Although Murtogh exhibits little wit, he is comic by virtue of his pretensions, and by his wild Irish mannerisms (Waters 43).

John Baldwin Buckstone Bibliography

Waters, Maureen. The Comic Irishman Albany, NY: State University of New York Press, 1984.

Gerald Griffin (1803-1840) IRELAND

Gerald Griffin was born in Limerick, Ireland but went to London in his youth. There he wrote some "admirable Irish stories" such as the humorous "The Loquacious Barber." His best known book is The Collegians, or, The Colleen Bawn. (O'Donoghue 234-239, 426).

Gerald Griffin Bibliography

O'Donoghue, David James, ed. The Humour of Ireland. London, England: Walter Scott, 1894; New York, NY: AMS Press, 1978.

James Clarence Mangan (1803-1849) IRELAND

Even though James Mangan was a Dubliner who had little formal education, his lyric Irish poetry came close to capturing the tone and the flavor of the lyric poetry of the seventeenth and eighteenth centuries (Greene 421). Mangan knew a number of languages, but his pretended translations from Turkish, Coptic, Hebrew, Arabic, and Persian are merely elaborate jokes. Mangan had a wonderful personality; and he received much encouragement to write from his admirers and from critics, but he wrote little (O'Donoghue 429).

James Clarence Mangan Bibliography

Greene, David H. "IRELAND: Literature." The Encyclopedia Americana: International Edition. Danbury, CT: Americana Corporation, 1978, 420-423.
O'Donoghue, David James, ed. The Humour of Ireland. London, England: Walter Scott, 1894; New York, NY: AMS Press, 1978.

Rev. Francis Sylvester Mahony (1804-1866) IRELAND

Reverend Francis Mahony was better known as "Father Prout," his pseudonym as a writer. He was one of the most admired contributors to Fraser, where he published his "Reliques." Mahony's "Elegy on Himself" is an especially humorous piece (O'Donoghue 242-243, 428).

Rev. Francis Sylvester Mahony Bibliography

O'Donoghue, David James, ed. The Humour of Ireland. London, England: Walter Scott, 1894; New York, NY: AMS Press, 1978.

Charles James Lever (1806-1872) IRELAND

Charles Lever was one of the most widely read of Irish novelists. He was a contributing editor of The Dublin University Magazine, and he also wrote for Blackwood's Magazine. Five of his most humorous pieces are "Bob Mahon's Story," "The Widow Malone," "The Girls of the West," "The Man for Galway," and "How Con Cregan's Father Left Himself a Bit of Land" (O'Donoghue 243-257, 427).

Charles James Lever Bibliography

O'Donoghue, David James, ed. The Humour of Ireland. London, England: Walter Scott, 1894; New York, NY: AMS Press, 1978.

Lady Dufferin (1807-1867) IRELAND

Lady Dufferin was the daughter of Thomas Sheridan, who was the son of Richard Brinsley Sheridan. Lady Dufferin's poems are frequently exquisite in their pathos, their humor, and their grace. One of Lady Dufferin's most humorous pieces is "Katey's Letter" (O'Donoghue 264-266, 424).

Lady Dufferin Bibliography

O'Donoghue, David James, ed. The Humour of Ireland. London, England: Walter Scott, 1894; New York, NY: AMS Press, 1978.

John Francis Waller (1809-1894) IRELAND

John Waller was born in Limerick, graduated from Dublin University in 1852, and held an important Government position in Dublin for a number of years. He was also the editor of The Dublin University Magazine for a while, and published a number of volumes of clever prose and verse. According to David O'Donoghue, Waller was one of the best authors of Irish songs. Waller wrote the humorous "Dance Light, for My Heart It Lies under Your Feet, Love" (O'Donoghue 267-271, 432).

John Francis Waller Bibliography

O'Donoghue, David James, ed. The Humour of Ireland. London, England: Walter Scott, 1894; New York, NY: AMS Press, 1978.

Sir Samuel Ferguson (1810-1886) IRELAND

Samuel Ferguson is considered to be one of Ireland's greatest poets. He graduated from Dublin University and became a member of the Irish Bar. He was an important contributor to Blackwood's Magazine, where he published both his humorous "Father Tom and the Pope," and his "The Forging of the Anchor" (O'Donoghue 267-271, 425). He wrote poetic renderings of legends and stories of the epic cycles in his Lays of the Western Gael (1865), Gongal (1872), and Deirdre (1880). Ferguson's depictions of these stories influenced later Irish authors (Greene 421).

Sir Samuel Ferguson Bibliography

Greene, David H. "IRELAND: Literature." The Encyclopedia Americana: International Edition. Danbury, CT: Americana Corporation, 1978, 420-423.
O'Donoghue, David James, ed. The Humour of Ireland. London, England: Walter Scott, 1894; New York, NY: AMS Press, 1978.

Edmund Falconer (1814-1879) IRELAND

Patrick O'Donnel is the hero in Falconer's Eileen Oge (1871). O'Donnel is a religious man, a man of honor, and a man who is chivalrous toward women. Brian O'Farrel is his comic foil. O'Farrel is a rogue who speaks with more of an Irish brogue than does O'Donnel. The play is filled with clichés about virtuous Irish girls and the stereotype of the impetuous Irishman. It incorporates scenes of singing and dancing, whisky drinking, and a good old Irish brawl (Waters 43).

Edmund Falconer Bibliography

Waters, Maureen. The Comic Irishman Albany, NY: State University of New York Press, 1984.

Joseph Sheridan Lefanu (1814-1873) IRELAND

Joseph Lefanu was one of the most widely read of Irish novelists. He graduated from Dublin University, received his M.D. degree at Louvain, and became a dispensary doctor in Ireland. He was the editor of The Dublin University Magazine from 1842 until 1845, and wrote many pieces for this magazine and for other leading periodicals of the day. Lefanu wrote a humorous piece entitled, "The Quare Gander" (O'Donoghue 279-288, 427).

Joseph Sheridan Lefanu Bibliography

O'Donoghue, David James, ed. The Humour of Ireland. London, England: Walter Scott, 1894; New York, NY: AMS Press, 1978.

James McKowen (1814-1889) IRELAND

James McKowen was born in Lamberg, near Lisburn in County Antrim, and received only an elementary education. He was employed as a thread manufacturer, and linen bleacher. He wrote mainly for papers in the North of Ireland, and was especially popular with people in Ulster. "The Ould Irish Jig" is one of McKowen's humorous pieces (O'Donoghue 271-273, 429).

James McKowen Bibliography

O'Donoghue, David James, ed. The Humour of Ireland. London, England: Walter Scott, 1894; New York, NY: AMS Press, 1978.

Edward Vaughan Hyde Kenealy (1819-1880) IRELAND

Edward Kenealy was born in Cork, graduated from Dublin University and became a member of the Irish Bar, though he was disbarred because of his conduct in the famous Tichbourne case. He often wrote for Bentley's Miscellany, and published a number of collections of his poetry. He was a vigorous journalist, and in later life became a member of parliament. Kenealy wrote the humorous "Table-Talk" (O'Donoghue 288-290, 426).

Edward Vaughan Hyde Kenealy Bibliography

O'Donoghue, David James, ed. The Humour of Ireland. London, England: Walter Scott, 1894; New York, NY: AMS Press, 1978.

Dion(ysius) Boucicault (c1820-1890) IRELAND

Boucicault wrote a comedy called "London Assurance" when he was only nineteen years old. According to David O'Donoghue, Boucicault was an admirable comedian as well as a dramatic writer (O'Donoghue 294-298, 423). The bulwark of authority in Dion Boucicault's plays is the parish priest, who is presented as an unassailable father figure. He is a "senex" figure, but one so powerful and respected that the comic hero does not dare to overturn him.

> Conn or Myles may tease the priest or slip a little whiskey into his "tay," but they acknowledge his superiority, and in any conflict the priest invariably prevails. At the conclusion of The Shaughraun, Father Dolan actually takes Conn by the ear and returns him to his mother, thus sealing his fate as a perennial adolescent. (Waters 56)

Boucicault was born in Dublin, and at an early age he was associated with the theatre (Waters 46). Boucicault's rogue makes for good drama. Boucicault was an amiable entertainer, full of passionate blarney for pretty women. He was fond of whiskey and liked telling good jokes.

> Each of Boucicault's rogues is linked to an aristocratic figure, usually an Irish rebel chief, for whom he risks his life. Their relationship suggests the traditional one of jester and king, but the Irish rogue is far more deferential than the medieval jester and his descendants, who bully and exploit their employers and delight in exposing their weakness and folly . . . . The "rogue" is articulate, good natured, fun loving, and [exhibits an] irrepressible élan vital. (Waters 47)

Dion Boucicault did much to establish the archetype of the stage Irishman, described by Maureen Waters as a merry, whiskey-drinking, pugnacious clown. Boucicault's characters reinforced the stereotypical Irishman as lazy, and fun-loving with a devil-may-care attitude--the very antithesis of Victorian respectability. Myles-na-Coppaleen in The Colleen Bawn (1860), for example, is a salmon poacher, an ex-convict, and a maker of bootleg whiskey. He is sly, and is as nimble as a fox. He is capable of listening at key holes and windows and of carrying forward his schemes with considerable success. Myles is as fond of playing with words as he is of dodging the main issue of a conversation. In typical Irish fashion, he does this by feigning ignorance or simplicity in order to throw his questioner off the scent. Myles will then double back and trap him in a snap of wit (Waters 48). Myles lives outside of the law and refuses to work. "He is adventurous, even heroic, in a highly melodramatic way and, like Phelim O'Toole, has a flattering tongue and an innate cunning that allowed him to wiggle his way out of many a compromising situation" (Waters 6).

Shaun Conn, another of Boucicault's characters, is an Irish Wanderer, or bodagh (comic vagabond). Shaun is constantly singing Irish songs, and playing tricks to amuse and confound his friends. He is a rogue who is addicted to knockabout comedy, which he finds useful in dodging the police as well as deceiving his "ould mother." He even presides at his own wake, "slyly emptying the whiskey jug while the keen is raised over the 'corpse.' " "The scene is sheer burlesque as Boucicault reflects little of the macabre found in folk tales and ballads" (Waters 50). All of Boucicault's rogues are wonderful talkers, as they tease women, or ease themselves out of difficult situations (Waters 51). During the trial scene in Arrah-na-Pogue: Arrah of the Kiss, for example, there is an uproar in the court which is attempting to convict Shaun of armed robbery. The comedy of this scene depends on Shaun's real and pretended ignorance as well as on his ability to create a thicket of language which those conducting the trial (none too bright themselves) have difficulty understanding.

MAJOR: Now, prisoner, are you guilty or not guilty?

SHAUN: Sure, Major, I thought that was what we'd all come here to find out. (Waters 52)

There is a similar "bull" in Boucicault's <u>Shaughraun</u> which contains the following dialogue:

CLAIRE: Did they bring him home insensible?

MRS. KELLY: No, Miss--they brought him home on a shutter. (Waters 52)

About this type of wordplay, Waters makes the following observation:

> In Boucicault's plays the values attached to standard English and to Irish English are curiously reversed. The speech of the peasants is not only comical, but witty and imaginative, while that of the upper classes--with the exception of Anne Chute and The O'Grady, who might have stepped out of Restoration Comedy--is devoid of resonance or feeling. (Waters 53)

As a tribute to Dion Boucicault's popularity, Joseph Holloway, describes the situation at the Queens Theatre, the traditional playhouse for Irish drama. The people in the audience "were so familiar with Boucicault's work that they could supply the appropriate line if an actor missed his cue" (Waters 56).

Dion(ysius) Boucicault Bibliography

O'Donoghue, David James, ed. <u>The Humour of Ireland</u>. London, England: Walter Scott, 1894; New York, NY: AMS Press, 1978.

Waters, Maureen. <u>The Comic Irishman</u> Albany, NY: State University of New York Press, 1984.

Richard Dalton Williams (1822-1862) IRELAND

Richard Williams was one of the earliest and one of the leading contributors to <u>The Nation</u>, usually using the penname of "Shamrock." His writings are often fierce and intense, but O'Donoghue feels that his real power lies in his humor and his parodies. Williams is the author of the humorous "Advice to a Young Poet" (O'Donoghue 290-291, 432).

Richard Dalton Williams Bibliography

O'Donoghue, David James, ed. <u>The Humour of Ireland</u>. London, England: Walter Scott, 1894; New York, NY: AMS Press, 1978.

Timothy Daniel Sullivan (1827-1914) IRELAND

Timothy Sullivan was a well-known politician, and one of Ireland's most widely read poets. Some of his songs have especially impressed themselves on Irish memory. His forté was the writing of political skits, which at one time were featured in the <u>Nation</u> newspaper, which he also edited. One of Sullivan's humorous pieces is named "Rackrenters on the Stump" (O'Donoghue 298-306, 432).

Timothy Daniel Sullivan Bibliography

O'Donoghue, David James, ed. <u>The Humour of Ireland</u>. London, England: Walter Scott, 1894; New York, NY: AMS Press, 1978.

Charles Joseph Kickham (1828-1882) IRELAND

Joseph Kickham was a poet of the people, and a powerful novelist. Such stories as "Sally Cavanagh," and "Knocknagow, or the Homes of Tipperary" give important insights into the home-life of the Munster people. Kickham was connected with The Irish People, a Fenian publication, and in 1865 he was arrested and sentenced to fourteen year's penal servitude, and this servitude shattered his health. "The Thrush and the Blackbird" is one of Kickham's most humorous pieces (O'Donoghue 314-320, 427).

Charles Joseph Kickham Bibliography

O'Donoghue, David James, ed. The Humour of Ireland. London, England: Walter Scott, 1894; New York, NY: AMS Press, 1978.

Charles Graham Halpine (1829-1868) IRELAND

Charles Halpine authored two volumes of verse some of which is very humorous. He was born in Oldcastle, the son of a Protestant clergyman. Halpine wrote a humorous piece called "Irish Astronomy" (O'Donoghue 320-322, 426).

Charles Graham Halpine Bibliography

O'Donoghue, David James, ed. The Humour of Ireland. London, England: Walter Scott, 1894; New York, NY: AMS Press, 1978.

James Joseph Bourke (1837-1894) IRELAND

James Bourke was born in Dublin, and his poems are widely known and appreciated throughout Ireland. Under the penname of "Tiria," Bourke wrote for a number of Irish newspapers for a period of at least thirty years. Bourke is the author of such humorous pieces as "O'Shanahan Dhu," and "Shane Glas" (O'Donoghue 329-333, 423).

James Joseph Bourke Bibliography

O'Donoghue, David James, ed. The Humour of Ireland. London, England: Walter Scott, 1894; New York, NY: AMS Press, 1978.

John Francis O'Donnell (1837-1874) IRELAND

John O'Donnell was an Irish poet. He began to publish his poetry at the age of fourteen, and in 1861 he moved to London where he wrote mainly for various journals, including those of Charles Dickens. "Paddy Fret, the Priest's Boy" is a humor piece written by James O'Donnell (O'Donoghue 322-329, 430).

John Francis O'Donnel Bibliography

O'Donoghue, David James, ed. The Humour of Ireland. London, England: Walter Scott, 1894; New York, NY: AMS Press, 1978.

Alfred Perceval Graves (1846-1931) IRELAND

According to David O'Donoghue, Alfred Graves is second in popularity only to Samuel Lover as a writer of humorous Irish songs. Not only has he written a number of good songs in a lighter vein, but he has also written some good songs that develop the emotion of pathos. Graves has done a great deal to make Irish music, and the Irish character better known to the world at large. "Fan Fitzgerl," and "Father O'Flynn" are two humorous pieces which Alfred Graves wrote (O'Donoghue 341-344, 426).

Alfred Perceval Graves Bibliography

O'Donoghue, David James, ed. The Humour of Ireland. London, England: Walter Scott, 1894; New York, NY: AMS Press, 1978.

Standish James O'Grady (1846-1928) IRELAND

Standish James O'Grady and Lady Gregory wrote popular renditions of many of the stories of earlier Irish mythology of the Ulster and Fenian cycles.

Standish James O'Grady Bibliography

Greene, David H. "IRELAND: Literature." The Encyclopedia Americana: International Edition. Danbury, CT: Americana Corporation, 1978, 420-423.

Charles Stewart Parnell (1846-1891) IRELAND

In 1875 Charles Parnell entered the English Parliament not as a Liberal, nor as a Tory, but as a member of the small Home Rule Party. Because of his shrewdness and his audacity, Parnell became a major manipulator of Parliament. The irony was that although Parnell fought tirelessly for Irish Catholics to have a major say in determining their own destiny, his accent was not that of Ireland, but was that of Cambridge University. Even though Parnell was the most significant symbol of Irish nationalism, he was himself a "Protestant landlord whose previous interests had been limited to cricket, geology and fox hunting." In addition to this, against all tenets of Irish Catholicism, he had an affair with Katharine O'Shea. When Captain William O'Shea, filed for divorce from his English wife, Katharine, he named Parnell as co-respondent. According to Thomas Flanagan, "O'Shea might have stepped out of one of Feydeau's Paris hotel room farces, complete with monacle, waxed mustaches and roguish ways. Panderer, liar, blackmailer, boaster, he lacked any redeeming trait, other than a fondness for such of his children as he had reason to believe might be his own" (Flanagan 2).

When Parnell died, his grave was marked by a massive boulder of Wicklow granite, and it bore only the single word, "Parnell." Since Parnell had passed into mythology, this single word represented a complex and potent legend, and it was an appropriate marker for the stern and incantory life it represented and symbolized (Flanagan 2).

Charles Stewart Parnell Bibliography

Flanagan, Thomas. "The Uncrowned King of Ireland." The New York Times Book Review September 4, 1994, 2, 21.

Kee, Robert. The Laurel and the Ivy: The Story of Charles Stewart Parnell and Irish Nationalism. New York, NY: Hamish Hamilton/Viking, 1994.

Lady Isabella Augusta Gregory (1852-1932) IRELAND

Lady Gregory's writing is filled with fantasy and imagination, qualities which are very common in Irish satire (Waters 24). Many of the characters in Lady Gregory's one-act plays are rustic clowns or fools, but they are wise fools (Waters 22).

> While it was earlier a common assumption that the peasant who couldn't speak English fluently was mentally and linguistically defective, Lady Gregory proposes that the problem is precisely the reverse. She satirizes the countryman's love of talk, his tendency to lose himself entirely in the play of imagination. The dialect of Cloon is marked by Gaelic rhythms and inflections and is intended to be amusing because of its variation from English; however, it is also rich in wit and imagery and unexpected associations. (Waters 24-25)

Much of Lady Gregory's comedy is generated by the static quality of Cloon, where her stories take place, and by the energy of the characters to create drama. out of the nonevents of their lives. In Spreading the News (1904), for example, there is a group of "foolish busybodies" who have nothing better to do than exaggerate a piece of misinformation into a full scale tragedy of murder and adultery. The story is based on the human capacity for self-delusion.

> No one comes forth with the least modicum of common sense or reason to put a stop to the gossip--there's too much pleasure in it. When the "dead" man appears on the scene, the people simply assume he's a ghost. At the finish the alleged murderer and his victim are taken off to jail together until the "real" corpse can be located. (Waters 25)

The central character in Hyacinth Halvey (1906) is not able to escape being held up as a model of moral conduct. Therefore, he steals a sheep and robs a church in a desperate effort to avoid the role that is being thrust upon him. Ironically, however, "his crimes are attributed to a local ne'er-do-well, who cannot escape his reputation either" (Waters 25).

The central theme of The Workhouse Ward is based on an old Irish proverb--"It is better to be quarrelling than to be lonesome." Michael Miskell and Mike McInerney are two old men in The Workhouse Ward who quarrel in order to pass the time. Each of these old men is skilled at hurling invective, and at deriding the character, the appearance, and the past life of the other. Each person attempts to cap the previous insult, thus coming as close as possible to physical combat or emotional violence and the resulting annihilation of the long friendship. "Each is testing the imagination and fury of the other in a combat of wit which is mutually exhilarating" (Waters 26). The story is also an illustration of a second Irish proverb--"It is conversation that keeps away death" (Waters 27).

Lady Isabella Augusta Gregory Bibliography

Waters, Maureen. The Comic Irishman. Albany, NY: State University of New York Press, 1984.

George Moore (1852-1933) IRELAND

Robert Langenfeld says that in Moore's Memoirs of My Dead Life (1906) part of the comedy is developed through the juxtaposition of pagan values with the conservative values of the establishment. Moore also castigates the church's abuse of authority. "In many ways a formative book, Memoirs foreshadows Moore's satiric masterpiece Hail and Farewell (1911) and his delightfully bawdy A Story-Teller's Holiday (1918)" (Langenfeld Memoirs 74). According to Langenfeld, all three of these pieces comically recreate what the serious minded Gogarty eventually learns. He leaves "the dead wisdom of codes and formulas, dogmas and opinions" and seeks "a vagrancy of ideas and affections" that accord with "the law of change which is the law of life" (Langenfeld Memoirs 76). Langenfeld also considers Moore's Confessions (1886) to be satiric, and perhaps even farcical in its approach. According to Langenfeld, "the humor in Memoirs never becomes caustic, as at times in Hail and Farewell, or raucous, as at times in A Story-Teller's Holiday" (Langenfeld Memoirs 79). Explaining the comic nature of Moore's turn-of-the-century writing, Langenfeld says:

> We see his mischievousness becoming more refined, achieving a very special humor where the comic effect is moderated by a tone of superior detachment, where the sarcastic phrase is sweetened by a polite smile, where indiscretion never degenerates into gossip, but always stays on the level of perfectly measured, aristocratic irony. (Langenfeld Memoirs 77).

Langenfeld feels that in the context of Moore's comic works, Memoirs is pivotal because

> It draws upon the autobiographical point of view, the humor and the themes in Confessions; on the Irish issues in The Untilled Field, on the style, the quest for escape from Ireland and Catholicism in The Lake, and it looks forward to very different comic approaches to similar topics in Hail and Farewell and A Story-Teller's Holiday. (Langenfeld Memoirs 88)

Like Hail and Farewell which would follow, Memoirs is a mock-heroic quest story. The mock-heroic theme is linked closely to Moore's purpose in Memoirs, which is "to use comedy to place conventional attitudes in question." According to Langenfeld, "the very notion of a modern heroic quest for love makes Moore sure of one thing: 'I was no longer a conventional citizen of the nineteenth century.' " But the quest was a quest for his pyjamas, as Moore employs exaggeration of the mock-heroic genre in order to laugh at the foolish proprieties associated with normal sexual relations. During his affair, the protagonist finds that no shop in Plessy carries pyjamas, though they do carry nightshirts, and these would be inappropriate. The irony is that pyjamas are necessary, and yet there is "no demand for the refinement of English pyjamas" (Langenfeld Memoirs 84).

In Memoirs, the irony of the situation gives rise to much of the humor. Moore is a mock-heroic lover pursuing a married woman whom he has been in love with for years. The consummation of his quest is nearly foiled by the fact that he can't find regalia which is heroic enough, but is rather to be found in his pyjamas. The irony is that Moore, who is a "great" author is sought out by a stunningly beautiful young lady from Texas, who wants Moore to sire "a race of 'great' authors for the culturally barren New World of Texas." According to Langenfeld, "Moore uses ironic situations to tease the stolidity of conventional sexual mores." Moore believes that there is a divinity in sexuality. He casts sexual love in a light of good-nature. He writes about it in a humorous vein which cheers those who believe as he does, and teases those who don't (Langenfeld Memoirs 81).

In "Resurgam," Moore writes about his own resurrection, but since the tale is comic and mock-heroic, the resurrection is not very Christ-like. Moore plans his own burial, and plans it as a "heroic spectacle" indeed. A funeral pyre is planned which is to be fifty feet high, saturated with scented oils, with all of his books functioning as his pillow. The fire would be seen for miles around. His mourners would be enjoying a magnificent feast as his corpse was burning, and they ate roasted meat, and drank wine, and wore bright colored clothes. At the same time, selections from the "The Marriage of Figaro" and excerpts from "The Valkyrie" would bring the evening to a close. Moore even makes elaborate plans for his remains. They would be placed in a granite vase, decorated with nymphs and satyrs of the saturnalia (Langenfeld Memoirs 86).

> He considers where his granite vase would be placed to ensure immortality. The bottom of the Pacific would be ideal, even though the "hero" knows that nothing lasts forever, even in the sea. Not only Moore but, of course, the earth itself will finally die and be absorbed into the sun, the sun into still greater suns. A new earth will form and "out of the primal mud" will come plants and animals. "Is this," asks Moore, "madder than Palestinian folklore?" (Langenfeld Memoirs 87)

Moore assumes the mock-heroic persona in order to "question whose madness is truly more mad: his comic, exaggerated vision of a comic theodicy, or the austere vision of the Judeo-Christian tradition" (Langenfeld Memoirs 87).

The function of A Story-Teller's Holiday is to recount Irish tales of priests and nuns in medieval Ireland in a comic and ironic manner that is highly reminiscent of Boccaccio's Decameron. These stories are designed to expose the hypocrisy of the church, "which often succeeds in subjecting an individual's judgment about his own sexual and emotional needs to the dictates of a religious order which forces people into orthodox ways of thinking and behaving" (Langenfeld Memoirs 88).

George Moore Bibliography:

Langenfeld, Robert. "George Moore's A Story-Teller's Holiday Reconsidered: Irish Themes Expressed through Comic Irony." Cahiers du Centre d'Etudes Irlandaises 9 (1984): 15-29.
Langenfeld, Robert. "Memoirs of My Dead Life: George Moore's Comic Autobiography." Éire-Ireland 21.1 (1986): 73-88.

William Boyle (1853-1874) IRELAND

William Boyle was one of the raciest of Irish authors. Boyle was born in Dromiskin, County Louth, and was educated at St. Mary's College in Dundalk. In 1874 he became a member of the Inland Revenue Department, and was stationed in Glasgow, Scotland. Boyle wrote the humorous "Philandering" (O'Donoghue 344-345, 423).

William Boyle Bibliography

O'Donoghue, David James, ed. The Humour of Ireland. London, England: Walter Scott, 1894; New York, NY: AMS Press, 1978.

Francis Arthur Fahy (1854-1935) IRELAND

Like William Boyle, Francis Fahy was one of Ireland's raciest and most humorous poets. Many of the poems which he wrote for Irish papers were signed "Dreoilin" (the wren), and in 1887 he published a collection of Irish Songs and Poems in Dublin. Fahy published some of his material in Songs of the Four Nations. The humorous "The American Wake," "How to Become a Poet," "The Donovans," and "Petticoats Down to My Knees" were all written by Francis Fahy (O'Donoghue 355-373, 425).

Francis Arthur Fahy Bibliography

O'Donoghue, David James, ed. The Humour of Ireland. London, England: Walter Scott, 1894; New York, NY: AMS Press, 1978.

William Percy French (1854-1920) IRELAND

William French was born at Clooniquin, County Roscommon, and graduated from Dublin University. In 1894, David O'Donoghue said that French was "one of the cleverest of living Irish humorists." He is the author of many humorous verses and stories which appeared in a small Dublin comic magazine named The Jarvey, which French at the time edited. Some of French's songs have become very popular, and he is also the author of the libretti of two operas. French wrote the humorous "The First Lord Liftinant" (O'Donoghue 347-355, 425).

William Percy French Bibliography

O'Donoghue, David James, ed. The Humour of Ireland. London, England: Walter Scott, 1894; New York, NY: AMS Press, 1978.

Oscar Wilde (1854-1900) IRELAND

James Joyce placed Oscar Wilde in the tradition of Irish comedy writers stretching from Richard Brimsley Sheridan and Oliver Goldsmith to George Bernard Shaw. He is also in the tradition of the English court jester (Waters 102). Wilde once said, "Humanity takes itself too seriously. It is the world's original sin. If the caveman had known how to laugh, history would have been different" (Nicholls vii). Hesketh Pearson said about Wilde that "No one ever said so many acute things in the guise of paradox. By shifting the viewpoint, he forced his listeners to look at life from unaccustomed angles and enlarged the boundaries of Truth. Though he owed something to La Rochefoucauld, he went deeper" (Pearson Life 176). In a book entitled Comedy of Manners, David Hirst discusses the development of this genre in the seventeenth century, and says that the genre had a renaissance in the nineteenth century with Oscar Wilde:

> With Wilde the dandy was reborn, and this figure was to reappear in the inter-war period and again in the 1960s. Both the "roaring," "gay" 1920s and the age of Hair and Carnaby Street were periods in which fashion, and notably male fashion, asserted themselves, and it is precisely in these times that the comedy of manners, dormant throughout the drab, unstylish 1940s and 1950s as through the Victorian era, again became a significant comic genre. (Hirst 3)

Hirst felt that it was Wilde, a contemporary of Meredith and Shaw, who was "best able to satirize the hypocrisy of his own age by exploring the dichotomy between word and deed. Fundamental to his plays--as to those of the late seventeenth century--is the vigorous rejection of puritan values." Hirst considers Wilde to have been the first of several homosexual writers in England who used social comedy to reveal the nature of sexual hypocrisy (Hirst 112).

The best moments in Wilde's comic plays occur when people talk about "important" things in totally inappropriate ways, as when Lord Arthur Savile approaches Herr Winckelkopf searching for an explosive clock, and Winckelkopf assumes that Lord Arthur is planning revenge against the police. He protests, "I am afraid I cannot do anything for you. The English detectives are really our best friends, and I have always found that by relying on their stupidity, we can do exactly what we like. I could not spare one of them" (Henkle 307).

In a book entitled, The Paradox of Oscar Wilde, George Woodcock develops the point that Wilde's life, his writing, and his thought are filled with apparent contradictions, and that is why many critics have considered Wilde to have been insincere. Woodcock feels he wasn't insincere; he was paradoxical. "I believe that Wilde was in fact a more earnest man than he or others believed, and that he was sincere in almost everything he did" (Woodcock 9). Woodcock goes on to say that Wilde loved the paradox because it suited a man of his peculiar duality of attitude. Wilde's only novel, The Picture of Dorian Gray (1891) showed Wilde's schizoid nature by dealing with the dual-image of a "doppelgänger." In Wilde's writing,

> there is the continual rivalry of paganism and Christianity, of the gospel of hedonism and the gospel of suffering. There is the contrast between his aesthetic clowning--which he himself admitted to be little more than posture--and the valuable critical theories expressed in his lectures and essays, and carried out in his own writing. There is the contrast between the delightful but often superficial nonsense that occupied so much of his conversation and drama, and the deep thinking on artistic, philosophical and social subjects that supported his outward brilliance. There is the contrast between the social snob, with his attitude of apparent flippancy towards the poor, and the social critic, whose ideas on political justice and attacks on existing relationships in society were of a truly subversive nature. And there is the contrast between the playboy whose antics brought about with a strange inevitability the crisis of Wilde's downfall, and the self-conscious "prophet" who emerged chastened from prison, only to be replaced again by the temporarily suppressed playboy of the last days in Paris. (Woodcock 12)

In The Picture of Dorian Gray, Erskine is a dinner-table wit who says such things as, "the way of paradoxes is the way of truth. To test Reality we must see it on the tightrope. When the Verities become acrobats we can judge them" (Murray 39).

Wilde posed as an antagonist, but he was not one.

> Wilde clowned and posed and indulged in pathetically sordid and ridiculous debauches. He was a social snob and could play the sedulous ape to any writer whose work he admired. Nevertheless, he undoubtedly possessed a gift for presenting important ideas in a fresh and striking way, and at times such ideas showed a deep wisdom. (Woodcock 10)

Sir William Rothenstein said of him, "He seemed to have read all books, and to have known all men and women . . . . He was remarkably free from malice. Moreover, I have met no one who made me so aware of the possibilities latent in myself" (Woodcock 11).

Some of Oscar Wilde's sayings are based on statements by William Butler Yeats, Samuel Butler, George Meredith, Sigmund Freud, and François La Rochefoucauld, but Wilde's sayings were more penetrating and more comprehensive than were the earlier statements (Pearson Life 177). Hesketh Pearson suggests that Oscar Wilde was like William Shakespeare's Falstaff in that he was not only able to be witty himself, but he also caused wit in others. Many people coined neat repartees at his expense, and in fact James Whistler had an "enduring animosity" of Wilde because of Wilde's "superiority as a man, a talker, and a wit," so that "no one else had a dog's chance against Oscar when he cared to exert himself" (Pearson Life 169). Not only Whistler, but also William Ernest Henley, George Bernard Shaw, and Edward Henry Carson were all born fighters who loved verbal combat. Wilde, on the other hand hated friction, and loathed argument, saying, "It is only the intellectually lost who ever argue." Wilde also had witty exchanges with Charles Ricketts and Wilfred Scawen Blunt. On one occasion in 1894, for example, Margot Asquith and her husband invited Oscar Wilde and Wilfred Scawen Blunt to the same luncheon, and after the luncheon Blunt said the following about Wilde's wit "Of all those present, and they were most of them brilliant talkers, he was without comparison, the most brilliant, and in a perverse mood he chose to cross swords with one after the other of them, overpowering each in turn with his wit, and making special fun of Asquith, his host that day, who only a few months later, as Home Secretary, was prosecuting him" (Pearson Life 170). Wilde's wit was effortless and spontaneous. He never dominated a conversation, and he never influenced the general direction that a conversation took. "Frivolity was the keynote to his wit. What other people took seriously he dealt with humorously; what they dismissed as trivial he treated with great solemnity. His favorite method of ridiculing conventional standards was to change a word or two in a proverb or cliché, and so add an aspect to truth" (Pearson Life 170).

Wilde's favorite subjects were friendship, religion, social expectations, sin, England, and youth vs. age. Of friendship he said, "Robert gave Harry a terrible black eye, or Harry gave him one; I forget which, but I know they were great friends" (Pearson Life 176). Of religion, Wilde said, "Prayer must never be answered; if it is, it ceases to be prayer and becomes a correspondence" (Nicholls 161). Arthur Balfour once asked him about his religious beliefs and he responded, "Well, you know, my dear Arthur, I don't think I have any. I am an Irish Protestant" (Nicholls 58). Of social expectations, he said, "Work is the curse of the drinking classes," "It is only by not paying one's bills that one can hope to live in the memory of the commercial classes," and "Consistency is the last refuge of the unimaginative" (Pearson Life 170-171). Of sin and crime, he said, "I can resist everything except temptation," "A community is infinitely more brutalized by the habitual employment of punishment than it is by the occasional occurrences of crime," "Wickedness is a myth invented by good people to account for the curious attractiveness of others," "Society produces rogues, and education makes one rogue cleverer than another" (Pearson Life 170, Nicholls 53). He said of one member of the Café Royal circle, "He hasn't a single redeeming vice." Of England, he said, "The English have a miraculous power of turning wine into water" (Pearson Life 170). Wilde was also concerned with youth versus old age. To a young writer he said, "It is a kind of genius to be twenty-one. To win back my youth, there is nothing I would not do--nothing . . . except take exercise, get up early, or be a useful member of the community" (Pearson Life 172). Wilde also said, "The tragedy of old age is not that one is old, but that one is young" (Pearson Life 177), and "The soul is born old, but grows young. That is the comedy of life. The body is born young, and grows old. That is life's tragedy" (Pearson Life 178). At one point, Wilde boasted that he could talk wittily on any subject. Hearing this boast, someone suggested that he talk wittily about the Queen, but Wilde smiled and said, "The Queen is not a subject" (Nicholls 53).

Most of Wilde's epigraphs are a mixture of fun and profundity. Hesketh Pearson suggests that only Sydney Smith could outdo Oscar Wilde as "the wittiest of humorists and the most humorous of wits." Wilde had the opinion that "seriousness is the only refuge of the shallow" (Pearson Life 171). During a lecture tour in America, an English newspaper wrote the story that Wilde had been seen in Boston on a beautiful sunny day wearing a mackintosh and carrying an umbrella. Wilde is said to have responded, "I hear that it is raining in London this morning." Sherard, one of Wilde's friends, asked him afterwards if there was any truth in the story. Wilde shook his head mournfully and replied: "A false report." "Ah, I thought so," Sherard said, very much relieved. Then Wilde continued, "Yes, I discovered later, and the discovery upset me a good deal, that the weather had been perfect in London that day . . . so my mackintosh and umbrella were really quite unnecessary" (Pearson Life 173).

Oscar Wilde's wit tended to be a bit confrontational. One day Wilde was walking with his friend Frank Harris along London's Jermyn Street, and they walked into an elegant florist shop. When a saleslady approached, Oscar asked her to remove several flower displays from the window. She did so, and then asked, "Sir. Will you take them or shall I send them?" and Wilde exclaimed, "Oh, I don't want any, thank you. I only asked to have them removed from the window because I thought they looked a trifle tired" (Nicholls 52).

In an essay entitled "The Decay of Lying" (1889), Wilde presents a mock dialogue between two supercilious aesthetes, Cyril and Vivian, who break up their serious conversations with a descant on the artificialities of Nature, and who smoke slim imported cigarettes. Vivian is a member of a club named "The Tired Hedonists."

> VIVIAN: We are supposed to wear faded roses in our button-holes when we meet, and to have a sort of cult for Domitian. I am afraid you are not eligible. You are too fond of simple pleasures.
>
> CYRIL: I should be black-balled on the ground of animal spirits, I suppose?
>
> VIVIAN: Probably. Besides, you are a little too old. We don't admit anybody who is of the usual age.
>
> CIRIL: Well, I should fancy you are all a good deal bored with each other.
>
> VIVIAN: We are. That is one of the objects of the club. (Ellmann 239)

"The Decay of Lying" is a nineteenth-century defense of art for art's sake. During Wilde's lifetime there were the same prejudices against art as there were against comedy. In an attempt to educate English readers and critics to appreciate artistic creation and improvisation for its own sake, Wilde wrote the following.

> Lying and poetry are arts--arts, as Plato saw, not unconnected with each other . . . . Many a young man starts in life with a natural gift for exaggeration which, if nurtured in congenial and sympathetic surroundings, or by the imitation of the best models, might grow into something really great and wonderful. He either falls into careless habits of accuracy . . . or takes to frequenting the society of the aged and well-informed . . . . The aim of the liar is to charm, to delight, to give pleasure. (qtd. in Ellmann 294, 305)

In Lady Windemere's Fan (1892) Lady Windemere never repents of her immoral lifestyle; yet she is never punished for it. It is Wilde's style to know what is expected and to do the opposite. Most Victorian plays would have this character regret her actions and become a moral and repentant woman, but that is not Lady Windemere's style, and she says to her husband,

> "I suppose, Windemere, you would like me to retire into a convent, or become a hospital nurse, or something of that kind, as people do in silly modern novels. That is stupid of you, Arthur; in real life we don't do such things--not as long as we have any good looks left, at any rate. No--what consoles one nowadays is not repentance, but pleasure. Repentance is quite out of date." (Wilde Three Plays Act IV)

The Importance of Being Earnest (1895), follows Wilde's belief that "we should treat all the trivial things of life very seriously and all the serious things of life with sincere and studied triviality" (Worth 154). This is demonstrated in the play's title where a character takes on the name of "Ernest" in order to escape from being in fact, "earnest." The Importance of Being Earnest is a comedy of manners in which high society is one of the targets. Lady Bracknell says about society, "Never speak disrespectfully of Society, Algernon. Only people who can't get into it do that" (Wilde Three Plays Act III). Earlier in the play, Lady Bracknell had been talking with Jack:

LADY BRACKNELL: Do you smoke?

JACK: Yes, I must admit I smoke.

LADY BRACKNELL: I am glad to hear it. A man should always have an occupation of some kind . . . . I have always been of the opinion that a man who desires to get married should know either everything or nothing. Which do you know?

JACK: I know nothing, Lady Bracknell.

LADY BRACKNELL: I am pleased to hear it. I do not approve of anything that tampers with natural ignorance. Ignorance is like a delicate exotic fruit; touch it and the bloom is gone. The whole theory of modern education is radically unsound. Fortunately in England, at any rate, education produces no effect whatsoever. If it did, it would prove a serious danger to the upper classes, and probably lead to acts of violence in Grovesnor Square. (Act I)

The Importance of Being Earnest is a play about names. Jack Worthing invents the name of Ernest so that he will have a justification for being anything but earnest. At the very end of the play, Jack Worthing finds out that Ernest is his real name and that in giving himself the name of Ernest, he has not lied at all. So Jack (Ernest) apologizes. "Gwendolyn, it is a terrible thing for a man to find out suddenly that all his life he has been speaking nothing but the truth. Can you forgive me?" (Abel 14). Algernon has also been using onomastics to lead a double life, as he has invented a sick friend named "Bunbury," and whenever he needs to escape social responsibilities he says that his friend is ill and that he must therefore leave to look after him. "Bunburism" is the term used for leading a double life deliberately. When a person leads a double life unintentionally, the term "hypocrisy" must be used (Abel 14).

In an article entitled "Wrong and Right: The Art of Comedy," Lionel Abel contrasts two types of humor, both of which have been studied by French critics. The Importance of Being Earnest contains hardly any instances of "l'esprit juste," defined by Abel as "wit through truth, through hitting the mark dead center." This is not the type of wit that is found in The Importance of Being Earnest. Instead, what is found in this play is "l'esprit faux," which is "wit through error, wit through missing the mark" (Abel 12). Abel gives an example of this "esprit faux" in a dialogue between Lady Bracknell and Algernon:

LADY BRACKNELL: It is very strange. This Mr. Bunbury seems to suffer from curiously bad health.

ALGERNON: Yes; poor Bunbury is a sad invalid.

LADY BRACKNELL: I must say, Algernon, that I think it is high time that this Mr. Bunbury made up his mind whether he was going to live or not. This shilly-shallying with the question is absurd. It shows a very ill-balanced intellect and a lack of decision that is quite lamentable. (Abel 13)

Many readers and critics have seen religious sermons and conventional social comment in The Importance of Being Earnest, even though Wilde was attempting pure comic caprice. Roger Henkle feels that Earnest is "as transparently agnostic as any work in English literature." He continues, "Can we possibly translate into a commentary on English society a drawing-room comedy in which one of the principal characters was discovered in a handbag in the cloakroom at Victoria Station and is therefore denied marriage to the woman he loves because, as her mother puts it, one could hardly imagine a girl brought up with the utmost care forming 'an alliance with a parcel?' " (Henkle 305-306).

On one occasion, Wilde watched the performance of The Importance of Being Earnest. Afterwards, he went backstage and called the company together. The company was afraid that Wilde would give them a tongue lashing, but instead, he stood before them, elaborately attired in browns, fawns, and tans, and said, "My dear, delightful company. I have just watched your performance and I wanted you to know that it reminds me of a play I once wrote" (Nicholls 164).

In The Paradox of Oscar Wilde, George Woodcock discusses Oscar Wilde's writing, and concludes that he was his best in writing dialogue, and this is especially true in his comedies.   But Wilde's "schizoid nature" exhibits a curious mingling of naïve sentimentality and sophisticated wit:

> Yet it is only in The Importance of Being Earnest that his verbal wit and satirical criticism of manners are allowed free play, unalloyed by sentimentality and unhindered by those melodramatic conventions which he seems to have had difficulty in abandoning. The hackneyed devices of fans and gloves and brooches around which the plots are woven, the tedious Victorian themes of self sacrificing mothers and injured wives which Wilde retained in all these early comedies, are in themselves banal enough, but when we come to such atrocious fragments as Mrs. Arbuthnot's exclamation in A Woman of No Importance, "Child of my shame, be still the child of my shame!" we must believe either that Oscar's ironic fun had run away with him and descended into burlesque, or that he really liked this kind of cheap effect, and that when his sentimental self perpetrated it, his critical self must have been looking the other way. (Woodcock 231)

Nevertheless, Wilde was able to reintroduce the comedy of wit and satire to the stage in the place of the melodrama which was so prevalent at the time. Wilde "brought comedy back to its genuine function of an ironical or satirical commentary on life" (Woodcock 233).

Wilde's biting sarcastic wit tended to offend certain types of people, and at one time he had to confront the skilled Edward Carson in defending his writing and his attitudes in court. The debate between these two ex-Trinity men was heated and witty. Carson asked if Wilde was of the opinion that there is no such thing as an immoral book, to which Wilde responded "Yes." Carson then asked if The Priest and the Acolyte was not immoral, and Wilde responded, "It was worse--it was badly written." Carson repeatedly provoked Wilde by using the word "pose," as in the question, "So far as your work is concerned, you pose as not being concerned about morality or immorality?" (Nicholls 179) Carson confronted Wilde with sentences Wilde had written, "Anything is good that stimulates thought, in whatever age," and "Pleasure is the only thing in life one should live for," and asked if he felt that these statements were true. Wilde responded, "I think that the realization of oneself is the prime aim of life, and to realize oneself through pleasure is finer than to do so through pain" (Nicholls 180). He also asked Wilde if he had said "The condition of perfection is idleness," and Wilde responded, "Oh, yes, I think so. Half of it is true. The life of contemplation is the highest life" (Pearson Life 180). Carson was a painstaking, persistent, and brilliant cross-examiner as he tried to damage Wilde's reputation. He produced a letter to Bosie Douglas, one of Wilde's friends, which contained phrases Carson felt were suggestive of Wilde's homosexuality. Carson quietly asked, "Can I suggest for the sake of your reputation, that there is nothing very wonderful in this . . . 'red rose lips' phrase of yours?" With a dig at Carson's Irishness, Wilde responded, "A great deal depends on the way it is read." Carson then read another of Wilde's sentences, "Your slim, gilt soul walks between passion and poetry," and asked Wilde, "Is that a beautiful phrase?" Wilde responded, "Not as you read it." Carson responded back, "But I do not profess to be an artist," and then he added, "and when I hear you give evidence, I am glad I am not." Then Carson shuffled through his papers and produced another letter from Wilde to the youthful Bosie, and asked, "Is that an ordinary letter, would you say?" Wilde responded with a taunt, "Everything I write is extraordinary. I do not pose as being ordinary" (Nicholls 183).

Wilde's wit was much more appreciated on the continent than it was in England. Firstly, his style had a certain lush ornateness, a lack of English restraint, which has always been more appreciated abroad than in Britain. And secondly, in a German public already used to the nihilism of writers like Nietzsche, Wilde's destructive epigrams must have found an appreciative audience. (Woodcock 235)

It is ironic that a writer as skilled as Wilde should have been so savagely treated by his own country. George Woodcock writes about Wilde's rejection in England and his acceptance elsewhere:

The hostility felt toward England over the Boer War helped to increase the repute of a man who was regarded by many people as the most distinguished victim of English perfidy. The fact that he ended his life in exile only helped to increase this continental idea of him as a kind of Prometheus figure, and it is significant that the most sensational stories of Wilde's misery and poverty in his last years came from French writers. (Woodcock 234)

It was not merely Oscar Wilde's words which were impressive. Equally impressive were his manner and his delivery. His formidable height and frame, and his attire added greatly to his impact. But his words were very witty, and they will be long remembered. It was Wilde who described a cynic as "a man who knows the price of everything and the value of nothing." And about bias he said, "It is only about the things that do not interest one that one can give an unbiased opinion; this is no doubt the reason why an unbiased opinion is always valueless." Wilde said that science "can never grapple with the irrational" (Woodcock 236), and Wilde also said, "People should not mistake the means of civilization for the end. The steam engine and the telephone depend entirely for their value on the use to which they are put" (Nicholls 56-57). On one occasion he met an old acquaintance he at first didn't notice. "My dear fellow," he said, "do forgive me, I didn't recognize you-- I've changed a lot" (Nicholls 59).

Throughout his life, Wilde concentrated on seeking pleasure. Even "at the height of his pleasure-seeking folly, and in the depths of his pitiful suffering, in his arrogance and his humility, he still sought the free development of his own self." The standard by which he measured his life and his art was "individual action." His life was a constant search for "the liberation of the human personality from all the trammels that society and custom have laid upon it" (Woodcock 239).

Wilde is a kind of latter-day representation, on an intellectual plane, of the Till Eulenspiegel myth. There is much in him of the classic fool whose antics are the mask for a biting criticism of established values, and whose vagaries disguise an essential wisdom. It is this element of folly that has caught the imagination, and has helped to give Wilde the influence his achievements as a writer would not have deserved. (Woodcock 238)

It has been said that eccentricity is the sign of a superior intelligence. Oscar Wilde was truly an eccentric. "His heavy features betrayed his delight in the almost alarmed reaction of the masses to his outlandish, but always elegant, attire." His frivolity was ever apparent, and as Hesketh Pearson has said, "good nature seemed to exude from him, pleasure to radiate from him, happiness to enfold him" (Nicholls 55). Max Beerbohm, the famous actor once prepared some cryptic notes to help in doing a literary portrait of Oscar Wilde. Beerbohm wrote:

Luxury--gold-tippedmatches--haircurled--Assyrian--waxstatue--hugerings-- fat white hands--not soigné--feather bed-pointed fingers--ample scarf--Louis

Quinze cane--vast Malmaison--cat-like tread--heavy shoulders--enormous dowager--or schoolboy--way of laughing with hand over mouth--stroking chin--looking up sideways--jollity overdone--but real vitality. (Nicholls 60) Beerbohm's caricature of Wilde continues: "The grand, lascivious, hulking figure in morning coat and pumps, the gaily festooned balloon of a man, displaying touches of mauve and 'decadent' yellow, riding above the common swell, blithely throwing overboard the ballast of convention." Roger Henkle contends that it is from Beerbohm's caricatures of Wilde that much of his image has been preserved (Henkle 297).

Oscar Wilde Bibliography

Abel, Lionel. "Wrong and Right: The Art of Comedy." Salmagundi. 28 (1975): 3-19.

Barth, Adolf. "Oscar Wilde's 'Comic Refusal': A Reassessment of The Importance of Being Earnest." Archiv für das Studium der Neueren Sprachen und Literaturen 216 (1979): 120-128.

Bergman, Herbert. "Comedy in Candida." Shavian 4 (1972): 161-169.

Catsiapis, Hélène. "Ironie et Paradoxes dans les Comédies d'Oscar Wilde: Une Interprétation." Thalia: Studies in Literary Humor 1.2 (1979): 35-53.

Ellmann, Richard, ed. The Artist as Critic: Critical Writings of Oscar Wilde. London, England: W. H. Allen, 1970.

Foster, Richard. "Wilde as Parodist: A Second Look at The Importance of Being Earnest." College English 18 (1956): 18-23.

Gagnier, Regenia. "Stages of Desire: Oscar Wilde's Comedies and the Consumer." Genre 15 (1982): 315-336.

Ganz, Arthur. "The Divided Self in the Society Comedies of Oscar Wilde." Modern Drama 3 (1960): 16-23.

Gregor, Ian. "Comedy and Oscar Wilde." Sewanee Review 74 (1966): 501-521.

Henkle, Roger B. "Wilde and Beerbohm: The Wit of the Avant-Garde, The Charm of Failure." Comedy and Culture--England--1820-1900. Princeton, NJ: Princeton University Press, 1980, 296-352.

Hirst, David L. Comedy of Manners. Volume 40 of The Critical Idiom. London, England: Methuen, 1979.

Howarth, Herbert. "The Joycean Comedy: Wilde, Jonson, and Others." A James Joyce Miscellany. Second Series. Ed. Marvin Magalaner. Carbondale, IL: Southern Illinois Univ Press, 1959, 179-194.

MacCarthy, Desmond. "Oscar Wilde." English Wits. Ed. Leonard Russell. London, England: Hutchinson, 1940 47-70.

Mikhail, E. H. "The French Influences on Oscar Wilde's Comedies." Revue de Littérature Comparée 42 (1968): 220-233.

Murray, Isobel, ed. The Picture of Dorian Gray, by Oscar Wilde. London, England: Oxford University Press, 1974.

Nicholls, Mark. The Importance of Being Oscar: The Wit and Wisdom of Oscar Wilde Set Against His Life and Times. New York, NY: St. Martin's Press, 1980.

Pearson, Hesketh. "Oscar Wilde." Lives of the Wits. New York, NY: Harper and Row, 1962, 222-247.

Pearson, Hesketh. Oscar Wilde: His Life and Wit. New York, NY: Harper, 1946.

Redman, Alvin, ed. The Wit and Humor of Oscar Wilde. New York, NY: Dover, 1959.

Rohse, Corinna Sundararajan. "The Sphinx Goes Wild(e): Ada Leverson, Oscar Wilde, and the Gender Equipollence of Parody." Look Who's Laughing: Gender and Comedy. Ed. Gail Finney. New York, NY: Gordon and Breach, 1994 119-138.

Schmidgall, Gary. The Stranger Wilde: Interpreting Oscar. New York, NY: Dutton, 1994.

Snider, Rose. "Oscar Wilde." Satire in the Comedies of Congreve, Sheridan, Wilde, and Coward. New York, NY: Phaeton Press, 1972, 74-94.

Waters, Maureen. The Comic Irishman. Albany, NY: State University of New York Press, 1984.

Wilde, Oscar. Three Plays: The Master Playwrights. London, England: Eyre Methuen, 1964.

Woodcock, George. The Paradox of Oscar Wilde. Folcroft, PA: Folcroft Library Editions, 1973.

Worth, Katharine. Oscar Wilde. London, England: Macmillan, 1983.

CHAPTER 6

Humor in 20th Century
Irish Literature: Early Authors

Edmund Downey (1856-1937) IRELAND

Edmund Downey was born in Waterford, the son of a shipowner and broker, and he signed his well-known stories as "F. M. Allen." Downey wrote such humorous pieces as, "Through Green Glasses," and "From Portlaw to Paradise." David O'Donoghue noted that these richly humorous Irish stories may be better known, but can hardly be considered superior to his excellent sea-stories such as "Anchor-Watch Yarns" (O'Donoghue 382-393, 424).

Edmund Downey Bibliography

O'Donoghue, David James, ed. The Humour of Ireland. London, England: Walter Scott, 1894; New York, NY: AMS Press, 1978.

George Bernard Shaw (1856-1950) IRELAND

When George Bernard Shaw was a child, he was called "Sonny." This is the name he had when he attended an educational institution sponsored by the Incorporated Society for Promoting Protestant Schools in Ireland. It was here that Sonny (Bernard Shaw) learned how properly to torture teachers. "He formed a secret society sworn to give topsy-turvy answers to questions asked by teachers and to play pranks with the text by putting in 'not' where the affirmative was called for and to compete always for the bottom place in class" (Winsten 20). In the Spring of 1871, Shaw went to work at the Land Valuation Office where his favorite topic of conversation was religion. When his fellow workers proclaimed that a world without God would be a "homeless chaos," George countered by saying that he had given up saying prayers and attending church and that he now felt a greater sense of moral responsibility than before "because the blame for what he did was on him and not on God" (Winsten 22). In truth, however, Shaw had not given up saying prayers, although it was true that he didn't pray to any specific deity (Winsten 22).

George Carr Shaw was George Bernard Shaw's father. The father had a "kind heart, a sense of humour, and a total lack of professional aptitude or commercial ability" (Pearson 1). Not wanting to get his hands dirty by entering into a retail trade, he bought a wholesale corn business, but before long one of his chief customers went bankrupt still owing the company a lot of money. This blow wiped out Shaw's father's partner, but George Carr, who was also ruined by this disaster had a different approach. Bernard describes his father's reaction as follows: "He found the magnitude of the catastrophe so irresistibly amusing that he had to retreat hastily from the office to an empty corner of the warehouse and laugh until he was exhausted." Bernard Shaw continued: "The more sacred an idea or a situation was by convention, the more irresistible was it to him as the jumping-off place for a plunge into laughter." When Bernard Shaw used to scoff at the Bible, his father would tell his son that the Bible was universally recognized as a literary and historical masterpiece. And after he had been giving evidence to support this view for quite a long period of time, Bernard would watch his father's eyes begin to twinkle, and he could see that an internal chuckle was starting to develop, and his eyes would wrinkle up: "He would cap his eulogy by assuring me, with an air of perfect fairness, that even the worst enemy of religion could say no worse of the Bible than that it was the damndest parcel of lies ever written. He would then rub his eyes and chuckle for quite a long time" (Pearson 2).

In 1961, John A. Mills wrote a dissertation entitled, "Language and Laughter: A Study of Comic Diction in the Plays of Bernard Shaw." This dissertation was published as a book by the University of Arizona Press in 1969. Mills has chapters about the major aspects of Shavian Comedy, and on the comic effects of the cockney dialect in Shaw's works, and on Shaw's linguistic satire, and on Shaw's automatism and word-play. In the chapter on "Linguistic Satire," for example, Mills makes the following statement:

> The humor in the speech of Shaw's cockney characters stems primarily from peculiarities of sound and word formation. Where word choice and arrangement figure in the effect, they do so by virtue of comic contrast with these oddities of sound. Elsewhere, Shaw uses vocabulary and syntax to achieve comic effects which have little or nothing to do with sound. (Mills 76)

Shaw tended to be a fast writer. It is said that he wrote The Admirable Bashville or Constancy Unrewarded in a single week. He was prompted by reports of several unauthorized American dramatizations of his 1881 novel about fighting, Cashel Byron's Profession. Shaw wanted to secure a quick copyright on Bashville, so he quickly dashed off a stage version, and paid to have it performed, thus protecting himself from further pirating. He wrote it in blank verse, because it was so "childishly easy" to do so. "I was enabled to do within the week what would have cost me a month in prose" (Mills 77-78). Bashville is a burlesque which contrasts elevated language with a homely topic. The elevated language is that of Elizabethan verse drama, and this clashes absurdly with the mock-heroic story of a prizefighter in love.

> Dread monarch: this is called the upper cut,
> And this a hook--hit of mine own invention.
> The hollow region where I plant this blow
> Is called the mark. My left, you will observe,
> I chiefly use for long shots: with my right
> Aiming beside the angle of the jaw
> And landing with a certain delicate screw
> I without violence knock my foeman out. (Mills 78)

In Bashville, Shaw dips deeply into Hamlet, as when he has his prizefighter begin an important match with the philosophical observation that "There's a divinity that shapes our ends, Rough hew them how we will. Give me the gloves" (Mills 79). Mills says that in The Admirable Bashville, and in The Dark Lady of The Sonnets, Shaw

> indulges in linguistic satire purely for its own sake. With Sergius, Morell, Marchbanks and Brassbound, on the other hand, he ridicules not only special

styles of speech, but the attitudes associated with them. Sergius, for instance, invites laughter not only because he talks like a Byron here but because he thinks and acts like one. (Mills 102)

Although Mills feels that Shaw is skilled as a satirist, he feels that he is much less skilled in his Automatism and Word-Play.

Word-play scarcely ever occurs in the major comedies, except in the punning names of characters, and even in the "Tomfooleries," other comic materials hold sway. But if Shaw uses the device less often than Shakespeare, he also uses it less skillfully and with considerably less comic force. Some of the more jarring specimens might be excused on the ground that they are so bad they are good. (Mills 130)

Mills claims that more often than not, Shaw's word-play is cumbersome, and clumsy in execution. Mills further claims that Shaw requires such elaborate machinery to get his joke set up and explained, that a lot of the fun is dissipated in the process. Shaw's word-play is forced, and it is also extremely unnatural, as when Tallboys speaks of "the colors" and the sergeant misinterprets the words as a reference to the regimental colors. We later learn that Tallboys was referring to the less-likely "watercolors." In Mills's opinion, this is so forced and unnatural an interpretation that the joke misfires (Mills 131). Mills also points out that most of the examples of Shaw's puns and word-play occur in his short plays, "trivial pieces" which he himself dismissed with subtitles such as "A Disgrace to the Author," or "A Piece of Utter Nonsense." According to Mills, Shaw's word-play could have been "similarly described" (Mills 132).

Stephen Potter considers Shaw to be "the chief pope and apostle of English humour." Potter considers Shaw to have been

the most Anglian thing which ever existed, mixed up as he was with such overwhelming Englishnesses as the Fabian Society and the West End Theatre, a strong touch of Jaeger puritanism, the lively but hopelessly unprofound and mechanistic religion of the Prefaces . . . , and a strong natural suspicion of artists as artists. (Potter 33)

Jacques Barzun says that it is frequently difficult to separate Shaw from his reputation, describing Shaw as "a man in a fog" (Barzun 159). Supporting this view, Joseph Wood Krutch says that in Shaw's last major plays, his optimism is "more a matter of temperament than of philosophical conviction" (Kaul 285). In the beginning, Shaw wrote pleasant plays in an attempt to revive the comedy that had been lost from the English stage for more than a hundred years. "But the relationship to tradition, however straightforward in the beginning, becomes in the end highly problematic" (Kaul 286).

George Bernard Shaw considered himself to be, like Henrik Ibsen, a realist and a naturalistic writer. In his The Quintessence of Ibsenism, Shaw predicted that "the woman's revolt would come first because the woman's enslavement was more complete than man's enslavement, but he also predicted that men would also learn to be subversive and come to understand the 'impossibility of duty' in due course" (Watson 128). In The Quintessence of Ibsenism, Shaw also comments of realism in literature:

Now the natural is mainly the everyday; and its climaxes must be, if not everyday, at least everylife, if they are to have any importance for the spectator. Crimes, fights, big legacies, fires, shipwrecks, battles, and thunderbolts are mistakes in a play, even when they can be effectively simulated . . . . Shakespeare had put ourselves on the stage but not our situations. Our uncles seldom murder our fathers, and cannot legally marry our mothers; we do not meet witches; our kings are not as a rule stabbed and succeeded by their stabbers; and when we raise money by bills we do not promise to pay pounds of our flesh. Ibsen supplies the want left by

Shakespeare. He gives us not only ourselves, but ourselves in our own
situations. (Kaul 44)

A. N. Kaul says that what Shaw calls natural should more properly be called comic.
Comedy deals with realism and naturalism in the same way that romance deals with
legacies and shipwrecks, and tragedies deal with fratricide, and incest (Kaul 44-45). In his
Quintessence of Ibsenism, Shaw notes that "the salvation of the world depends on the men
who will not take evil good-humoredly, and whose laughter destroys the fool instead of
encouraging him" (Smith 4).

In an article entitled "Shaw's Paradox: Use in Dystopia," Alice Rayner points out
that for Shaw, paradox rules, and there is not always a clear distinction between right and
wrong. Shaw's villains are just as conscientious as are his heroes, if not more so.

> Ibsen and Shaw may share a distrust of the simple divisions between right
> and wrong, good and evil that dominated the melodramas of the nineteenth
> century, and they may share the idea that drama ought to be instrumental in
> changing the moral perceptions of its society; but they differ insofar as
> Ibsen's judgments are fundamentally pathetic and appeal to our sympathies
> and Shaw's judgments are rational and appeal to our minds. (Rayner 110)

The prevailing assumption during Shaw's day was that comedy should punish the wicked
and reward the virtuous; however, Shaw's comedy is based on the impossibility of
separating the wicked from the virtuous (Rayner 111-112). "Shaw delights in his
contradictions; he revels in the disturbance of the peace. He refuses to let us know what
he thinks because his own skill at dialectic could overturn even his own assertions" (Rayner
113). Shaw refused to resolve his paradoxes, and many critics are therefore confused by
the aesthetic of his plays. Shaw claims to be a revolutionary and in fact recognizes comedy
as a special kind of revolution: "All very serious revolutionary propositions begin as huge
jokes. Otherwise they would be stamped out by the lynching of their first exponents"
(Rayner 114).

Shaw was an enigma, and different critics saw different things in his writings. A.
W. Gomme says that Shaw was a moralist.

> Shaw has himself said that art ought to be didactic . . . . Moreover he has
> been, quite definitely, an active politician--a vigorous member of political
> societies, a speaker at street corners, a member of a borough council. And
> he is nothing if not autobiographical: he writes a long preface to every play,
> in which he tells us his opinions on its main theme. (Abel 7)

Edmund Wilson, however, disagrees with A. W. Gomme's assessment of Shaw as a
moralist.

> The political writing of Shaw does not drive you into taking up a position
> as the greatest socialist writing does: indeed, before he has finished, he has
> often seemed to compromise the points which you had imagined he was
> trying to make . . . , both his intelligence and his sense of justice have
> prevented him from assailing the capitalist system with such intolerant
> resentment and unscrupulous methods as Voltaire trained on the church.
> With Voltaire, it is the crusader that counts; with Shaw, it is the dramatic
> poet. (Abel 8).

Reed Whittemore feels that there are two distinct-and-contrasting "armies of words"
that can be used to describe Shaw's writing. One army of words would include "illusion,
romance, chivalry, convention, fiction, sentiment, unreason, and morality." In contrast, the
other army of words would include "facts, hard facts, actuality, reason, and realism" (Kaul
294). Lionel Abel resolves these conflicting opinions of Shaw's writing by describing the
following paradox: "There is hardly a right side for the author of comedy, but there is often
a right side for Bernard Shaw, and he happens to be the greatest" master of comedy in the

English language" (Abel 9). Eric Bentley says that

> Shavian comedy is parodistic in a way, or to an extent, that Plautus, Jonson, and Mollière were not. These others, one would judge, took a convention they respected and brought it to the realization of its best possibilities. Shaw took conventions in which he saw no possibilities--except insofar as he would expose their bankruptcy. (Kaul 295)

Harold Hobson suggests that Shaw's plays fall into four main groups. In his first group, Arms and the Man (1894), The Devil's Disciple (1900), and You Never Can Tell (1912), Shaw attacks romanticism by writing about soldiers who think chocolate is more important than fire-arms, and about young people who make love in terms of chemical formulas. In the second group, Major Barbara (1905), Mrs. Warren's Profession (1898), The Doctor's Dilemma (1906), Getting Married (1908), Heartbreak House (1917), and Widowers' Houses (1893), Shaw discusses problems of social organization. In the third group, St. Joan (1923), The Apple Cart (1929), On the Rocks (1937), In Good King Charles's Golden Days (1939), and Too True To Be Good (1932), Shaw discusses problems related to leadership and government. And in the fourth group, Man and Superman (1903), and Back to Methuselah (1921), Shaw discusses the proposition that mankind can achieve salvation during their own time and according to the rules of material existence "before the Life Force disgustedly sweeps them into oblivion." There is a fifth category, Pygmalion (1912) and Candida (1913), which cannot be boiled down to the solving of a simple philosophical problem, but these are considered by most critics to be his best work (Hobson 283).

Shaw's Candida (1856) is filled with humor tinged with sympathy and comprehension, especially in such comedy types as Prossy, the star-crossed lover (Potter 35). Candida appears to progress through a love triangle involving a married woman, her husband, and her romantic lover. There is a dramatic confrontation, and a return to the husband. In the climactic scene that reveals the mystery, Candida reverses all the traditional expectations, as the husband's strength is shown to be weakness; the lover's weakness is shown to be strength. "The paradox settles the outward events, which have ceased to matter" (Watson 125).

Arms and the Man (1894) was the first of what Shaw himself called his "pleasant plays." It is an anti-romance set during the Balkan wars in the 1880s. Bluntschli, the Swiss officer in Arms and the Man carries chocolate in his revolver holster rather than cartridges. "The cool cynicism of this 'hero,' so the critics of the day objected, makes him not only wildly improbable but also politically neutral and martially inglorious" (Kaul 287). The two main comic characters in this play are Raina Petkoff and Sergius Saranoff. These characters are "not the victims of romance so much as its willful and highly self-conscious votaries" (Kaul 287). Bluntschli and Louka, Raina's servant girl, are very cynical and disillusioned. Once they have acknowledged their disillusionment they can provide a less high-minded, and genuine love for the final comic resolution. When Raina learns that Sergius, her fiancé, has defied orders to make the charge, she exclaims "I am so happy!" But this romantic mood is interrupted by the entrance of Bluntschli, who unlike the "tall romantically handsome" Sergius is described as a man "of middling stature and undistinguished appearance," with a "hopelessly prosaic nose" (Kaul 289). Bluntschli is unromantic and unheroic, and not only does he take refuge in a lady's bedchamber, but he threatens her with a revolver to make sure that she doesn't betray him to his pursuers (Kaul 289).

Both Nicola and Bluntschli are described as men of cool temperament and keen intelligence, men who have no illusions. The servant and the hero have the same capacity to remain unflustered in trying situations, and they both have the ability to "accept intended insults as compliments or at least exact descriptions with which they have no quarrel" (Kaul

302):

> LOUKA: (<u>with searching scorn</u>) You have the soul of a servant, Nicola.
>
> NICOLA: (<u>complacently</u>) Yes: that's the secret of success in service.

Compare this dialogue with that between Raina and Bluntschli:

> RAINA: (<u>furious: throwing the words right into his face</u>) You have a low
> shopkeeping mind. You think of things that would never come into
> a gentleman's head.
>
> BLUNTSCHLI: (<u>phlegmatically</u>) That's the Swiss national character, dear
> lady. (Kaul 302)

Shaw is satirizing war when he has Bluntschli answer Mrs. Petkoff's objection by saying, "My rank is the highest known in Switzerland: I am a free citizen." And he is parodying the medieval or chivalric tradition in the following dialogue between Sergius and Raina.

> SERGIUS: Dearest: all my deeds have been yours. You inspired me. I
> have gone through the war like a knight in a tournament with his
> lady looking down at him!
>
> RAINA: And you have never been absent from my thoughts for a moment.
> (<u>Very solemnly</u>) Sergius: I think we two have found the higher love
> . . . .
>
> SERGIUS: My lady and my saint! (<u>He clasps her reverently</u>).
>
> RAINA: (<u>returning his embrace</u>) My lord and my--. (Kaul 290)

In his notes to <u>The Devil's Disciple</u> (1900), Shaw describes General Burgoyne as follows:

> Burgoyne . . . is a man who plays his part in life, and makes all his points,
> in the manner of a born high comedian . . . . His peculiar critical
> temperament and talent, artistic, satirical, rather histrionic, and his fastidious
> delicacy of sentiment, his fine spirit and humanity, were just the qualities to
> make him disliked by stupid people because of their dread of ironic criticism
> (Gatch 130)

A. M. Gibbs feels that the controlling metaphor of <u>Man and Superman</u> (1903) is developed in the antithetical relationship between the play's comedy, and its philosophy:

> The centre of the play's comic philosophy, lies in the uniqueness of its
> principal male protagonist. Sexual attractiveness--and eventual dominance,
> in this oddly Darwinian comedy--is associated not with the sentimental and
> melancholy man of feeling in the Romantic tradition, nor with the rampant
> and insatiable seducer of the Don Juan legend, nor with the military hero,
> but with the politically alert, breezy, affable, vulnerable and humorous
> revolutionist. (Gibbs 174)

<u>Man and Superman</u> is subtitled, <u>A Comedy and A Philosophy</u>. The "man" of the title relates to the play, and the "superman" relates to the dream within the play. A. M. Gibbs feels that "the play and the dream are mutually modifying and mutually illuminating, and the 'philosophy,' that complex amalgam of views on politics, evolution, art, the relations of the sexes, and human nature in general which emerges from the work, is partly defined in its import and directions by the shape and development of the comic action" (Gibbs 162). The debate in the Dream ranges over a wide variety of topics, but two central areas of conflict can be isolated. In the first place, there is the fundamental opposition between the Devil, who has a life-denying viewpoint, and Don Juan [John Tanner], who has a life-affirming viewpoint. The Devil and Don Juan disagree not so much in the facts themselves as in the stances which they take towards these facts. For the Devil, "man measures his strength by his destructiveness," but for Don Juan, strength is measured by pleasure and creativity. "What Shaw presents as Hell in fact is very close to the pleasures

that Mozart's Don Juan is enjoying before he goes to Hell" (Gibbs 170). "Don Juan/Tanner presents in opposition . . . a belief in the possibility provided by man's creative and intellectual energies" (Gibbs 171). In the Dream, Don Juan differentiates between masculine and feminine forms of creativity, and sees them as essentially hostile to each other. This is why Ann's final wooing of Tanner is presented as a titanic struggle of wills.

> What the Dream does for the play is to brace its affirmative comedy with the profoundly skeptical diatribe against man with which Shaw arms the devil. What the play does for the Dream is to subject its lofty idealism and philosophizing to the test of social realities, to place it in a context in which imposing concepts like the Life Force can be comically punctured (as by Ann's saying "it sounds like the Life Guards"); or in which a Quixotic defence of unmarried motherhood can be upset by the discovery that the mother in question is in fact married. (Gibbs 172)

In the Dream, the brigands are presented more as political and racial types than as individuals. These stereotypes form a comically impressionistic picture of political ferment on a world scale and of stultifying fictious debate, as can be seen in the dialogue between Mendoza and Tanner:

> MENDOZA . . . [posing loftily]: I am a brigand: I live by robbing the rich.
> TANNER [promptly]: I am a gentleman: I live by robbing the poor. Shake hands.

The comic pattern of Man and Superman closely follows Northrop Frye's chapter on comedy in his Anatomy of Criticism:

> What normally happens is that a young man wants a young woman, and his desire is resisted by some opposition, usually paternal, and that near the end of the play some twist in the plot enables the hero to have his will. In this simple pattern there are several complex elements. In the first place, the movement of comedy is usually a movement from one kind of society to another. At the beginning of the play the obstructing characters are in charge of the play's society, and the audience recognizes that they are usurpers. At the end of the play the device in the plot that brings hero and heroine together causes a new society to crystallize around the hero. (Gibbs 162)

This is not only a description of what Frye referred to as "New Comedy" which developed out of Greek and Roman theatre; it is also a description of Shaw's Man and Superman. There is an abundance of paternal figures in the play, one of whom is the deceased Mr. Whitefield, to whose authority Ann demurely and strategically appeals throughout.

Man and Superman is based on Milton's Paradise Lost, and it is also based on Wolfgang Amadeus Mozart's Don Giovanni. The play begins with a description of the provisions of Mr. Whitefield's will. The problem is that the joint guardians of the will are the conservative Ramsden and the radical Tanner. Ann and Tanner want to get married; however Ramsden opposes this marriage, and favors instead a match between Octavius Robinson and Ann, as did the deceased Mr. Whitefield. Shaw's stage direction describing Octavius in Act I is of interest: "Mr. Robinson is really an uncommonly nice looking young fellow. He must, one thinks, be the jeune premier; for it is not in reason to suppose that a second such attractive male figure should appear in one story" (Gibbs 163-164). However, Shaw follows this with a description which shows that Shaw wanted Octavius to appear not as a matinee idol, but rather as a parody of a matinee idol:

> The slim, shapely frame, the elegant suit of new mourning, the small head and regular features, the pretty little moustache, the frank clear eyes, the wholesome bloom on the youthful complexion, the well brushed glossy hair, not curly, but of fine texture and good dark color, the arch of good nature

in the eyebrows, the erect forehead and neatly pointed chin, all announce the man who will love and suffer later on. (Gibbs 194)

It is only a few minutes after this description of Octavius that John Tanner enters. It becomes immediately obvious that Tanner is a second strong contender for the position of "jeune premier," as he arrives on the scene and introduces a complicating factor in audience expectations. Tanner appears in the dream sequence as Don Juan, and his argument can be seen as a defence of comedy as opposed to tragedy, melodrama, and romance (Gibbs 164).

> The two visible shows of life, in hell and on earth, are not so much alike as they are the reverse versions of each other. Hell is "the home of the unreal"; it is a theater that calls us, in the words of its manager The Devil, "to sympathize with joy, with love, with happiness, with beauty--." But such a claim, Juan argues, can only be a cheat under the existing circumstances. If in hell people "talk of nothing else but love" and "think they have achieved the perfection of life," it is only "because they have no bodies." This is sheer "imaginative debauchery," like, as he later adds, "sitting for all eternity at the first act of a fashionable play, before the complications begin." (Kaul 312)

Don Juan progresses from the romantic man to the man of experience and finally to the philosophical man. "The reason why one takes this philosophy as a confession of disillusionment or a satirical fantasy rather than a solution is that bodiless self-contemplation seems as much of an imaginative debauch as the illusions of hell: both are equally devoid of moral content and equally repulsive" (Kaul 314). The Devil's warning is "Beware of the pursuit of the Superhuman: it leads to an indiscriminate contempt for the Human" (Kaul 314).

Lionel Abel considers Man and Superman to be one of Shaw's greatest comedies, in fact one of the finest of any author in the twentieth century. John Tanner is the play's central figure, and functions as the play's "raisonneur."

> He is not especially comical except for one rare moment at the play's climax. It is the other characters in the play who provide the moments of humor. All the same, it would be wrong to think of Tanner simply as the play's raisonneur, for if the ideas he expresses are adequate to that role, the same cannot be said of his actions. Now the actions of Ann Whitfield, on the other hand, are in support of and realize the ideas expressed by John Tanner, though the ideas she puts into words are a continual denial of everything for which John Tanner says he stands. Who is the raisonneur of the play? John Tanner for what he says; Ann Whitfield for what she does. (Abel 11-12)

In The Shavian Playground, Margery Morgan suggests that the "will" at the beginning of Man and Superman is Shaw's "central, strategic pun." There is, for example, wordplay involving different senses of the term "will" in the climactic scene between Tanner and Ann in Act IV:

> TANNER: Your father's will appointed me your guardian, not your suitor. I shall be faithful to my trust.
>
> ANN: [in low siren tones]. He asked me who I would have as my guardian before he made that will. I chose you!
>
> TANNER: The will is yours then! The trap was laid from the beginning.
>
> ANN: [concentrating all her magic]. From the beginning--from our childhood--for both of us--by the Life Force.
>
> TANNER: I will not marry you. I will not marry you.
>
> ANN: Oh, you will, you will. (Gibbs 166)

Gibbs suggests that the end of the play can be seen as a victory of the will, both in the sense of a legal instrument and in the sense of the volitional influence of the old society, "and an ironic contradiction of Tanner's affirmation in the Dream of the potential of the individual human will to promote evolutionary change" (Gibbs 166).

According to A. N. Kaul, the comedy of Man and Superman

> is a comedy of love that depends for its effect and even its purpose on the overturning of romantic convention--in this case the large-scale convention that regards and requires women to be the reluctant quarry and men the relentless pursuers in the chase or game of love. To John Tanner, the hero of Man and Superman, love is not a game at all, nor even the chase of a weak and helpless female by a strong and imperious male, but rather a deadly combat in which all the purpose, strength, and ferocity lie on the side of the woman. (Kaul 305)

In Man and Superman the roles of hero and heroine are reversed. Part of the fun of the play is based on the fact that Ann Whitefield, the heroine assumes the role of a "womanly woman," and she plays this role for all that it is worth:

> She pleads the helplessness of her situation and her own gentle weakness and uncertainty. Left an orphan, she claims that she has nowhere to turn except to her two appointed guardians and the wishes of her father--which to her are "sacred," she herself being "too young, too inexperienced" to decide any question whatsoever. (Kaul 306)

In reality, however, Ann is able to wrap everyone around her little finger. John Tanner, the hero of the play is able to see through Ann's façade: "He not only sees through what he at one point calls 'her confounded hypocrisy' but sees through to the deadliness underneath. To him she is 'an ironclad' pretending to be 'at the mercy of the wind and the wavers,' a 'boa constrictor,' and a 'Bengal tiger' " (Kaul 306).

There are two plots in Man and Superman. In the first plot there is the marriage of Violet and Hector, which is at first presented not as a marriage, but rather as a passionate escapade involving a romantic but illegitimate pregnancy threatening disaster for Violet.

> Later, when Hector's identity as the legal husband becomes clear, there still remains the possibility of disinheritance by Hector's father, the American millionaire. Yet Violet has proceeded all along not only legally but with the coolest of heads: "You can be as romantic as you please about love, Hector: but you mustn't be romantic about money." (Kaul 307)

The second plot concern's Octavius's poetic and eternal devotion to Ann. He worships the ground she treads on. But Ann Whitefield's pursuit of Tanner is more "the real thing." Ann Whitefield is one of the most impressive heroines in all of English comedy "combining something of the wit, the resourcefulness, and the artfulness of Shakespeare's comic heroines and the fine womanly strength and beauty of a Sophia Western. In Tanner, too, we may see something of Tom Jones's irrepressibility, expressed in him as the sowing of intellectual wild oats." Even Shaw's Don Juan, Tanner's double in the play, is licentious only in philosophical terms (Kaul 308).

One of the important aspects of Man and Superman is "The Life Force":

> "I am in the grip of the Life Force," Tanner cries at the end, when he surrenders to the charm and persistence of Ann. While he has come to realize at last, like any comic hero, that he loves the heroine, he expresses this ordinary fact mixed up with a good deal of extraordinary philosophy. "I love you. The Life Force enchants me: I have the whole world in my arms when I clasp you." (Kaul 309)

But this is how Tanner describes his marriage: "This afternoon is to renounce happiness, renounce freedom, renounce tranquillity" in order to surrender jointly to a force which represents life's higher creative purpose in order that out of their marriage may be born--the superman (Kaul 309).

At the request of William Butler Yeats, Shaw wrote <u>John Bull's Other Island</u> (1904) as a patriotic contribution to the repertory of the Irish Literary Theatre. He wrote it specifically for production in the Abbey Theatre in Dublin. However, Shaw notes in the "Preface" that Yeats got rather more than he bargained for, since the play was at that time beyond the resources of the new Abbey Theatre (<u>Island</u> v). <u>John Bull's Other Island</u> made fun of both the Irish and the English. "English audiences very naturally swallowed it eagerly and smacked their lips over it, laughing all the more heartily because they felt that they were taking a caricature of themselves with the most tolerant and largeminded good humor" (<u>Island</u> vi). Shaw comments on his own Irishness:

> When I say that I am an Irishman I mean that I was born in Ireland, and that my native language is the English of Swift and not the unspeakable jargon of the mid-XIX century London newspapers. My extraction is the extraction of most Englishmen: that is, I have no trace in me of the commercially imported, North Spanish strain which passes for aboriginal Irish. I am a genuine typical Irishman of the Danish, Norman, Cromwellian, and (of course) Scotch invasions. (<u>Island</u> viii)

Shaw adds that "England cannot do without its Irish and its Scots today, because it cannot do without at least a little sanity" (<u>Island</u> ix).

In the "Preface" to <u>John Bull's Other Island</u>, Shaw also comments on the logic of home-rule for Ireland.

> America, as far as one can ascertain, is much worse governed, and has a much more disgraceful political history than England under Charles I; but the American Republic is the stabler government because it starts from a formal concession of natural rights, and keeps up an illusion of safeguarding them by an elaborate machinery of democratic election. And the final reason why Ireland must have Home Rule is that she has a natural right to it. (<u>Island</u> xxxvii)

In <u>Major Barbara</u> (1905), Undershaft succeeds because he does not confuse morality with business; Cusins succeeds because he does not confuse purity with virtue, and Major Barbara succeeds because she does not confuse femininity with selfhood. This is a feminist play, for the roles of the two men are clearly subsidiary to that of Major Barbara (Watson 125). The language of <u>Major Barbara</u> is aphoristic and aggressive in nature (Rayner 119). In Shaw, single-minded characters are rare. What the play teaches, in fact, is that characters must learn how to assimilate the attitude of paradox and contradiction if they are to survive (Rayner 121).

Adolphus Cusins in <u>Major Barbara</u> is a Professor of Greek. The humorous and scholarly Cusins nicknames Andrew Undershaft "Mephistopheles," thereby calling attention to the fact that like Goethe's antagonist, Undershaft "does good with evil intentions" (Gatch 132). Undershaft "appears to hold mutually exclusive perspectives in simultaneous view. As a character he is a paradoxist." After many years of being away from his family, Undershaft remarks, "My difficulty is that if I play the part of a father, I shall produce the effect of an intrusive stranger; and if I play the part of a discreet stranger, I may appear a callous father" (Rayner 121).

> Undershaft is for Shaw a positive figure representing positive values, though in a paradoxical form. A capitalist, he represents Socialism; a munitions maker, he represents peace; disinheriting his son, he represents paternal wisdom and justice, and giving his daughter Barbara a serious lesson in cynicism, he sets her on the right way to a proper spiritual life. (Abel 11)

The name of Lady Britomart, in Major Barbara is an allusion to Britomart in Spenser's Faerie Queene. Lady Britomart silently acknowledges the benefits of the munitions factory and clears her conscience by stating her opinion., "Charles Lomax: you are a fool. Adolphus Cusins: you are a Jesuit. Stephen: you are a prig. Barbara: you are a lunatic. Andrew: you are a vulgar tradesman. Now you all know my opinion; and my conscience is clear, at all events" (Rayner 122).

Andrew Untershaft (Saint Andrew) justifies having a munitions factory in the following way:

> I love the common people. I want to arm them against the lawyers, the doctors, the priests, the literary men, the professors, the artists, and the politicians . . . . I want a power simple enough for common men to use, yet strong enough to force the intellectual oligarchy to use its genius for the general good. (Rayner 104)

Untershaft says that the world will scrap its obsolete steam engines and dynamos, "but it won't scrap its old prejudices and its old moralities and its old religions and its old political constitutions" (Kaul 325).

It is unclear whether the play Major Barbara is describing a dystopia or a utopia. A dystopia for Shaw is not a world which is evil, but one which is monolithic. "Shaw uses his paradoxical habit not viciously but genially. Unlike the satirist who implies a division between right and wrong, Shaw attempts to go beyond these moral categories to suggest a division between morality and reality. The world of conventional morality is the dystopian world of illusion" (Rayner 124). The play is a perfect place for Shaw to present his concept of "utopia," for in a play there is a place for paradox, and a place for "discussion which can go on indefinitely, never coming to rest in a specific social world." "Utopia and dystopia, then, constitute another paradox in Shavian terms, for the presence of a dystopia makes the projection of a utopia necessary, and finally Shaw seems to want to correct that dystopia through his utopian vision" (Rayner 125). But in Shaw's utopian play it is Shaw who is in control. He asks his audiences to be passive receptors--to listen intently to what he has to say. What Rayner says is true: "The irony of Shaw's 'unresolved paradox' is that it creates a monolithic aesthetic form that reflects, in a way, the very dystopian monolith of moral certainty that the plays presume to correct" (Rayner 126).

In The Doctor's Dilemma (1906), Shaw reinforces the tragic effects by his introduction of humor and humorous characters at the most dramatic moments. But Shaw's humor here is much more than just a compliment to the tragedy. There is, for example, a long stage direction at the climactic time of the death of Dudebat in which a comic journalist is introduced. There is another long and rambling stage direction, which Stephen Potter describes as moderately funny. However, "the intrusion of this ridiculous Guy Fawkes casts a chill of doubt over the tragic climax of the play, and puts Shaw as an artist under suspicion" (Potter 34).

The classic conclusion of most comedies is that a wedding takes placed. This classic ending is also to be found in Getting Married (1908); however, there is a difference, because in the Shavian view, the marriage is not the simple ritual solution expected in comedy. In Getting Married, the men find the status quo less intolerable than do the women.

> The bride has a Christlike objection to letting marriage interfere with her work for justice and salvation. Lesbia wants children but no husband. Leo wants a ménage à trois ("Well, I love them both.") or better: "I should like to marry a lot of men. I should like to have Rejjy for every day, and Sinjon for concerts and theatres and going out in the evenings, and some great austere saint for about once a year at the end of the season, and some

perfectly blithering idiot of a boy to be quite wicked with." Mrs. George, the mystic and philanderer, wants her marriage to stand like a rock while she flits off with various lovers and writes passionate letters to the Bishop about meeting him in heaven. (Watson 119)

According to Gladys Crane, Hypatia Tarleton in Shaw's Misalliance (1910) takes a comic journey from being a rebellious daughter to becoming a conventional woman. Many of Shaw's most rebellious characters are women, probably because in Victorian times women had much more to rebel against than did men. The "misalliance" referred to in the title of Shaw's play is between Hypatia Tarleton and Bentley Summerhays (Crane Misalliance 480):

> In the opening scene of the play, Bentley starts an argument with Johnny, Hypatia's brother, in the course of which Johnny loses his temper and tells Bentley that no one in the family likes him. Bentley's reactions are hilariously juvenile as he calls Johnny a beast, a brute, a cad, a bully, and a swine, and, when Johnny threatens to spank him, throws himself on the floor and screams. (Crane Misalliance 481)

Hypatia asks Bentley what's the problem, and tells him not to cry, but Hypatia's words make Bentley appear even more childish, "There, there, pet," she says, "It's all right: Don't cry . . . Johnny will go to the doctor; and he'll give you something to make it well." Bentley's weakness is visually demonstrated when he is escorted from the room between Hypatia and her mother. Hypatia is the antithesis of her mother. Hypatia is cold-blooded and practical while her mother is a romantic. When Hypatia is asked if she loves Bentley, she responds, "Oh, how could anybody be in love with Bunny? I like him to kiss me just as I like a baby to kiss me." When asked why she wants to marry Bentley rather than marrying someone she loves, Hypatia's answer is revolutionary, as she responds that a woman should never marry the man she is in love with because, "it would make a perfect slave of you" (Crane Misalliance 481). Mrs. Tarleton, Hypatia's mother, describes Bentley as "overbred, like one of those expensive little dogs," and says that she herself prefers "a bit of a mongrel . . . whether it's a man or a dog; they're the best for everyday."

Johnny, Hypatia's brother, is dedicated to principles of business. He is totally practical in his mind set as he self-righteously insists that everyone should toe the mark of conventional morality. Johnny's view is that "an open mind is all very well in clever talky-talk, but in conduct and in business give me solid ground." Hypatia assumes an attitude of superiority over Johnny.

> Her most devastating comment on Johnny's inferior intelligence is her wish that Johnny could wag his tail or put back his ears to express approval or disapproval, since his talking conveys nothing more than that anyway. Hypatia delights in her intellectual superiority over Johnny; Johnny delights in the scrapes Hypatia's bad manners cause her and enjoys the discomfort of the men with whom she is involved. (Crane Misalliance 487)

Later in the play there is a scene in which Hypatia finds herself alone with Lord Summerhays, a man who, even though he is older than her father, misunderstands Hypatia's attempts to ingratiate herself with her future father-in-law. He thinks instead that she is flirting with him, and therefore he proposes to her. "Hypatia's delight in having provoked Lord Summerhays's proposal is that of being considered an attractive, adult woman ready for marriage, yet her reactions throughout the scene are those of a child who has managed to get power over an adult." In an attempt to get Hypatia to pay more attention to him, Lord Summerhays calls her a "glorious young beast," a term which he considers derogatory, but which Hypatia hears as a compliment. Hypatia repeats this expression twice, for "Glorious young beast expresses exactly what I like to be." The broad comedy of this scene results from the antithesis of Hypatia's vigor and Summerhays's delicacy (Crane

<u>Misalliance</u> 482-483).

Joey Percival's plane crashes into Mr. Tarleton's garden, and Hypatia also has an encounter with this gentleman.

> Hypatia's shameless advances to Joey are comic for two reasons: first, for the reversal of roles of man the pursuer, and woman, the pursued; and second, for the reversal of expectations in Hypatia's complete lack of manners and Joey's attempts to mold the situation into something reasonable according to social standards. Joey is comic, too, in assuming the female role in his somewhat prudish, old-maidish responses to Hypatia's advances . . . . Joey tries to reason with Hypatia but she has an answer for his arguments. Finally, Joey's condescending remark, "Really, Miss Tarleton," provokes her to slap him; his involuntary response is to swear at her. Having "lost his cool," he thoughtlessly sits down while she is standing and Hypatia triumphantly seizes on his accidental lapse of decorum with "Really, Mr. Percival, really, really, really." (Crane <u>Misalliance</u> 483)

Gladys Crane feels that Hypatia's merciless teasing of Lord Summerhays, and her shameless pursuit of Joey make Hypatia an irresponsible child (Crane <u>Misalliance</u> 484).

The relationship between Hypatia and her father is one of exasperation. Mr. Tarleton loses all his dignity as he wrangles with Hypatia. When Mr. Tarleton is outwitted, he resorts to futile assertions of parental authority, telling Hypatia to hold her tongue, but she responds in kind telling him to keep his temper.

> Finally, as Joey points out, Tarleton has reached the stage where the next logical move is to strike Hypatia; Tarleton admits that if Hypatia doesn't get out of his reach he will "thrash the life out of her." The height of the irony in Hypatia's treatment of Tarleton is her offer to let him thrash her "just really and truly for the fun of it and the satisfaction of it." (Crane <u>Misalliance</u> 485)

Crane suggests that this is the comic inversion whereby the child offers to help the parent feel better by permitting herself to be spanked, and that this offer dramatizes Hypatia's superior emotional control in the situation (Crane <u>Misalliance</u> 485).

The plane that crashes in Mr. Tarleton's garden has two passengers rather than one-- Joey, and Lina--and it is ironic that Mr. Tarleton is trying to seduce Lina at the same time that Hypatia is trying to seduce Joey. In order to emphasize the irony of this situation, Shaw places these two scenes back to back. "In both scenes Joey and Lina attempt to set Hypatia and Tarleton straight as to correct behavior in the situation" (Crane <u>Misalliance</u> 486).

<u>Fanny's First Play</u> (1911) is a play which presents two bourgeois households--the Gilbeys and the Knoxes. These households are both dignified, being long associated in business, and in the time frame of the play the two houses are about to be further consolidated by marriage. Bobby Gilbey, who is rebellious against the strictness of his home and against the pietism of his Catholic tutor is about to marry Margaret Knox, who is threatened by Bobby's preference for Dora Delany, who is described by Katherine Gatch as a "daughter of joy and of the proletariat" (Gatch 133-134):

> After a too joyful evening Dora lands herself and Bobby in jail for disorderly conduct. Meanwhile, Margaret, on her way home from an evangelistic meeting, with spirit set free, picks up a French naval officer and goes dancing with him. In a police raid, Margaret, like Bobby, goes to jail. The dialectical farce is brought to a hilarious synthesis when a way is found for a happy future by the Gilbeys's monumental butler, Juggins, who reveals at the crisis that he is the brother of a duke, and that he is doing penance by servitude for having insulted a member of the working class. (Gatch 134)

The plot thickens as the audience discovers that Juggins has fallen in love with Margaret Knox, "who appeals more than ever to his aristocratic tastes for having lost her middle-class conventionality in Holloway Gaol" (Gatch 134).

In Androcles and the Lion (1912), where "the odor of blood arises from the arena," Shaw must resort to fantasy in order to preserve the comic tone. Ironically, the force that can be used against the Caesars is the Christian humility of Androcles and the blood of the martyrs; this power is greater that mighty Caesardom. "Androcles and his lion go waltzing off together in symbolic synthesis. The lion, like the Untershaft gunpowder, is an authentic Christian symbol of Christian" (Gatch 135).

Shaw's Pygmalion (1912) is based on a Greek legend in which Pygmalion, the King of Cyprus sculpted a statue of a beautiful woman named Galatea. The King fell in love with the statue, and prayed to Aphrodite for a wife resembling the statue, and Aphrodite made the statue come to life. Lerner and Lowe later transformed Shaw's play into a musical, My Fair Lady with the same characters--Eliza Doolittle (the flower girl who becomes a duchess), Freddy Eynsford-Hill (who is in love with Eliza Doolittle), Colonel Pickering (the linguist from India who places a bet with Henry Higgins that he can't change Eliza Doolittle into a lady), Henry Higgins (who does change Eliza into a lady), and Alfred Doolittle (Eliza's father) (Nilsen 35). Not only Shaw's characters, but also much of his logic, and his turn of phrase also ended up in My Fair Lady. In the 1942 preface to Pygmalion, Shaw wrote "it is impossible for an Englishman to open his mouth without making some other Englishman despise him." When this was transformed into the musical by Lerner and Lowe, it became: "An Englishman's way of speaking absolutely classifies him. The moment he talks he makes some other Englishman despise him" (Nilsen 43).

The idea of a man's molding a woman into something perfect, and her subsequent transformation is a common theme. It can be seen in Ovid's Metamorphosis, W. S. Gilbert's comedy Pygmalion and Galatea, William Morris's poem cycle The Earthly Paradise, and the recent film entitled Educating Rita. With some variation, this is also the theme of Pinnochio (Nilsen 36-37). Shaw's Pygmalion was a story about a "creation," but only a superficial creation. Shaw, like Molière, believed that people are more impressed by the trappings (language, dress, manners) than by the real person. But unlike Molière, Shaw believed in "creative evolution." Molière's "doctor" never became a real doctor, but Shaw's "lady" may very well have become a real lady (Nilsen 39).

Heartbreak House (1917), which was subtitled, A Fantasia in the Russian Manner on English Theatre was the hinge between Shaw's early plays and his late plays (Gatch 135). In this play, much of the mysticism is achieved through the old man who is constantly trying to reach the "Seventh Degree of Concentration," which in reality is nothing more than a particular concoction made out of rum. The women in Heartbreak House are totally fearless as bombs explode around them, as they view war in the same way that they would view a football game. In fact, as the final curtain goes down, they are hoping for the "terror and beauty of another air raid" (Watson 126).

The dialogue between Adam and The Serpent in Part I of Back to Methuselah (1921) establishes the play as hopeful, and therefore a comedy:

> ADAM: (Angrily) How can I help brooding when the future has become
>   uncertain? Anything is better than uncertainty. Life has become
>   uncertain. Love is uncertain. Have you a word for this new misery?
> THE SERPENT: Fear. Fear. Fear.
> ADAM: Have you a remedy for it?
> THE SERPENT: Yes. Hope. Hope. Hope. (Kaul 320)

Back to Methuselah simplifies the Don-Juan-in-Hell theme which was earlier presented in Man and Superman. Here the Don-Juan-in-Hell theme blossoms into the full-blown utopia, but a utopia which is satire-driven. "The argument that man was not created but had evolved into his present state, and that therefore further biological progress was not only possible but was the only possible progress--becomes a trick of satire, a way of affirming the very premise that is overtly denied" (Kaul 315) Shaw once observed, "I deal with all periods, but I never study any period but the present, which I have not yet mastered and never shall" (Kaul 322).

Back to Methuselah, which is subtitled A Metabiological Pentateuch, begins with Adam and Eve in the Garden of Eden, and concludes in the year 31,920. By this time, Don Juan's heaven is already almost here.

> Not only has man willed and finally achieved the power to live forever, barring physical accidents, but the aged inhabitants of the earth, the Ancients, have become masters of reality to the extent to which they are, in Juan's words, "omniscient, infallible, and withal completely, unilludedly self-conscious." If they are not gods yet, it is only because they still have bodies. (Kaul 316-317)

It is Lileth's last speech which both closes the play and extends the play to a still more hopeful future: "after passing a million goals they press on to the goal of redemption from the flesh, to the vortex freed from matter, to the whirlpool in pure intelligence that, when the world began was a whirlpool in pure force" (Kaul 317). In the year 31,920, human babies are not born, but rather they are hatched out of large eggs at the age of about seventeen. Such a system is able to circumvent not only marriage, but in fact all kinds of sexuality as well. In addition, science and art are relegated to the status of childish games, and are treated with a certain amount of contempt. In fact, "dolls" is the word used by the Ancients both for products of science and for products of art, in addition to being the word being used for the human body (Kaul 317-318). At the beginning of Part V, Chloe, the child maiden, turns away from love, as she asks her disconsolate lover, "Have you ever thought about the properties of numbers?" (Kaul 318). After Back to Methuselah, Shaw wrote mainly farces interlaced here and there with all kinds of fantasy.

A. N. Kaul considers Saint Joan of Arc (1923) to be Shaw's finest play because it is a completely serious play, and at the same time it is filled with wit and humor and is free from humbug. Kaul feels that Shaw often manufactured a kind of humbug in his writing, which he substituted in place of the humbug he was exploding. Shaw tended to deal in "intellectual slights of the hand, twists of argument, and promotion of novel theories which have the brave air of revelations that no one will believe, not even the author" (Kaul 321).

Most writers before Shaw, including Mark Twain, saw Joan of Arc as a martyr whose judges were corrupt men who tricked and trapped her into false submissions. But Shaw does not see the situation in this way. "Joan's judges were as straightforward as Joan herself, and it cannot be too clearly understood that there were no villains in the tragedy of Joan's death. She was entirely innocent; but her excommunication was a genuine act of faith and piety; and her execution followed inevitably" (Kaul 324).

Barbara Watson notes that in our society there is a distinction between a role and a stereotype. "Soldier is a role; bishop is a role; shepherd is a role; even saint is a role; but woman is an antirole and therefore a woman must be a rebel or nothing." Watson notes that being a woman is not a role, it is a stereotype, not in fact a role, but rather the denial of a role (Watson 124). In Shaw's St. Joan, "a real element in Joan's martyrdom is her inability to conform to the role assigned to her as a woman" (Watson 124).

The Apple Cart (1929) was subtitled, A Political Extravaganza. This play demonstrates the ironic pattern that Shaw had mentioned earlier in his statement, "I deal in the tragi-comic irony of the conflict between real life and the romantic imagination" (Gatch 127). In The Apple Cart, King Magnus "returns almost on time to his work and his placid maternal wife whom Orinthia calls an old cabbage, with a remark no male chauvinist could have dreamed up: 'Besides, all these old married cabbages were once roses; and, though young things like you don't remember that, their husbands do' " (Watson 127).

Like The Apple Cart, Too True to be Good (1932) is also subtitled, A Political Extravaganza (Gatch 136). In this play Private Meek is Shaw's tribute to his friend Lawrence of Arabia, who at this time was calling himself T. E. Shaw.

> Meek's knowledge of dialects, his ingenuity and omnipresence, his motorcycle, his headgear, and his habit of demoting himself to the ranks are Lawrence to the life. The satire on the military mind of Tallboys, who aggravates the dangerous friction between the white and dark races, is integral to the scheme of this political extravaganza. The intellectual grasp of international relations, as Shaw understands it, amounts to common sense and humanity raised to the degree of genius in experts like Lawrence--but the numskulls and water-colorists remain in command. (Gatch 138)

Sweetie, the nurse in Too True to be Good is a "promiscuous vulgarian" who masquerades as a countess. "She is a Shavian inversion of the postwar women of high social position and promiscuous habits." In this same play, Aubrey is an allusion to Aldous Huxley. This can be seen by Aubrey's relation to the nineteenth-century Elder, by his twentieth-century associates, by his return to religion, and by his eloquent despair. Elder is, of course, an allusion to Aldous Huxley's older brother, Thomas. Shaw felt a sense of tragicomedy in the plight of both generations of Huxleys. Elder (Thomas Huxley) rushes out of the museum to keep from going mad, as he demands a "solid footing in dogma." However, he suddenly realizes that "the only trustworthy dogma is that there is no dogma" (Gatch 139).

Gatch feels that Shaw critics are missing the point if they assume that Aubrey's despair was Shaw's despair. Many Shaw critics quote Aubrey, "I am by nature and destiny a preacher. I am the new Ecclesiastes," and again, "I must preach and preach and preach no matter how late the hour and how short the day, no matter whether I have nothing to say--." But Gatch notes that Shaw separates himself from his characters. In one of the Malvern Festival programs he singled out one of his critics, Joseph Wood Krutch, when he said,

> I find it hard to forgive him for saying that I announced, in . . . Too True To Be Good, that world affairs are now irremediable, and that mankind is damned beyond hope and redemption . . . . The despair of the shell-shocked young gentleman-burglar-clergyman, who made such a pitiful attempt to be happy by spending a lump of unearned money, is not my despair . . . . I made him a good preacher to warn the world against mere fluency, and the result was that his talking took Mr. Krutch in. He must be more careful next time. (Gatch 140-141)

In The Millionairess (1936), an Egyptian doctor agrees to marry the heroine because her pulse is "irresistible." He describes it as "a pulse in a hundred thousand" (Kaul 320). The heroine in The Millionairess has "the galvanic energy that marked the conductors of the Life Force in the early comedies." Epifania, the millionairess, has an unholy and appalling vitality, but she is mean, bullying, avaricious, and a law unto herself. She makes money by instinct and bosses everyone (Gatch 145). Epiphania's sexual vitality is as ruthless as is her appetite for power. As Epifania extends her wrist, the Egyptian doctor automatically puts his finger on her pulse and takes out his watch, exclaiming, "Ooooh!! I have never felt such a pulse. It is like a slow sledge hammer . . . . It is the will of Allah . . . . You are a terrible woman; but I love your pulse. I have never felt anything like it before" (Watson 123).

On the Rocks (1937) is a farce having to do with the love affairs of the Prime Minister's children. David is the Prime Minister's "overbred son," who is about to marry Aloysia Brollikins, a "bounding daughter of the proletariat." Aloysia has won many scholarships and is politically more literate than is the Prime Minister. The message of On the Rocks relates specifically to Sir Arthur Chavender, the Prime Minister, whose week-end conversion to a radical philosophy satirizes political amateurs during the depression (Gatch 142). Nevertheless, the satire deals not so much with the Prime Minister, as it does, by implication, with the audience who votes for him. Thirty years earlier Shaw had said, "What our voters are in the pit and the gallery, they are in the polling booth."

> The curtain falls on the sound of shattering glass and the singing of the unemployed, "England, arise! the long, long night is over"; but in ironic counterpoint comes the thwacking sound of police batons. The real horror implied in the ending of On the Rocks is expressed in the formidable title of its preface, "Extermination." Critics have shuddered in alarm at this preface without seeing that it modulates from irony to direct appeal and back again without warning, in the manner of Swift. Had Shaw called it "A Modest Proposal for the Extermination of the Politically Irresponsible," readers might have heard the overtone of the first subheading, "Killing as a Political Function." (Gatch 144)

Edmund Wilson has called The Simpleton of the Unexpected Isles "Shaw's only really silly play." About this evaluation, Katherine Gatch notes that Shaw was actually satirizing silliness, and she further notes that "although Shaw may be credited with having intended The Simpleton to provoke a revulsion against silliness, this play must be counted as experiment that brought art to the vanishing point" (Gatch 144). According to Gatch, The Simpleton of the Unexpected Isles "conveys the feeling that the failure of this civilization is a farce of simple-minded folly, not a twilight of the gods" (Gatch 145). The idea of selective breeding, which was treated with comic effect in Man and Superman was also developed in The Simpleton of the Unexpected Isles. Kaul describes this play as "a full-fledged farce of a eugenic group marriage leading to the establishment of a 'Superfamily' " (Kaul 320). Geneva (1938) is a play in which Battler, Bombardone, and Flanco, three farcical dictators, are summoned to a court of pure justice. The play shows that a world that can synthesize the powers of three such dictators is very far in the future. The machinery for international cooperation, is, in fact, in the hands of superpatriots like Begonia Brown (Gatch 146). Buoyant Billions was Shaw's last play, and A. N. Kaul describes it as a search for the "mathematical hormone" (Kaul 320).

In an article entitled "The New Woman and the New Comedy," Barbara Bellow Watson indicates that by placing women at the center of his dramatic structures, Shaw radically changed the structure of comedy itself (Watson 114). Watson goes so far as to say that "Shavian drama deals preeminently with the conflict between the individual woman's humanity and the rigidity of the sex role assigned to her" (Watson 115). Watson adds a significant insight in her discussion of the Old Comedy. She notes that if the traditional pattern of conflict is between the spontaneous desires of the young protagonists and the stiff resistance of the old, and if the marriage of young lovers is the goal and the triumph, then the desired conclusion is simply a wedding, a reciprocal process by which society accedes to lovers and they accede to society. This has been earlier demonstrated by Northrop Frye and others. Watson adds, however, that "at this point the young ones begin to become the old ones. The young lover, once wedded, becomes a shareholder in the status quo, and old father in the bud" (Watson 116).

Shaw's characters not only change; they evolve. "Shaw sees society, and even nature, as capable of genuine evolution, of an escape from recurrence, and his comedy reflects that view in its very structure." The women in Shaw's comedies tend to be enterprising, audacious, aggressive and self-assured, and in Shaw's comedies, it is the women who secure all the desired outcomes through their wit and daring in such plays as St. Brassbound's Conversion, St Joan of Arc, Major Barbara, Pygmalion, Mrs. Warren's

Profession, and Misalliance (Watson 121, 124). According to Watson, "Shaw never flinches from strong women. Where most men see in strong women a threat to themselves, Shaw sees in them a hope for the world" (Watson 126).

According to Watson, there is an important category of women in Shavian drama who escape from marriage and from the tyranny of love. On realizing that they have escaped marriage, these women often display a swoon of relief that drops other women into a lover's arms. In Captain Brassbound's Conversion, for example, Lady Cicely is a gifted moralist and tactician who finds herself almost mesmerized into marriage in the last minutes of the action but, reprieved for the final curtain, cries, "How glorious! How glorious." In Pygmalion, many directors are tempted "to sweep Eliza into the arms of Professor Higgins in an illogical and irrelevant final embrace," but Watson feels that this would weaken the story. The curtain falls on a new kind of consummation, not a woman losing herself in marriage, but rather a woman finding herself in her own abilities (Watson 117).

In Shaw's comedies, the strong characters, what Barbara Watson calls the "Vital Geniuses," tend to be androgynous, whether they are men or women.

> They are seldom husbands in the true sense. Husbands tend toward the bombastic or uxorious. Fathers and grandfathers come off much better. In Major Barbara, Heartbreak House, Cashel Byron's Profession, The Millionairess, and elsewhere, fathers show a certain verve. It is only a step from father to Caesar, who is paternal toward the infantile Cleopatra. Like the paternal, encouraging, instructive manner of King Magnus, his power, which is his detachment, which is his wisdom, is part of an androgynous consciousness. No conventional masculine traits like aggression, vengefulness, violence appear in the vital genius, just as no conventional feminine traits appear in the vital woman. Androgyny appears to be the key to the new humanity. (Watson 128)

"Social Darwinism," or "creative evolution" was the metaphor which drove many of Shaw's works:

> In association with Harley Granville-Barker, Mr. Shaw produced Man and Superman in London in 1905. Man and Superman definitely established Mr. Shaw's fame with the general public, and, together with a group of revivals, led to a collective reconsideration of his earlier work. What he was really driving at became clear to thousands who had not hitherto troubled to think of him otherwise than as a political fanatic or a buffoon. The doctrine of "creative evolution" which underlies this play was seen as the guiding social philosophy of all his work. (Roberts 8)

"Creative evolution" was a major theme of Back to Methuselah in which Shaw investigated various religious and philosophical themes with which he was obsessed, in this case not just "creative evolution," but "eternal creative evolution." Pygmalion continues this theme of "creative evolution." Shaw had a passion for reforming the world and he was not above being didactic to do so. He had a contempt for those who preached art for art's sake, and once remarked, "For art's sake alone I would not face the toil of writing a single sentence. If you don't like my preaching, you must lump it. I really cannot help it" (Roberts 10).

Like Oscar Wilde, George Bernard Shaw was an epigramist. If it is true that humor is a product of the emotions, while wit springs from the mind, then Shaw is clearly witty rather than humorous. His aphorisms, which can be found in a wide range of sources, normally view the world from a slightly skewed perspective, and are generally quite insightful.

> Do not do unto others as you would they should do unto you. Their tastes may not be the same. (O'Farrell 56)

> We learn from experience that men never learn anything from experience. (Katz and Arbeiter 210)

> A government that robs Peter to pay Paul can always depend upon the support of Paul. (Peter 10)

Shavian epigrams such as these are constantly turning up in a very wide range of sources. Anecdotes involving Shaw are just as ubiquitous. It is said that Isadora Duncan proposed marriage to Shaw by writing to him, "With my beauty and your brains we would produce the perfect child." Shaw is said to have responded, "Madam, I am flattered--but suppose it turned out to have <u>my</u> beauty and <u>your</u> brains?" (Wilde 3; MacHale 40). A similar story is told about Bernard Shaw and Winston Churchill. Shaw sent Churchill a ticket to the premiere of one of his plays with a note reading, "I'd be glad to see you among the audience." Churchill returned the ticket with a note of his own: "I apologize for not being able to attend the premiere. I will gladly come to a later night--if there is one." At this point, Shaw sent Churchill <u>two</u> tickets for a different evening and wrote, "I'll be glad if you come to the show accompanied by a friend--if you have one" (Ziv 9).

Budding young authors were constantly sending Shaw manuscripts for publication, or to receive his critical comments. To one author he wrote, "The covers of your book are too far apart." To another author, who had pasted two leaves of her manuscript together and then had complained when he returned the manuscript with these leaves still pasted together that he hadn't read the entire manuscript, Shaw responded, "You don't have to eat a whole egg to know it's rotten" (Wallace 153). Shaw treated publishers in the same way that he treated budding authors. One of his publishers sent him a telegram which read, "Send manuscript. If good will send check." Shaw responded, "Send check. If good will send manuscript" (Helitzer 125).

Shaw once wrote, "if you want to tell a person the truth, make him laugh or he'll kill you" (Helitzer 29), and "The reasonable man adapts himself to the world. The unreasonable man persists in trying to adapt the world to himself. Therefore, all progress depends on the unreasonable man" (Helitzer 129).

These witticisms and retorts can be seen as the end result of Shaw's preoccupation with "creative evolution." What began as an experiment to show how language can affect perception, ended up by showing how language can change behavior (Nilsen 42).

In an article entitled, "The Last Plays of Bernard Shaw: Dialectic and Despair," Katherine Gatch concludes as follows: "In all Shaw's late plays the ironic relationship between the magnitude of the themes and the triviality of the treatment is calculated; the political extravaganzas are tragicomedies, concerned with grotesque disproportion between the gigantic problems and the pygmies who deal with them" (Gatch 146-147).

A common criticism of Shaw's plays, both the early ones and the late ones, is that they are all talk and no plot (Gatch 127). Katherine Gatch suggests that the structure of Shaw's plays was derived from Hegel and Marx, and could be stated as: "Thesis, Antithesis, and Synthesis." Gatch says that the essence of the Hegelian dialectic is change. Much of Shaw's humor is derived from what Bergson describes as "the mobility of the intelligence conforming exactly to the mobility of things . . . the moving continuity of our attention to life" (Gatch 128-129).

Harold Hobson suggests that "the disturbance of complacency is one of the two cardinal features of Shaw's wit." Boanerges, the working man Cabinet Minister of <u>The Apple Cart</u>, asserts confidently that the workers will never throw him over. He tells Magnus, "No king on earth is as safe in his job as a Trade Union official." Talking about the union members, he continues, "I tell them that they have the vote, and that theirs is the kingdom and the power and the glory. I say to them 'You are supreme: exercise your power.' They say, 'That's right! Tell us what to do;' and I tell them. I say, 'Exercise your vote intelligently by voting for me.' And they do." (Hobson 305)

> According to Hobson, the second cardinal feature of Shaw's wit is its good-nature. He satirizes marriage; but he does not hate it, like Strindberg. He ridicules theories of medicine in The Doctor's Dilemma; but he does not hate them, as Chesterton, for example, hated them in the figure of Dr. Warner in Manalive. He finds men and women and their associations and activities absurd and foolish and inefficient, but he neither despises them nor would rejoice in their final failure. He makes wit as good-humoured as humour. (Hobson 306)

Because of these qualities of Shaw's writing, he had an important impact on the twentieth century. As late as 1940, Hobson was able to say, in a book entitled English Wits that Shaw's plays "are now more widely produced than anyone's but Shakespeare's" (Hobson 284).

George Bernard Shaw Bibliography

Abel, Lionel. "Wrong and Right: The Art of Comedy." Salmagundi 28 (1975): 3-19.

Austin, Don. "Comedy through Tragedy: Dramatic Structure in Saint Joan." Shaw Review 8 (1965): 52-62.

Barzun, Jacques. "Bernard Shaw in Twilight." George Bernard Shaw: A Critical Survey. Ed. Louis Kronenberger. New York, NY: World, 1953.

Couchman, Gordon W. "Comic Catharsis in Caesar and Cleopatra." Shaw Review 3.1 (1960): 11-14.

Crane, Gladys. "Shaw's Comic Techniques in Man and Superman." Educational Theatre Journal 23 (1971): 13-21.

Crane, Gladys. "Shaw's Misalliance: The Comic Journey from Rebellious Daughter to Conventional Womanhood." Educational Theatre Journal 25 (1973): 480-489.

Dukore, Bernard F. Bernard Shaw, Playwright. Columbia, MO: Univ of Missouri Press, 1973.

Evans, James E. "Irish Comic Literature." Comedy: An Annotated Bibliography of Theory and Criticism, Metuchen, NJ: Scarecrow Press, 1987, 177-182.

Frank, Joseph. "Major Barbara--Shaw's Divine Comedy." Publication of the Modern Language Association 71 (1956): 61-74.

Ganz, Margaret. "Humor's Devaluations in a Modern Idiom: The Don Juan Plays of Shaw, Frisch, and Montherlant." Comedy: New Perspectives. Ed. Maurice Charney. New York, NY: New York Literary Forum, 1978, 117-138.

Gatch, Katherine Haynes. "The Last Plays of Bernard Shaw: Dialectic and Despair." English Stage Comedy: English Institute Essays 1954. Ed. W. K. Wimsatt, Jr. New York, NY: Columbia Univ Press, 1955, 126-147.

Gibbs, A. M. "Comedy and Philosophy in Man and Superman." Modern Drama 19 (1976): 161-175.

Helitzer, Melvin. Comedy Writing Secrets. Cincinnati, OH: Writer's Digest Books, 1987.

Hobson, Harold. "George Bernard Shaw." English Wits. Ed. Leonard Russell. London, England: Hutchinson, 1940, 279-306.

Katz, Marjorie, and Jean Arbeiter. Pegs to Hang Ideas On. New York, NY: M. Evans, 1973.

Kaul, A. N. The Action of English Comedy: Studies in the Encounter of Abstraction and Experience from Shakespeare to Shaw. New Haven, CT: Yale Univ Press, 1970.

Kornbluth, Martin L. "Shaw and Restoration Comedy." Shaw Bulletin 2.4 (1958): 9-17.

McDowell, Frederick P. W. "Politics, Comedy, Character, and Dialectic: The Shavian

World of John Bull's Other Island." Publication of the Modern Language Association 82 (1967): 542-553.

MacHale, Des. Irish Love and Marriage Jokes. Cork, Ireland: Mercier, 1977.

Mills, John A. Language and Laughter: Comic Diction in the Plays of Bernard Shaw. Tucson, AZ: University of Arizona Press, 1969.

Nilsen, Don L. F. "The Pygmalion Story: A Recurring Theme." The Leaflet 90.2 (1991): 34-47.

O'Donoghue, David James, ed. The Humour of Ireland. London, England: Walter Scott, 1894; New York, NY: AMS Press, 1978.

O'Farrell, Padraic. G. B. Shaw: Gems of Irish Wisdom. Cork, Ireland: Mercier, 1980.

Park, Bruce R. "A Mote in the Critic's Eye: Bernard Shaw and Comedy." University of Texas Studies in English 37 (1958): 195-210.

Parker, William. "Broadbent and Doyle: Two Shavian Archetypes." Aspects of the Irish Theatre. Eds. Patrick Rafroidi, Raymonde Popot, and William Parker. Paris, France: Eds. Universitaires, 1972, 39-49.

Pearson, Hesketh. "Bernard Shaw." Lives of the Wits. New York, NY: Harper and Row, 1962, 248-268.

Peter, Laurence. The Peter Plan. New York, NY: Morrow, 1976.

Potter, Stephen. "S.B. and G.B.S." Sense of Humour. New York, NY: Henry Holt, 1954.

Rayner, Alice. "Shaw's Paradox: Use in Dystopia." Comic Persuasion: Moral Structure in British Comedy from Shakespeare to Stoppard. Berkeley, CA: University of California Press, 1987.

Reardon, Joan. "Caesar and Cleopatra and the Commedia dell'Arte." Shaw Review 14 (1971): 120-136.

Roberts, James L. Pygmalion and Arms and the Man. Lincoln, NE: Cliffs Notes, 1959.

Robinson, Fred Norris. "Satirists and Enchanters in Early Irish Literature." Studies in the History of Religions Presented to Crawford Howell Toy. Eds. David Lyon and George Moore. New York, NY: Macmillan, 1912, 95-130.

Shaw, Bernard. John Bull's Other Island and Major Barbara: Also How He Lied to Her Husband. London, England: Archibald Constable, 1907.

Shaw, Bernard. The Quintessence of Ibsenism. New York, NY: Hill and Wang, 1961.

Shaw, Bernard. "Tolstoy: Tragedian or Comedian." The London Mercury 4 (1921), 32.

Smith, B. L. O'Casey's Satiric Vision. Kent, OH: Kent State University Press, 1978.

Speckhard, Robert R. "Shaw and Aristophanes: Symbolic Marriage and the Magical Doctor/Cook in Shavian Comedy." Shaw Review 9 (1966): 56-65.

Thackeray, W. M. The English Humorists: Charity and Humour: The Four Georges. New York, NY: Dutton, 1912.

Ussher, Arland. Three Great Irishmen: Shaw, Yeats, Joyce. New York, NY: Devin-Adair, 1953.

Wallace, Irving, David Wallechinsky, Amy Wallace, and Sylvia Wallace. The Book of Lists 2 New York, NY: Morrow, 1980.

Watson, Barbara Bellow. "The New Woman and the New Comedy." Fabian Feminist: Bernard Shaw and Women. Ed. Rodelle Weintraub. University Park, PA: Pennsylvania State Univ Press, 1977 114-129.

Whittemore, Reed. "Shaw's Abstract Clarity." Comedy: Meaning and Form. Second Edition. Ed. Robert W. Corrigan. New York, NY: Harper and Row, 1981 415-246.

Wilde, Larry. The Last Official Irish Joke Book. New York, NY: Bantam, 1983.

Winsten, Stephen. Jesting Apostle: The Private Life of Bernard Shaw. New York, NY: E. P. Dutton, 1957.

Ziv, Avner. Personality and Sense of Humor. New York, NY: Springer, 1984.

Douglas Hyde (1860-1949) IRELAND

Douglas Hyde was born in Kilmactranny, County Sligo, the son of the Reverend Arthur Hyde. He graduated from Dublin University, where he had a brilliant career. Hyde is one of the foremost contemporary Irish writers, and was a master of the Gaelic tongue. He was also a well known scholar and folk-lore enthusiast, and has published fine collections of Irish folk tales and popular songs of the West of Ireland. Hyde was also a clever writer of verse, both in Irish and in English (O'Donoghue 426). Hyde was a professor of Irish at the National University from 1909-1932. He was also the poet and literary historian who founded the Gaelic League (Greene 421).

Douglas Hyde Bibliography

Greene, David H. "IRELAND: Literature." The Encyclopedia Americana: International Edition. Danbury, CT: Americana Corporation, 1978, 420-423.
O'Donoghue, David James, ed. The Humour of Ireland. London, England: Walter Scott, 1894; New York, NY: AMS Press, 1978.

Patrick Joseph McCall (1861-1919) IRELAND

Patrick McCall was like many other Irish poets in balancing his time between the writing of original Irish poems and translating poems from the original Gaelic language. The son of a Dublin grocer, McCall was educated at the Catholic University School in Dublin, and for many years was a frequent contributor to the Dublin Nationalist press. A good selection of his poems has been published under the title of Irish Noinins, and many of his stories have appeared in The Shamrock of Dublin. Such humorous pieces as "The Dance at Marley," "Fionn MacCumhail and the Princess," and "Tatther Jack Welsh" were written by Patrick McCall (O'Donoghue 393-405, 429).

Patrick Joseph McCall Bibliography

O'Donoghue, David James, ed. The Humour of Ireland. London, England: Walter Scott, 1894; New York, NY: AMS Press, 1978.

Edith Ann Somerville (1861-1949) IRELAND

Edith Somerville and Violet Martin (under the penname of Martin Ross) published their first comic story in 1898 in Badminton Magazine. The story was entitled "Great Uncle McCarthy," and was the first installment of Somerville and Ross's Irish R.M. stories. "Great Uncle McCarthy" is a Gothic tale in which the mysterious shuffling at night on the upper floors gives evidence of a "pervading sub-presence," which Major Yeates believes is the ghost of his landlord's great-uncle McCarthy. Yeates eventually discovers that he is the unwitting host of some elderly real-life McCarthys who, with the aid of the housekeeper, have made themselves at home in the attic, helping themselves not only to Yeates's home, but to his food and whiskey as well. (Waters 16) In this story, as in other Somerville and Ross stories, Yeates is the butt of the joke. "He is frequently duped by local people who know much more about a given situation than he does. They connive and collaborate all the while covering their tracks by a pretense of ignorance or ineptitude or superstitious fear" (Waters 17).   In "The Waters of Strife," the mother of a man accused of murder is called as a witness; however, "Bat Callahan's mother had nothing to fear from the inquiry. She was by turns deaf, imbecile, garrulously candid, and furiously abusive of the principal witness" (Waters 18).

The Irish R.M. stories "have been among the most popular and successful works of comic fiction to have come out of Ireland." These stories are episodic, and are filled with realistic Irish-English dialect humor as well as some rather fantastic occurrences (Cahalan 87). Although the Irish R.M. stories began appearing in 1898, they were not published all together until 1928 (Cahalan 88).

> Their protagonist, Major Sinclair Yeates--a well-educated, well-meaning chap with some Irish blood--is sent from England, in classic Irish fictional fashion, to remote southwestern rural Ireland as a resident magistrate--an archaic legal post whose closest American equivalent is the justice of the peace. There he and subsequently his wife, Philippa, encounter many unforgettable Irish characters who really run the area, particularly Flurry Knox and his grandmother Mrs. Knox, and participate in many race Irish pastimes, most of which center on hunting. (Cahalan 89)

Cahalan feels that Flurry's Grandmother, Mrs. Knox, is probably the most dominant character in all of the R.M. stories. Mrs. Knox is the impressive "mater familias" of the "Big House of Aussolas," and Mrs. Knox is much cleverer than any man. "What she stands for is Edith's feminine ideal--a matriarch" (Cahalan 99). Mrs. Knox is patterned very closely on Mrs. Martin (Violet Martin's mother), who "could also be an outrageous character in her own right, provoking in her daughter a remarkably loud laugh that her collaborator, Somerville, often described as penetrating." Violet Martin describes her mother as follows:

> "Mama" was completely unselfconscious and eccentric about her clothing. In 1892 her daughter described at length how at one point "Mama" was wearing, on top of everything else, a red kettle holder that she had been unable to find around the house, and at another point a woman came up to her in the street and alerted her to the fact that "her sponge and sponge bag were hanging from her waist at the back." (Cahalan 100)

Cahalan then continues, "The unforgettable fictional Mrs. Knox is a close copy of the unforgettable actual Mrs. Martin" (Cahalan 100).

It is from the perspective of Major Yeates, the Resident Magistrate in the Irish R.M. stories that the comedy develops (Waters 15). James Cahalan suggests that the reason Somerville and Ross chose Yeates, an Anglo-Irishman, to be both the central victim and the narrator of the story is so that the Irish Ascendancy could laugh at itself. More specifically, this was a case of two women (Somerville and Ross) making fun of an Anglo-Irish man (Yeates). The comedy is greatly leavened by the fact that Yeates himself participates in the laughter as he narrates the story. He has the maturity to be able to laugh at himself (Cahalan 89).

In The Comic Irishman, Maureen Waters indicates that in the comedy of Somerville and Ross there is a racist consciousness at work, and that they contributed to the stereotype of the Irish countryman as a "tricky clown" (Waters 20). In contrast to this view is that of James Cahalan--that "far from being 'racist' victimizers Somerville and Ross were victimized women who nonetheless managed to become successful, and that intermixed in the R.M. stories with a nostalgia for a dying way of life was a subversively gendered portrait of strong, vital women" (Cahalan 90). Elizabeth Stanley Trotter supports this point of view. In an article entitled "Humor with a Gender," Trotter argued that "men tend to laugh 'at' while women tend to laugh 'with,' avoiding ridicule and often aligning themselves with the victims of jokes, as Somerville and Ross do by making Major Yeates their narrator" (Cahalan 90-91).

Major Yeates, the Resident Magistrate in the Somerville and Ross Irish R.M. stories, seems to be grounded to some extent on the real William Butler Yeats, whom Ross had met at Coole. Cahalan states, "there remains the slight, teasing possibility that their Major Yeates might have been named partly as a private joke at the poet's expense." The fact is that Ross met Yeats in 1896, just two years before the R.M. stories started to appear, a time when Yeats was just becoming famous. Martin was fascinated by Yeats, saying, "He is a little affected and knows it--He has a sense of humour and is a gentleman" (Cahalan 95). Five years later, in 1901, Ross was again in Coole, and again ran into Yeats, reporting in a letter to Somerville as follows: "I liked him . . . . He is not at all without a sense of humour, which surprised me . . . . But he doesn't approve of humour for humour's sake-- (here Miss Martin [Ross] said beautiful things about humour being a higher art) I will tell you more when we meet" (Cahalan 96).

Somerville and Ross didn't like Yeats's "shadowy romanticism," and their character, Major Yeates, is often lost in his own reveries. "It would not have been out of character for Somerville and Ross to have a private little joke--rather along the lines of their use of the language of the 'Buddhs' as a confidential comic code--protecting themselves by keeping quiet about it and by spelling their Major's name 'Yeates' rather than 'Yeats' " (Cahalan 96). We know that Yeats himself was interested in The Irish R.M., as Lady Gregory wrote a letter to Ross in 1915 saying that she was slow in reading The Irish R.M. because she was reading it aloud to W. B. Yeats. When the name of "Major Yeates" was mentioned, W. B. Yeats anxiously asked if it was spelt with a second "e," and when he was told that it was, he "gave himself up to uninterrupted enjoyment" (Cahalan 96).

Major Yeates is symbolic of the Anglo-Irish Ascendancy, but it is "an Ascendancy on the descent." Cahalan calls Flurry Knox a "half-sir," that is, "a Protestant who outfoxes Yeates and nearly everyone else, and who is in fact as much a part of Somerville and Ross's own social stratum as Yeates." Flurry is Master of the Fox Hounds. Both Yeates and Flurry are outmatched by the women, for it is the women who are really in control of the Big House. "In terms of gender as well as class, the R.M. stories are subtly and deliciously subversive." Cahalan says that there is also a great deal of comedy in the R.M. stories that has to do with linguistic registers--shifting between "Yeates's impeccably standard Oxford English and the racy dialogue of such characters as Mrs. Cadogan" (Cahalan 97).

The story entitled "Poisson d'Avril" is about a wedding feast. An enormous salmon has been promised for this feast, and as it is being transported by carriage over the fifteen or so miles, with much banging and bumping, "the salmon slowly churned its way forth from its newspaper, and moved along the netting with dreadful stealth" (Waters 21). One of the stylistic features in the Irish R.M. Stories is the use of such deflated similes as "the friend of her youth," or "the small, rat-like head of Bill's kitchen-maid." But the Somerville and Ross similes are overstated rather than understated. In "Poisson d'Avril," one character says, "That one has a tongue that'd clip a hedge!" (Cahalan 98). And in "The Bosom of the McRorys" Somerville and Ross write that Bobby Bennett's dancing is "a serious matter, with a Cromwellian quality to it, suggestive of jack boots and the march of great events" (Cahalan 99).

Another humorous feature of the stories is the reversal of roles.

> Yeates is often ordered about while women cook, clean, and socialize, as in "A Royal Command," where he complains that his cigarettes, "in common with every other thing that I wanted, had been tidied into oblivion. From earliest dawn I had heard the thumping feet, and the swish of petticoats, and the plying of brooms." (Cahalan 98)

According to Cahalan, Somerville and Ross were effective in the women's suffrage movement because they were able to "laugh by proxy." In a book entitled The Book of

Negro Humor, Langston Hughes says, "Humor is laughing at what you haven't got when you ought to have it. Of course, you laugh by proxy" (Cahalan 102). Although Somerville and Ross are only laughing by proxy, they are indeed laughing, and this is possible only because they forgive the R.M. They even allow the R.M. to narrate their stories, following the pattern of identification and role-reversal with the comic victim that is a humor device especially developed by women. "If Major Yeates is made a fool of, we are nonetheless permitted to emerge from the R.M. stories liking him" (Cahalan 102).

Maureen Waters considers Major Yeates to be in the tradition of the Rustic Clown, but with a difference. Yeates is a cunning clown. Although he may blunder in speech, he is extremely inventive and skillful in protecting his own interests. Waters feels that Yeates is in the long tradition of "tricky servants" who contrive to turn the tables on their alleged masters (Waters 13). Somerville and Ross do much to reinforce the traditional English-Irish stereotypes. "Through Yeates's eyes the Irish often appear vigorous and imaginative, but they are also unreliable, highly emotional, manipulative, verbally very clever clowns." In contrast, "Yeates and his English wife, Philippa, are discreet, polite, conventional people, more fitted to accept than to alter circumstances. It often seems that the clash of cultures provides the only real excitement in their lives" (Waters 17).

The tone in the Irish R.M. stories is very skeptical. In these stories,

> . . . wily Irish clowns seem bent on pulling down every outpost of civilization. In the face of their contempt for English government and their adherence to a more primitive, but always more inspired way of life, Yeates's system of reason and moral order is doomed to failure. The best he can do is maintain an ironic distance while bending to the inevitable. (Waters 20)

Waters continues.

> Rejecting the sentimental comedy of the previous era, Somerville and Ross wrote with a biting humor and satire which reflects their kinship with Jonathan Swift, Maria Edgeworth and John Synge. Somerville and Ross have that firm grasp of detail and economy of plot essential to good satire. Their precisely polished prose is distinguished by metaphor which is often original and zany in character. Even their hunting stories, which seem tedious today, are redeemed by flashes of wit. (Waters 21)

Somerville and Ross rose their voices in defense of their class. They wrote many fine comic sketches including the excellent The Real Charlotte (1894). Ann Weekes says that "no other nineteenth-century Irish novel spans such a wide section of, nor delves so deeply into, Irish society" (Weekes 20). The narrators have more than a single vision, and the work constantly forces the reader to consider the narrators' biases and prejudices toward their characters, and in fact to consider the perspective to be "narrationally contaminated" (Weekes 21).

Edith Somerville and Martin Ross were two late-Victorian women trying to invade the male provinces of satire and hunting. They very much needed each other's input to be able to succeed in this endeavor. In 1889, Ross was writing to Somerville about the difficulties facing women writers, and said, "I am not man enough for a story by myself" (Cahalan 94). It is interesting to note that the collaboration between Somerville and Ross was so close that when Ross died in 1915, Somerville still insisted on publishing everything under their joint names, believing that she was still able to maintain some sort of a mystical communication with Ross (Cahalan 93).

Edith Ann Somerville Bibliography

Cahalan, James M. " 'Humor with a Gender': Somerville and Ross and The Irish R.M."

Éire-Ireland 28.3 (1993): 87-102.
Trotter, Elizabeth Stanley. "Humor with a Gender." Atlantic Monthly 130.6 (December, 1922): 784-787.
Waters, Maureen. The Comic Irishman. Albany, NY: State Univ of New York Press, 1984.
Weekes, Ann Owens. "Somerville and Ross: Ignoble Tragedy." Irish Women Writers: An Uncharted Tradition. Lexington, KY: University Press of Kentucky, 1990, 60-82.

Martin Ross (Ne: Violet Florence Martin)(1862-1915) IRELAND

See EDITH ANN SOMERVILLE.

Martin Ross (Violet Florence Martin) Bibliography

Cahalan, James M. " 'Humor with a Gender': Somerville and Ross and The Irish R.M." Éire-Ireland 28.3 (1993): 87-102.
Trotter, Elizabeth Stanley. "Humor with a Gender." Atlantic Monthly 130.6 (December, 1922): 784-787.
Waters, Maureen. The Comic Irishman. Albany, NY: State Univ of New York Press, 1984.
Weekes, Ann Owens. "Somerville and Ross: Ignoble Tragedy." Irish Women Writers: An Uncharted Tradition. Lexington, KY: University Press of Kentucky, 1990, 60-82.

Frank Mathew (1865-1924) IRELAND

Frank Mathew's first literary work was his biography of the eminent English judge, Sir James Mathew, Frank's uncle; the piece was entitled "The Apostle of Temperance." Mathew wrote a number of admirable Irish stories which appeared in The Idler. These were later collected into a volume called At the Rising of the Moon. The stories are very graphic in their detail. One of Mathew's humorous pieces was entitled, "Their Last Race" (O'Donoghue 405-409, 429).

Frank Mathew Bibliography

O'Donoghue, David James, ed. The Humour of Ireland. London, England: Walter Scott, 1894; New York, NY: AMS Press, 1978.

William Butler Yeats (1865-1939) IRELAND

In one way, W. B. Yeats was to Ireland what the Brothers Grimm were to Germany, in that he was an avid collector of fairy tales and folk tales of the Irish peasantry. He was especially interested in the trooping fairies, the changelings, the merrow, the solitary fairies, ghosts, witches and fairy doctors, Tyeer-Na-N-Oge, saints and priests, giants, Kings, Queens, Princesses, Earls, and robbers, and The Devil (Yeats vii-viii). In fact, Mary Thuente goes so far as to say that "Irish folklore was the most important impulse behind one of the most distinctive literary movements of the century, the Irish Literary Renaissance. Yeats and his associates repeatedly claimed that it was a revival of interest in Irish folklore that had made their work possible" (Thuente xi). In the Irish peasant tradition, ancient Irish gods had often become human heroes, and sometimes they became mock-heroic giants, as in William Carleton's tale, "A Legend of Knockmany," which Yeats included in his first anthology of Irish folklore, Fairy and Folk Tales of the Irish Peasantry (1888). Yeats, however, made some changes to the Carleton poem. In Carleton's story, Finn and Cuchulain are mock-heroically portrayed as giants with Finn using the trunk of a huge fir tree as a walking stick, and with a neighbor wanting to borrow some butter, and Finn's wife throwing the neighbor a piece about the weight of a couple of dozen mill-stones across a valley which was four miles wide. For both Carleton and Yeats, the plot turns on broad comedy and trickery. When Cuchulain arrives at Finn's pleasant Irish cottage, Finn pretends to be a baby in order to get under Cuchulain's skin. In Carleton's tale, Cuchulain's stature depends on the strength of his magic finger; however when Yeats rewrote his series of plays about Cuchulain, he portrayed Cuchulain as the embodiment of tragic passion and heroic energy. Of the two treatments, Carleton's was the more comic (Thuente 22).

In his Treasury of Irish Poetry, Yeats referred to Irish poets who seek "to express indirectly, through myths and symbols, or directly in little lyrics full of prayers and lamentations, the desire of the soul for spiritual beauty and happiness" (Marcus 259). In 1892, William Butler Yeats and some other Irish writers founded the influential Irish Literary League.

One of the first legendary poems which Yeats wrote was "The Madness of King Goll" (1887). Yeats's father did a picture of Yeats as King Goll to accompany the poem, and in later years Yeats humorously recollects the incident, saying that he wrote for boys and girls of twenty but he was always thinking of myself at that age. This was the age Yeats was when his father painted him as King Goll. Yeats had a very youthful appearance, and he also looked very desirable with his dreamy eyes and his great mass of black hair; nevertheless, no women noticed the picture at the time. The picture hung in the Yeats drawing room throughout his life, and Yeats considered it to be "a pathetic memory of a really dreadful time" (Marcus 242).

Another early legendary poem which Yeats wrote was The Wanderings of Oisin (1887). The principal source for this poem was an eighteenth-century Irish poem attributed to Michael Comyn; however, Yeats greatly reshaped the material and made significant structural alterations. In Comyn's poem, for example, Oisin visited only two places, a Land of Virtues and a Land of Youth, stopping at the former on the way to the latter. Yeats, in contrast, writes about three places: the Island of the Living (which corresponds to Comyn's Land of Youth), the Island of Victories (similar to Comyn's Land of Virtues), and the Island of Forgetfulness. In an 1889 letter to Catherine Tyhnan, Yeats justified this tripartite division: "There are three incompatible things man is always seeking--infinite feeling, infinite battle, infinite repose--hence the three islands" (Marcus 243). Another difference between Comyn's poem and Yeats's poem is that in Comyn's poem Oisin fights a battle with a Fomorian giant, but Yeats turned this giant into a demon of unspecified nationality, thus paving the way for the interpretation of this demon as representing England, with the maiden he holds captive corresponding to Ireland. The dance and the rose are important symbols for Yeats, and both of these symbols are developed in The Wanderings of Oisin. "Dancing constitutes the main activity of the immortal inhabitants of his first island; and in the course of their dancing he had them come to a grove of 'damask roses' which, because they never decay, represent the eternality of life there" (Marcus 247).

In a slim volume named Rosa Alchemica (1897), Yeats developed a special way of exploiting the literary situation by fabricating texts that seem to gratify the sensibility of the nineties but in fact are gentle satires of this period (Helmling 233).   Yeats was also a leader in the founding of the Irish National Literary Society and in 1899, with the performance of Yeats's Cathleen Ni Houlihan, and Martyn's The Heather Field, the Abbey Theatre was founded, and the Irish dramatic movement was thereby launched in Dublin

(Greene 421). It was probably Yeats more than any other Irish author who was responsible for the literary revival in Ireland, though according to Gregory Castle, Yeats credits O'Grady with this distinction. He saw that Ireland was in a dilemma, and in 1892 he wrote in a letter published in United Ireland, "Can we not build up a national literature which shall be none the less Irish in spirit from being English in language?" Yeats was trying to make a "golden bridge" between the old and the New in Ireland (Greene 420-421). In 1909 Yeats wrote in his diary that "Supreme art is a traditional statement of certain heroic and religious truths, passed on from age to age, modified by individual genius, but never abandoned." In an often quoted letter, Yeats said, "Man can embody truth but he cannot know it. You can refute Hegel but not the Saint or the Song of Sixpence" (Clark 7).

In "Adam's Curse" which is part of Yeats's A Vision (1926), there is a shocking discovery that it is not always the author who is in control of the meanings in a poem. In a bitterly comic re-evaluation of the importance of books, Yeats wrote a poem in which targeted lovers get their experiences from books rather than from real life. These lovers would "sigh and quote with learned looks" the things that had happened to other people and were later recounted in "beautiful old books." But now that practice had been revealed as a sham (Helmling 231). Steven Helmling states that the deflating effect of the last line of this poem gives the reader a double vision, and allows a recognition of the possibility of "submitting once cherished notions to the mockery and laughter of a new self." The deflation of the last line is instantaneous, and this is typical of Yeats's poetry. This process occurs so frequently in Yeats's poetry that it's possible to consider this poem as a prototypical paradigm of a comedy that is uniquely Yeatsian in its style and effects. This is a comedy of ironic self-discovery, a comedy where contradiction and inconsistency are rhetorical devices with considerable value and effect (Helmling 231). Helmling calls this comic technique "a comedy of discovery;" however, the "discovery" is never complete or final. It is a discovery of something symbolic. About this type of discovery, Thomas Carlyle said, "In a symbol, there is concealment, yet revelation" (Helmling 232).

Helmling suggests that Yeats became skilled at "uttering the preposterous without fear of contradiction." In fact, Sir Edmund Gosse and Gilbert Murray were unable to respond to Yeats when he suggested that a mutual acquaintance was being followed around by a green elephant (Helmling 233). Although much of the humor in A Vision may be unintentional, Steven Helmling points out that Yeats's naive stance might be part of the humor. This humor is not only perfectly conscious and intentional for Yeats, but in addition, it is a well-conceived and emphatic type of strategic put-on in which the humor suddenly results in a "knowing wink" from Yeats to the reader, and this wink lets the reader in on the joke. Many critics have missed this put-on reading, and Helmling feels that this is an irony which Yeats would have enjoyed (Helmling 236). After reading A Vision, Ezra Pound wrote that when he had been at Rapallo he tried very hard to convince Yeats that he should not publish it. He told Yeats it was rubbish. So what Yeats did was to publish it anyway, and he added a note in the preface saying that Pound considered the piece to be rubbish (Helmling 237).

A Vision is an unacknowledged practical joke, in the tradition of Jonathan Swift's "Discourses," his "Meditations," and his "Proposals." It is also a practical joke in the general tradition of the "Irish Bull." "The joke is on literary critics, whose ginger solicitousness in dealing with the problem of Yeats's beliefs emerge as more and more distinctly risible." Helmling describes A Vision as "heroic," "gay," and "quixotic," "rising ebulliently out of the stony rubbish of the disillusioned postwar wasteland." The implausibility of The Vision "lends intensity to the ferocity of Yeats's witness" (Helmling 243).

A Vision is a strange and ironic blend of the factual with the fictional. It also has both a factual and a fictional author. The factual author is W. B. Yeats. The fictional counterpart is Giraldus, the author of <u>Speculum Angelorum Et Hominum</u>, whose picture is presented in the form of a woodcut. One of Yeats's more "literal-minded" characters notes that this picture bears a strong resemblance to Yeats himself. Of course Yeats is here putting the reader on. According to Steven Helmling, the smile in the woodcut is "inscrutable;" the eyes are "shifty;" and the general visage is "crafty." Furthermore, "his hand is extended towards us, proffering, no doubt, a mystic and revelation-bearing manuscript; his ancient glittering eyes are gay with the assurance that he knows more than we, and always will. He is laughing at us" (Helmling 239).

"The Phases of the Moon" is about two characters named Robartes and Aherne, who stand beneath Yeats's tower, as they look up at his window, which is lit by a lamp. They mock the futility of Yeats's work. "He has found, after the manner of his kind,/ Mere images," sneers Robartes, "and now he seeks in book or manuscript what he shall never find." What Yeats seeks, it is implied, can be found not in books or manuscript in the high tower, but outside, in nature, in experience, on the muddy road where Robartes and Aherne are journeying (Helmling 242).

Yeats not only blurs the boundaries of fact and fiction in his pieces, but he does the same in the prefatory matter. In the Preface to <u>A Vision</u>, Yeats gets into elaborate exchanges, quarrels, commiserations, etc. with his fictional characters. In "Stories of Michael Robartes," Yeats makes "giddy fun" of a number of senex figures (Helmling 241). In the Preface to the 1938 edition of <u>A Vision</u>, there is a "A Packet for Ezra Pound" and "Stories of Michael Robartes and his Friends: An Extract from a Record Made by His Pupils." These sections contain two different accounts of how the manuscript of <u>A Vision</u> came into existence. The reader is supposed to assume that the first account is the truth and the second account is a lie, because the second one is so extravagantly farcical in tone (Helmling 234). "Stories of Michael Robartes" is a "tale-within-a-tale-within-a-tale" in which "narrators enter, succeed one another, and spin yarns within yarns." Daniel O'Leary is the first narrator; he is an excitable character, and is probably a caricature of Yeats himself (Helmling 237). The second narrator is John Bond and the third narrator is Mary Bell. Their stories involve their deception of Mary's husband, an eccentric who has dropped out of the human rat race in order to work for the "redemption of birds." O'Leary believes that this redemption will occur when cuckoos are able to build nests. O'Leary says that he decided to devote his life to the cuckoos, and goes on to say that his great objective was to persuade them to make nests; but for a long time the cuckoos were so obstinate that he almost despaired. But then the birth of a child renewed his resolution (Helmling 238).

The child was the son of his wife, but the child's father was John Bond. The wife, who is determined to sustain her husband's illusions, presents him, on his deathbed, with a counterfeit cuckoo's nest, carefully "crafted after the best scientific knowledge (furnished her by Bond) of what a cuckoo's nest would be like if cuckoos built nests" (Helmling 238). According to Helmling, Yeats's wit is evident as he orchestrates this fable in a way that the reader's attention moves from a bogus bird's nest to a mysterious ivory box from which is produced with appropriate ceremony, "an egg the size of a swan's" (Helmling 239).

"Crazy Jane on the Day of Judgment" is third in a series of twenty five poems called "Words for Music Perha's" in a collection of poems entitled <u>The Winding Stair</u> (1933). Crazy Jane is the speaker of the seven poems in the series (Clark 8). According to Yeats, the character of Crazy Jane is loosely based upon an old lady who lived in a little cottage near Gort in Ireland. This old lady loved flower gardens, and was an eloquent speaker. One of her most memorable performances was a description of how a mean wife of a Gort shopkeeper was so concerned about the price of a glass of wine that she despaired of the human race and drunk. When she did during that druncken spree have achieved "epic magnificence." She is the local satirist and one to be reckoned with (Clark 9). The

Crazy Jane that Yeats is here alluding to was in real life called Cracked Mary. As Yeats presents her, she curses the Bishop; she tells how Jack the Journeyman took her virginity, and how she leaves her door unlatched to him. She tells how her body is like a road for men to pass over, and how she embraces foul as well as fair, because "Love has pitched his mansion in / The place of excrement" (Clark 9).

Steven Helmling feels that "textual flimflam" is an important aspect of Yeats's comedy, and that it is especially prevalent in the middle phase of Yeats's career, "though its roots are discernible in the deliberately contrived ambiguities of Yeats's nineties verse" (Helmling 245). Yeats coined the phrase, "tragic joy." "This is paradox, not antithesis; and we are heightening a paradox, not enforcing an opposition, when we note that if Yeats's joy is tragic, his rage and despair are also comic, a sort of battered kettle at the heel" (Helmling 246).

William Butler Yeats Bibliography

Clark, David R. "That Black Day": The Manuscripts of "Crazy Jane on the Day of Judgement". Portlaoise, Ireland: Dolmen Press, 1980.

Deane, Seamus. "Yeats and the Idea of Revolution," and "O'Casey and Yeats: Exemplary Dramatists." Celtic Revivals: Essays in Modern Irish Literature--Joyce, Yeats, O'Casey, Kinsella, Montague, Friel, Mahon, Heaney, Beckett, Synge. Winston-Salem, NC: Wake Forest University Press, 1985, 38-50, and 108-122.

Forrester, Arthur M. An Irish Crazy-Quilt: Smiles and Tears, Woven into Song and Story. Boston, MA: A. Mudge and Son, 1891.

Greene, David H. "IRELAND: Literature." The Encyclopedia Americana: International Edition. Danbury, CT: Americana Corporation, 1978, 420-423.

Helmling, Steven. "Yeats's Esoteric Comedy." The Hudson Review 30 (1977): 230-246.

Lentricchia, Frank. The Gaiety of Language: An Essay on the Radical Poetics of W. B. Yeats and Wallace Stevens. Berkeley, CA: University of California Press, 1968.

Marcus, Phillip L. Yeats and the Beginning of the Irish Renaissance. Ithaca, NY: Cornell University Press, 1970.

Thuente, Mary Helen. W. B. Yeats and Irish Folklore. Totowa, NJ: Gill and Macmillan/Barnes and Noble, 1980.

Ussher, Arland. Three Great Irishmen: Shaw, Yeats, Joyce. New York, NY: Devin-Adair, 1953.

Yeats, William Butler, ed. Fairy and Folk Tales of the Irish Peasantry. London, England: Walter Scott, 1888.

Seumus MacManus (1869-1960) IRELAND

Seumus MacManus is one of the legendary Irish Seanchai, or story tellers; he is much beloved throughout the twentieth century. His Story of the Irish Race (1921) is an excellent example of his story telling technique.

Seumus MacManus Bibliography

MacManus, Seamus. The Story of the Irish Race: A Popular History of Ireland. Old Greenwich, CT: Devin-Adair, 1921.

John Millington Synge (1871-1909) IRELAND

David Greene says that the astringent realism and satire in John Synge's plays made him a persona non grata among a generation of extreme Irish nationalists both in Ireland and abroad (Greene 422). Nevertheless, John Synge cursed the English language, a language in which a man cannot swear without being vulgar (Reid 80). Although Synge was a turn-of-the-century writer, Ann Saddlemyer says that his insistence on "the worms and the clay," his restoration of "personal humor," his "general wit," and his transcendence of naturalism into the realm of the absurd places him squarely in the twentieth century (Saddlemyer 31).

C. S. Faulk considers John Synge's vision to be mythic, paradoxical, and romantic. "Synge's gift is catalytic rather than static, and his dramatic image, like Shakespeare's, is frequently mock-ritualistic, sometimes in so serious a way that irony disappears momentarily into ritual again" (Faulk 432). Faulk agrees with Herbert Howarth who claimed that it was Synge rather than Yeats who changed the direction of the Irish Renaissance (Faulk 433). Yet it was Yeats who gave Synge the important advice, "Give up Paris. Go to the Aran Islands." Synge did go to the Aran Islands, and it was there that he developed an interest in Gaelic speech and folklore that was romantic, but only paradoxically so.

> It was directly romantic, perhaps partly in a modern way, but also in a way very close to the spirit of the early romantic movement. Synge was thrilled by what seemed to him an almost Elizabethan richness in Gaelic speech and literature, a quality which made it possible to unite the colloquial and the poetic in dramatic dialogue. (Faulk 434)

In the Gaelic lore of the Aran Islanders Synge found an unselfconscious stoicism, but he found more. In addition to the strength and endurance of the Aran Islanders he found "gaiety, raciness, elasticity of imagination, physical and moral nerve, astonishing innocence, and a powerful weather of temperament, genuinely attuned to the elemental world of rocks and stones and ocean" (Faulk 434).

Synge noted the brutal aspects of Irish culture, but he associated them not with pity, but with reality and joy. He associated them with the goat presiding over an Irish fair, and with a deity manifesting carnal desires, and with the excitement of lust and rage and the sudden blow. According to Faulk, one of the functions of Synge's comedy is to exorcise pity (Faulk 435). A very important characteristic to be found in Gaelic literature, folklore, and folk culture is the uninhibited, primitive, archaic play spirit.

> This spirit grows out of the Gaelic failure to distinguish between the natural and the supernatural, the trickster and the magician. It informs the artistry of Aran Islands story-tellers, whose stories, even those accepted as literally true, were stylized, but given a special quality by the fluctuation between credulity and skepticism which characterized the narrator and the audience alike. (Faulk 437)

Faulk notes that something very like the archaic play spirit was a vitalizing element in English Elizabethan drama, especially in the plays of Shakespeare, but he also notes that it disappeared almost completely after the seventeenth century, and that it was Synge and other Irish playwrights who reestablished it (Faulk 437).

> Synge was one of the first modern writers to really understand the value of archaism--its mocking, lyrical laughter, its almost impersonal grief, or its free embroidery of wishful thinking--as a transient, irresponsible, but genuine relief from the refined, isolated, madly sensitive personality frequently cultivated in and by romantic art. (Faulk 438)

Faulk talks about what he calls the "masks of Dionysus" that appear in Synge's writing.

These masks are a threat to order and purpose, but they are a source of joy, and they can be found in "the parricide; the roaring, drunken tyrannous father; the widow who has destroyed her man; the beggars who will to be blind; the tinkers who see the beasts of the field as the best models for human life; the vagrant who wins an attractive woman from the man of property who probably could not have loved her even in his youth." These are the comic masks of Dionysus (Faulk 439).

Ann Saddlemyer notes that the language of In the Shadow of the Glen (1903) came from the servant girls in the kitchen by way of some fortuitous chinks in John Synge's bedroom floor. Synge claimed that his writing is mild compared with the wild language and ideas in the kitchen below, or compared with "the fancies one may hear on any little hillside cabin in Geesala, or Carraroe, or Dingle Bay" (Saddlemyer 9).

James Pierce notes that In the Shadow of the Glen is neither a comedy nor a tragedy, but rather a combination of both. The comic elements are not fully exploited in the present and the tragic elements are projected into the future after the curtain has fallen (Pierce 129). In the Shadow of the Glen, like Playboy of the Western World to follow, tells of the "resurrection" of a dead man. In this case the husband is only pretending to be dead in order to cheat his wife into admitting her infidelity. Nora, the wife, is affected by her gloomy environment, by the dreariness and drudgery of her life in the glen. It is her husband, Dan, who counterfeits death, but it is Nora who suddenly realizes that "he has been dead all the time." Dan's resurrection is dramatic irony, but it is another kind of epiphany as well, as Nora realizes the grimness and absurdity of the situation. As Dan rises from the dead, Nora says to her prospective lover, "You'll be sitting up in your bed--the way himself was sitting . . . . It's a pitiful thing to be getting old, but it's a queer thing surely . . . . It's a queer thing to see an old man sitting up there in his bed, with no teeth on him and a rough word in his mouth" (LeBlanc 53).

In The Well of the Saints (1905), a saint restores Martin Doul's eye sight; however, the gift of sight proves more painful than the affliction of blindness. Doul's first error when he regains his sight is to mistake the pretty Molly Byrne for Mary, his ugly and deformed wife (Orr 49).

In Synge's The Playboy of the Western World (1907) joy springs from the sheer exuberance of creation embodied in Christy Mahon, the emerging hero (Waters 90). Christy is a "comic hero" who confronts his own tyrannical father and literally overturns him to win his own autonomy, freedom, and manhood (Waters 8). Maureen Waters suggests that The Playboy is a "comic version of the oedipal theme." If he is to become a man, Christy must do more than rebel against his father; he must "slay him symbolically and ritualistically" (Waters 68-69). And in "slaying" his father, Christy becomes a comic hero.

> Given the dreary lives of the people of Mayo, bound fast by poverty, custom and religion, it is little wonder that they are attracted by a man who has committed a violent and revolutionary act. The fantastical and the unexpected had occurred, and Christy is hailed as a heroic and, above all, a manly figure. As an outlaw he enjoys celebrity as well as protection from the police. He represents freedom and energy; he is a man who might well revitalize a community in which chastity is the highest virtue and the wake a central ritual. (Waters 70)

The two controlling images of The Playboy are death and resurrection. These are also the two controlling images of the Irish wake.

> Until well into the nineteenth century funeral games, including kissing and mock marriages, evidently originating in obscure rites of fertility, were an essential feature of the keen or ritual crying of the mourners. In The Playboy, therefore, it is not surprising that activity shifts back and forth

between the courting of Pegeen and Kate Cassidy's wake. (Waters 70)

Christy Mahon is a comic hero, but he is also related to the "poet-fool," an archetype in twelfth-century Ireland, and to the "playboy" an archetype of eighteenth-century Ireland. Both of these archetypes are calculating in their donning of the comic mask. Seeing himself through the eyes of his new adoring audience, Christy begins to understand that he has a new position in society. He is gradually transformed from a country fool into a comic hero. As he responds to the demands of the Mayo people, he is given to greater and greater leaps of imagination and daring.

> The bare story of his one single blow: "I just riz the loy and let fall the edge of it on the ridge of his skull." increases in drama and savage detail: "He gave a drive with the scythe, and I gave a lep to the east. Then I turned around with my back to the north, and I hit a blow on the ridge of his skull, laid him stretched out, and he split to the knob of his gullet." With a little more encouragement, he achieves mythic proportions as "a gallant orphan cleft his father with one blow to the breeches belt." (Waters 72)

But Christy's father is a very vital person, who springs to life again and again, and who makes his own version of the assault rather profitable by retelling the story to anyone who will listen, in return for a few drinks or a night's lodging. Christy's father is not only not destroyed, he is not even defeated. He accepts his new role, in the spirit of play, and uses his own "death" for his own purposes (Faulk 441). Old Mahon's image is by turns "archaically titanic, grotesquely profane, enraging, pathetic, awesomely and hilariously resilient, and finally, benign" (Faulk 442).

When Christy's father "returns from the dead," Christy is "nearly speechless with rage." He curses his father for not having died as he was supposed to.

> To be letting on he was dead, and coming back to his life, and following me like an old weasel tracing a rat, and coming in here laying desolation between my own self and the fine women of Ireland, and he a kind of carcass that you'd fling upon the sea . . . . May I meet him with one tooth and it aching, and one eye to be seeing seven and seventy divils in the twists of the road, and one old timber leg on him to limp into the scalding grave. (Pierce 127)

Christy and his father's mutual ability to produce a macabre story emphasizes the similarity between father and son. Both are rogues; and both are imaginative and resilient comic figures (Waters 77).

Although Christy is a peasant and a comic figure, he is a hero as well, because he has challenged all comers and defended his new concept of himself. "One begins by laughing at him, as one laughs at the earlier clowns, but is eventually won over to his point of view. Christy's gift for language, which always tends to be comical in its extravagance, recalls the other prodigious talker, Denis O'Shaughnessy." Waters notes that there is a "dramatic correlation between Christy's development as a poet-hero and his growing mastery of language" (Waters 72). The language in The Playboy is not English, but is Gaelic-English--a language which is more flexible, more expressive, and more potent in its rhythm than is English. "It is language remarkable for its flights of extravagant fancy, its metaphor and its economic phrasing, its use of images which are strange to the modern sensibility because they reflect the remote, primitive life of the people of Connemara" (Waters 73-74). C. S. Faulk argues that in general Synge's sympathetic characters are not fully creative artists or symbols of aestheticism. "although they respond to language, and they know or learn how to use it in exciting or funny or touching ways, they use it as a weapon against unpalatable facts, not for art's sake" (Faulk 444).

In the final scene, Christy is denounced as a liar, and there is an attempt to force him back into his earlier role of idiot and fool. But by this time Christy has discovered his own powers, and he can subdue his father and leave the community behind, "denouncing them in turn as 'the fools' of Mayo." Such a situation is consistent with a common theme of many primitive cultures whereby the madman comes to be regarded as the visionary (Waters 78).

James Pierce notes that most critics have treated Christy Mahon as a bona fide hero in a comic romance, or as a mock hero in a comic farce. Pierce, however, feels that Mahon is an anti-hero, and he considers The Playboy to be a tragicomedy.

> What seems to develop along the traditional lines of comedy concludes in a manner quite opposite of comedy: rather than the expected marriage of comic hero and heroine and the unification of society, there is estrangement, and, although youth does triumph over age, the effect of this triumph is hardly comic unity. (Pierce 122)

Pierce considers Synge's view to be neither comic nor tragic, but rather tragi-comic, or ironic. But in order to see the play as ironic, there needs to be a point of reference, or what Pierce calls a touchstone. Pierce points out that Synge provides such a touchstone in his other ironic plays. Nora is the touchstone in The Shadow of the Glen (1903); Maurya is the touchstone in Riders to the Sea (1904); Mary Doul is the touchstone in The Well of the Saints (1905); Deirdre is the touchstone in Deirdre of the Sorrows (1910). and Mary Byrne is the touchstone in The Tinker's Wedding (1911). Pierce feels that it is the Widow Quin who is the touchstone in Playboy of the Western World (1907). Pierce sees the Widow Quin as an "ironic backdrop" to the play against which all other of the play's points-of-view are shown to be incomplete, and without which the play is a hopelessly enigmatic puzzle, since contradiction is a central theme in the play. Most critics see the Widow Quin as a delightfully comic old schemer, a "parody of the wise old woman figure with her greater knowledge of the situation and her shrewd sense of how to handle it for her own ultimate benefit" (Pierce 123). The Widow Quin is more however. She is more aware than any other character in the novel of the boundary between fact and fancy. "The Widow Quin, the only realist in this Mayo community, serves as the touchstone of the play, the only reliable commentator on The Playboy world" (Pierce 124). Since they provide the landmark against which all other observations are measured, the Widow Quin's cynically comic observations serve to establish the ironic course and tone of the play. Everyone else is awed by Christy Mahon's killing of his father, but the Widow Quin displays only "warmly humorous curiosity." This immediately separates her from the other, more easily impressed characters in the play. Synge says that the Widow Quin sizes Christy up immediately for what he is: "looking at him with half-amused curiosity," and then she says, "Well, aren't you a little smiling fellow? It should have been great and bitter torments did rouse your spirits to a deed of blood . . . . It'd soften my heart to see you sitting so simple with your cup and cake, and you fitter to be saying your catechism than slaying your da." In this short scene, the Widow Quin sizes up Christy just by looking at him. She also warns that Pegeen, with her bad temper and her sharp tongue, would be tongue-lashing Christy within a week (Pierce 125).   According to Pierce, the Widow Quin turns out to be right about everything and everyone in Mayo. "She knows the immature, flighty, headstrong kind of girl Pegeen is. She immediately recognizes the not particularly heroic, but quite human qualities of Christy. And, though she never complains of it, she seems quite aware of the potential cruelty of the Mayo people." The Widow Quin displays a mild and sympathetic humor. She often teases, but not cruelly. The Widow Quin is "the only one among the villagers who is not fascinated by the cruelty of others" (Pierce 126).

Most critics see Pegeen Mike and the Widow Quin to be antithetical characters; however Pierce suggests that these two characters have much more in common than not. Pegeen is about twenty years of age, and the Widow Quin is only about ten years older. "This single difference, and the difference in experience and awareness that it implies, forms the basis of their personality differences--namely that Pegeen is youthfully and sometimes cruelly impetuous, whereas the Widow is patiently and sympathetically mature." Furthermore, Pegeen Mike and the Widow Quin are "the liveliest and most personally demanding women in the village. They demand more of life than any man in Mayo can provide." Also, both Pegeen Mike and the Widow Quin are attracted to Christy Mahon (Pierce 131-132). Furthermore, Pegeen is growing up fast. When she observes the actual murder of Christy Mahon's father, she says, "there's a great gap between a gallous story and a dirty deed" (Pierce 132). Pierce sees Pegeen as a younger version of the Widow Quin (Pierce 131).

Pierce considers Synge to be at his ironic best in Playboy of the Western World but this is true only if we see the play through the eyes of the Widow Quin.

> We not only can, but must accept the existence of seemingly contradictory interpretations. Christy has lived up to the romantic ideals of the western world--and he is therefore a hero. Yet in terms of the play's broader perspective, the ideals of the western world are empty fantasies, not worth living up to--and he is therefore not a hero. (Pierce 133)

The other characters in the novel don't fully recognize the shallowness of the heroic ideal.

> Only the Widow Quin seems fully aware, and her tragic "moment" has already passed, since she has rejected the shallow fantasies of this falsely romantic world even before the start of the play. Moreover, the overriding tone of the Widow Quin's presentation is not tragic but satirically comic, just as the overriding structure of the play is not that of tragedy but of ironic romance. (Pierce 133)

In his Preface to The Tinker's Wedding (1911), Synge admitted that the object of the play was "to laugh at the country people, albeit without malice" (Saddlemyer 9). There is a divided vision of reality in The Tinker's Wedding. Synge assumes the traditional stance of a satirist as he considers the established social and moral order from a point of view that obeys and establishes its own code of values (Leblanc 55). Gérard Leblanc says that at the end of Synge's plays, his heroes, tramps, tinkers, vagrants, and playboys all leave the stage "confident in the merits and potentialities of their own outlook." The same is true of his sympathetic figures which represent the establishment. At the end of The Tinker's Wedding for example there is the following stage direction, "They rush out leaving the Priest master of the situation" (Leblanc 51).

John Synge had a love for and an understanding of Ireland, but his vision was more than a local one. It is ironic that "the very man whom debate kept pushing into a tight Irish corner was in fact the first of the playwrights to achieve a European reputation. During his lifetime, Synge's plays were translated and produced on the continent, and discussed as far away as Australia" (Saddlemyer 10).

John Millington Synge Bibliography

Bessia, Diane E. "Little Hand in Mayo: Synge's Playboy and the Comic Tradition in Irish Literature." Dalhousie Review 48 (1968): 372-383.

Deane, Seamus. "Synge and Heroism." Celtic Revivals: Essays in Modern Irish Literature--Joyce, Yeats, O'Casey, Kinsella, Montague, Friel, Mahon, Heaney, Beckett, Synge. Winston-Salem, NC: Wake Forest University Press, 1985, 51-62.

Faulk, C. S. "John Millington Synge and the Rebirth of Comedy." Southern Humanities Review 8 (1974): 431-448.

Greene, David H. "IRELAND: Literature." The Encyclopedia Americana: International Edition. Danbury, CT: Americana Corporation, 1978, 420-423.

Leblanc, Gérard. "Ironic Reversal as Theme and Technique in Synge's Shorter Comedies."
    Aspects of the Irish Theatre. Eds. Patrick Rafroidi, Raymonde Popot, and William
    Parker. Paris, France: Eds. Universitaires, 1972, 51-63.
Orr, John. Tragicomedy and Contemporary Culture: Play and Performance from Beckett
    to Shepard. Ann Arbor, MI: University of Michigan Press, 1991.
Pierce, James C. "Synge's Widow Quin: Touchstone to the Playboy's Irony." Éire-Ireland
    16.2 (1981): 122-133.
Reid, Alec. "Comedy in Synge and Beckett." Yeats Studies 2 (1972): 80-90.
Saddlemyer, Ann. J. M. Synge and Modern Comedy. Dublin, Ireland: Dolmen, 1968.
Waters, Maureen. The Comic Irishman Albany, NY: State University of New York Press,
    1984.

CHAPTER 7

Humor in 20th Century
Irish Literature: Mid Authors

Sean O'Casey (1880-1964) IRELAND

Maureen Waters says that Sean O'Casey's world is filled with shrews, eccentrics, boozers, parasites, and other clowns representing "a rag-tag assembly scraped from the very bottom of the refuse pits of Dublin." Waters feels that the most memorable of these clowns are Fluther Good in The Plough and the Stars, and Captain Jack Boyle in June and the Paycock (Waters 151).

In a book entitled, O'Casey's Satiric Vision, B. L. Smith notes that Sean O'Casey wrote twenty-two satiric plays. These are divided into four categories. The first category is the "Irish Plays," which include The Shadow of a Gunman (1923), Juno and the Paycock (1924), and The Plough and the Stars (1926). The second category for Smith is the "Colored Plays," including The Silver Tassie (1928), Within the Gates (1933), Purple Dust (1940), and Red Roses for Me (1944). Smith entitles his third category of O'Casey satire as "Finale and Encore," and lists among others Oak Leaves and Lavender: A Warld on Wallpaper (1947), Cock-a-Doodle Dandy (1949), The Bishop's Bonfire (1955), and The Drums of Father Ned: A Mickrocosm of Ireland (1960). Smith's fourth category is named "Encore," and includes Behind the Green Curtains (1961), Figuro in the Night (1961), and The Moon Shines on Kylenamoe (1961) (Smith vii-viii). Smith feels that it is the satire which gives both continuity and unity to the kaleidoscopic variety of O'Casey's work. He also feels that the satire ranges from incidental, as in The Shadow of a Gunman, to a sustained satiric barrage, as in The Bishop's Bonfire and Behind the Green Curtains.

> O'Casey's first three major plays (The Shadow of a Gunman, Juno and the Paycock, and The Plough and the Stars) are called tragedies; his next is experimental tragicomedy (The Silver Tassie); then, he enters the morality play world (Within the Gates, The Star Turns Red) which gives way to the frankly fantastic (Red Roses for Me, Purple Dust, and Cock-a-Doodle Dandy). (Smith 3)

According to Smith, O'Casey's satire is developmental, and doesn't emerge as fully developed until the end of O'Casey's transitional period (Smith 3). O'Casey's satiric targets were traditional establishment figures representing the Church, Business, and Politics, but O'Casey's satire was not hostile. His satiric vision included plenty of room for joy and laughter, and for having a good time, and loving life in the process (Smith 3). O'Casey's villainous targets tend to be general rather than specific. They are "businessmen, quarrelsome Irishmen, newly powerful politicians, officers of the church, army personnel."

In other words, they are "all those who would (by choice or through ignorance) halt change or deny the joys of life to the living" (Smith 6-7). "It is not necessary to wear a uniform to be a villain, but virtually all of O'Casey's evil men do wear either clerical, political, or military uniforms. O'Casey's satire juxtaposes the good and the evil components of his comic world" (Smith 175). For O'Casey's villains, laughter is allowed only if the target of the laughter is the foibles of the common man. The laughter is frowned on and thought to be unseemly when it makes fun of superstitions, creeds, or customs (Smith 182).

Smith suggests that as O'Casey's plays become progressively more satiric, the settings become progressively more universal. "By the last period, each setting (however specific) is macrocosmic; each character type (however Irish) is representative of some aspect of mankind, and the poet's satiric weapons (however destructive) are directed toward the improvement of the comic world he portrays" (Smith 175). O'Casey's characters sprang out of the grim slum settings of national and social deprivation and misery. They lived in constant contact with dire poverty, chronic illness, futile revolt, insanity, and violent death, extreme elements that could easily have made for pathetic oversentimental melodrama, but which O'Casey turned into tragi-comedy. Such an environment made for the easy development of mock heroic characters (White 288).

The targets of O'Casey's satires were the man-made evils of the world, evils which were caused by men, and could only be cured by men. These targets ranged from the repressive religionists like Farther Domineer, Purple Priest, and Bishop Malarkey, through repressive militarists like Kian, which, by the way, is an anagram for Cain. Hitler and his fascists were another target, as were the Auxiliaries and the Black and Tans and the argumentative civilian populace. Even good men who have lost their way like Sailor Mahan and Manus Moanroe are targets. And interspersed among these targets are to be found "the antics of the delightful Fluther Goods, Joxer Dalys, and Angela Nightingales" (Smith 12). It is interesting to note that O'Casey's satiric portraits of inadequate fathers are similar whether these fathers are earthly fathers or fathers of the church. In both cases the targets are shown to be "selfish, arbitrary, domineering, and essentially unaware of what their children really need" (Smith 177).

O'Casey's satire suggests that it is man himself who has created dystopia here on earth, and it will have to be man himself who deals with it. Jack Boyle is constantly talking about the "chassis" (crisis) of the universe, and Juno exclaims "Ah, what can God do agen the stupidity o' men?" The answers to Juno's question "vary from the drunkenness and joy of Joxer Daly and Jack Boyle (Juno and the Paycock) to the political involvements of Ayamonn Breydon and Red Jim (Red Roses for Me and Star Turns Red) to the dancing and cavorting of the Cock and Maid Marion (Cock-a-Doodle Dandy)" (Smith 5). In The Silver Tassie Harry Heegan says, "The Lord hath given and man hath taken away." This is an echo of Juno's "Ah, what can God do agen the stupidity o' men?" (Smith 7). O'Casey's target, from his earliest to his latest satire, is mankind. "In O'Casey's vision, organized religion, nationalistic organizations, and politics are all mad games played by mad men" (Smith 7). As a satirist, O'Casey uses laughter as a weapon against all who would destroy social order for selfish gains and all who would perpetuate the chaos of social disorder for personal profit." O'Casey, as a man, viewed laughter as a weapon against evil surely, but also as "wine for the soul" (Smith 15). "The more insistent a character is that his view is clear and that his answer is right, the more ridiculous and potentially dangerous he is. In O'Casey's world, hollow poses and empty façades, like hollow statues and empty promises, are to be laughed at rather than adored--ridiculed rather than endured" (Smith 180-181).

It is interesting to note that O'Casey's characters are often identified by the clothes they wear.

His priests, soldiers, and successful businessmen are suitably costumed.

Whenever a character takes himself too seriously or assumes the symbolic value of his costume to be overly impressive, he is comic. Hence, the soldiers who hide their fears behind the gaudy costumes of the Foresters and the Irish Citizens Army (Plough and the Stars) are as foolish as those who wear the formal attire and the top hat of the DeValerian politician (Cock-a-Doodle Dandy, Bishop's Bonfire, Drums of Father Ned, etc.). O'Casey bitterly satirizes the wearers of Trilby hats and bowlers as reflectors of and worshippers of public opinion, as a sick society's leaders, and as its touchstones of success (Within the Gates, Cock-a-Doodle Dandy, Behind the Green Curtains, etc.). (Smith 178)

There are characters in Cock-a-Doodle Dandy and The Drums of Father Ned which transform the world, and they are appropriately dressed in brilliantly colored costumes. These characters use paint, flowers, song, and magic to dress up the drab world. The goodness of the Brown Priest is also symbolized by the color of his habit, and is contrasted with the colorful habit of the materialistic and very powerful Purple Priest (Smith 179). Sean O'Casey himself chose to wear laborer's clothes, and this choice earned him much criticism from other members of the Gaelic League, because he attended their meetings "untidily dressed, and was once asked to wait outside as he was not suitably clad to appear before the Dean of St. Patrick's." B. L. Smith indicates that O'Casey brought a new audience to the Abbey Theatre in Dublin, an audience that was "more concerned with seeing than with being seen" (Smith 179).

E. H. Mikhail and John O'Riordan's The Sting and the Twinkle contains fifty-four interviews about Sean O'Casey. Joseph Stein's interview was entitled, " 'It Was Fun,' said Sean O'Casey" (86-89), and Donal Foley's interview was entitled, "O'Casey Out to Make them Laugh" (90-91). The title of the anthology represents O'Casey's bitter-sweet nature, waspish at times, and dove-like at other times; the title comes from an interview with W. J. Weatherby entitled, "The Sting and the Twinkle" (Mikhail and O'Riordan viii, 2). The tragicomic muse is evident throughout these interviews, as it is in other biographies of O'Casey, with such titles as The Flying Wasp (1937), The Green Crow (1956), Under a Colored Cap (1963), and Blasts and Benedictions (1967). On the evening of a major production of a new play or at the launching of a special festival of a group of his best-known plays, he was frequently in a hilarious mood, and he would sometimes regale his astonished audience with a rousing, "roysterin' " song. Mikhail and O'Riordan note that O'Casey's stage characters "are endowed with the same sonorous accomplishments; they break into song when the audience least imagines" (Mikhail and O'Riordan 3).

Many O'Casey critics consider him to have been narrow and bitter; however Jac MacGowran, who played major roles in some of his later plays said, "He was a wonderfully expansive man to talk to, full of good humour. Within half an hour of your meeting him, he would want to sing ballads. He wanted to create joy and be surrounded by joy. He used his plays as a platform for his belief and never gave up until the end of his days." Denis Johnston said, "he was a very good mimic, acting out the stories he told you. He was really Joxer Daly." After reading The Silver Tassie (1928), O'Casey's great anti-war play, George Bernard Shaw told O'Casey he was a "Titan," but then he went on to add, "You really are a ruthless ironfisted blaster and blighter of your species!" (Mikhail and O'Riordan 4-5).

When asked why he left Ireland, O'Casey responded as follows: "I have a good deal of courage, but not much patience, and it takes both courage and patience to live in Ireland. The Irish have no time for those that don't agree with their ideas, and I have no time for those who don't agree with mine. So we decided to compromise, and I am coming here [Devon, England]" (Mikhail and O'Riordan 5).

Although many Irish writers react against the stereotype of the comic Irishman, Sean

O'Casey and Brendan Behan both exploited the stereotype.

> O'Casey's characters are entertaining precisely because of their colorful rhetoric, their outrageous postures, and the song and dance routines from the music hall, but they are the maimed survivors of economic and social breakdown, retreating behind a verbal screen and refusing to come to terms with the demands of the world around them. (Waters 93)

Maureen Waters says that O'Casey is a satirist who uses colorful Dublin slang to puncture the romantic concept of Ireland with its mystique of war (Waters 93).

In The Shadow of a Gunman (1923), Mr. Gallagher's attempts at eloquence always gets him into such knots as "my unvarnished respectability. Consider also the following dialogue from the same play.

> MRS. HENDERSON: Them words is true, Mr. Gallicker, and they aren't.
> For to be wise is to be a fool, an' to be a fool is to be wise.
>
> MR. GALLAGER: (with deprecating tolerance). Oh, Mrs. Henderson,
> That's a parrotox.
>
> MRS. HENDERSON: It may be what a parrot talks, or a blackbird, or for
> the matter of that, a liar--but it's what Julia Henderson thinks . . . ."
> (White 286).

Another comic device which O'Casey uses in The Shadow of a Gunman is the logical fallacy, as in the following anachronistic non-sequitur: "Upon my soul! I'm beginnin' to believe that the Irish People are still in the stone age. If they could they'd throw a bomb at you" (White 287).

Sean O'Casey had a tragicomic talent whereby he was able to combine realism with humor even in his earliest plays--The Shadow of a Gunman (1923), Juno and the Paycock (1924), and The Plough and the Stars (1926). These plays were very successful. Many critics believe, however, that these plays are "fumbling efforts, made memorable by extraordinary language and characterization" (Coakley and Felheim 265). Maureen Waters suggests that O'Casey's two best plays, Juno and the Paycock, and the Plough and the Stars are the ones most fashioned by his own harsh experience, including his association with the labor movement, the Gaelic League, and the Irish Citizen Army (Waters 147). In these plays, the language bristles with aggressiveness. "It has a needling, restless quality, intended to prick, to deflate, to keep the listener slightly off balance. The sheer love of invective is carried to far greater extremes by O'Casey than by any of the other Irish writers" (Waters 150).

In The Silver Tassie, O'Casey began to use the symbolization that was so much more characteristic of his later plays. James Coakley and Marvin Felheim, however, suggest that the symbolization process started earlier, in 1924, with the publication of Juno and the Paycock, and they substantiate this claim by suggesting that this play is written in the tradition of Plautus's classical theatre. They note, for example that both Plautus and O'Casey were writing for audiences familiar with war, "hence, the subject of war, long borne, could become, and was, both ludicrous and searing." "As the Dubliners of O'Casey's day were to the British, so Plautus's Romans were to the Greeks." The urban setting of Athens was for Plautus what the Urban setting of Dublin was for O'Casey (Coakley and Felheim 265). Consider also the classical allusion in the title of O'Casey's play: Juno and the Paycock. "The obvious allusion to the Queen of the Gods, traditionally surrounded by peacocks, firmly plants the central symbol of the play's action. Yet O'Casey, in mock heroic fashion, distorts the legend by surrounding his Juno with a peacock neither noble nor beautiful, but vain and bibulous" (Coakley and Felheim 266).

The gods of Mount Olympus are also represented in Juno and the Paycock. Charles Bentham, the antagonist, is a satiric representation of the snooty, and presumptuous Englishman.

Bentham proclaims his beliefs in the Prawna, "the vital force in man." At once, however, the sceptical Boyle debunks all religions, all gods, insisting that the Irish people "know more about Charlie Chaplin an' Tommy Mix." The gods, then, are present in Juno. And O'Casey's characters will deride them often, yet turn to them in fervent appeal when all else has failed. (Coakley and Felheim 266-267).

Charley Bentham is a "stage Englishman," but he is also a cad. He seduces Mary Boyle and then he abandons her. When Mary says, "My poor little child that'll have no father!" Mrs. Boyle responds, "It'll have what's far betther--it'll have two mothers" (Waters 157).

In Juno and the Paycock there is also a saturnalian juxtaposition of tragedy and comedy. In Act II, the Boyles are celebrating their financial expectations by decorating their tenement room with new furniture--including a gramophone, as they entertain Mr. Bentham, Mary's fiancé. They are joined by Joxer Daly and by Mrs. Madigan, and there is a great deal of singing and drinking. One type of humor which O'Casey uses involves having his characters go into long tirades of irrelevant detail. When Mrs. Madigan is presented to Mr. Bentham, Mary's boyfriend, for example, she responds as follows:

"An' I'm goin' to tell you, Mr. Bentham, you're goin' to get as nice a bit o' skirt in Mary, there, as ever you seen in your puff . . . . I remember, as well as I remember yestherday, the day she was born--of a Tuesday, the 25th o' June, in the year 1901, at thirty-three minutes past wan in the day be Foley's clock, the pub at the corner o' the street." (White 286-287)

And on she goes.

Another comic device which O'Casey uses is the recurring expression to identify a particular character. For example, Joxer Daly seems to have only one adjective--"darlin'," and he therefore talks about "a darlin' song, a darlin' song," and about "a darlin' word, a darlin' word." Joxer also does strange things to proverbs and other folk expressions. "For want of a nail the shoe was lost, for want of a shoe the horse was lost, an' for want of a horse the man was lost--aw, that's a darlin' proverb, a darlin' proverb" (White 288). Joxer also has the chameleon ability to switch his opinion whenever such a switch is to his advantage:

BOYLE: Father Farrell stopped me to-day an' tole me how glad he was I fell in for the money.

JOXER: He'll be stoppin' you often enough now; I suppose it was "Mr." Boyle with him?

BOYLE: You're seldom asthray, Joxer, but you're wrong shipped this time. What you're sayin' of Father Farrell is very near to blasfeemey. I don't like any one to talk disrespectful of Father Farrell.

JOXER: You're takin' me up wrong, Captain; I wouldn't let a word be said agen Father Farrell--the heart o' the rowl, that's what he is; I always said he was a darlin' man, a darlin' man. (White 288)

Still another O'Casey comic technique is inflated language. Captain Boyle talks about sailing from the Gulf of Mexico to the Antarctic Ocean, and about seeing things "that no mortal man should speak about that knows his Catechism," but Juno responds to Jack Boyle's calling himself a captain: "Everybody callin' you 'Captain,' an' you only wants on the wather, in an oul' collier from here to Liverpool, when anybody, to listen or look at you, ud take you for a second Christo For Columbus" (White 287).

Captain Boyle's comic reversals as he tries to outwit his wife provide much of the farcical humor of Juno and the Paycock.

He is so obviously irresponsible and self-indulgent in his maneuvers to avoid work. For all his talk of mastery and adventure, he is the universal guilty husband trying to cope with a strong minded wife. His attempts to outwit her are utterly transparent, but as quickly as she corners him, he slips away under cover of an even more preposterous story . . . . Boyle's avowals, denials, pleas, alibis are delivered with an irritable air of self importance. Like the comic figures before him, he is a grand talker. (Waters 155)

However, this joyous scene is interrupted by the Tancred funeral party, which passes down the stairs just outside of Boyle's living room. This is a very ironic and dramatic blending of comedy and tragedy. Of course the Boyles are too concerned in their own joys to waste time in sympathy for Mrs. Tancred, so they return to their celebration.

This revelry is now interrupted by "Needle" Nugent, the tailor, who reminds them of the funeral procession passing by. The record, "If you're Irish, come into the Parlour," gives way to a sacred tune, which drifts up from the street. Surely this is the essence of Saturnalia: the intermingling of religious feeling and secular excitement. the final irony is supplied by the entrance of a young man who brings the message of retribution to Johnny Boyle--"No man can do enough for Ireland!" (Coakley and Felheim 268)

O'Casey does here what the Greeks had done earlier. He juxtaposed war with religion in a modern rendition of the rites of Saturn. There is a similar saturnalian juxtaposition at the end of the play. The Boyles have lost all hope for their inheritance, and in fact have accumulated additional debts. Mrs. Boyles is trying to hold back her tears over the death of her son, Johnny, while at the same time trying to think about a future of caring for her pregnant but unwed daughter. In contrast, Captain Boyle, the paycock, is completely indifferent to these tragic details, as he drinks with his buddy Joxer Daly, both of them mouthing a variety of useless proverbs, and thus reducing the situation to comic absurdity (Coakley and Felheim 268). O'Casey has a penchant for burlesques and a willingness to reduce his villainous straw men to absurdity and to endow them not with dialogue but with poisonous platitudes offset by his equal willingness to reduce his heroes to absurdity by utilizing essentially the same technique. (Smith 175)

Juno and the Paycock is not just an allusion to classical Greek life and letters; it is a parody allusion. Mr. Boyle doesn't have the beauty or the grace of a real peacock. And the allusion to the Greek goddess in Juno's name is also a bit far-fetched, as Mr. Boyle explains: "Juno was born an' christened in June; I met her in June; we were married in June, an' Johnny was born in June, so wan day I says to her, You should ha' been called Juno, an' the name stuck to her ever since" (Coakley and Felheim 270). The curtain falls on Juno and the Paycock with the words of Captain Jack Boyle as he makes the drunken revelation that "th' whole worl's . . . in a terr . . . ible state o'. . . chassis!" (Smith 176).

The Plough and the Stars (1926) is a tragi-comedy dedicated "to the gay laugh of my mother at the gate of the grave" (White 289). In Act III, Bessie and Mrs. Gogan use Mrs. Sullivan's pram to cart off their stolen goods. This is followed by tragic scenes of war and death, but there is also the comic singing of the drunken Fluther Good, who had stolen a half-gallon of whisky (Croakley and Felheim 267). It is ironic, of course that Fluther Good continually drinks while he also continues to vow temperance (Smith 12). Fluther Good's use of the term "drogatory" is also interesting. Not only is it an example of a malapropism, but in addition, it is a leitmotif--a way of identifying Fluther Good. "Fluther uses the adjective 'drogatory' seventeen times [in The Plough and the Stars] and manages to do so wrongly each time" (White 286). Maureen Waters considers Fluther Good to have been O'Casey's most ingratiating comic figure. He boasts and drinks while he solemnly swears to remain sober. "In the company of men he is as scrappy as a bantam rooster, and though he bears the scars of previous battles, including a broken nose, what he obviously relishes most is the preliminary argument, the dual of wit. He is a master of brinkmanship" (Waters 151). Although he is uneducated, and although he comically misuses words, Fluther Good is something of a philosopher. He is capable of true insight, especially regarding the relations between men and women:

> MRS. GOGAN: . . . . She dresses herself to keep him with her, but it's no use--afther a month or two, th' wondher of a woman wears off.
>
> FLUTHER: I dunno, I dunno. Not wishin' to say anything derogatory, I think it's all a question of location; when a man finds th' wondher of one woman beginnin' to die, it's usually beginnin' to live in another. (Waters 151)

Fluther is always true to character. When the war reaches the streets near the tenement, Fluther joins a band of looters, and what he chooses to loot, of course, is a barrel of whiskey. "Without a family to support, Fluther is detached from the usual domestic concerns. He lives from day to day with little money and little ambition, but a great deal of bouyant humor, an excellent defense against a poverty ridden world. He is in the play to provide comic relief" (Waters 152). Maureen Waters states that Pearse's impassioned call to arms is set in contrast to a series of farcical collisions between Bessie Burgess and Mrs. Gogan, between the Covey and Peter, and between the Covey and Fluther. "The result is black Irish comedy" (Waters 153). O'Casey also has Mrs. Gogan taunt Peter in a comical way in The Plough and the Stars. When Peter parades around in a ceremonial green uniform complete with sabre and plume, Mrs. Gogan responds, "Th' loveliest part of th' dress, I think, is th' ostrichess plume . . . . When yous are goin' along, an' I see them wavin' an' noddin' an waggin', I seem to be lookin' at each of you hangin' at th' end of a rope, your eyes bulgin' an' your legs twistin' and jerkin', gaspin' for breath while yous are tryin' to die for Ireland" (Waters 178).

The prostitute Rosie Redmond in The Plough and the Stars is an ironic figure who solicits clients all the time that Pearce is delivering his impassioned speech. "The equation is obvious. Each is a seducer of men, and in the context of the scene, Rosie is the more sympathetic figure because she is more honest and direct: she gives full value for money received" (Waters 154). O'Casey uses the character of Rosie Redmond to strike at both sides of the opposing political factions, noting that "Redmond" is the name of the Irish leader who preached moderation and parliamentary reform, and Rose is a traditional name for Ireland.

> It is little wonder that Dublin audiences were enraged and that some of them climbed up on the stage of the Abbey Theatre to get their hands on Fluther. This scene underscores the fact that Irishmen were drawn to the nationalist movement by the sheer spectacle, the sheer self-indulgence of the parades, the music, the speeches, the sense of importance that they generated. (Waters 154)

In this scene, Fluther's boasting and posturing parody the actions of the Irish rebels, thereby reducing their tragic sacrifice to a clown-like foolishness (Waters 155).

Coakley and Felheim say that The Plough and the Stars is a blend of tragedy and comedy and this blend of tragedy and comedy is well within the tradition of Greek saturnalia. "The imminence of war and its fury are matched by the revelries of the people, who steal, drink, and sing, ecstatic activities which parallel the absurdities and violence of war, all ritualized by the dramatist" (Croakley and Felheim 267). In The Plough and the Stars the vanity and the immediate excitement of untempered patriotism destroy the most basic and meaningful human relationships--those between friends, those between husband and wife, and those between mother and child.

The Silver Tassie (1928) is subtitled, "A Tragi-comedy in Four Acts." It deals with the effects of World War I on a group of Irish slum dwellers. These slum dwellers are extremely individualized, as they "bicker and joke in typical Irish rhythms." Harry Heegan is established as the symbol of youthful vigor. He has been a football hero, and he is also very popular with the women. During the war, however, he has lost the use of the lower half of his body, and by the third act, set in a hospital, he is no longer a symbol of life. The final act of The Silver Tassie is set in a dance hall, and of course dance is a traditional ending for a comedy. But in The Silver Tassie the festivities cannot begin as long as Harry is present (Pasachoff 42).

Naomi Pasachoff feels that the plays which O'Casey wrote between the time he was fifty and seventy years old are the most exuberant works in his canon. These plays include Within the Gates (1933), Purple Dust (1940), and Cock-a-Doodle Dandy (1949). These plays are all dominated by the celebration of life, despite the constant assaults on it by all those who would like to undermine the celebration (Pasachoff 41). Within the Gates is an exuberant play as it develops O'Casey's recurrent theme of the affirmation of life through song and dance. It is the Dreamer who, in Act I, Scene I, establishes the message of the play: "Will none of you ever guess that man can study man, or worship God, in dance and song and story!" The Dreamer is aligned with the forces of fertility and life against the forces of drought and death. O'Casey uses both song and dance as basic symbols (Pasachoff 43). B. L. Smith feels that Jannice is the only vital personality in Within the Gates. This is O'Casey's first play which deals from beginning to end with the interplay between those who are for, and those who are against, the celebration of life, and with their responses to song and dance. Pasachoff feels, however, that the attempt to celebrate life in Within the Gates is a bit too imposing, and the results are sometimes unintentionally comical.

> The Chorus of children, who appear dressed as trees in the very beginning of Scene I, suggests to the reader nothing so much as a kindergarten pageant. There are many other passages in the play that border on the embarrassing. Also, even in a non-naturalistic play it is disturbing to discover that two characters have the same name: not only the Atheist, but also the Gardener is named Ned. (Pasachoff 47)

The Flying Wasp (1937) has a long and humorous subtitle, as follows: "A laughing look-over of What Has Been Said about the Things of the Theatre by the English Dramatic Critics, with Many Merry and Amusing Comments Thereon, with Some Shrewd Remarks by the Author on the Wise, Delicious, and Dignified Tendencies in the Theatre of To-day" (O'Casey i).

In Purple Dust (1940), Poges, a speculator in stock, is attempting to acquire 500 shares in a cement company. He reasons that the shares are bound to jump as soon as "the bombing starts seriously." But there are no longer any shares available, and Poges remarks that "One wouldn't imagine there'd be so many trying to cash in on splintered bodies," forgetting for the moment that he was planning to do just that (Pasachoff 49). Some of the names in Purple Dust are humorously appropriate. Canon Creehewel's name is a pun on "cruel," and "Father Domineer" also is appropriately named. O'Casey describes him as follows: "He is trying to smile now, but crack his mouth as he will, the tight, surly lines of his face refuse to furnish one" (Pasachoff 57).

Purple Dust is a comic fantasy, in which the threats to life are comic caricatures of people we never take seriously. O'Killigain, for example, enters singing a life-affirming song that "puts to shame the mock pastoral of the Englishmen and their party." Dancing is also important in the play, and the imagery of dance occurs over and over in O'Killigain's speech. He claims that the sight of Avril dancing makes him want to dance to, as his thoughts become "as jaunty an' hilarious as your little dancin' feet" (Pasachoff 50). Even though the play hints darkly at the existence of many people who are incapable of living a spontaneous and joyous life, it nevertheless ends exuberantly (Pasachoff 48).

The primary satiric target in Purple Dust is

> the rationalistic English mind, with its incumbent faith that empire, heritage, and culture will somehow muddle through. The decaying mansion is a

museum to such bumbling: its residents (Stoke and Poges) are living embodiments of Gray's country churchyard, and their aims are to glorify England by putting it back together as it was in the good old days. (Smith 10)

Stoke and Poges have mercenary values, but they are hopelessly outmatched by the realistic Irishmen led by O'Killigain. Purple Dust is a farce comedy in which an Irish salesman convinces Poges that a huge grass roller is easy to handle, but it gets out of control and crashes through a wall when Poges attempts to maneuver it. Another farcical element is when Stoke and Poges buy a cow from an Irishman, and when it chases them, they mistake it for a bull and run for cover, shooting the cow dead in the process. Still another farcical element is the methodical destruction of the mansion by the workmen--the ceiling, the walls, the door frames, and the heirlooms. Finally, it is farcical when Stoke falls off from a spirited horse, and his "lassie o' th' house" goes off riding naked with his rival O'Killigain. When rain comes, it doesn't dampen the spirits of the Irish O'Killigain, Avril, O'Dempsey, or Souhaun. Instead, "It is a healing and life-giving rain which will wash away the purple dust of the dead past and send the dabblers in antiquity out of a land which is not theirs: Purple Dust hits, of course, at the adoration of the old outworn things, and leans towards new thought and young ideas" (Smith 11).

In Oak Leaves and Lavender: A Warld on Wallpaper (1947) the tragedy almost overwhelms the comedy. There is the blitz of London, and the crumbling Ireland, and the apparently unstoppable military strength of Germany.

The call to arms that this play is does provide, of course, slapstick and farfetched laughter, but his main thesis is that the bumbling, stumbling Prufrocks, in the face of crisis, are able to unite and defend themselves heroically against the military barrage hurled by Germany. (Smith 9)

Mikhail and O'Riordan consider Cock-a-Doodle Dandy (1949) to have been O'Casey comedy at its flamboyant best (Mikhail and O'Riordan 10). The play takes place in Nyadnanave, a "town of fools." In this town lives Michael Marthraun, a man nearly seventy years of age who was once a small farmer and is now "owner of a lucrative bog." Cock-a-Doodle Dandy is a dark play, but it is nevertheless a comedy celebrating and affirming life. In this play, song and dance are important not only to the form of the play but to its content as well. Pasachoff notes that the characters in this play are defined by their attitudes to song, dance, and the merry life in general. "Dance is on the minds of the play's characters throughout most of Cock-a-Doodle Dandy. The three women spend much of their time preparing for the fancy-dress ball planned for that night. The costume ball takes on symbolic importance in the antagonistic response it elicits" (Pasachoff 53-54).

The Bishop's Bonfire (1955) is subtitled A Sad Play within the Theme of a Polka. In this play, song and dance are again important motifs, as the central message of the play deals with the struggle for and celebration of life. The message, preached by Father Boheroe, is that "merriment may be a way of worship" (Pasachoff 61).

O'Casey's heroes are young and strong, and they are gifted with song, dance, and an appreciation for the joys of life. These young heroes combat the hate-drenched values of the establishment. They combat the Fillifogues, the Binningtons, and the McGilligans, and the young win. But O'Casey's satire is more sophisticated than this.

O'Casey's didacticism is more than offset by his humor and his capacity to present even the straightest preachment in brilliantly funny episodes. Moreover, the antihero, not the hero, is perhaps his most significant contribution to the theatre: the antics of Joxer Daley, Captain Boyle, and Fluther Good, together with those of Bernadette Shillayley (The Drums of Father Ned), Angela Nightingale (Bedtime Story), and the saucy vital wenches of Cock-a-Doodle Dandy underline the basic themes of those plays.

(Smith 14)

In "The Power of Laughter: Weapon Against Evil," O'Casey states explicitly what he so often stated implicitly in his plays--"that those who deny or condemn laughter as evil are themselves to be feared, that laughter reveals the greatest dangers in those areas where it is forbidden." Talking about laughter, O'Casey states:

> No one can escape it: not the grave judge in his robe and threatening wig; the parson and his saw; the general full of his sword and his medals; the palled prelate, tripping about a blessing in one hand, a curse in the other; the politician carrying his magic wand of Wendy windy words; they all fear laughter, for the quiet laugh or the loud one upends them, strips them of pretense, and leaves them naked to enemy and friend. (qtd. in Smith 13)

Two things remained constant in all of O'Casey's plays. One was his ability to create good drama. The other was his ability to create laughter. For O'Casey, laughter is a shared joy, and when O'Casey is laughing with his audience, the laughter becomes a weapon against evil (Smith 182).

B. L. Smith said that O'Casey wrote tragi-comedies, morality plays, sad plays, and tragedies, but he was "first and foremost a satirist" (Smith 12). On the basis of the interviews they collected in The Sting and the Twinkle, Mikhail and O'Riordan say that O'Casey's work is filled with gaiety and flamboyant freedom, ideals which he cherished and defended vigorously and relentlessly throughout his long life. "He remained, to the end, an incorrigible rebel, but a colourful one" (Mikhail and O'Riordan 10). For O'Casey, drama was the most important thing in life, and he was able to explain his dramatic success quite succinctly: "A play worthy of the theatre must be able to withstand the terror of Ta-Ra-Ra-Boom-Dee-Ay" (White 289).

Sean O'Casey Bibliography

Coakley, James, and Marvin Felheim. "Thalia in Dublin: Some Suggestions about the Relationships between O'Casey and Classical Comedy." Comparative Drama 4 (1970): 265-271.

Cowasjee, Saros. "The Juxtaposition of Tragedy and Comedy in the Plays of Sean O'Casey." Wascana Review 2.1 (1967): 75-89.

Daniel, Walter C. "Patterns of Greek Comedy in O'Casey's Purple Dust." Bulletin of the New York Public Library 66 (1962): 603-612.

Deane, Seamus. "O'Casey and Yeats: Exemplary Dramatists." Celtic Revivals: Essays in Modern Irish Literature--Joyce, Yeats, O'Casey, Kinsella, Montague, Friel, Mahon, Heaney, Beckett, Synge. Winston-Salem, NC: Wake Forest University Press, 1985, 108-122.

Mikhail, E. H., and John O'Riordan, eds. The Sting and the Twinkle: Conversations with Sean O'Casey. New York, NY: Barnes and Noble, 1974.

O'Casey, Sean. The Flying Wasp New York: Benjamin Blom, 1937.

Pasachoff, Naomi. "O'Casey's Not Quite Festive Comedies." Éire-Ireland 12.3 (1977): 41-61.

Smith, B. L. O'Casey's Satiric Vision. Kent, OH: Kent State Univ Press, 1978.

Waters, Maureen. "The Paycocks of Sean O'Casey." The Comic Irishman. Albany, NY: State Univ of New York Press, 1984, 149-160.

White, M. C. "Language and Humour in O'Casey's Abbey Plays." Literary and Linguistic Aspects of Humour. Barcelona, Spain: Univ of Barcelona Dept of Languages, 1984, 285-290.

James Joyce (1882-1941) IRELAND

James Joyce was such a cheerful and amiable child that his family gave him the nickname of "Sunny Jim." Stanislaus often tells how Jim's good humor and gaiety were obvious in his interests and pleasures. James would study upstairs for hours, and then he would come down " 'in high good humour,' sustained by a 'joyous certainty' in his ability. Such confidence and 'frank hilarity' endured through university, where 'his loud laugh was characteristic and occasionally disconcerting.' So often do we hear about Jim's gay pranks that Stanislaus runs out of synonyms for good cheer, amusement, and laughter" (Bell 34).

Mockery is a key element in much of James Joyce's writing. His greatest mockers are Shaun-Justius, Buck Mulligan, and the nameless narrator of "Cyclops" in Ulysses. "Shem at times plays a necessary if unsympathetic role in Ulysses and the Wake. Joyce had to learn to incorporate him into his art before it could have the wholeness, harmony, and radiance that he aspired to" (Polhemus 298).

Maureen Waters suggests that James Joyce is the most Irish when he "violates the bounds of good sense, good taste, and even sanity for the sake of a jest" (Waters 90). Waters also says that Joyce acquired a taste for satire as he matured as a writer, and he used his satiric skills with increasing intensity against the objects of his indignation, namely,

> the writers who formed a circle of influence in Dublin who were to establish the Abbey Theatre and provide a new direction in literature. They must have been fully astonished at the caricatures etched by Joyce in his Swiftian lampoon, "The Holy Office." Assuming the role of Catharsis-Purgative, he wittily and arrogantly mocks the key figures of the Revival as overly romantic, effusive, out of touch with the human condition. (Waters 96)

Much of Joyce's ferocious mockery was directed at particular individuals, and this was very much in the tradition of the Irish satire of his day. In his writing, Joyce drew freely from Irish myth and folklore, and fully exploited the stage Irish tradition, especially in his fashioning of his great comic epic Finnegans Wake (Waters 109). In addition, Joyce carries his jest to ludicrous extremes, seldom attempting to answer the charges of his Gaelic critics to respond to the complexity of his subject (Waters 108). Dubliners (1925) is a book of short stories, the most important of which is "The Dead." In an article entitled "Comic Design in Joyce's 'The Dead,' " John MacNicholas notes that this story is filled with humorous misunderstandings, and minor failures and gaffes, many of which are hilarious. These are conveyed in a narrative tone that stands aloof, presenting no evidence whatever of an understanding of the mistakes (MacNicholas 56). Lionel Trilling goes so far as to suggest that the title of the story, "The Dead," refers not so much to Michael Furey as it does to Gabriel Conroy, to the guests at the Christmas party, and in fact to all of the people of Ireland, for "it is better to have died as Michael Furey died than to have lived after the fashion of Gabriel Conroy and all the other guests at the Christmas party [without passion]" (MacNicholas 57). MacNicholas says that the structure of the party scene establishes "The Dead" as comic or life affirming. "The structural purpose of the party scene is not to alienate us from Gabriel and his society but to give a necessary ballast to his fleeting vision of the impalpable other world" (MacNicholas 57).

Gabriel, a pompous self-serious person, tells a funny story about Patrick Morkan's horse, which seems to be in an invisible harness, what MacNicholas calls "a very Irish harness" because it "draws Morkan helplessly in circles about the statue of William of Orange, a militarily successful oppressor of Ireland." This has a vividly ironic effect because Patrick Morkan was driving "out from the mansion of his forefathers" in order to see a military review. Gabriel's story is insightful but not bitter, and it is funny. There was something of a "comic poetic justice in the manner it deflates the pompous Grandfather

Morkan. The comic overtones are analogously extended to Gabriel himself" (MacNicholas 61).

In "The Dead," Molly Ivors and Mr. Browne are presented as antithetical characters at the party. "Miss Ivors has immersed herself in what Gabriel (and Joyce) regards as a cultural atavism. She champions the Irish Revival with an abrasive arrogance." It is an example of dramatic irony when she accuses Gabriel of being a "West Briton," since she does not know what the reader knows--that Gabriel is "uncomfortable about the West because he considers Gretta's background inferior to his own" (MacNicholas 58).

Mr. Browne is a central symbol in "The Dead." Irishmen use the color "brown" as a code word for the paralysis of Ireland. Paradoxically, Mr. Browne is both omnipresent and excluded. He is excluded because he is the only person at the party with only a last name, and the only Protestant. Gabriel, Gretta, Kate, Julia, Mary Jane, Freddy, and Lily are all referred to by their first names, but the reader is never told what Mr. Browne's first name is (MacNicholas 59-60). There is also a certain social distance between Mr. Browne and the other party guests, and this is conveyed through the constant repetition of the expression "Mister." But even though Mr. Browne is excluded, he is nevertheless ubiquitous. Mary Jane says, "Browne is out there, Aunt Kate;" and Aunt Kate responds, "Browne is everywhere." Aunt Kate lowers her voice, and Mary Jane laughs at her tone. Then Mary Jane continues, "Really, he is very attentive," and Aunt Kate adds, "He has been laid on here like the gas . . . all during the Christmas" (MacNicholas 59). Gas is a noxious, potentially inflammatory substance; it is associated with death. Browne's irritating personality is omnipresent--"Brown is everywhere. He pervades the atmosphere; he is too attentive, too gallant. His characterization is actuated by a Johnsonian humour: he is too full of himself, flatulent. He functions as a comic foil to Gabriel, who also is pompous, full of himself" (MacNicholas 59).

Another function of the character Mr. Browne is to "instigate a convivial if rude chaos, the kind of genial disorder which produces comic non sequitur behavior throughout the entire evening." Joyce's tone is indeed satiric, but it is gentle. For example, when Freddy retells his joke for Mr. Browne before dinner, the two men enjoy their mirth so much that the story itself can hardly be finished (MacNicholas 60). Not only is the interior of "The Dead" comic, but the ending is comic as well, since it involves "the extraordinary shift in narrative tone coloring Gabriel's final thoughts." This shift "is entirely pertinent to an evaluation of the story's comic movement" (MacNicholas 62).

In an article entitled "The Comic Structure of Joyce's Ulysses," Michael Klug demonstrates how Joyce criticism pulls in opposite directions. The novel can be viewed either as a "psalm of comic joy," or as a "cold and indifferent anatomy of a dead world." One group of critics argues that the novel ends happily, emphasizing the final union of Stephen Dedalus and Leopold Bloom and Bloom's reconquest of his wife. Other critics, however, see the novel ending in a "drift of futility and despair." These critics insist that Stephen and Bloom end up facing the same insurmountable problems they had had to start with. Klug says, however, that in order to see the conflicts and the resolutions in Ulysses as comic, the reader should look at the novel in terms of Northrop Frye's framework for comedy. For Frye, "traditional comedy often ends in a public 'party or festive ritual,' usually a marriage ceremony, which signals the emergence of a new society that is to 'crystallize around the hero'." In Ulysses, Bloom

> . . . is able to defeat the forces which keep him from his rightful bride and isolate him from his community. He gains a full state of comic communion with his restored society and in so doing wins control of that society and its future, since he along with his comic bride shall create and shape the future. Finally he is able to act out his triumph in a public way and embody it in the public ritual of marriage. (Klug 64)

Bloom is a clown. He is "a Chaplinesque figure, a schlemiel or Pierrot le Fou, comically henpecked and cuckolded, a combination bound to inspire mockery." While Bloom is describing a constellation in the sky, Lenehan gleefuly bumps Molly's bosom. Bloom is often mocked, that even his wife has noticed that people are "making fun of him . . . behind his back." Even the label on Bloom's hat mocks him: "High grade ha."

> Bloom sometimes aggravates his "image problem" by preaching to his cohorts, in his "Herr Professor Liutpold Blumenduft" mode, claiming the moral or informed position. He prefers tennis to boxing, deplores violence, pities women, children, and animals, and remains maddeningly sober: not, in short, a real Irish man. More insufferable to most people than Bloom's foolish pedantry and pontification is his hopeless effort to put a lid on gaiety and revelry, thus becoming another stock comic butt, a killjoy or party pooper. (Bell 41-42).

Bloom engages in weird introspections. He wonders, "Do fish ever get seasick?" (Bell 50). He assumes the perspective of a flock of pigeons which ask, "Who will we do it on? I pick the fellow in black. Here goes." Bloom progresses from being a simple fool who gets slapped to one of Paul's "fools for the sake of Christ." Bloom's middle name, Paula, in fact reminds the reader of Paul the apostle, who was an advocate of folly (Bell 51). Bloom himself is a religious symbol, and in "Circe" when a deadhand writes on the wall that "Bloom is a cod,"

> It conveys several jocoserious implications. Cod is slang for joker or fool, scrotum or penis--and, as such, the subject of Panurge's loving tribute. But cod also suggests the traditional Christian icon, a fish, and puns on God. Bloom's childhood nickname reinforces this cluster of associations. He was called "Mackerel" which, like "Cod," has both sacred and mundane connotations. (Bell 52)

Robert Bell suggests that one way to describe "Circe" is as a comic gospel: "Bloom descends, declares the new Bloomusalem, raises many dead souls, endures mockery and sacrificial death, and rises from the dead" (Bell 53).

Bloom sees life as a stream, ongoing like comedy, not truncated like tragedy or static like satire (Bell 46). Bloom sees the functioning of the human body not with satiric contempt, nor with tragic anguish, but with acceptance and joy (Bell 47). He believes in "enjoying nature now," and adds, "What harm?" Earlier works like Gargantua and Pantagruel, Gulliver's Travels, Tom Jones, and Tristram Shandy refer to defecation; however, no hero before Bloom has so thoroughly enjoyed a bowel movement. Bloom's first episode begins with his savoring the tang of urine, and ends with his wiping his bum. Bloom isn't so much erotic as he is polymorphously perverse, taking infantile delight in his body. "Hope it's not too big--bring on piles again. No, just right. So. Ah! . . . Life might be so." Bloom regards going to the bathroom as a kind of creativity. This same attitude carries over into taking a bath. In his mind's eye, he saw "his pale body inclined in it at full, naked, in a womb of warmth, oiled by scented melting soap, softly laved. He saw his trunk and limbs riprippled over and sustained, buoyed lightly upward, lemon yellow: his navel, bud of flesh: and saw the dark tangled curls of his bush floating, floating hair of the stream around the limp father of thousands, a languid floating flower" (Bell 48).

Leopold Bloom's wife, Molly, shares many comic traits both with the Wife of Bath, and with Moll Flanders. "Like Moll Flanders, she is constantly casting up accounts and taking inventory, defining herself through what she wears and eats. Both utter conventional pieties and refer regularly to God, the soul, religion, and spirituality, in relentlessly prosaic and unconvincing language" (Bell 58). Both are also preoccupied with body parts and functions. Robert Bell talks about Molly Bloom's body-allusions in Ulysses.

A page doesn't pass without reference to "my bottom" (18:53), "me behind"

(18:122), the "big hole in the middle of us" (18:151-152), "my neck"
(18:173), "my ring hand" (18:313), "my eyelids," "my heart" (18:321, 330),
"my teeth . . . fingers . . . throat . . . belly" (18:430-50), "my piss . . . the
skin underneath . . . my finger" (18:462-65), "my head . . . my chest"
(18:522-29), "titties" (18:536), "nipple . . . breast . . . behind . . . legs . . .
eyes . . . tongue . . . lips" (18:569-94), and so on. (Bell 55)

Bell says that "passing water is one of Molly's contributions to the 'stream of life,' " and
refers to this as her "chamber music" (Bell 56-57). Molly talks about being in her skin
hopping around. "I used to love myself then stripped at the washstand." Molly is clearly
an exhibitionist. Even though Molly has only a little wit, she has a ready, a broad, and a
deep sense of humor. Molly likes to laugh and she also enjoys the memory of laughter.
"I was in fits of laughing with the giggles I couldn't stop . . . youre always in great humour
[Josie] said" (Bell 57).

Another aspect of the comic in Ulysses is that Bloom and Stephen are both comic
heroes. They are both alienated from the women who are the symbols of their lives.

Stephen's conflict is established in his relation to his dead mother. He
cannot accept his connection to her by acknowledging his sonship, nor can
he fully reject her by burying her memory or eradicating her image as it
lives on within his own features. His conflict with his mother shapes his
conflicts with his church, his country, and finally human history itself
because he sees the Church, Ireland, and human history as so many dead
mothers. (Klug 65)

Stephen's relationship with his mother, Mae Dedalus, is the same as his relationship with
the Church. "He can neither serve nor escape service." Stephen also sees the country of
Ireland in terms of the mother metaphor. For Stephen, Ireland is seen as "Gummy
Granny," and as "the old sow that eats her farrow."

The first indication of Stephen's conflict with Mother Ireland appears in the
Telemachus episode where he sees a "milkwoman" with her "unclean loins"
and "shrunken paps" as a personification of his barren country. Although
Stephen thinks of her as a wrinkled witch on a toadstool and watches the
"wandering crone" in "scornful silence," his feeling toward her is not simple
rejection. He is personally injured because she "slights" him while deferring
to Haines, the conquering Englishman, and Mulligan, the traitorous
Irishman. (Klug 67-68)

It is ironic that Stephen would feel jealous of someone he so abhors. It should also be
noted here that body parts and functions figure prominently in Joyce's comic vision, even
for Stephen, who "resists and resents the body that imprisons his immortal spirit." Stephen,
therefore, is the opposite of both Leopold and Molly Bloom in this regard (Bell 55).

Mother metaphors are common in Ulysses. The sea is one of the dominant symbols
in the "Proteus" episode, and Stephen sees the sea as "Our Mighty Mother." Time is also
seen in terms of the mother metaphor; time is the "mighty mother who has swallowed up
the dead past, as containing all men and at the same time contained within all men" (Klug
69). Stephen also sees Molly as the living representation of his dead mother, "still capable
of fruition, as a replacement for the dead mother who has dominated his experience." To
Bloom she offers the living and unavailable wife as a replacement for his masochistic
dreams of the "lost one" (Klug 80).

Bloom's conflict is similar but different. It is dominated not by his mother, but by
his wife, Molly. He cannot acknowledge his connection to Molly by serving her in the role
of a husband and a sexual partner. But he is also unable to deny his connection to her by
escaping from her memory (Klug 65). Bloom feels that he can regain Molly only by
ending her adulterous affair with Blazes Boylan (Klug 72). Bloom "views his race, his

nation, and finally all human history as so many barren lands, which he can neither touch to life nor abandon to sterility" (Klug 65). For Bloom the role of father and creator of life is attractive, but he is repelled by his fear of the human involvement that such a role demands. "Like Stephen, Bloom is cut off from the feminine source of life and at the same time inescapably bound to it. Just as Stephen is haunted by the image of the dead mother Bloom is haunted by the image of the lost Molly." Bloom is able to recall the "pleasant old times" a time when he was fully alive and shared Molly's bed as husband and father. But in his mind he continually returns to his failures as a husband and a father. "He constantly remembers Molly and his earlier life with her in terms of gardens, flowers, perfumes, fruit, and similar images of growth and fertility" (Klug 70).

> Garden imagery dominates the description of Bloom's "final satisfaction" as he climbs into bed, a "land of promise," "redolent of milk and honey," and proceeds to celebrate his possession of the rich fruit of Molly's body by kissing in turn each of the "plump mellow yellow smellow melons of her rump." However even in this moment of "final satisfaction," Bloom has no illusions of exclusively possessing Molly, the female source of life. In fact his "satisfaction" partially stems from his sense of the "ubiquity" of Molly's "posterior female hemispheres," their availability to all men in all "habitable lands and islands explored or unexplored." (Klug 78)

Just as Bloom sees his successes with Molly as a husband and father in terms of garden imagery, he sees his subsequent separation from Molly in contrasting images of desert and wasteland (Klug 70).

In developing the argument that Ulysses is a comic novel, Michael Klug notes that Bloom and Stephen both have attraction-repulsion relationships with women, and further notes that if this is a comic novel, the comic resolution Bloom and Stephen reach must in some way relate to their paradoxical attitudes about women, and this is indeed the case:

> Bloom introduces Stephen to his wife, Molly. First of all he shows Stephen a "faded photo" of Molly, "with her fleshly charms on evidence in an open fashion, as she was in the full bloom of womanhood." After allowing Stephen to "drink in the beauty for himself," Bloom lectures Stephen on the "female form in general." This passage and a later one which describes Bloom's Utopian hopes of establishing an opera company featuring Molly and Stephen clearly indicate that he is trying to hand his wife over to his younger companion. (Klug 75)

Later, in the garden of Bloom's back yard, Bloom and Stephen are "attracted" toward a "visible luminous sign" coming from Molly's upstairs window. At Stephen's suggestion the two heroes urinate while gazing up at Molly's window with their reproductive organs "elevated to the projected luminous and semi-luminous shadow" of Molly. Bloom and Stephen are "offering up their praise to Molly and in so doing acknowledging their acceptance and affirmation of the female figure" (Klug 76). This image is problematic to many critics, but is in no way problematic if Ulysses is seen as a comic novel (Klug 75).

Klug sees the denouement of Ulysses as clearly comic. Like traditional comic heroes, Stephen and Bloom each resolves his conflict by atonement with the comic bride, and each thereby "insures himself a controlling part in creating a new society of the future." It should be pointed out, however that neither Bloom's nor Stephen's conflict is fully resolved. "Their union with the comic bride is incomplete as a comic resolution because it ends in a transitory state, because it costs the two heroes a partial loss of identity, and finally because it does not culminate in a significant comic action" (Klug 82).

The final episode of Ulysses can also be interpreted in a number of ways, but according to Klug the comic interpretation is the best.

In this final episode Molly opens herself to both Bloom and Stephen and thus acknowledges their _partial_ claim to her. Some able critics have attempted to show that Molly finally decides to return to her husband or that she finally chooses Stephen, who returns after the action ends to reclaim his prize. Both of these arguments satisfy our normal desires to see the comic hero triumph, but both are unconvincing and force us to ignore Molly's essential nature. She never _finally_ chooses any one man, for she is as Joyce describes her [a] "sane full amoral fertilizable untrustworthy engaging limited prudent indifferent Weib." (Klug 78-79)

Molly shows a sexual interest in "some nice looking boy," a coalman, a bishop, a dog, a black man, a sailor, and any number of other males who cross her consciousness. Even her final "yes," which some critics see directed solely toward Bloom, is a universal "yes," because Molly is a symbol of feminine fertility, and "in this capacity she stands at the end of the quest of Bloom and Stephen for creative reconciliation with the feminine source of life" (Klug 79). Molly sees herself as a "fair field and no favor" and will never become the property of any single man. "It is probably this indifference to the ego of individual men that has provoked individual critics to attack her" (Klug 79).

Bloom is a paradoxical character. He hates being a Jew; he hates Ireland; he hates the universe. He sees all three as "sterile wastelands inhabited only by the dead and dying." But at the same time he is attracted to the fact that he is Jewish, Irish, and human, and he is filled with the sporadic hope of restoring each of these qualities to life.

Bloom finds Ireland the "land of the setting sun" in which the inhabitants are slowly "dropping into a hole one after the other." As he rides through Dublin in Dignam's funeral cortege, he sees the city as a graveyard of broken monuments to the unsuccessful past and discovers the symbol of "old Ireland" in the "saddened angels, crosses, broken pillars, family vaults, [and] stone hopes praying with upcast eyes" that litter Glasnevin cemetery. (Klug 73)

Because Bloom hates himself so much, he tries in his mind to exaggerate his own importance.

In his wildest moment of self-inflation [he] sees himself successively as the Lord Mayor of Dublin, the successor to Parnell, and "the world's greatest reformer," who will lead Ireland out of bondage and into the promised land, inaugurate the reign of the "law and mercy," establish the "New Bloomusalem in the Nova Hibernia of the future," and finally restore the whole world to "universal brotherhood" with all the benefits of "free money, free love, and a free lay church in a free lay state." (Klug 74)

Robert Bell says that _Ulysses_ (1922) is "never simply optimistic and joyful; it is also skeptical, even suspicious, especially of uncritical optimism and reassuring conventions" (Bell 23). In _Ulysses_ Simon Dedalus is the comic Irishman, the storyteller, the archetypal humorist. He is "a born _raconteur_ if ever there was one." Stephen, in contrast, "stubbornly resents and distrusts Simon's garrulous, glib wit, mostly borrowed from John Joyce, whose importance in contrast, James Joyce frankly and generously acknowledged: 'Hundreds of pages and scores of characters in my books came from him. His dry (or rather wet) wit and his expression of face convulsed me often with laughter' " (Bell 31).

In a book entitled ULYSSES as a Comic Novel, Zack Bowen develops many of the same points that Klug had developed earlier, saying that many of the readers and commentators of _Ulysses_ have demonstrated that the dilemmas, the ambiguities, and the lack of definitive answers in _Ulysses_ make it something of a tragedy. After Carl Jung had read _Ulysses_, he responded in the following way:

Everything is desouled, every particle of warm blood has been chilled, events unroll in icy egoism. In all the book there is nothing pleasing, nothing refreshing, nothing hopeful, but only things that are grey, grisly, gruesome, or pathetic, tragic, ironic, all from the seamy side of life and so chaotic that you have to look for thematic connections with a magnifying glass. (Bowen ix)

Cheryl Herr made a similar assessment:

The reader finds in Ulysses the grand themes of Western literature: the son's search for the father, the father's search for the child he can never truly know to be his offspring, the artist's struggle for recognition and cash, the quest for romantic love, the often unsatisfying domestication of that love, the acceptance of death, the human battle with betrayal and despair . . . . It is a book about a writer's vexed relationship to a land plagued with poverty, dominated by an oppressive foreign government, and hostile to its own prophets. (Bowen xi)

Despite the comments of Carl Jung, Cheryl Herr, and many other like-minded critics, however, Zack Bowen considers Ulysses to be a comic novel. Ulysses draws its roots from antique origins and comic traditions. It celebrates life. It produces laughter, and in so doing, it follows a long a glorious, and a "purposefully dishonorable" tradition.

The first chapter employs Suzanne Langer's biological-cultural approach to comedy in terms of natural philosophy . . . . The second chapter explores the history and theory of comedy as the oldest, most fundamental literary form, one in which the mature Joyce exercised his literary genius most profitably . . . . The third chapter deals with the central issue of linguistic parody and its comic implications, particularly for the second half of Ulysses, and the fourth chapter treats comic themes, characters, and techniques that Joyce shared with Rabelais, Cervantes, and Sterne. The concluding chapter emphasizes the role of the reader in determining what is or is not comic, and how comparisons and parallels from serious works such as the Divine Comedy can infuse comic meaning into Ulysses. (Bowen xiii)

About Stephen Dedalus in Ulysses Joyce said, "He laughed to free his mind from his mind's bondage" (Polhemus 313). The Stephen Dedalus of Stephen Hero, and of Portrait of the Artist as a Young Man and of Ulysses had a young friend named Cranly, who was detached, critical, and catalytic. In real life, Cranly was a very close friend of James Joyce by the name of J. F. Byrne, who wrote an autobiography entitled, The Silent Years: With Memoirs of James Joyce and Our Ireland. In the Forward of this book Harvey Breit wrote that many Joyce readers had long wanted Byrne to write an autobiography, but that he had chosen to remain so silent "that he had literally disappeared from the scene" (Breit ix).

The impact of Byrne was honesty; not wit, or intelligence, or kindness, or shyness, or malevolence, but honesty. There was some deep gratification for me in that; there still is. I can almost laugh aloud with pleasure and amusement when I construct for myself the invariable image of our talks; the question asked, the short intense pause, the question answered, as simple as you could want it without it falling into insufficiency, as direct and candid, as bearing the stamp of himself, the blood of his being. (Breit x)

One of the comic devices which James Joyce employed in the novel Ulysses was the juxtaposition of polarities. Bloom is contrasted with Stephen; Bloom is contrasted with the Dubliners. Bloom's uncensored stream of consciousness is contrasted with Gerty Macdowell's popular-press prose. There is also the ironic Cyclopean giganticism contrasted with the Cyclopean myopia. Such polarities "create marvelous absurdities, incongruous images, resonating energies, and multiple perspectives" (Polhemus 299).

Just as "metempsychosis" is a problem word for Molly, "parallax" is a problem word for Bloom in <u>Ulysses</u>. In fact, some critics define <u>Ulysses</u> in terms of these two words. "The words refer to two different kinds of change with which <u>Ulysses</u> is concerned; the change which converts an Odysseus into a Leopold Bloom, and the change which converts the reader's view of Boylan as seen through Bloom's eyes to that as seen through Molly's eyes" (DiBernard 82).

In an article entitled, "Parallax as Parallel, Paradigm, and Paradox in <u>Ulysses</u>," Barbara DiBernard considers parallax to be the viewing of an object from different perspectives, and describes the parallax metaphor in terms of Bloom, who sees all women in terms of Molly. During his sexual interlude with Gerty, he thinks of Molly having her period, of Molly's violet garters, and he speculates that he can't be so bad-looking if Molly was attracted to him. While talking to Mrs. Breen, a former admirer of his, he looks at her and thinks, "Only a year or so older than Molly." In "Circe," Mrs. Breen amorously confronts him, Bloom answers as if he were at home answering Molly's questions about how his day had gone. While listening to the song <u>Martha</u> in "Sirens," Bloom thinks of Molly and her meeting with Boylan, and even Lydia Douce's stroking the beerpull triggers an association with Molly (DiBernard 74).

Another example of parallax in <u>Ulysses</u> is that Stephen and Bloom are living through similar experiences, but from radically different vantage points.

> Stephen starts out on a symbolic level, while Bloom begins on a literal level. Seen in this way, they are not two different people, but the two eyes of the person performing Ball's experiment. When one eye is closed, we see things through the other and assume it to be a true view. However, when we look at things through the other eye, the objects seem to have moved. They are displaced. The "true" view can only be obtained by taking this displacement into account. Hence, we often find Bloom and Stephen reacting to similar situations or thinking similar thoughts, but we must keep in mind whose stream of consciousness we are in, which eye we have open, to interpret things accurately. (DiBernard 79)

Through the parallax metaphor, the reader is given a multiple perspective not only on various persons and events, but also readers get a radical change in point of view from chapter to chapter. The first type of parallax can be seen in the scene on Howth as remembered very differently by Bloom and Molly. The Glencree dinner is also remembered very differently by Bloom, Lenehan, and Molly. The second type of parallax can be seen in Joyce's deliberately shifting his point of view. Joyce wrote in a letter to Harriet Weaver that "the task I set myself technically in writing a book from eighteen different points of view and in as many styles, all apparently unknown or undiscovered by my fellow tradesmen, that and the nature of the legend chosen would be enough to upset anyone's mental balance" (DiBernard 80).

Proteus fascinated Joyce because Proteus is the "King of Flux."

> The myth of the shifty old man of the sea told him how hard it is to find and hold onto any meaning and permanence when mind and matter alter shape so fast. In the "Proteus" episode of <u>Ulysses</u>, Joyce gives us Stephen Dedalus's consciousness, racing hot with energy as he visits the sea but is yet unable to give form to the whirl of his brilliant imagination. (Polhemus 300)

In <u>Ulysses</u> Joyce satirized the efforts of W. B. Yeats, Augusta Gregory and John Synge to achieve a true Anglo-Irish synthesis by creating a literature in English which drew on the Gaelic world for its inspiration (Waters 95). In <u>Ulysses</u> Joyce uses the most extreme forms of ridicule in order to discredit the political as well as the literary goals of Irish nationalism. The Cyclops scene illustrates Joyce's tactics as a satirist, as Joyce links the Irish capacity for heroic gesture with the Irish capacity for porter. Giantism is the structural principle of the chapter, but it is a spurious giantism, as can be seen in the character of the citizen, who is petty, malicious, and ignorant, "all wind and piss like a tanyard cat" (Waters 97). The citizen has a tendency to speak in hackneyed patriotic phrases, and is responsible for some of the macabre humor in Ulysses (Waters 98). Joyce treats the Revival as just one more comic manifestation of Irish nationalism. In the opening chapter of Ulysses, Buck Mulligan mocks the new Revival Art as pretentious, and hence "snot green" (Waters 104). Buck Mulligan's wit is not liberating, nor is it life affirming, even though Joyce's satire is generally in the tradition of liberation and life affirmation. But Buck Mulligan is often comic, even though his purpose is to negate or destroy. Furthermore, Buck Mulligan "seems less and less entertaining as the day wears on" (Waters 106).

In his Jocoserious Joyce, Robert Bell suggests that Buck Mulligan is a great deal more complicated and important to the novel than Joyce critics generally recognize (Bell 11). Buck provides much of the humor, satire, and playfulness of Ulysses. Bell indicates that as Ulysses progresses, the spirit of folly becomes more and more persistent, pervasive, and "Buck-like." Buck is the novel's élan vital, its court jester, its gifted clown. Buck has a "blithe broadly smiling face," and "eyes, from which he had suddenly withdrawn all shrewd sense, blinking with mad gaiety" (qtd. in Bell 12). Bell says that for Buck as for such Shakespearean clowns like Touchstone, Mercutio, and Feste, "a bit of Buck's wit goes a long way" (Bell 12). It is Buck who mocks the subjects that concern James Joyce, and preoccupy Stephen Dedalus--Ireland, religion, sex, paternity, and creativity (Bell 13). Like Shakespeare's fools, Buck is more important than his brief appearance "on stage" would suggest. "He stands apart from the main action and acts, to some extent, as a privileged commentator upon the action" (Bell 16).

Buck Mulligan is preoccupied with bodily functions.

> Buck jokes about prepuces, making water, or "rotten teeth and rotten guts" (1:412), "that's all done with a purpose" (6:735): his jibes incessantly link the sublime and the bodily, as when he coins his own Homeric epithets: "The snotgreen sea. The scrotumtightening sea" (1:78). Most important, it is Mulligan who dubs Stephen "poor dogsbody" (1:112). This characteristically blasphemous inversion sticks in Stephen's mind, as well it should, for it summarizes the part of himself that disgusts and appalls him. (Bell 36)

It is interesting to note that Joyce, like Buck, had a "devilish talent for clowning." He appeared in a number of amateur theatricals, and was clearly someone who "loved and studied his Pierrots, Harlequins, Grocks, and Chaplins" (Bell 22). When Joyce played charades, he would provoke roars of laughter with his clowning, sometimes imitating a look of blank imbecility, weeping, and blowing his nose loudly (Bell 23).

The legendary Finn MacCool appears as a hyperbolic leprechaun, swollen to monstrous proportions (Waters 97). Finn is described as a "broadshouldered deepchested stronglimbed frankeyed redhaired freely freckled shaggybearded widemouthed largenosed longheaded deepvoiced barkneed brawnyhanded hairylegged ruddyfaced sinewyarmed hero" (Waters 98).

Malachi (Buck) Mulligan is a character who plays the role of a mock priest in the opening chapter of Ulysses. He celebrates Mass with a bowl of shaving cream, a mirror and a razor. Buck Mulligan's gaiety and pleasure in the physical world is counterbalanced by Stephen Dedalus's tragic and introspective mood (Waters 102).

> Mulligan not only penetrates Stephen's defenses, he strikes at values central to Irish culture. His assault is invariably comic, but the hostility beneath the jester's mask is never quite concealed. Mulligan's parody of the Mass is an excellent device for ridiculing Stephen's moral seriousness, but it also allows

> Mulligan to dominate, to force Stephen into the role of acolyte, who must carry first the shaving bowl and then the food which is offered around in a kind of communion feast. In ridiculing Catholicism Mulligan is typically blasphemous or obscene, as in the "Ballad of Joking Jesus": "I'm the queerest young fellow that ever you heard / My mother's a jew, my father's a bird . . . ." (Waters 103)

According to Maureen Waters much of the brilliant satire of Ulysses was directed at this character. "The name of Malachi (Buck) Mulligan is rich in associations, many of them ironic, which particularly fit him for the role of 'Schlagfertig' or striking wit" (Waters 99-100). The term "buck" implies a kind of "dandy" or "fop," and this

> links Mulligan with his primrose waistcoat to Oscar Wilde and the aesthetes of the 1890's, the yellow decade. Mulligan's narcissism and concern with dress, his witty, epigrammatic style, the hint of homosexuality ("manner of Oxenford"), all suggest the decadent mode of the fin de siècle . . . . The most characteristic trait linking Mulligan to Wilde is, however, a propensity for clowning, the need to perform, to wear a mask. Early in his career Wilde deliberately attracted the attention of the public through his eccentric manner and dress, the famous knee breeches, the velvet coat, the sunflower boutonnière. (Waters 102)

Ulysses contains a large number of intentional mistakes.

> Fritz Senn says that Ulysses tends to counteract whatever it has been doing, contradict whatever it has been saying. No book is more systematic in its schemas, correspondences and cross-references. Yet it is also designed to create various kinds of uncertainty . . . . The paradox lies in the fact that the design is effective in this respect because it is so systematically organized. (Deane 126)

As Bloom is walking past the tombstones of Glasnevin cemetery to visit Parnell's grave, he thinks that "Eulogy in a country churchyard ought to be that poem of Wordsworth or Thomas Campbell." Of course Bloom is wrong. The author is Thomas Gray, and the poem is "Elegy in a Country Churchyard." Bloom is making a joke by punning on the word "elegy." He develops the joke further by suggesting that tombstones would be more interesting if they recorded what the dead people had done during their lives. He reads the name of a woman, and suggests for example, that the note on her tombstone should read something like, "I cooked good Irish stew" (Deane 126).

Much of the laughter in A Portrait of the Artist as a Young Man (1928) is threatening, mirthless, scornful, or jeering in tone. It is almost always other people who laugh, and it is almost always Stephen who ponders. "O how could they laugh about it that way?" Stephen sometimes "tried to share their merriment"; however "he felt himself a gloomy figure" (qtd. in Bell 29). James Joyce himself was painted by many portrait artists, and he once told Patrick Tuohy, "Never mind my soul. Just be sure you have my tie right" (qtd. in Zois 22).

John Bishop indicates that the "simplest way of reading Finnegans Wake (1939) is to see it as one protracted and extremely funny little-moron joke, but with one important twist: the little moron turns out to be an altogether representative Western Man." Marion Robinson considers the humor in Finnegans Wake to be essentially non-verbal, or pre-verbal, or in Joyce's own words, the humor is "non-day" and "non-sense" (Robinson 96). The fun of Finnegans Wake comes from knowing that it is the thoughts of the sleeping Humphrey Chimpden Earwicker, whom Robinson describes as a "motionless Gulliver bound within his own body and unable to control the Lilliputian antics dimly sensed therein" (Robinson 97). "The jokes at Joyce's 'Fillagain's chrissormiss wake' are strikingly like the humor in old Irish texts like Táin Bó Cuailnge: grotesque, unnerving, macabre, irrational--

and very funny" (Robinson 97). The Táin is much funnier than are most classic national epics. Marian Robinson notes that "there are not a lot of laughs in Beowulf or the Nibelungenlied." But Finnegans Wake is like Táin Bó Cuailnge in discussing uncontrollable forces like reproduction and bodily functions and even death as epic material. And it also relies on the wild, exaggerated, and funny if ultimately deadly gyrations of its heroes and heroines in battle (Robinson 97). At one point in the last battle of Táin, Fergus responds, "By god, you have picked a bad time for this." At this point Mebd relieves herself, and the gush "dug three big channels, each big enough to take a household." This demonstrates Marian Robinson's point that there is no aspect of life that is too sacred to escape the mockery of Irish laughter. There is an echo of Táin Bó Cuailnge in Finnegans Wake as Shem and Shaun are in the same type of combat as were Ferdia and Cuchulainn in the Táin. "The Warring brothers of Humphrey Chimpden Earwicker's 'blacked out mind' meet at least seven times in various guises in personal confrontations simultaneously both comic and threatening."

> Like Cuchulainn and Ferdia, Shem and Shaun, from their first appearance to their last, exchange insults and boasts--both funny and threatening--and emerge unscathed, or rapidly healed, after each devastating combat until the final struggle. Shem, like Ferdia, consistently loses the battles with his invincible brother, Shaun/Cuchulainn. Beginning with the Mutt and Jute episode in the first chapter and ending with the brothers' appearance as Muta and Juva in the final chapter, Joyce surrounds their eternal battle with the same sort of bizarre, grotesque imagery found in the Táin in the ludicrous and terrifying single combats of Ferdia and Cuchulainn. Shem and Shaun are the comic, nighttime version of Ferdia and Cuchulainn in Joyce's "funny funereels." Shaun, "the fine frank fairhaired fellow of the fairytales," is analogous to the sun-god Cuchulainn. (Robinson 98)

In "The Mookse and the Gripes" confrontation of Finnegans Wake, Shaun (the Mookse) is described as "having flabelled his eyes, pilleoled his nostrils, vacticanated his ears and palliumed his throat." The word "vacticanated" is a compression of "Vatican" and "vaccinated," and Robinson suggests that it also means "made vacant" since this would describe Shaun's aural distortion. This image, like the image of Cuchulainn, is grotesque, nonsensical, threatening, and comic. When Shaun is the Ondt in the tale of "The Ondt and the Gracehoper," he displays a frenzy of eating. He ate "all the whilepaper, swallowed up the lustres, devoured forty flights of styearcaeses, chewed up all the mensa dna seccles, made mundballs of the ephemerids and vorasioused most glutinously with the very timeplace in the ternitary--not too dusty a cicada of neutriment for a chittinous chip so mitey." Joyce provides his reader with a "nightmare image of a giant bug devouring walls and staircases as well as months and centuries" (Robinson 99).

On the battlefield, Cuchulainn had a warp-spasm which is described in Táin as follows:

> His body made a furious twist inside his skin, so that his feet and shins and knees switched to the rear and his heels and calves switched to the front . . . . On his head the temple-sinews stretched to the nape of his neck, each mighty, immense, measureless knob as big as the head of a month-old child. His face and features became a red bowl: he sucked one eye so deep into his head that a wild crane couldn't probe it onto his cheek out of the depths of his skull; the other eye fell out along his cheek. His mouth weirdly distorted: his cheek peeled back from his jaws until the gullet appeared, his lungs and liver flapped in his mouth and throat, his lower jaw struck the upper a lion-killing blow, and fiery flakes large as a ram's fleece reached his mouth from his throat. His heart boomed loud in his breast like the baying

of a watch-dog at its feed. (qtd. in Robinson 102)

Joyce's description of the body makeup of Shem/Ferdia at the beginning of Chapter Seven in Finnegans Wake parodies Cuchulainn's body makeup.

> An adze of a skull, an eight of a larkseye, the whoel of a nose, one numb arm up a sleeve, fortytwo hairs off his uncrown, eighteen to his mock lip, a trio of barbels from his megageg chin . . . , not a foot to stand on, a handful of thumbs, a blind stomach, a deaf heart, a loose liver, two fifths of two buttocks, one gleetsteen avoirdupoider for him, a manroot of all evil, a salmonkelt's thinskin, eelsblood in his cold toes, a bladder twistended . . . (Robinson 103)

Joyce's parody does not have the same tone as the original. Shem's imagery is fish-like, referring to eel's blood and salmon scales, because he is in essence cold-blooded. Shaun/Cuchulainn, however is filled with hot-blooded power. "Where Cuchulainn's hair is 'twisted like the tangle of a red thornbush' and spiked with bristles 'as it stood up on his scalp with rage,' Shem's is scanty and lank" (Robinson 103). Nevertheless, both Finnegans Wake and Táin Bó Cuailgne are totally within the tradition of Irish humor, in that both inextricably mix "suffering and sport, pathos and play in the 'druidful scatterings' of these struggles on the 'cabracattlefield of slaine,' like 'so many unprobables in their poor suit of improssable' " (Robinson 106).

Barbara DiBernard notes that the "thunder words" that signal the end of one cycle and the beginning of the next in Finnegans Wake are all composed of 100 letters each. Zack Bowen uses such evidence as the linguistic incongruities, the parody, the general tone and demeanor, and the hilarious celebration of life as support for classifying Finnegans Wake as a comic novel (Bowen ix). Oliver St. John Gogarty describes Finnegans Wake as "the most collosal leg-pull in literature" (Deming 675). James Joyce describes Finnegans Wake as "a shitty piece of writing and an indecipherable riddle of cacophony." He laughs at his own effort and burlesques his Wakean voice squalling away incomprehensibly to the world (Polhemus 317). Finnegans Wake is filled with sexual allusions, some of them rather gratuitous. Rather than writing "that is to say," for example, Joyce shortens the expression to "t.i.t.s.," thus giving the word a double meaning, for "t.i.t.s." means "tits" too, and this expression (like many others in Finnegans Wake) tells us that "Joyce's writing gave him the libidinous pleasure of breasts" (Polhemus 319).

Finnegans Wake is filled with obscure allusions and punning diction and convoluted syntax. Robert Polhemus suggests that "Wakean language is to Joyce's comic faith what Latin is--or was--to the Roman Catholic Church." In both cases,

> we have to grapple with the language. We can't take it for granted; we have to slow down and struggle with its multiplicities, its connections, its patterns. Joyce's insiders' language, so hard to follow, implies a militant emotional defiance, 'us against the Philistines,' a spirit that underlies much comedy as well as religion . . . . Reading the Wake seriously is a perpetually frustrating struggle for meaning and light and a continuing act of faith. (Polhemus 328)

Finnegans Wake is a novel which merges animate and inanimate life: "babbling, bubbling, chattering to herself, deloothering the fields on their elbows leaning with the sloothering slide of her, giddygaddy, grannyma, gossipaceous Anna Livia." Joyce wants to express his interconnectedness with water, and with earth. "The fields, resting 'on their elbows,' become humanized, but voice and thought have become hydraulic" (Polhemus 326-327). Finnegans Wake is described by Robert Polhemus as a "comic Bible" in that it "offers, in its joking, punning way, knowledge and understanding of all things first to last, promise of aggregate immortality, reconciliation to personal fate, and the experience of holy mystery" (Polhemus 295). In Finnegans Wake Joyce uses the dream format "as a wonderful joke played on proud, narrow rationalism and moral smugness. In the chaos, the homage to the unspeakable, the bawdy sexuality, the uncontrollable absurdity, and the multiple significance of dreams, he finds our common and manifold humanity" (Polhemus 308). In uninhibited playful dreamlike fashion, Joyce plays on the multiple meanings of words. The word "mummy" for example carries with it meanings related to death, life, and humanity, but it also means "mother." "One single term connotes the fact that out of the mother comes new life, and out of death comes memory." The word "mummy" occurs in a monolithic sentence about one page in length (Polhemus 309).

Polhemus feels that the crux of the protean comedy of Finnegans Wake is the flux.
> Something is always in the process of becoming something else: words turn into other words, meanings become other meanings, people, places, and times become other people, places, and times. Voices, elements, and language are constantly changing and flowing. One of Joyce's names in the Wake for the whole circulating, recycling, evolving, dreamlike nature of being is "collideorscape." (Polhemus 299)

Polhemus considers the "Shem" section of Finnegans Wake to be a "comic masterpiece." Polhemus notes that "Shem is as short for Shemus as Jem is joky for Jacob" (Polhemus 300). Like Proteus, Shem is a shape-shifter. He gets formed by "putting truth and untruth together" (Polhemus 302).
> "Shem" is both a farcical portrait of an artist as a ridiculous man and the clownish odyssey of mental and physical wandering from Dublin to Paris to Trieste, from Eden to Dublin, from birth to death and resurrection, from condemnation to redemption, from genesis to revelation, from era to era, from civilization to civilization, from dream stage to dream stage. Like the whole Wake, it is the story and vision of a Humpty-Dante, a universal, human--not divine--comedy, telling of a momentous but fortunate and very funny fall. (Polhemus 295)

Joyce gives Shem's rival, Shaun-Justius, the power of "the word." In describing the House O'Shea (or O'Shame), known as "the Haunted Inkbottle," Shaun begins with the exclamation, "My wud!" He then describes the contents of the room:
> . . . fluefoul smut, fallen lucivers, vestas which had served, showered ornaments, borrowed brogues, reversibles jackets, blackeye lenses, family jars, false hair shirts, Godforsaken scapulars, neverworn breeches, cutthroat ties, counterfeit franks, best intentions, curried notes, upset latten tintacks . . . , twisted quills, painful digests, magnifying wineglasses, solid objects cast at goblins, once current puns, quashed quotatoes, messes of mortgage, crocodile tears, spilt ink, blasphematory spits, stale shestnuts . . . . (qtd. in Polhemus 303)

In this surrealistic writing, Joyce is not merely having Shaun describe the things that surround him. This is a novel of ideas, and the purpose of the passage is to "allude to everything that could possibly exist and be thought, said, or written and make it funny."

This is a catalogue of Joyce's mental and physical life, a table of contents for Joyce's universe. "Between each pair of relentless commas, Joyce casts one more mudpie brick for his new Tower of Babel, and each one radiates with meaning and energy" (Polhemus 304). In Joyce's universe, language, material objects, the human body, literature, and Joyce's own work and imagination come together. "Everything fuses in the act of creation so that dead objects, clichés, waste products, old words, suddenly convey new life and burn with new meaning and animating mockery" (Polhemus 305). The constant punning in Finnegans Wake fuses many images and meanings simultaneously. Polhemus suggests that this type of free-flowing, unstructured language is "in one sense a metaphor for the psychological phenomenon of the dream" (Polhemus 307).

Shaun-Justius is full of himself. He loves conformity and hates otherness. Since he is unable to change himself, he wants to change everything into himself--or kill it. Shem, Shaun's rival, is an artist. Shem may be just as egotistical as Shaun, but since he is a creator he is able to change himself and change everything else, "to feel and speak as objects, making himself literally the spokesman for all life and being. In his final speech, the comic artist-hero brings the merciful gift of linguistic imagination" (Polhemus 322-323).

Through the character of Shaun-Justius, Joyce mocks the tyranny of other people's judgments over ourselves. Shaun represents certain people's boiling dissatisfaction with other people.

> In the rhetorical irony of Shaun's voice, Joyce justifies our rebelliousness toward the highness that despises lowness: "take your medicine . . . . Let me finish! Just a little judas tonic, my ghem of all jokes, to make you go green in the gazer," says Justius, trying to execute Shem. The allusion may remind us that it is the Shauns of the world who gave the orders to poison Socrates, crucify Christ, stone Stephen, burn Bruno, gas the Jews, and conduct the Inquisition and Party purges. (Polhemus 320)

There is comic irony in Shaun's vicious attack on the creative artist Shem: "nomad, mooner by lamplight . . . , an Irish emigrant the wrong way out . . . , an unfrillfrocked quackfriar, you semi-semitic serendipitist, you Europasianised Afferyank!" (qtd. in Polhemus 321). The voice of Shaun is the voice of Joyce's critics--Gogarty, Pound, H. G. Wells, Alfred Noyes, Wyndham Lewis, Stanislaus Joyce, and everybody else who reproached his writing. "Shaun alludes to almost every knock that Joyce ever got" (Polhemus 321).

The "Shem" chapter is mainly a hostile account of the disgraceful career of Shem by his brother and foremost enemy--Shaun. But this chapter is also heavily grounded in Joyce's own reality.

> Much of the abuse is made up of pastiches and parodies based on derogatory reviews of Joyce's books and remarks and deeds of those who acted toward him with enmity. Shem is an exile, a heretic, a bohemian, a plagiarist, a fornicator, and a fetishist who smells, shirks, refused to get married, and has delusions of grandeur. According to Shaun, he commits all seven deadly sins and breaks each of the Ten Commandments. He makes ink from his own excreta. (Polhemus 296)

Polhemus feels that the folly of Shem in Finnegans Wake is the folly of James Joyce, for Shem is Joyce incarnate, Joyce's "word" is Shem's "my wud." "He does not omit the most ridiculous and shameful things about himself, nor does he pretend that he has reformed into respectability, has triumphed and left behind the old flawed self, as the authors of 'confessions' so often do. He admits his own comic lowness and plays with it without exculpating himself." Joyce directly or indirectly alludes to every personal fault he can dredge up--the nasty things his disparagers charged against him, his alcoholism, his conceit, his laziness, his selfishness, his callous behavior to those who loved him, even his incestuous feelings for his own daughter. Polhemus goes so far as to suggest that much of the comedy and the confession of "Shem" comes out of Joyce's sexual exhibitionism. And Joyce is not just using the "old tactic of defensive self-mockery and discrediting his critics by having the egregious Shaun speak their views . . . . It is part of the drama of 'Shem,' the Wake, and Joyce's comic gospel that the criticism is in some ways true and must be faced and accepted" (Polhemus 315).

As a creative artist, Shem provides many examples of what Joyce termed the "epiphany," a concept which splices together psychology, religion, art, and, in Finnegans Wake, humor. "Epiphany," is the sudden expression of divinity, and this idea so moved Joyce that he adapted the term to his own purposes, to mean "a sudden spiritual manifestation, whether in the vulgarity of speech or of gesture or in a memorable phrase of the mind itself." For Joyce, the moment of epiphany is when someone recognizes that the relations of the parts of an object or idea are exquisitely interrelated. When the parts are adjusted to the special point, we recognize that it is that thing which it is. "Its soul, its whatness, leaps to us from the vestment of its appearance [e.g. from the printed page]" (Deming 213). The epiphany is a sudden revelation. Paul was blind; and then he could see. Joyce sanctified the pun, for in the pun there was the epiphany. In the pun, we see the point, or we get the joke. "And it is remarkable how similar that moment is to accounts of quick, blissful, religious illumination."

> Every darkly obscure new word in the Wake carries with it a potential comic epiphany. Take, for instance, the striking, sprawling pun of Mercius's, "astroglodynamonologos." The Jesuit scholar Robert Boyle explicates it this way: "Mercius's word for his own artistic vocation, or rather for himself as artist, is drawn . . . from the opening of St. John's gospel with its description of the ideal priest . . . . It combines the words for star, aster; cave-dweller (literally, hole-seeker), troglodyte; source of power, dynamo; lonely speaker, monologos; and the word, logos." (Senn 139)

Polhemus suggests that the prayer that ends Book II, Section I of Finnegans Wake "recapitulates the drift of Mercius's soliloquy and itself flows out of those 'prolonged laughter-words,' " "quoiquoiquoiq . . . ." The prayer reads as follows:

> "O Lord . . . . Lord, heap miseries upon us yet entwine our arts with laughters low!
> Ha he hi ho hu.
> Mummum." (qtd. in Polhemus 336)

At the climax of "Shem," Mercius dream-talks the long and flowing sentence that ends that chapter (Polhemus 308).

> The speech that ends the chapter conveys the all-encompassing joke of imagination and form as well as anything can. Shem, his "joky" quality, Mercius, the lifewand, and the miraculous speech of the dumb culminate in the sound of laughter, what Joyce calls "prolonged laughter words": "Quoiquoiquoiquoiquoiquoiquoiq!" Justius had earlier taunted Shem to "move me . . . to laughter," and that is just what finally happens. (Polhemus 312)

Polhemus explains that "Quoiquoiquoiquoiquoiquoiquoiq" is a "laughter-word that conveys bemusement, obscurity, the cacophony of critics, and the babble out of which flow the dialectic of our being and our malleable verbal ability" (Polhemus 333-334).

Robert Bell says that the protagonist in Joyce's Stephen Hero (1944) may be satirical toward the world, but he is humorless about his role in it. "He could always suck melancholy from an egg" (Bell 29). The concept of "epiphany" is very well described in Stephen Hero. Stephen describes an epiphany as sudden illuminations caused by trivial, sometimes even arbitrary, events (Beja 13). When Stephen uses the word "epiphany," he is referring to a sudden almost spiritual manifestation, and this could be either in the vulgarity of speech or gesture or in a memorable phrase. Stephen believed that it was the function of scholars to record these epiphanies with extreme care, because they are "the most delicate and evanescent of moments." Morris Beja adds that even though "epiphany" is a theological term it is not necessarily a religious concept (Beja 14). Beja furthermore points out that there are two major types of epiphanies: the "retrospective" epiphanies, and the epiphanies of "the past recaptured" (Beja 15). Joyce was fascinated by the fact that triviality is significant, and he once said to his brother, "It is my idea of the significance of trivial things that I want to give the two or three unfortunate wretches who may eventually read me" (Beja 16). It was Joyce who developed the concept of epiphany, but it is a concept that has influenced many later writers as well. Since Joyce, authors have used epiphanies for many different functions. James Joyce and Virginia Woolf used epiphanies to mark climaxes in a narrative. William Faulkner, Virginia Woolf, and Alain Robbe-Grillet used epiphanies to suddenly recapture the past in flashbacks that reveal some necessary background to the developing story. In <u>Death of a Salesman</u>, Arthur Miller used epiphany in having Willy Loman relive various moments of his past. Events in the story trigger Willie Loman's mind into flashbacks that are so real that he sees them as actually occurring events. Epiphanies were also used in France in the early "New Wave" films, especially in Alain Resnais's <u>Hiroshima, Mon Amour</u> and <u>Last year at Marienbad</u>. Finally, epiphanies serve as a unifying and integrating device that instantaneously brings together many of the main threads of a novel (Beja 22). When characters receive epiphanies, they "transcend themselves and see into the truth of things." In some ways Bloom and Mrs. Dalloway may not be very bright, but when they have moments of insight, that insight serves their creators well (Beja 23).

Trevor Griffiths describes Joyce's <u>Comedians</u> (1976) as follows:

> A real comedian--that's a daring man. He <u>dares</u> to see what his listeners shy away from, fear to express. And what he sees is a sort of truth, about people, about their situation, about what hurts or terrifies them, about what's hard, above all, about what they <u>want</u>. A joke releases the tension, says the unsayable, any joke pretty well. But a true joke, a comedian's joke, has to do more than release tension, it has to <u>liberate</u> the will and the desire, it has to <u>change the situation</u>. (Griffiths 20)

Joyce described his <u>Exiles</u> (1978) as a comedy in three acts. He also described it as "three cat and mouse acts" (Maher 461). The comedy in <u>Exiles</u> is based on the startling number of inconsistencies and misunderstandings that take place whenever two or more characters come together (Maher 462). R. A. Maher considers <u>Exiles</u> to be a "cacophony of man's illogical behavior" (Maher 473).

> All four characters are speaking of events that took place nine years before the play opens. Apparently there were two triangles, the first consisting of Richard, Robert, and Beatrice, and the second of Richard, Robert, and Bertha. Richard ran away with Bertha, and Robert and Beatrice remained behind in Ireland. Beatrice's attraction to Robert waned when she discovered that he was "a pale reflection" of Richard. The play probes the theoretical question of the couples' possible mismating. Should Richard have married Beatrice, and Robert Bertha? (Maher 464-465).

Maher explains that Beatrice and Bertha are the more human counterparts of Richard and Robert, "with Beatrice clearly seeing through Robert but admiring Richard, and Bertha clearly seeing through Richard but admiring Robert. In the final act, Richard and Robert continue to hold their poses, but Bertha effects a reconciliation with Beatrice" (Maher 474).

Especially in James Joyce's later writings, there is an antiauthoritarian and playful tenor. In addition to this, these later writings are tremendous enough in scope to break free of repression. Joyce's satire, his experiments with parody, language and style, his stress on human communication, and on the necessity of union with nature, and his surprising tolerance, all have precedent in the great comic tradition of the preceding (nineteenth) century (Polhemus 295). This has led William York Tindall to say:

> If the eighteenth century, supposedly the age of wit, found Swift and Sterne too witty, the plight of Joyce in our age was more desperate. Never needing the assurance of a crowd, he stood apart from those who are not only solemn but serious about it. Yet, like Shaw, Joyce was most serious and most profound when at his gayest. His humor is the proof of understanding the sign of equanimity. (qtd. in Bowen xii)

James Joyce Bibliography

Beja, Morris. Epiphany in the Modern Novel. Seattle, WA: University of Washington Press, 1971.

Bell, Robert H. Jocoserious Joyce: The Fate of Folly in Ulysses. Ithaca, NY: Cornell University Press, 1991.

Bluemel, Kristin. "The Feminine Laughter of No Return: James Joyce and Dorothy Richardson." Look Who's Laughing: Gender and Comedy. Ed. Gail Finney. New York, NY: Gordon and Breach, 1994 161-172.

Bowen, Zack R. Ulysses as a Comic Novel. Syracuse, NY: Syracuse University Press, 1989.

Breit, Harvey. "Forward." Silent Years: An Autobiography with Memoirs of James Joyce and Our Ireland. by J. F. Byrne. New York, NY: Farrar, Straus, and Young, 1953, ix-xi.

Deane, Seamus. "Joyce and Stephen: The Provincial Intellectual," "Joyce and Nationalism," "Joyce and Beckett." Celtic Revivals: Essays in Modern Irish Literature--Joyce, Yeats, O'Casey, Kinsella, Montague, Friel, Mahon, Heaney, Beckett, Synge. Winston-Salem, NC: Wake Forest University Press, 1985, 75-107 and 123-134.

Deming, Robert H. Ed. James Joyce: The Critical Heritage. New York, NY: Routledge and Kegan, 1970.

DiBernard, Barbara. "Parallax as Parallel, Paradigm, and Paradox in Ulysses." Éire-Ireland 10.1 (1975): 69-84.

Griffiths, Trevor. Comedians New York, NY: Grove, 1976.

Howarth, Herbert. "The Joycean Comedy: Wilde, Jonson, and Others." A James Joyce Miscellany. Second Series. Ed. Marvin Magalaner. Carbondale, IL: Southern Illinois Univ Press, 1959 179-194.

Ingersoll, Earl G. "Irish Jokes: A Lacanian Reading of Short Stories by James Joyce, Flann O'Brien, and Bryan MacMahon." Studies in Short Fiction 2 (Spring, 1990): 237-245.

Klug, Michael A. "The Comic Structure of Joyce's Ulysses." Éire 11.1 (1976): 63-84.

MacNicholas, John. "Comic Design in Joyce's 'The Dead.' " Modern British Literature 1.1 (1976): 56-65.

Maher, R. A. "James Joyce's Exiles: The Comedy of Discontinuity." James Joyce Quarterly 9 (1972): 461-474.

Polhemus, Robert M. "Joyce's Finnegans Wake (1924-39): The Comic Gospel of 'Shem'." Comic Faith: The Great Tradition from Austen to Joyce. Chicago, IL: Univ of Chicago Press, 1980, 294-337.

Robinson, Marian. "Funny Funereels: Single Combat in Finnegans Wake and the Táin Bó Cuailnge." Éire-Ireland 26.3 (1981): 96-106.

Santos, Antonio Raul de Toro. "Algunas Consideraciones sobre el Humorismo de James Joyce." Literary and Linguistic Aspects of Humour. Barcelona, Spain: Univ of Barcelona Dept of Languages, 1984, 233-238.

Schlossman, Beryl. Joyce's Catholic Comedy of Language. Madison, WI: University of Wisconsin Press, 1985.

Senn, Fritz, ed. New Light on Joyce Bloomington, IN: Indiana University Press, 1972.

Ussher, Arland. Three Great Irishmen: Shaw, Yeats, Joyce. New York, NY: Devin-Adair, 1953.

Waters, Maureen. "James Joyce and Buck Mulligan." The Comic Irishman. Albany, NY: State Univ of New York Press, 1984, 95-109.

Zois, Joelle. "Portraits of the Artist: A Review of Joyce Images (Norton, 1994), Edited by Greg Vitello." New York Times Book Review Oct. 9, 1994, 22.

Brinsley MacNamara (né John Weldon)(1890-1963) IRELAND

In 1910, John Weldon was a bit player in the Abbey Theatre. During that year, Lennox Robinson had Weldon change his name to "Brinsley MacNamara" because "Weldon" didn't sound Irish enough (MacDonnell 56).

The Valley of the Squinting Windows (1918) is a vitriolic exposé of rural Irish manners and customs that caused MacNamara to be labeled "the great pioneer of realism in Irish fiction," and it is because of this reputation that many critics have considered The Irishman to be realistic Irish fiction as well. Benedict Kiely considers this to be

> the fatal error of supposing that because a novel dealt uncharitably with uncharity and savagely with parochialism, and because it touched on two seductions, and ended with a bloody murder, it was a realistic novel. But "realism" is a method of using material, not a description of the material used, and a murder or a seduction or a satire on a village postmistress can be as genuinely matter for fantasy as a man changing into a donkey or a pooka with a good fairy in his pocket. (Kiely 93-94)

So MacNamara's book entitled The Irishman is misread by those who consider it to be realistic fiction. The book is not a realistic book about "the Comic Irishman." Rather it is a satire targeting the literary treatment of "the Comic Irishman." And it is subtle, because it is not targeting English authors, but is rather targeting Anglo-Irish authors like George Birmingham, Dorothea Conyers, Edith Ann Somerville, and Martin Ross. It should be noted that even though Birmingham, Conyers, Somerville, and Ross were somewhat Irish in their heritage and their thinking, they weren't as thoroughly Irish as MacNamara, who wrote from the inside looking out, rather than from the outside looking in. The Anglo-Irish authors observed the quaint idiosyncracies of the Irish peasant. They treated the characters as bibulous, sly, and witty, but in no way truly human, sensitive, or equal; their treatments were therefore superficial. So when Brinsley Macnamara treats "the Comic Irishman" in this same way, he is satirizing the whole Irish literary movement in order to illustrate his condemnation of "peasant realism." MacNamara, however, doesn't have enough distance from his subject to make the satire work.

> Most of the sketches are satirical in intention; some are bitingly comic; others are sympathetic and compassionate. But it must be acknowledged that the majority of these portraits smack more of caricature than of in-depth satirical studies. This is one of the weaknesses of the novel. In The Irishman, MacNamara has produced caricature, the weapon of the young and angry, instead of satire, the weapon of the mature moralist. (MacDonnell 54)

The Irishman is an attempt to satirize the whole Irish literary movement, by a novel which on the surface looks like an Irish novel written in a highly realistic mode (MacDonnell 55).

In The Irishman, Martin Duignan is an actor who applies for a job at the Tower Theatre (in real life the Abbey Theatre). He is introduced to Mr. Augustus Connell (in real life Lennox Robinson). Mr. Connell explains how the Abbey theatre is different from other theatres:

> Our players fit so perfectly into our plays. As a matter of fact, they are specially constructed for them. Take the case of a certain person, for example, who writes by far the most of the plays we produce here. He is quite unable to write a line of his lines without a constant manipulation in his mind of the character who is destined to deliver it. (MacDonnell 56)

Compare this to an analysis by Dorothy Macardle of how the Abbey Theatre was operating during this period of time.

In order to change their programme every week the company resorted to frequent revivals at short intervals and to the revival of those plays which they could perform with most facility. Their range became restricted; their excursions from the cottage interior rarely led them farther than to a tenement room, a lodging-house bedroom or a "parlour" in "the suburban grove," and the dramatists followed suit. For years we have seen plays performed which, quite obviously have been written, not only for the Abbey Theatre, but for the Abbey players--for this actor's lift of an eyebrow and that actress's toss of the chin--and even for the Abbey property-room. I have heard the property man, in a tone of indignant protest, rebuking a new author who had made a demand considered exorbitant--"a mug with a black pig on it" was the direction in the script. The author was categorically instructed as to what was and what was not in the property-room, "So that another time you won't write ad-lib." (Macardle 126-127)

Brinsley MacNamara's and Dorothy Macardle's remarks are very similar, and to some extent, William Butler Yeats, John Synge, and Lady Isabella Gregory (early patrons of the Abbey Theatre) were targets of that criticism. MacNamara especially lampooned these early "realists" by saying that what these authors considered to be Irish country speech had not been studied first-hand and through intimate contact. MacNamara even referred to Synge's peasant dialogue as "crack-in-the-floor realism." And in The Irishman, Augustus Connell requires Martin Duignan (in real life Brinsley MacNamara as a character) to take an oral examination over a sheet of "Irish Peasant Expressions" that were "prevalent in Tower Theatre" (in real life the Abbey Theatre) plays. "This litany of stereotypical Abbey lines signifies that MacNamara believed the Abbey had become cliché ridden well before 1910. He wittily mimics the gamut of early Abbey playwrights' purple patches, obviously familiar enough then to merit satiric censure" (MacDonnell 58). MacDonnell resented the fact that authors before him had characterized the Irish peasant by such superficial aspects as his peculiar turns of phrase, by what he said rather than by what he did. This was consistent with "the language obsession of the Gaelic League" (MacDonnell 58). MacDonnell listened to the speech of the Irish peasants in play after play at the Abbey, and he concluded that this was not the speech of the Irish peasant.

It had the ring of the speech of the peasant . . . , but it was not the speech of the men who went into Glannidan every evening and remained drinking in the gloom of the pubs . . . . He listened to their humor, but it was the humour which comes from flights of the mind, and the humour he had known in Glannanea was something which came most often from a petty satisfaction of some low spite when one man got the better of another through the exercise of a little animal cunning. It was seldom that any one laughed in Glannidan, but they were always grinning (Blyth 92).

The "Comic Irishman" is a standard stereotype on the English stage. The "Comic Irishman" is also a standard stereotype on the Irish stage. Paul Smith makes the following insightful observation of how the Irish were able to change the stereotype of the "Comic Irishman."

By the 1940s the Abbey did chase out the red-headed, beady-eyed, flat-nosed, freckled and crafty gombeen dressed in a tight-fitting, short-sleeved and trousered suit of large checks and twirling a shillelagh; but, alas! it replaced him with a bowler-hatted, whey-faced, crafty and provincial civil servant dressed in a tight-fitting, short-sleeved and trousered suit of black. (Hogan 15).

What MacNamara was attempting to show in The Irishman is that in pursuing the goal of "reality," what the Abbey had done, instead of finding truth, was the "interring of one kind of stage Irishman and replacing him with another" (MacDonnell 60). In discussing the importance of The Irishman, MacDonnell concludes by saying, "acerbic insights intertwine with prophecy and droll humor to produce a valuable satiric novel." MacNamara's first-hand analysis of the early Abbey realities proves peculiarly appropriate today. MacNamara "viewed life on a bias with a multifacetedness which was to find its finest expression in tragi-comic fantasies, informed by his long, low chuckle of the mind" (MacDonnell 64).

Brinsley MacNamara Bibliography

Blyth, Oliver. The Irishman. London, England: Everleigh Nash Company, 1920.
Hogan, Robert. After the Irish Renaissance Minneapolis, MN: University of Minnesota Press, 1967.
Kiely, Benedict. Modern Irish Fiction. Dublin, Ireland: Golden Eagle Books, 1950.
MacCardle, Dorothy. "Experiments in Ireland." Theatre Arts 18 (February, 1934): 126-127.
McDonnell, Michael. "Stereotypes and Caricatures of the Abbey Theatre (1910) in The Irishman by Brinsley MacNamara." Éire-Ireland 24 (1989): 53-64.

Kate O'Brien (1897-1974) IRELAND

Kate O'Brien is a Gaelic-Irish novelist who attempted to articulate a woman's position in the new Ireland (Weekes 21). The Ireland which O'Brien writes about is Catholic, Gaelic, and middle-classed. O'Brien notes the irony that in this Ireland of the rebel Eamon De Valera, the women are no more free than are the women in the England of Queen Victoria (Weekes 22). Kate O'Brien wrote such works as Without My Cloak (1931), The Anteroom (1934), Mary Lavelle (1936), Pray for the Wanderer (1938), The Land of Spices (1941), The Last of Summer (1943), That Lady (1946), The Flower of May (1953), As Music and Splendour (1958), My Ireland (1962), and Presentation Parlour (biographical sketches) (1963).

Kate O'Brien Bibliography

Weekes, Ann Owens. "Kate O'Brien: Family in the New Nation." Irish Women Writers: An Uncharted Tradition. Lexington, KY: University Press of Kentucky, 1990, 108-132.

Elizabeth Dorothea Cole Bowen (1899-1973) IRELAND

Regina Barreca feels that Elizabeth Bowen's humor is like much women's humor in questioning, mocking, and demystifying the world of inherited and institutionalized power (Barreca 109). During her writing years of 1923 until 1968, Bowen deployed a kind of humor which Judy Little calls "renegade humor," a kind of humor that was also used effectively by Virginia Woolf and Muriel Spark. Barreca says that Bowen's humor is the humor of the "ruthless observer" (Barreca 110), as she skillfully intermingles the apparently contradictory forces of humor and anger. Bowen's satire is not corrective in purpose. In fact, her work is fascinatingly enigmatic because she mimics the accents of the ruling class; "she mirrors power only to ridicule it" (Barreca 111). Barreca feels that Bowen's humor demonstrates "a profound awareness that the accepted pattern has no necessity." Bowen's female characters are especially aware that "life is a series of arbitrary, closely guarded assumptions based on the most flimsy and transient foundations" (Barreca 113). Bowen herself says that "to write is always to rave a little," and in Bowen's writings there is a linking of madness, and hysteria, and matriarchy, and witchiness with the comic (Barreca 114). In Bowen's works, there is also a close relationship between violence and humor. Nevertheless, some critics (for example Hermione Lee and James Ginden have classified her work as "comedy of manners," but with an "underlying pull of fatality." Barreca suggests that such a view needs to be modified to include the subversive aspects of Bowen's comedy; Barreca would prefer to classify Bowen's work as "resistance writing." She says that Bowen looks at life from a "wildly sideways" perspective (Barreca 115).

Susan Lanser feels that Bowen's writing is humorous partly because she writes with a double voice. When she says, "the condition of being a woman in a male-dominant society may well necessitate the double voice, whether as a conscious subterfuge or as a tragic dispossession of the self." Lanser continues that Bowen's "deployment of decorum in staid and elegant drawing-rooms, however, actually challenges the ideology of manners." Then Lanser explains Bowen's double voice by saying, "Her female characters both embody and rail against domestic codes" (Lanser 157). Regina Barreca considers Bowen's female characters to be "laughing Medusas." Judith Wilt describes them as "laughing at the edge, withholding fertility, humility, community" (Wilt 180). Barreca says that one of Bowen's most dangerous comedic strategies is "avenging innocence" (Barreca 120). Barreca adds that Austen's "scathing wit and subversive humor" are echoed by Bowen. The humor of both of these authors is cloaked in the beginning, but it is "eventually revealed as both deadly and accurate" (Barreca 121).

The sensitive people in The Hotel (1928) "feel spikes everywhere and rush to impale themselves" (The Hotel 77). In this novel God is seen as "an enormous and perpetually descending Finger and Thumb" (The Hotel 89).

Elizabeth Bowen's The Death of the Heart (1938) takes place in Victorian times. In the novel, both of Portia's parents have died, and since she is only sixteen years old, and the half sister of Thomas Quayne, she comes to live with the Quaynes at Windsor Terrace. Thomas and Anna Quayne are in their thirties; they are well to do; and before Portia comes into their lives, they are childless. The novel is about Portia's way of getting along with her adoptive parents and their friends and associates (Coles 110). "The Death of the Heart" is a provocative title for a novel to have, and the chapter headings are equally provocative: "The World," "The Flesh," and "The Devil." Although Windsor Terrace is very proper, it is sad and is suffering from emotional deterioration. Thomas feels that his marriage to Anna is a fantasy. He thinks of it in terms of "what they might do together if both of them were different" (Coles 111).

During her stay at Windsor Terrace, Portia has been keeping a diary, and Anna discovers this diary and reads from it. She finds the comments to be irresistible, yet nerve-racking, and she feels that they are both distorted and distorting in their nature. She tells a friend that "either the girl or I are mad." Portia is a keen observer; she misses nothing, and records everything. Portia has a keen instinct for the phony and the pretentious, regardless of how solid and permanent an appearance the adults manifest, so sixteen-year-old Portia, with her diary, is keeping a keen watch on the adults around her. Coles feels that there is a certain irony here, because Bowen is keeping a sort of diary of her own while the story unfolds (Coles 113). "Bowen is not afraid to show Portia contending with most of those seven deadly sins: at the very least, pride, covetousness, lust, anger, and envy. One could even make a case for sloth" (Coles 151).

At one point in The Death of the Heart Portia buries her face in Eddie's shoulder as they ride in a taxi, and she says, "No, don't kiss me now." Eddie doesn't understand, and asks, "Why not now?" and Portia explains simply, "Because I don't want you to." Eddie doesn't leave it at that, and asks the barbed question, "You mean that I didn't once when you did?" Regina Barreca considers this little conversation to be a "delicate moment, done with extreme caution and expertise, like the balancing of an orange on the rim of a plate" (a trick also mentioned in The Death of the Heart) (Barreca 112).

In The Death of the Heart, Bowen is really talking about "youth." There is a constant conflict between youth and the adult world. Youth tend to be "selfish, turned in on themselves, demanding, spoiled, naive, dangerously ignorant and susceptible to the blandishments of--well dozens of dangerous propagandists or ideologues." But The Death of the Heart shows the other side of this issue: "Someday the devils of this world, the whole Windsor Terrace crowd, residents and visitors alike, will be seen for the killers they are, and summarily banished, or at the least stripped of their considerable authority over the lives of the world's Portias" (Coles 153).

In The Heat of the Day (1949), Bowen explains "the joke or agony" without seeing anything strange about the juxtaposition of "joke" and "agony" (Barreca 115). The mad woman in The Heat of the Day refuses to embroider roses in the traditional way not because she is out of pink wool, but rather because "there are purple roses." She complains that nobody believes her, and yet she persists in her belief that "I could lead you to the very place in the garden and show you the bush. There is only one; it's not my fault if there are no others in the world" (Heat 240). The mad woman's defiance is her weakness; but it is also her strength. "Defiance forms the bridge between the richness of chaos and the richness of comedy in Bowen's work. Anger and humor establish their own authority, with defiance as the manifestation of rage and humor as its voice" (Barreca 122). Even the innocence of children in The Heat of the Day is a target of Bowen's satire, as she tends to portray them as "engaged innocently in some act of destruction--depetalling daisies, puffing at dandelion clocks, trampling primrose woods, rioting round in fragile feathered grown-up hats . . . or knocking down apples from the bough" (Heat 234).

British manners are a target of satire in To the North (1950), where the reader is told that a typical British outing consists of traveling "twenty-five miles [to sit] on a stump of the Roman villa, their feet in a pit" (To the North 59). Marriage is also a source of much of Bowen's satire. In To the North, Gerda Bligh is described as "not really a fool, she was an honest girl . . . with a tendency to hysteria. Having read a good many novels about marriage, not to speak of some scientific books, she now knew not only why she was unhappy but exactly how unhappy she could still be" (To the North 51). Gerda and her young husband have a bitter argument during a weekend in the country. "Their attention to one another was almost lover-like. They broke off conversations at dinner to glare compellingly at one another across the table; they dogged one another about the house and garden to see what the other was doing and interfere" (To the North 60).

The men and the women in Bowen's novels tend to have a very different notion of humor. When they view women's humor, the men say with authority, "That's not funny." Bowen's men simply don't understand why women find particular things funny, and furthermore, they don't approve of women's humor. In To the North, Sir Mark is attending a party about the Channel tunnel, and he speaks condescendingly to a young woman there who responds, "But I am a shipping agent." Sir Mark cannot take this statement seriously, and assumes that she is making a joke. It doesn't occur to him that she is indeed a business woman, so he responds, "Ha-ha. Hum. Very good, yes, ha-ha!" with his thumbs under his lapel, and his eyes anxiously looking round the room (To the North 130).

Markie's wit in To the North is contrasted with Emmeline's "divine humourlessness." Nevertheless, contrary to Markie's assessment, Emeline has "an exquisite and finely tuned sense of humor, what the narrator calls 'a profound irony' " (Barreca 126). Markie considers Emmeline to be an "adorably comic," object rather than a producer of her own wry humor. He sees her not as someone who acts, but rather as someone who is acted upon. Emmeline asks Markie if most of his friends are amusing, and he responds that they are not. Emmeline then says, "I expect they are. But as you're amusing yourself you might not notice' " (To the North 182). Emmeline says that she likes Markie because "he is so funny" (To the North 48); however, Celia counters by saying that listening to Markie be clever is "like watching something catch too many flies on its tongue" (To the North 49).

At one point in To the North an airplane flying overhead makes it difficult to converse, so Markie scribbles to Emmeline, "You must know what I want; all I want: if I COULD marry, it would be to you" (To the North 138). Barreca notes, however, that Markie never intends to marry her (Barreca 128), and when Emmeline loses her virginity to Markie in a Paris hotel, Markie once again emphasizes that people "like you and me" do not marry. Markie adds, cheerfully, "If I shot anyone, I am the sort of man I should shoot;" Markie feels that by saying this line he has absolved himself of all responsibility towards the woman who has just become his lover (Barreca 129).

Eva in Eva Trout; or, Changing Scenes (1968) is a giant both literally and figuratively. She is so physically large as to have an overwhelming presence, but she is also awkward, a little out of kilter, and not able to find a proper form (Barreca 114). The narrator in Eva Trout is somewhat judgmental. This narrator says that Iseult Smith had been a townswoman, and a reader of D. H. Lawrence as well, so her husband was "lucky not to come out worse than he did" (Eva Trout 16). In Bowen's writing, women are frequently accused of being humorless and unlaughing; they have a kind of wicked and subversive humor, however, which is potently dangerous, and necessary to the spirit of rebellion. These are the moments which are described in Eva Trout as those when it is "fatal to laugh" (Barreca 125).

The Last September (1979) is the story of the demise of a Big House, and the parallel release from Eden of a young girl during the 1920 Irish Troubles. This seems appropriate as a Bowen text because the relationship between these two events is more than coincidental (Weekes 21).

Elizabeth Dorothea Cole Bowen Bibliography

Barreca, Regina. " 'The Joke or Agony': Elizabeth Bowen's Comic Vision." Untamed and Unabashed: Essays on Women and Humor in British Literature. Detroit, MI: Wayne State University Press, 1994.

Bowen, Elizabeth. Eva Trout. New York, NY: Alfred A. Knopf, 1968.

Bowen, Elizabeth. The Heat of the Day. New York, NY: Alfred A. Knopf, 1949.

Bowen, Elizabeth. The Hotel. New York, NY: Alfred A. Knopf, 1952.

Bowen, Elizabeth. To the North. New York, NY: Alfred A. Knopf, 1950.

Coles, Robert. "Youth: Elizabeth Bowen's The Death of the Heart." Irony in the Mind's Life: Essays on Novels by James Agee, Elizabeth Bowen, and George Eliot. Charlottesville, VA: University Press of Virginia, 1974, 107-153.

Lanser, Susan. "Toward a Feminist Narratology." Feminism: An Anthology of Literary Theory and Criticism. Eds. Robyn R. Warhol and Diane Priced Herndl. New Brunswick, NJ: Rutgers University Press, 1991, 610-629.

Weekes, Ann Owens. "Elizabeth Bowen: Out of Eden." Irish Women Writers: An Uncharted Tradition. Lexington, KY: University Press of Kentucky, 1990, 83-107.

Wilt, Judith. The Laughter of Maidens, the Cackle of Matriarchs: Notes on the Collision Between Humor and Feminism. Gender and the Literary Voice. Ed. Janet Todd. New York, NY: Holmes and Meier, 1980, 1-74.

CHAPTER 8

Humor in 20th Century
Irish Literature: Late Authors

Patrick Kavanagh (1904-1967) IRELAND

Darcy O'Brien said that Patrick Kavanagh had the same ability as Frank Sinatra, Dylan Thomas, Pablo Picasso and the Marx Brothers to arouse the emotions to a screaming pitch--for or against him (Waters 137). Kavanagh was a careful observer of the small details of everyday life. The style of both his prose and his poetry is quite plain, and he has the ability to catch the rhythms of country speech. Rather than presenting the heroic and extravagant playboy, Kavanagh presented the poet as a wise fool, an archetype which has roots in Middle Irish literature (Waters 138). Patrick Kavanagh was an Irish-Free-State poet who blended the traditional languages of regional loyalty and Catholicism with the adversity language (English) in a body of work which "expresses contentment at the spectacle of an ordinary but still miraculous world" (Deane 16). In discussing his penchant for satire, Kavanagh tells about the "furious enthusiastic hatred which is a form of love" (Waters 90). Kavanagh used the term "buck lep" to describe the actions of a man who is "eager to display his merit and exuberance as a true Gael." The "buck lep" is performed by leaping high into the air with a shout, at the same time striking both of the heels hard against the buttocks (Waters 92).

The central theme of <u>Tarry Flynn</u> (1949) is sexual frustration. Tarry has had very little experience with women and this fact is the basis for a great deal of self-mockery. Tarry's notion of impressing a woman is to lecture her on philosophy or canon law so that she won't suspect him of lewd intentions (Waters 142). There is great irony in the fact that Tarry is regarded as a troublemaker, since he is actually a timid and conservative character. In the novel a crisis develops because of the local ability to change insignificant and trivial details into full scale drama. "Absurdly enough, Tarry is implicated in both a seduction and an attempted murder as rumor is fed by neighbors delighted at the prospect of a little diversion. No one is interested in the truth, including his own family; his mother denounces him for not keeping in with the priests." Tarry, in his patched trousers with the crotch reinforced with overcoat buttons, is the traditional Fool. He is mocked on all sides, and is particularly the target of women. Furthermore, there is a great disparity between Tarry's perception of himself as a lusty and eloquent man of consequence, and the towns people's perception of him as a contemptible fool (Waters 145).

Much of the satiric humor of <u>Tarry Flynn</u> derives from the disproportionate amount of fury that is expended on trivial matters. There is an "absurd jealousy over a small field," and there is also "eternal scheming to win a minor advantage or to deceive a neighbor"

(Waters 138). Tarry Flynn lives in Drumnay, a static and closed society in which very little of importance ever happens. The height of excitement there would be the occasional sermon on sexual sin. Kavanagh satirizes the romantic traditions about rustic life. Kavanagh's folk characters are not the open hearted, jolly, musical and extravagant characters we would expect; rather, they are cautious, embittered, spiritually and mentally impoverished. There is a strong element of realism in Tarry Flynn, but the tone is nevertheless that of comic satire. Details are piled up on top of one another and are exaggerated in the process until the very excess is laughable. There are no ordinary people in Drumnay, since everyone is characterized as grotesque. Kavanagh writes:

> Between the three Flynn girls there was little to choose. They were all the same height, around five feet two--low-set, with dull clayey faces, each of them like a bag of chaff tied in the middle with a rope--breasts and buttocks that flapped in the wind. When they were unwashed and undressed in the morning a stranger passing seeing them would hardly be able to say who was who.

This quote is typical of Kavanagh's writing in containing "a comic energy of the language with its pungent metaphors and needling tone" (Waters 139). Tarry Flynn is also filled with sharp and scatological wit which displays a delight in exposing human folly. The people in Drumnay don't tend to lose themselves in conversation nor do they tend to fantasize. Although they love gossip and melodrama, they are firmly planted in the Irish earth. Tarry Flynn's mother is ambitious and she treats Tarry much as Christy Mahon's father treated Christy--contemptuously.

> She continually scolds him like a child, belittling him, stressing his foolishness, and in every way keeping him dependent upon her despite his twenty-six years. She represents the persisting grip of parental authority in rural areas where men often did not marry until middle age. The most telling signs of Tarry's emasculation at her hands are the patched trousers she forces him to wear, which look like "they had been torn by mad dogs and patched by mad women;" the crotch is distinguished by large buttons that he tries to conceal from young women by walking sideways. (Waters 140)

Tarry Flynn is an earthy novel whose satiric humor is mainly associated with Mrs. Flynn's shortsighted and furious struggle to help Tarry advance in life. She has a biting tongue, and can always find an appropriate metaphor to skewer the immediate object of her wrath. For example, a local woman who has an eye on Tarry is summarily dismissed as "that old pot walloper." Mrs. Flynn is tough minded, suspicious, and shrewd. She so much enjoys a quarrel that she is continually stirring up trouble in her own household. Like many other Irish comic characters, she has a gift for the dramatic, as she makes herself "the center of a crisis by investing the minutiae of domestic and parish life with terrible significance." Like Sean O'Casey's Mrs. Gogan, Mrs. Flynn relishes the possibility of any scandal or disaster (Waters 141).

Patrick Kavanagh Bibliography

Deane, Seamus. Celtic Revivals: Essays in Modern Irish Literature--Joyce, Yeats, O'Casey, Kinsella, Montague, Friel, Mahon, Heaney, Beckett, Synge. Winston-Salem, NC: Wake Forest University Press, 1985.

Kavanagh, Patrick. Tarry Flynn. Middlesex, England: Penguin, 1978.

Waters, Maureen. "Patrick Kavanagh and Tarry Flynn." The Comic Irishman. Albany, NY: State Univ of New York Press, 1984, 137-148.

Molly (Mary Nesta Skrine) Keane (1904-) IRELAND

Molly Keane (M. J. Farrell) began writing seriously in the 1930s. Her early work was both daring and colorful. Keane wrote such books as Taking Chances (1920), Mad Puppetstown (1931), Devoted Ladies (1934), Full House (1935), The Rising Tide (1937), Two Days in Aragon (1941), Queen Lear (1989), Treasure Hunt (1990), and Conversation Piece (1991). Keane's Good Behaviour (1981) is a black comedy which "testifies to the variety as well as the continuity within Irish women's fiction." It is a satire which widens Elizabeth Bowen's presentation of a young girl's awakening by glancing across fifty years to the last September of Anglo-Ireland. Good Behaviour is a caricature, but it is also "a needed corrective, or widening, of Bowen's picture" (Weekes 22).

Molly Keane Bibliography

Weekes, Ann Owens. "Molly Keane: Bildungsroman Quenelles." Irish Women Writers: An
    Uncharted Tradition. Lexington, KY: University Press of Kentucky, 1990, 155-173.

Samuel Barclay Beckett (1906-1989) IRELAND

According to John Orr, it was Beckett who developed the dialogue of paired characters, each of which contributed to half of the total personality. "Here the balanced land symmetrical ciphers of dialogue are the offspring of vaudeville clowns and the great comics of the silent cinema. Yet their voices clearly speak a language of dark times amidst hilarity and confusion" (Orr 49). One of Beckett's most successful rhetorical techniques is what Frederik Smith called "verbal slapstick" (Smith 43). "His syntax typically tries to contain words that resist violently the rational attempt to bring them together into the same sentence or paragraph. The result is that incongruous meanings and tones and voices crash into one another with the same frequency as automobiles in a Mack Sennett comedy" (Smith 43-44). Beckett's symbols--rocking chairs, bicycles, crutches, hats, pencils, windows, doors, pots, and sacks--take on a life of their own, as do his other words and expressions. Words "seem to exist only to bring about the downfall of the speaker's or writer's self-confident syntax. The anarchy of objects in silent film becomes the 'unbridled gibberish' (Malone's term) or 'wordy-gurdy' (the Unnamable's term) of Beckett's relentless verbal comedy that his personae quite understandably seek to make silent" (Henkle 44).

Beckett is fascinated with etymology, and in order to read Beckett, the reader must constantly be aware of what Henkle calls the "lexical field," defined as "a word's complex of related words, level of usage, social register, age, and tone" (Henkle 44). In opposing lexical fields, Beckett is, of course, also opposing values and points of view. "It is here that he parts company with the satirist. Rather than using one vocabulary to belie another-- the way Swift and Pope do, for example--Beckett sets one vocabulary over against another simply as a way of showing that both value systems are viable as well as arbitrary" (Henkle 54).

A rhetorical technique which Beckett frequently uses is the establishment of a local lexical context, along with the attendant expectations on the reader. Beckett then inserts within this lexical context a few words that don't jibe in meaning or tone with the lexical environment. These words therefore shockingly and humorously alter the significance of the context. Henkle gives the name of "verbal slapstick" to what Beckett does, and he gives an example from Murphy.

> "Love requited," said Neary, "is a short circuit, a ball that gave rise to a
>   sparkling rally."

"The love that lifts up its eyes," said Neary, "brings in torments; the craves
for the tip of her little finger, dipped in lacquer, to cool its tongue--is
foreign to you, Murphy, I take it."
"Greek," said Murphy.
"Or put it another way," said Neary; "the single brilliant, organised, compact
blotch in the tumult of heterogeneous stimulation."
"Blotch is the word," said Murphy.
"Just so," said Neary. (Beckett Murphy 5-6)

Here in order to define "love requited," Neary uses an electrical metaphor (short circuit),
a lyrical style (being in torments, that craves for the tip of her little finger), and an
academic description (the tumult of heterogeneous stimulation). But all of these metaphors,
though slightly askew are nevertheless weirdly appropriate. But then we come to the
colloquial "blotch," "at which point Murphy seems to know precisely what he means"
(Henkle 45).

Beckett explains how the various stages of humor correspond to "successive
excoriations of the understanding." According to Beckett's guide, the early stages involve
"the ethical laugh" at what is good, and "the intellectual laugh" at what is not true. Here
there is an implied criticism. In fact, Beckett's early works tend to be critical of both God
and of existence. This is why "his youthful iconoclasm and comic genius are given full
rein in More Pricks than Kicks (1934) and Murphy (1936)." After this the humor becomes
blacker and more cruel. In Molloy (1947), and its sequel Malone Dies (1948), the narrator
may be tiring, but in order to continue writing, he deploys such pastimes as comical sexual
adventures, moments of euphoria on a bicycle, and many digressions and jokes in order to
stave of "accidia" (Topsfield 128-129).

A comparison of the writings of Samuel Beckett with those of James Joyce is
inevitable. Beckett was very much influenced by Joyce, and almost everything he wrote
was either purposefully like what Joyce wrote, or purposefully different. Joyce and Beckett
shared a mischievous sense of fun, and both were driven by their countrymen to a kind of
manic laughter.

Their closest relationship, though, is in the realm of irreverence, wild
comedy and non sequiturs, which, for them, mirror life. Their humour was
formed in Dublin, the home of such wit and wordplay, blasphemy and
obscenity, parody and paradox. Like Joyce, Beckett observes his fellow
creatures, and finds comic material in their confusions. Most of all they
share the joy of comic language. (Topsfield 16)

Joyce plays with language, saying, "That's enough of finicking with Finnigan and fiddling
with his faddles" (qtd. in Topsfield 16). And Beckett plays with language by calling one
of his works "Foirade" in French and "Fizzles" in English. He said he just "farted out" the
work, and defines his title for the Oxford English Dictionary as "the action of breaking
wind quietly . . . a failure or fiasco" (Topsfield 16). Some of Beckett's puns work across
languages; others just don't. Valerie Topsfield notes that in Murphy Beckett developed an
English pun that doesn't work well in French, for "Murphy is most off his rocker when he
is on his rocker" (Topsfield 34). Beckett's and Joyce's fascination with language is
comically described by Beckett's character Watt, who is obsessed with words. The narrator
in Watt says, "Watt's need of semantic succour was at times so great that he would set to
trying names on things, and on himself, almost as a woman hats" (Beckett Watt 79).

Valerie Topsfield indicates that Beckett had an "inbuilt sense of fun," especially in
his early works where his childlike humor is filled with wit and wordplay. There are many
jokes in these early works, and some are well-worn, like the one about the barmaid at
which Belacqua laughs until he cries, and the other one about the vicar who dies laughing
(Topsfield 1). Beckett loved the Irish earth, and this shows through in his parody of the

scriptures when he says, "It was always from the earth, rather than from the sky, notwithstanding its reputation, that my help came in time of trouble" (Four Novellas 56).

In his early works, Beckett's characters demonstrate a comic verbal elegance that is based on sophisticated vocabulary and reference. The titles of these early works, like the works themselves, contain puns: Whoreoscope, More Pricks than Kicks, "Enueg," and Murphy (where Beckett declares, "In the beginning was the pun").

> In these works, an intellectual laugh springs from linguistic techniques that are indifferent or irrelevant to truth: polished paradox, sneering irony, twisted quotation, erudite jargon. Even the heavier humor of misplaced literalism is lightly and elegantly applied. Beckett's wit glitters mainly in parody, where the tone is sometimes riotously, sometimes grotesquely, out of key with its subject. (Cohn 292-293)

Samuel Beckett wrote that "the mirthless laugh is the laugh of laughs, laughing at that which is unhappy, at suffering and, ultimately, at death." This is why so much of Beckett's humor is macabre humor (Mercier 4). Like James Joyce, Samuel Beckett was in love with language. In contrast to James Joyce, however, Samuel Beckett was a minimalist writer (Deane 129). In Beckett's plays there are few characters, no action, no time change, no place change, and no props. In Waiting for Godot they wait for Godot.

Deane suggests that in Beckett's writing, forms of narrative are often supplanted by the techniques of meditation (Deane 127). Beckett's protagonists are old fools who are in the tradition of being "slapped." But Beckett writes in such a way that the reader laughs not only at the fool who gets slapped, but laughs also at the slapper, and at the slap itself. Beckett's protagonists also exhibit other features in the tradition of the fool. Physically they are freaks; they inspire an idiocy that borders on wisdom; and they are alienated from society (Cohn 284). Mrs. Williams in Human Wishes expresses the darkly humorous outlook of the maimed characters in Beckett's later works. Mrs. Williams hears something she was not supposed to hear, and responds, "I may be old, I may be blind, halt and maim, I may be dying of a pituitous defluxion, but my hearing is unimpaired" (Topsfield 12).

Beckett's protagonists tend to have ridiculous compulsions. There is Murphy and his rocker; there is Molloy on his compulsive voyage; there is Malone in bed; there is the Unnamable in limbo; there are "uprooted" Gogo and Didi beside their "rooted" tree; there are the defenseless Hamm and Clov in their shelter; there is the partner of Pim and/or Bom in the mud; there are Winnie and Willie on the scorched earth beneath a blazing sun. All of these absurd tableaux evoke laughter at the physical situation, and require pity for the metaphysical situation (Cohn 290). Beckett's heroes are "limp rags of life lost in a stone-cold universe" (Cohn 291). We may laugh at the leg ailments, the verbal difficulties, the ignorance, and the passions of Beckett's heroes, but our laughter is quite nervous and anxious (Cohn 296). When Beckett changed from English to French, "the cultivated English smile explodes into a Rabelaisian guffaw when pedantic jawbreakers give way to Basic-French-and-dirty-words" (Cohn 293). Beckett's French heroes, although they are "trapped between birth and death" are just as funny as are his American characters (Cohn 292). Laughter (or the absence of laughter) is an important element in Beckett's works. In Waiting for Godot (1952) it hurts Vladimir to laugh. In Endgame (1958) Hamm muses, "You weep, and weep, for nothing, so as not to laugh." In Embers (1959) Henry is able to laugh only a "long horrible laugh." In Comment c'est (1961) there is a crawling creature which at first wants to laugh all the time, then wants to laugh only sometimes, then three times out of ten, four out of fifteen, but he finally settles for "trois quatre rires reussis de ceux qui secouent un instant ressuscitent un instant puis laissent pour plus mort qu'avant" (three four successful laughs of those that shake one an instant revive one an instant then leave one more dead than before).

Ruby Cohn says that from his earliest writing on, Beckett uses callousness and cruelty to evoke a "bitter ethical laughter."

An execution amuses Belacqua Shuah; the sadistic routines of the Magdalen Mental Mercy-seat are itemized for our amusement; and all the heroes of Beckett's French fiction invite our laughter at their savage drives--Moran's towards his son, Molloy's towards his mother, Malone's towards his creations, the Unnamable's towards his creators. Vladimir and Estragon turn their stichomythic humor to suicide and murder. Hamm and Clov engage in verbal torture, to their and our ironic appreciation. In Comment c'est all men are paradoxically and statistically revealed as both victim and executioner, and the more one suffers, the more wildly one laughs. (Cohn 287)

There are many places throughout Beckett's works where he makes mild fun of Pythagoras's theory that "certainty lies in numbers" (Topsfield 17). Molloy has a problem of how to manipulate sixteen sucking stones from one pocket to another so that he can be sure that he will suck them in strict rotation (Reid 89). In Murphy there is an episode involving the comic application of mathematical formulas in the feeding of five biscuits to a single dog, where Murphy considers the twenty different permutations in the order of eating them himself. This relates to one of Beckett's favorite philosophical principles, first stated by Democritus: "Nothing is more real than nothing" (Topsfield 18). Beckett's writing was influenced by the movies. Valerie Topsfield feels that Vladimir and Estragon are wearing Charlie Chaplin's clothes, that Krapp slips on a banana peel, and that in Watt there is a pun on the "hardy laurel" (Topsfield 29).

In 1929 Beckett wrote a satire by the name of "Che Sciagura," which was based on a bawdy line from Voltaire's Candide. In 1931, Beckett wrote a parody of Corneille's Le Cid entitled, The Kid, and this was performed at Trinity College in Dublin in 1931, with Beckett himself (brandishing an umbrella as if it were a sword) in the role of Don Diège (Topsfield 36). Beckett's first novel was begun in Paris in 1932. The title is a play both on Tennyson's poem and Henry Williamson's novel, A Dream of Fair Women. Beckett's version is entitled A Dream of Fair to Middling Women.

The motto of Beckett's first novel, More Pricks than Kicks (1934), was "Hope for the best and expect the worst" (Topsfield 6). The novel is a rich collection of droll anecdotes, some autobiographical, about the 'sinfully indolent' Balacqua Shuah, beginning with his student days at Trinity College, Dublin, and ending with his death in early middle age (Topsfield 38). This collection of stories is rich in satire and in verbal wit. Maureen Waters considers all of Beckett's early work to be filled with verbal wit and playfulness (Waters 121-122). In More Pricks that Kicks Beckett twists plots for comic effect as "Belacqua abandons a damsel in distress, urges his fiancee to take a lover, is himself the object of a lady's lust, and is finally supplanted in the arms of his third wife by his best friend" (Cohn 288).

Beckett was interested in the opposing philosophies of Heraclitus, "the sad philosopher," and Democritus, "the laughing philosopher," and Valerie Topsfield suggests that it is Democritus's philosophy of being amused by the follies of society which is associated with such Beckett clowns as Bim, Bom, and Grock of More Pricks than Kicks. It is appropriate that the pessimistic Belacqua, who fears death and is about to undergo minor surgery, wonders whether he should choose the humorist Democritus, or the pessimistic Heraclitus as his patron philosopher. He decides on Democritus because, "He would arm his mind with laughter, laughter is not the word but it will have to serve." Ironically, Belacqua's fear of death is well grounded, for his anaesthetist has returned from a wedding and is still drunk, and he misadministers the anesthetic (Topsfield 17). Beckett develops humor in the trivial and vulgar incidents which make up Belacqua's career by elaborately analyzing these vulgarities. This type of satire embellishes the commonplace with a wealth of observation, alternated with sudden brusqueness. (Topsfield 37-38). Beckett's humor is a curious blend of colloquialism and coarseness with high sophistication, and in fact Beckett himself considered More Pricks than Kicks to be nothing more than "juvenalia." Balacqua's trouble is that he cannot grow up. His childishness is the source of a large portion of the comedy. Balacqua himself is rather charming. Beckett describes him as "a kind of cretinous Tom Jones." In considering Balacqua's infantile outlook on life, consider the following comic description about how he makes a sandwich: "He laid his cheek against the soft of the bread, it was spongy and warm, alive. But he would very soon take that plush feel off it, by God, but he would very quickly take that white look of its face" (Beckett Pricks 11).

Many of the stories told in More Pricks than Kicks are humorous. In "What a Misfortune," James Skyrm is described as "an aged cretin' who gnashes his teeth without ceasing at invisible spaghetti." Topsfield considers Skyrm to be a forerunner of many of Beckett's later grotesques (Topsfield 40). "Love and Lethe" is black comedy which is rich in double entendres (Topsfield 41). The humor in "Walking Out" is somewhat savage. The title is a pun meaning not only "walking out" in the sense of courting but also "walking out" in the sense of escaping. In love, as in all other matters, Belacqua has a lack of commitment, and it is from this quality that Beckett draws much of his "seemingly heartfelt saturnine humour" (Topsfield 43).

In Our Exagmination, a collection of essays on Joyce's Finnegans Wake published in the 1930s, Purgatory is described by Beckett as "a flood of movement and vitality," much more productive than "the static lifelessness of unrelieved viciousness" which is Hell, or "the static lifelessness of unrelieved immaculation" which is Paradise (Our Exagmination 22). Beckett is aware of Joyce's influence on his own [Beckett's] writing. In Our Exagmination Beckett's description of Joyce's style could just as well be a description of his own style: "Here form is content, content is form. You complain that this stuff is not written in English. It is not written at all to be read, or rather it is not only to be read. It is to be looked at and listened to. When the sense is sleep, the words go to sleep, when the sense is dancing, the words dance" (Our Exagmination 14).

In 1935 Beckett wrote an article entitled "Censorship in the Saorstat," which was a satirical attack on the censorship laws in the Irish Free State (Topsfield 37). Despite its grotesqueries, Maureen Waters finds Murphy (1938) to be a very funny book (Waters 121). It is a novel of ideas. As Murphy himself puts it, he wishes he could "live inside his own head, and not be distracted by his passion for Celia and ginger biscuits" (Murphy 131). Murphy is very systematic, as can be seen by the way he eats his biscuits. His biscuits came in the standard five-pack grouping labeled Ginger, Osborne, Digestive, Petit Beurre, and anonymous respectively. "He always ate the first-named last, because he liked it best, and the anonymous first, because he thought it very likely the least palatable" (Coetzee 22-23). John Coetzee suggests that although the logic in Murphy is very rigorous--in fact too rigorous--the structure is comically flippant, and that this is a way for the author to express his flippant attitude toward the subject. There are many authorial asides in Murphy like, "It is most unfortunate, but the point in this story has been reached where a justification of the expression 'Murphy's mind' has to be attempted," or "All the puppets in this book whinge sooner or later, except Murphy, who is not a puppet." Coetzee suggests that comedy of this sort is ironic, and is meant to keep sentiment at a distance (Coetzee 25). In Murphy, Beckett develops the risus purus, the ability to laugh at something which is not happy, and not merely to "whinge." Beckett has said that in this way Murphy prefigures Waiting for Godot. Murphy is based on situations that are normally considered tragic; however these situations are "lightened by cruelly comic or incongruous remarks, which mock despair." Murphy has a mocking tone, and is an intellectual tour de force. "Much of the fun lies in the high-spirited word-play, puns, altered aphorisms, witty incongruities and outrageous irony.   There is some very acute characterization, and appreciation of human absurdities" (Topsfield 44).

In Murphy, Beckett is very fond of the punning riddle. For Beckett, the answer to the question, "Why did the barmaid champagne?" is "Because the stout porter bitter." Beckett also enjoyed the inverted cliché, like "Murphy, unable to believe his ears, opened, his eyes," or "he now told her all about them (his heart attacks), keeping back nothing that might alarm her" (Waters 118).   Murphy is an ironic and playful novel in which Murphy is portrayed as an "irrational man drifting through a Newtonian world of mechanical lust and mechanical action" (Waters 110). Beckett's Murphy is like Swift's Gulliver's Travels in that it is written in the tradition of Menippean satire, a genre which deals less with people than with intellectual attitudes. Representing the archetype of philosophus gloriosus, Murphy is something of a self-parody. He is a highly stylized character who is committed to a rigid (though not rigorous) system of ideas. Maureen Waters considers Murphy to be "the most eccentric of our Irish comic figures," and notes that in Ireland, "murphy" is a slang term for "a potato." She further notes that the name of Murphy is associated with "Murphy's Law," whereby if anything can go wrong, it will (Waters 111).

Murphy rejects Irish puritanism, believing that physical craving must be appeased, and never repressed, if the mind is to be free (Waters 112). As Murphy grows older, he becomes more and more convinced that his mind is a closed system, "self-sufficient and impermeable to the vicissitudes of the body." Waters notes that it is on this delusion which much of the macabre humor of the book relies. Murphy is a sort of mock saint. He considers freedom not as the right to choose, but as the absence of all desire. The other characters in the novel move briskly to accomplish their desired goals; however Murphy is always procrastinating, always allowing himself to drift along propelled more by accident than by intention (Waters 113). A very funny scene in the novel occurs when Murphy literally goes off his rocker and lands on his head, with his bare backside exposed. He is totally unable to free himself from his bonds, and remains in this situation, muttering to himself, until Celia rescues him (Waters 114). Celia is pretty and she is young. She would prefer to stay with Murphy because she loves him, and because she considers prostitution to be a boring profession. Murphy proposes marriage to Celia, and Celia accepts; however, Murphy's scheme of petty fraud will not support two people, so Murphy must go to work. When Murphy dresses himself in order to seek employment he again demonstrates his inimitable style. He dresses in a suit which is green with age, and he wears a lemon bow tie. He is "content to expose himself vaguely on the fringes of the better-attended slave market." In this scene Murphy attends meticulously to the details of his dress, and as a result he comes across as a caricature of the dandy (Waters 114).

Unlike the work that follows it, Murphy has an ironic and humorous tone (Waters 112). Murphy has a richly comic tone with humorous set pieces not only about the order of biscuit eating, but also about Murphy's horoscope, and about Neary's Passion in the Post Office (Reid 89). Maureen Waters suggests that Samuel Beckett's Murphy is to some extent a parody of James Joyce's Stephen Dedalus (Waters 91). Beckett warned that literary criticism is different from book-keeping (Reid 84). And it is therefore humorous when Murphy has a great debate on the order in which he should consume the five biscuits of his lunch. Waters suggests that with Murphy, Beckett emerges as a master of the comic style. In this novel, Beckett is especially adept at providing the reader with unexpected language expressions, as well as unexpected character and situation. In Murphy the style is witty and precise, and Waters agrees with Vivian Mercier that a major source of the comedy is the "disparity between Beckett's irrational and fairly grotesque characters and the formal, balanced, Latinate speaking style" (Waters 117).

Murphy has to make rounds every twenty minutes at the Magdalen Mental Mercy Seat hospital, where he works, and it is Mr. Endon's chess playing that makes these rounds bearable, because he is able to return after each round to make a move in the game. Rounds finished on time were called "virgins," and rounds finished ahead of time were called "Irish virgins." Because of the on-going chess game, Murphy was very fast in finishing his rounds. "Never in the history of the MMM had there been such a run of virgins and Irish virgins as on this Murphy's maiden night" (Topsfield 46).

The minor characters in Murphy are characterized partly by their obsessions--mainly sex and alcohol. The comedy in Murphy usually fits Henri Bergson's definition, since it is "the effect of the mechanical encrusted upon the living." Neary, in love, is described as follows:

> There he sat all day, moving slowly from one stool to another until he had completed the circuit of the counters, when he would start all over again in the reverse direction. He did not speak to the curates, he did not drink the endless half-pints of porter that he had to buy, he did nothing but move slowly round the ring of counters, first in one direction, then in the other, thinking of Miss Counihan. (Beckett Murphy 56)

Miss Counihan is a stereotype of the nineteenth-century Irish brute with her "low breasts and high buttocks." As a Dubliner, Beckett identifies the aspects of provincial life with County Cork, and says that Miss Counihan is "exceedingly anthropoid even for Cork." At another point in Murphy Beckett says, "I say you know what women are." and then asks, "Or has your entire life been spent in Cork?" (Waters 120).

In the concluding chapters of Murphy the comic tone becomes increasingly macabre. the characters are forced to undergo various indignities, "among which death is merely a bad joke." Murphy expires in flames. His upstairs neighbor slashes his throat with a razor. The disposal of Murphy's dead body is presented as a triumph of economy and bureaucratic efficiency, as Miss Carridge, Murphy's landlady, stages an attack of hysteria, thereby attracting the police and thus avoiding a doctor's fee. The police in turn deposit the body in an ambulance, saying that he must still be alive, since it is a misdemeanor to put a corpse, even a fresh one, into an ambulance (Waters 118-119).

In Murphy Beckett is following a long history of comic tradition by laughing at the physically abnormal. The beautiful Celia is the only character in the novel who is not in some way physically deformed. "The romantic Neary is covered with sores, literally as well as figuratively. Cooper, Neary's dipsomaniac servant, has one eye and can neither remove his hat or sit down. Even the animals are abnormal" (Waters 119).

Samuel Beckett was like James Joyce in liking to take pot shots at the Revival. Murphy's last wish is that his ashes be flushed down the w.c. during a performance of the Abbey Theatre (Waters 120). What happens instead, however, is that Murphy's ashes are scattered "in a busy London bar--in crooked comic comment on Murphy's teetotaling, solipsistic life" (Cohn 288). There is a macabre laugh sounded at Murphy's wake, where the birthmark on his bare burnt buttock is viewed by "17 eyes," and also later when his "body, mind, and soul" are scattered over the barroom floor (Waters 179).

Beckett's comedy after Murphy becomes increasingly bleak--what Maureen Waters describes as "true humour noir." At the same time as Beckett was writing Murphy in English, he was composing bitter and violent poems in French like "La Mouche." Beckett once explained to Lawrence Harvey that he started writing in French in order to "rid himself to the nuances of the Anglo-Irish idiom and the consequent temptation to rhetoric and virtuosity" (Waters 121).

In 1945 Beckett began writing in French. He wrote the nostalgic "Premier Amour," and then the bitter "L'Expulse," "La Fin," and "Le Calmant" (Topsfield 58). Eleuthéria: Drame Bourgeois was written in 1947, but it was never published. It would have been performed in 1950 but it had such an elaborate set and so many characters (seventeen) that it was too expensive. One of the characters is a member of the audience who adds his point of view to the debates going on stage. The first half of the play is conventional and almost banal as it parodies the structure of the "well-made play." It imitates the tone of the bourgeois theatre of the period. The second half becomes lighter in tone, faster in pace, and anarchical in structure; it becomes a play by Pirandello (Topsfield 70-71). The play opens in the salon of the Krap family, a view of a typical Parisian female conversation between Madame Krap, Victor's mother, her sister, Madame Piouk, and Madame Meck, who are paying a call on her. The connotations of the names immediately reveal the comic intentions of the play (Topsfield 71). The title is an oxymoron, since "Eleuthéria" means "Freedom," and the play is about the impossibility of achieving freedom, but the need to continue seeking it by staying outside of society.

The title character in Molloy (1951) begins his journey on a bicycle, which is an important symbol of freedom in Beckett's works. The bicycle has a horn, and this adds to Molloy's delight.

> To blow this horn was for me a real pleasure, almost a vice. I will go further and declare that if I were obliged to record, in a roll of honour, those activities which in the course of my interminable existence have given me only a mild pain in the balls, the blowing of a rubber horn--toot!--would figure among the first . . . . This should all be written in the pluperfect (Beckett Molloy 78).

Molloy has a vague recollection of observing two strangers, A and C, who cross each others paths. Molloy doesn't know either man, nor does he come to know them, but as a storyteller he hypothesizes because C possesses a stout stick he must be using this stick to defend himself. And from that, it follows that C "went in fear." "Yes, he saw himself threatened, his body threatened, his reason threatened" (Henkle 36). The tone of Beckett's Molloy is often dark and pessimistic. Molloy, like much of Beckett's other writing, is calculated to arouse indecision in the reader:

> In the same episode from Molloy we are told that the gentleman (A or C) observed by Molloy lifted the pomeranian dog (although he is not sure that it was a pomeranian), "drew a cigar from his lips and buried his face in the orange fleece, for it was a gentleman, that was obvious." Just for a moment, "it" seems to refer to the dog, not the man. Although the reader recovers quickly, the next sentences introduce uncertainty again: "Yes, it was an orange pomeranian, the less I think of it the more certain I am." The word "it" here, and in many other instances, is constantly forcing the reader to adjust the meaning of the text. (Deane 125)

Molloy tries to tell his story, but the account stalls. "I am perhaps confusing several different occasions, and different times." "And perhaps it was A one day at one place, then C another at another, then a third the rock and I, and so on for the other components, the cows, the sky, the sea, the mountains" (Henkle 36).

The digressions account for much of the humor of Molloy. There is, for example, a seven-page anti-bean-counting joke in Molloy's problem of how to manipulate sixteen pebbles from one pocket to another so that he can be absolutely certain that he will suck them in strict rotation. Alec Reid considers this to be one of the most brilliant and sustained pieces of comic literature (Reid 89).

The first love affair which Molloy mentions is with a chamber maid, but he later denies that it happened. "I should never have mentioned her . . . . Perhaps there was no chambermaid." Then he is struck with the philosophical impact of his thinking, and even invents a title for this possibly non-existent love story-- "Molloy, or life without a chambermaid" (Topsfield 77). Molloy also makes love with Ruth, or Edith, he's not certain which. Not only is Molloy unsure of the name of his lover, but he is unsure of other details as well: "Molloy cannot be sure it was love, nor with a woman, nor of her name, nor in what orifice, nor how long it lasted" (Henkle 35).

Moran is in search of his son, Molloy, but he never finds him. He ends up in defeat with only his umbrella, his bag, and fifteen shillings. But he laughs at his misery, and he transcends his situation as he combines the poetic with the scatological as he humorously remarks that he seemed to be drawing toward himself "as the sands toward the wave, when it crests and whitens, though I must say this image hardly fitted my situation, which was rather that of the turd waiting for the flush" (Beckett Molloy 174).

Malone Dies: A Novel (1951) is a sequel to Molloy. This is the second book in a trilogy, the third one being The Unnamable. Beckett explains that this Trilogy can be seen as three phases of a single existence: Prime (Molloy), Death (Malone Dies), and Limbo (The Unnamable). The Narrator in Malone Dies says, "Now it is a game I am going to play, I never knew how to play until now" (Beckett Malone Dies 8). The purpose of the "game" is to pass time as he waits to die, and he does this by telling himself stories, producing an inventory, by "making the tot" (Malone Dies 10), and by thinking about writing his memoirs, though he calls this last activity a joke (Malone Dies 12).

In Malone Dies, Malone invents stories, the first of which is a parody of the bourgeois narrative of ordinary experience. It is the tale of the Saposcats. Malone also tells a tale about love between two old people named Macmann and Moll. The story is filled with caprice, with "Macmann trying to bundle his sex into his partner's like a pillow into a pillow-slip, folding it in two, and stuffing it in with his fingers." It is curiosity more than passion or the mating instinct which is stiring these "cold embers." Macmann is obsessed with Moll's tooth, on which is carved the image of the crucifixion. "The sight of her so diminished did not damp Macmann's desire to take her, all stinking, yellow, bald and vomiting, in his arms." According to Roger Henkle, this parody "must be said to be the comic highpoint of Malone Dies" (Henkle 37).

Malone is lying immobile as he is waiting to die, and he decides to tell three stories to pass the time. One story is to be about an animal, probably a bird; the second story is to be about a man and a woman; and the third story is to be about a thing, probably a stone. The story about the animal is never told, although he does tell a joke about some vultures. Outside of his window there are all sorts of birds. "They come and perch on the window-sill, asking for food! It is touching. They rap on the window-pane with their beaks. I never give them anything. But they still come, what are they waiting for?" Then, realizing that he is dying, he adds as a grim jest: "They are not vultures" (Beckett Malone Dies 13). There is also a joke about a parrot, which in attempting to say "Nihil in intellectu quod non prius in sensu," but the parrot can only say "Nihil in intellect" plus some unintelligible squawks (Topsfield 82).

The story about the stone is even more tenuous, as he never actually comes to grips with it. But the story about the man and woman is illuminating. In particular, the story is about the Lamberts, but in general it is about the harsh life led by poor peasants. Mr. Lambert is an inarticulate killer of pigs, who is alive and vital only during the killing season, at which time he alarms his sick wife and children with detailed accounts of his pig-killing exploits (Topsfield 83). In Malone Dies there is also a darkly comic account of MacMann's love affair with his keeper, Moll. There is much bawdy humor as this relationship develops, especially in regard to their ineffectual coupling. The reader is told that was only natural that "they should not succeed at first shot, given their age and experience," but "warming to their work," they did eventually obtain "a kind of somber gratification" (Beckett Malone Dies 85).

Words are a problem for Malone, and he is fascinated by the phrase "Nothing is more real than nothing." Malone believes that he will have to go on uttering words to the end. He believes that if he ever stops, "It will be because there is nothing more to be said, even though all has not been said, even though nothing has been said." Malone tells himself that he should not be discouraged, alluding to the crucifixion by saying, "One of the thieves was saved, that is a generous percentage" (Beckett Malone Dies 83). The important thing for Malone is that writing must go on. He tries to "recognize the good in the bad, the bad in the worst, and so grow gently old all down the unchanging days and die one day like any other, only shorter" (Topsfield 87).

John Coetzee considers the name L'Innommable (The Unnamable) (1952) to be an expression of the inability to maintain the "separation of creator and creature, namer and named, with which the act of creating, naming begins." In 1949 Beckett wrote "To be an artist is to fail" (Coetzee 26). In The Unnamable, the narrator describes the ear as "two holes and me in the middle, slightly choked" (Beckett The Unnamable 72). The eye is also described comically. "The eye, likewise. Ah yes there's great fun to be had from an eye, it weeps for the least thing, a yes, a no, the yesses make it weep, the noes too, the perhaps particularly" (Beckett The Unnamable 92). The narrator continues, "I don't believe in the eye either, there's nothing here, nothing to see, nothing to see with, merciful coincidence when you think what it could be, a world without spectator, and vice versa, brr! No spectator then, and better still no spectacle, good riddance" (Beckett The Unnamable 92). The Unnamable is the third novel in Beckett's Trilogy. Paradoxically, it is the narrator's search "to put an end to things, an end of speech" that keeps him writing (Beckett Unnamable 16). The narrator's chief diversion in The Unnamable, like that of his predecessors, is the telling of stories. He calls these stories "facetiae," and he says that he would like to finish with his "troop of lunatics," his "ponderous chronicle of moribunds" who "let him down, as media of expression" (Topsfield 90). The narrator has lost faith in telling stories. He says that there's no point in telling yourself stories to pass the time, because they don't pass the time.

> The Unnamable says that when you have nothing left to say, you talk of time, seconds of time. There are some people, he says wistfully, who "add them together to make a life. I can't." All he knows about time is that it piles up about you deeper and deeper, "your time, others' time, the time of the ancient dead and the dead yet unborn," and it buries you "grain by grain." (Topsfield 91)

The Unnamable demonstrates Beckett's contention that not only is there nothing new to say, but that there is not even a new way to say it. It is always just the same old slush that is constantly being churned and rechurned. The narrator quips, "Now it's slush, a minute ago it was dust, it must have rained" (Beckett The Unnamable 121). The narrator refers to this rechurning of words as the "wordy-gurdy" (The Unnamable 117). The narrator is pleased to find occasional silences--which he calls truces--in the battle of the words. The narrator feels that he must keep going until the end, which, he postulates will be neither a bang nor a whimper. He thinks it might be a laugh. It will end "in a chuckle, chuck, chuck, ow, bapa." He practices with "yum, hoo, plop, pss," which are words that express pure emotion. "Bing bang, that's blows, ugh, pah . . . . Ohh, ahh, that's love, enough." Then there is a joke of Malone's, "It's tiring, hee hee" (The Unnamable 126). The Unnamable has a special name for his own writing. He calls it "pidgin bullskrit" (Henkle 50).

Tom F. Driver describes Beckett's En Attendant Godot (Waiting for Godot: A Tragicomedy) (1952) as "Pascal's Pensées performed by the Fratellini Clowns" (Topsfield 20). Beckett's humor was based in tragicomedy. It is mainly visual and physical, and it is based on the humor of vaudeville, the music hall, and the circus. In Waiting for Godot the following dialogue takes place:

> VLADIMIR: Charming evening we're having.
> ESTRAGON: Unforgettable.
> VLADIMIR: And it's not over.

ESTRAGON: Apparently not.
VLADIMIR: It's only the beginning.
ESTRAGON: It's awful.
VLADIMIR: It's worse than being in the theatre.
ESTRAGON: The circus.
VLADIMIR: The music hall.
ESTRAGON: The circus (Godot 41).

Waiting for Godot uses automatism, exaggerations, repetitions, and circularity of plot, and Topsfield feels that these are the "essence of comedy" for Bergson (Topsfield 21). Because the clowns in Waiting for Godot would not accept their fate "as true tragic heroes would," he uses the subtitle "A Tragicomedy;" tragicomedy is the comedy of the human condition. The main theme of Waiting for Godot is, of course, waiting, a theme that has already been established in Malone Dies. Estragon says, "Nothing happens, nobody comes, nobody goes, it's awful" (Beckett Waiting for Godot 94). Talking about the scenery, Vladimir says, "It's indescribable. It's like nothing. There's nothing," but then he adds a ray of hope. "There's a tree." The tree is Estragon's and Vladimir's axis mundi. They meet at the tree; they watch it; they hide behind it; when they are frightened they even make jokes about it. They decide the tree is a willow tree; they think that the tree must be dead, and joke, "no more weeping" (Topsfield 96). In Waiting for Godot it is Pozzo who claims that there is a constant amount of laughter in the world, so that if some people laugh, other people must stop laughing. Pozzo then laughs at this observation. "The noise of his mirth is darkly mordant, and after it we can imagine the smiles it wipes from the faces of others" (Orr 58).

When Vladimir and Estragon become bored, they try to invent diversions. One such diversion is a music-hall routine involving hats.

ESTRAGON: Let me see (he takes off his hat, concentrates).
VLADIMIR: Let me see (he takes off his hat, concentrates). Long silence.
Ah! (They put on their hats and relax). (Topsfield 97)

Later they go into another hat routine. A long stage direction tells them how to rotate three hats between them, and there is extra funny business when Vladimir minces around the stage like a mannequin, until they tire of the game (Topsfield 97).

Estragon describes their conversation as "blathering about nothing in particular," but they are nevertheless ingenious about finding new topics. One exchange goes as follows: "Oh, pardon!" "Carry on." "No no, after you." "No no, you first." "I interrupted you." "On the contrary." However their unnatural politeness angers them and they soon become abusive: "Morpion." "Sewer rat." "Curate." "Cretin." "(with finality) Crritic!" After this, there is a reconciliation scene: "Now let's make it up." "Gogo!" "Didi!" "Your hand!" "Take it!" "Come to my arms!" "Your arms?" "My breast!" "Off we go!" They embrace; then they separate; then there is silence. Vladimir sums up this weird exchange with the words, "How time flies when one has fun!" (Beckett Waiting 76).

To pass the time, Didi tries to remember the Gospel story about the three thieves. Didi can't remember the story, so he hopes that Gogo will be able to jog his memory. But Gogo responds blankly, because the Bible is a distant memory for him. He says, "I remember the maps of the Holy Land. Coloured they were. Very pretty. The Dead Sea was pale blue. The very look of it made me thirsty. That's where we'll go, I used to say, that's where we'll go for our honeymoon. We'll swim. We'll be happy." According to John Orr, the humor of this quote lies not only in the quick change from the sacred to the profane, but also in the "blissful forgetting of the original source, the trace of pleasant memory without its object" (Orr 55). Much of the tragicomic pathos in Waiting for Godot comes from the half-told stories and the interruptions which insure that they will never be fully told. There is also the humor of the parallel between the two thieves and Didi and

Gogo, which the audience is led into realizing. "Both are damned by a fate they cannot control and rely on the miracle of a last-minute intervention." The parallel, however, is not a perfect one, since the thieves want to be saved from death, and from hell, while Didi and Gogo want to be saved from "the boredom of living" (Orr 56).

At the end of the play, Estragon and Vladimir decide to hang themselves tomorrow, but even here there is a trouser-dropping scene that provides light relief.   Their talk about the double suicide is very funny.

> The tensions between the life-urge and death result in the bawdy thought that hanging would result in an erection, which momentarily cheers the would-be suicides. Then there is the comic argument whether Vladimir should go first because he is heavier (he is not), as Estragon says: "Gogo light--bough not break--Gogo dead. Didi heavy--bough break--Didi alone." (Beckett Waiting 99)

Much of the humor of Waiting for Godot lies in the long, boring, pseudo-intellectual speeches. Beckett is using parody to produce a monotonous effect that is meant to reflect the monotony of everyday life, and mankind's passive acceptance of this monotony (Topsfield 34). The tone of the play can be seen from the following excerpt.

> ESTRAGON: Let's go.
> VLADIMIR: We can't.
> ESTRAGON: Why not?
> VLADIMIR: We're waiting for Godot.
> ESTRAGON: Ah! (Beckett Complete 71)

This type of dialogue goes on during the entire play. At the end of the play they are still waiting:

> VLADIMIR: Well? Shall we go?
> ESTRAGON: Yes, Let's go.
> [They do not move]
> Curtain. (Beckett Complete 71)

In Texts for Nothing (1954) the qualities of tragedy and comedy are discussed. "Tears, that could be the tone, if they weren't so easy, the time, tone and tenor at last" (Beckett Texts 35). But the narrator doesn't weep, for he says that comedy is more suitable. He says that a laugh can distance the horrors, and everything can become a game (Beckett Texts 28). In Texts for Nothing there are ghosts of Murphy (18), of Mercier and Camier and Vladimir and Estragon (18), of Molloy and Malone, who he says were happy even though they were mere mortals (23), of Pozzo (27) and of himself as Watt (37).

Much of the humor in Texts for Nothing is based on wit and wordplay. The undeveloped character is waiting to be written, and he echoes a joke from First Love when he says that in purgatory a person can believe himself dead if he "makes no bones about it" (Texts 24). Another joke is about when he is away for a while and then returns. "Peekaboo, here I come again, just when most needed, like the square root of minus one" (Texts 54). The narrator also uses a comical food image when he "thinks he may utter another guzzle of words, but piping hot" (Texts 52). Valerie Topsfield considers Texts for Nothing to be an "impasse" in Beckett's life. The narrator says "there's nothing like breathing your last to put new life in you" (Texts 10), and continues that a laugh distances the horrors, "especially of oneself, and everything becomes a game" (Texts 29).

Watt (1953) is filled with verbal repetition, flat contradiction, and ambivalent irony (Cohn 293). In Watt it is the earnest seeker for the meaning of life that is parodied and ridiculed. Here, there are serious undertones, and the humor tends to be cruel. A seeker should be a free thinker, but Beckett's seeker depends on conventional ideas, and this is the basis for the paradox of Watt (Topsfield 48). The author of Watt is named Samuel, and the narrator is named Sam. Sam follows Watt around, taking down his words in a little notebook, and he pieces Watt's story together in a fragmentary book. According to John Coetzee, Sam belongs both inside of the fiction, as he walks around the grounds of an asylum with Watt, and outside of the fiction as the representative of the author. And what he records is sometimes not true to real life, nor does it have credibility in the novel. Sam reports to Watt, for example, that Kate is "a fine girl, but a bleeder," and then adds, "Haemophilia is, like enlargement of the prostate, an exclusively male disorder. But not in this work" (Coetzee 25).

The main themes of Watt are cruelty, the nature of the deity, and difficulties of communication, and the tone varies from devil-may-care wit, to gallows comedy, to uninhibited fantasy (Topsfield 50). Watt discovers three important things about Mr. Knott. The first is that Mr. Knott's slops have to be emptied "before sunrise, or after sunset, on the violet bed in violet time, and on the pansy bed in pansy time, and on the rose bed in rose time." The second is that whenever Watt gives up one of his duties, such as supervising the dog who eats Mr. Knott's leftover food, there is no punishment--no thunderbolt. The third is that Mr. Knott "needed a witness." But Watt was an imperfect witness, so he wasn't of much value in this regard (Beckett Watt 65).

Arthur was another of Mr. Knott's servants and "witnesses." He had a small fat clown-like appearance, and in order to relieve tensions he would make up stories about Louit and Bando. Louit, is a failed scholar who ends up by running a company which produces an aphrodisiac called "Bando." Before the impotent gardener, Mr. Graves uses this product, he is described as moody, listless, and constipated. But when he uses the product he changes into "a popular nudist, regular in [his] daily health, almost a father, and a lover of boiled potatoes" (Topsfield 53). In the "Addenda" to Watt there is an anecdote about Arthur which illustrates his sense of fun. He laughed so heartily at a particular aphorism that he was obliged to lean against a shrub for support, which joined him heartily in the joke. When Arthur asked an old man what the shrub was called, the old man replied, "That's what we calls a hardy laurel" (Beckett Watt 253).

The characterization in Watt involves wit and wordplay, and is an important aspect of the comedy. Every day Mr. Nolan would thoroughly read the penny newspaper, and then he would gallantly place the newspaper in the ladies room. The narrator described this as "spending a penny." There is, for example, some light-hearted fun, concerning Mr. Nolan the station-master, "whose spirits always rose as he reached the station in the morning," and rose again, as he left in the evening: "Thus Mr. Nolan was assured twice a day, of a rise in spirits" (Topsfield 54). Much of the wordplay in Watt is notable. "Cute of the roob" is said instead of the correct "root of the cube." and "pissabed" is a word used instead of the more usual "dandelion." When the narrator commented on the dark color of the sky he added that it was probably because the usual "luminaries" were absent. Sam the narrator also comments that Mr. Graves always pronounced the words "third" and "fourth" as if they were "turd" and "fart" (Topsfield 56).

In Watt Beckett juxtaposes various inkhorn terms, often invented, with basic vulgar Anglo-Saxon terminology. Examples of inkhorn terms in Watt include "irrefragable," "obnubilated," "tardigrade," "dianoetic," "contunded," "equidependency," "subaxillary," "funambulistic," "pneumogastric," and "anathematisation." But in this same novel can be found such vulgar earthy items as "turd," "scum," "snug," "puke," "prog," "dung," "bugger," "muck," "suckers," and "pissabed." "The style of the novel is a disorienting mix of high and low, proper and vulgar, intellectual and physical" (Henkle 46).

Watt has an affair with Mrs. Gorman, a fishwoman who would call on Thursdays and sit on Watt's knee as she drank stout. But Mrs. Gorman did not always sit on Watt; sometimes Watt sat on Mrs. Gorman. In fact, there is a page of permutations of these positions, after which the narrator slyly comments, "Further than this, it will be learned with regret, they never went, though more than half inclined to do so on more than one occasion," because "Watt had not the strength and Mrs. Gorman had not the time" (Beckett Watt 140).

Much of the humor in Watt is sick, disgusting, and/or cruel, as it deals with the various diseases of the Lynch family, the death of the dog O'Connor, the killing of birds, etc. "The laugh here is not the distanced laugh at what is unhappy, but a kick at God and the cruelty of existence. The diseases of the Lynch family are so many and so awful that they become black comedy" (Topsfield 52). Beckett describes the thirteen members of the Lynch family as repellent and diseased, but Beckett's attitude nevertheless remains ambivalent, and his tone remains comic. "Then there was Joe's boy Tom, aged 41 years, unfortunately subject alternately to fits of exaltation which rendered him incapable of the least exertion, and of depression, during which he could stir neither hand nor foot" expresses a tragi-comic and grotesque tone that continues throughout the novel (Topsfield 12).

In Watt, Beckett defines the three important kinds of laugh which mark the three stages of philosophical progression--the bitter, the hollow, and the mirthless (Topsfield 1). According to Ruby Cohn, Arsene, Watt's predecessor and mentor at Mr. Knott's house, is the best in terms of laughing. Arsene's characterization of "the bitter, the hollow, and the mirthless" laugh suggests the complexity of Beckett's own laughter distinctions (Cohn 286).

> The bitter laugh laughs at that which is not good, it is the ethical laugh. The hollow laugh laughs at that which is not true, it is the intellectual laugh . . . . But the mirthless laugh is the dianoetic laugh, down the snout--Haw!--so. It is the laugh of laughs, the risus purus, the laugh laughing at the laugh, the beholding, saluting of the highest joke, in a word the laugh that laughs--silence please, at that which is unhappy. (Watt 48)

Arsene is using wordplay to suggest that there is certainty behind our uncertainties when he refers to "the shadow of purpose, of the purpose that budding withers, that withering buds, whose blooming is a budding withering" (Watt 57).

To some extent, Watt is a reaction to Schopenhauer's statement that we would be able to live in peaceful non-existence if only we could silence the will. Beckett disagrees, and uses a comic image to explain why he disagrees. According to Beckett if the will is silenced, life would begin to "ram her fish and chips down your gullet until you puke, and then the puke down your gullet until you puke the puke, and then the puked puke, until you begin to like it." For Beckett the real problem lies in "beginning to like it" (Topsfield 21).

1956 was an important year for Beckett. This is the year he wrote Fin de Partie, and produced first drafts of All that Fall, Krapp's Last Tape, Comment C'est, Happy Days, and The Gloaming. All that Fall (1957) was first commissioned for the BBC. This is a short play for radio written in the tradition of earthy Irish black humor. There are many bawdy and bizarre innuendoes in the play, in which the uncertainty of the human condition is made quite comic. The play has the same sense of the ridiculous that is found in plays written by O'Casey or Synge (Topsfield 113). "Descriptions are homely and funny. Mrs. Rooney sees her shape as 'a big fat jelly slopped out of a bowl,' and Mr. Rooney sees her as a blancmange. When Miss Fitt affects not to see her, she inquires whether her cretonne dress is so becoming that she 'merges into the masonry' " (Topsfield 114). Mrs. Rooney and Miss Fitt get stuck trying to go up some steps, and Mrs. Rooney remarks, "Now we are the laughing stock of the twenty-six counties." This is a kind of self-parody which comically helps prepare the reader for the tragedy which is to come (Orr 50). The shocking ending to All that Fall occurs when the train is late. It plays on a juxtaposition of salvation with childlessness, of barrenness with procreation, as the boy Jerry catches up with Mr. Rooney to give him back an object which he has dropped. The boy tells Mrs. Rooney the reason for the train's delay which her husband had been unable to give her. A small child had fallen out of one of the train cars and, onto the tracks, and under the wheels. Mr. and Mrs. Rooney "have ironically missed out on the death of childhood just as they have missed out on its birth" (Orr 51).

Endgame: A Play in One Act (1957), like Murphy, uses the chess game as a metaphor for life (Topsfield 109). The purpose of life is not to win the game--which is impossible--but to use dialogue to delay the end of the game. Beckett uses banter, fantasy, nostalgia, old jokes, comic exchanges and black humor to produce this tragicomedy which in many ways is similar to Waiting for Godot. "The likeness to Waiting for Godot is not fortuitous. Beckett told Roger Blin that Hamm and Clov are Didi and Gogo at a later date, 'at the end of their lives' " (Topsfield 110).

Beckett uses a wide variety of humor devices in Endgame. There is the most intellectual humor, the risus purus, the defiant laugh at what is unhappy. This type of humor reaches its apogee in Endgame where Beckett gives the reader special insight. When Nagg sniggers at Hamm's misery, Nell rebukes him, saying, "One mustn't laugh at these things . . . . Nothing is funnier than unhappiness, I grant you that. But--." This "But--" shocks Nagg, and then Nell continues, "Yes, yes, it's the most comical thing in the world. And we laugh, we laugh, with a will, in the beginning. But it's always the same thing. Yes, it's like the funny story we have heard too often, we still find it funny, but we don't laugh any more" (Beckett Endgame 20). Beckett has made the statement that this is the most important sentence in this particular play (Topsfield 112).

In Endgame the characters are completely isolated. There is no real hope. The characters laugh at each other; they cause pain. Hamm is blind and sits in a wheel chair and Clov can't sit down, and follows all of Hamm's orders. Nagg and Nell, Hamm's parents, have lost their legs in a bicycling accident and are kept in trash cans, separated from each other. Nell seems to die, but the audience is not certain. In any case, if she did die, she is the only female character, so life stops there; it is the end of the game. Clov wants to leave, but just stands by the door; he never leaves. Beckett explained why his characters don't leave: "When you're trapped on stage you stay, not because you don't want to leave, but because there's simply nowhere else to go. Outside of here it's death" (Brater 85).

Beckett describes the paradoxes in Proust (1957), which result from the recapturing of experience, as being "the real without being merely actual, ideal without being merely abstract, the ideal real, the essential, the extra-temporal" (Joyce Proust 75). In Proust, Beckett attempts to express the inexpressible, or as he puts it he wants to "eff the ineffable." "What we know partakes in no small measure of the nature of what has so happily been called the unutterable or ineffable, so that any attempt to utter or eff it is doomed to fail" (Beckett Watt 61). Beckett's frustration with his failure to complete all of his thoughts is described as being like the madness that holds in a "conversation with the furniture" (Topsfield 32-33).

John Orr considers Krapp's Last Tape (1958) to "go to the limits of the ludic theatre." The entire play is based on an epiphany which the audience recognizes, but the Older Krapp refuses to recognize--the passion of the tape-voice's ordered and lyrical description of love-making in the drifting punt. This has an effect on the audience, but not on Old Krapp, who is no longer able to respond to the tape. For Krapp, it is an example of "paradise lost." Krapp plays this part of the tape twice. "As if to emphasize the infinite regress into which he has been trapped; Krapp is then made to record his comments on the 'stupid bastard' he had taken himself to be thirty years previously" (Orr 68). This is a prime example of what John Orr calls "Irish amnesia." "Forgetting is both an attribute of modern consciousness locked in the horizons of the present and an attribute of Beckett's Anglo-Irish consciousness, amnesiac in exile . . . . It prompts Beckett to write his plays in French and translate them back into English" (Orr 71).

Krapp's Last Tape has contrasting light and dark tones to explore the tension between tragedy and comedy in the tradition of Pirandello. It develops the idea that a single person has a "multiplicity of selves," by observing Krapp at various stages in his life (Topsfield 116-117). Much of the paradoxical nature of Krapp's Last Tape comes from the frequent juxtapositions of the dark with the light. As the middle-aged Krapp is waiting for his mother to die he notices the nursemaid's "incomparable bosom." Old Krapp romantically recalls Effi Briest, and his own love, as he shifts to his present love, "the old whore." "The paradox is especially poignant at the end, when the middle Krapp's voice gloats over the fire in him now, and old Krapp, listening to it, regrets the human relationships he exchanged for the 'fire,' which he feels now is reduced to ashes" (Topsfield 118).

Comment C'est (How It Is) (1961) was originally entitled Pim. The somber tone is frequently lightened up by wit and wry comedy. How It Is is written in three parts: before Pim, with Pim, and after Pim (Topsfield 120). The narrator remains certain of only four things. The first is that "the mud and the dark are true" (158). The second is that he is alone in the mud and the dark, alone with his sack. "I beg your pardon no no sack either no not even a sack with me no" (159). The third thing he knows is that there are only a few things that remain for him--"a few words yes a few scraps yes" (160). And the fourth thing he knows is that he will die, and that his death will bring a positive relief (Topsfield 125).

In How It Is, the reader runs across nonce forms like "subprefecture," "imbrication," "lubricious," "acervation," "exactitudes," "infinitudes," "inexistence," "hypo," "intorse," "malar," "thenar," "bo," "meatus," "procumbency," "capillarity," "agglutinated," "piriform," "sinistro," "untorturable," "unbutcherable," "prepensely," "scissiparous," "buccinators," and "revictuallings." In a tone of understatement, Roger Henkle notes that "many of these words are not to be found in the OED." However, the fact that so many of these difficult words can be found in the concordances to Ulysses and Finnegans Wake suggests that "Beckett has never, really, moved permanently out of the shadow of James Joyce" (Henkle 50). In How It Is Beckett talks about "bits and scraps from various vocabularies and voices," adding that "My whole life [is] a gibberish garbled six-fold" (Beckett How It Is 134).

Happy Days: A Play in Two Acts (1961) has an ironic title, as the days are not all that happy. Valerie Topsfield considers the subtitle, A Low Comedy, to be the key to the play, since it echoes the cruel sexual humor of Watt. Winnie, like Watt, is in a wilderness which she doesn't understand, so she "makes a pillow of old words," and imposes a series of rituals and habits onto her baffling existence, welcoming the intermittent bell, because it is the only thing that seems to give structure to her day. In Happy Days, Winnie asks Willie after a laugh, "How can one better magnify the Almighty than by sniggering with him at his little jokes, particularly the poorer ones?" (Cohn 286). In Happy Days Winnie waits. She occupies her time putting on her hat, her lipstick, or filing her nails. She is buried up to her waist in the first act, up to her chin in the second, by life's troubles. There is no third act.

Beckett's First Love (1970) is bitterly ironic, and it is peppered with obscenities and is in addition "ruefully nostalgic." It was written earlier, but was not published until 1970, because that is when the woman who had inspired the story died (Topsfield 58). About this piece, Valerie Topsfield says that this is "the funniest of the novellas." She adds that First Love begins with a two-and-a-half page macabre digression in the form of a soliloquy about cemeteries, which begins, "Personally I have no bone to pick with graveyards." The narrator enjoys picnicking in cemeteries, because his sandwich, or his banana always tastes better when he is sitting on a tomb. (Topsfield 59) He also enjoys readings the epitaphs. "There are always three or four of such drollery that I have to hold on to the cross, or the stele, or the angel, so as not to fall" (Topsfield 59).

The protagonist of First Love, who doesn't have any place to stay, meets Anna/Lulu who volunteers the information that she has a room. "Who has not a room?" he brusquely responds, and then adds, "Ah, I hear the clamour." She continues that she really has two rooms and a kitchen, to which he responds, "At last conversation worthy of the name," and he decides to move in with her (Topsfield 61). But Anna/Lulu is a prostitute, and the sound of her clients annoy the protagonist, who says, "I couldn't make out if it was always the same gent or more than one. Lovers' groans are so alike, and lovers' giggles." He confronts her with the rhetorical question, "So you live by prostitution?" She responds by saying, "We live by prostitution" (Beckett First Love 56).

The action of Mercier and Camier (1970) begins with a comic passage which describes how Mercier and Camier have just missed each other. First one, and then the other, arrived at the appointed place, but they didn't arrive at the same time, and rather than remaining each left to seek the other (Topsfield 68). Mercier and Camier is an example of Beckett's search for the risus purus. Here one member of the couple is short, the other member is tall, and together they resemble Vladimir and Estragon in Waiting for Godot. Mercier is the live wire, and Camier is the dead weight. In Mercier and Camier Beckett develops such antithetical paradoxes of existence as good vs. evil, negation vs. affirmation, tragedy vs. comedy (Topsfield 63-64). In one very dark passage, life is compared to the trash in the pocket of an abandoned raincoat, where there might be a mixture of "punched tickets, of all sorts, spent matches, scraps of newspaper bearing in their margins the obliterated traces of irrevocable rendez-vous, the classic last tenth of pointless pencil, crumples of soiled bumf, a few porous condoms. Life in short" (Beckett Mercier 66). In Mercier and Camier the juxtaposition of pathos and humor can almost be considered the leitmotif of the novel (Topsfield 65). Since Mercier and Camier are both improvisational clown characters, they provide much of the risqué and inconsequential comedy. Mercier and Camier discover that bars make it much easier for them to await the dark (Topsfield 66). Some of the dialogue is highly reminiscent of Waiting for Godot. Camier asks, "Do you not know where we are going?," and Mercier replies, "What does it matter where we are going? We are going, that's enough" (Beckett Mercier 90). Since the goal of their journey is undefined, Camier asks the direction, and Mercier merely responds, "Crooked ahead" (Beckett Mercier 185).

Roger Henkle considers The Lost Ones (1972) to be a novel riddled with clichés, and sometimes in parody fashion, these clichés are piled on top of one another, as in the following excerpt: "From time immemorial rumour has it or better still the notion is abroad that there exists a way out" (Beckett The Lost Ones 17-18).

> Beckett's aim here is to compose a sociological report and to pass it off as a novel, and his diction must therefore be kept as refrigerated as possible. What humor there is in this book thus depends upon the momentary and of course quite unexpected use of a single word that suddenly melts the ice. Terms such as "fury," "fancy," "ferment," "precocious," "mite," "famished," "throbbing," "buckle to," "murk," "devoured," "vacation," "succulence," "frenzies," and most certainly "goose bumps" are in the context of this detached diction decidedly out of place. These words come as thunderbolts to his otherwise intellectualized description of some Godot Figure's no-exit cylinder. (Henkle 52)

The Gloaming (1974) was written in 1956 but was not published until 1974. In this play, A as a blind man, and B as a cripple have different aims, needs, and perspectives. In their fight for existence, they find that they need each other's help, so the cripple suggests that they set up house together, since they are "made for each other." This is a typical Beckettian touch of black humor. The mordant humor of the play is based on the tension between B's need for love, and A's disgust for the human race. But the themes of loss and adaptation are also humorously treated. "A says that before his lost violin he had a harp, which he also lost. B jests that, now he has lost the violin, he will tell someone else one day that, before he had a harmonica, he had a violin, and taunts A: when he has lost the harmonica he may be reduced to having to sing" (Topsfield 108).

In Beckett's latest works, "Arsene's three laughs are merged; the ethical laugh is aroused by cruelty, the intellectual laugh by ignorance, but cruelty and ignorance dissolve in suffering. Bitter and hollow laughter are drowned in mirthless, dianoetic laughter--the only possible reaction to the impossible human situation, in which we live" (Cohn 293). Aristotle wrote that comedy and irony paint men worse than they are. This is certainly true in Beckett's case, for Beckett's comic ironist is "ugly, small, poor, cruel, ignorant, miserable, and infinitely vulnerable. It is above all in that vulnerability that we recognize ourselves. As long as man remains ugly, small, poor, cruel, ignorant, miserable, and vulnerable, Beckett's ironic works will have lively and deadly relevance for us" (Cohn 299).

Samuel Barclay Beckett Bibliography

Beckett, Samuel. Endgame. London, England: Faber and Faber, 1964.
Beckett, Samuel. First Love. London, England: Calder and Boyars, 1973.
Beckett, Samuel. Four Novellas: "The End," "The Expelled," "First Love," "The Calmative." London, England: John Calder, 1977.
Beckett, Samuel. The Lost Ones. New York, NY: Grove, 1972.
Beckett, Samuel. Malone Dies. London, England: Calder and Boyars, 1975.
Beckett, Samuel. Mercier and Camier. London, England: Calder and Boyars, 1974.
Beckett, Samuel. Molloy. London, England: Calder and Boyars, 1976.
Beckett, Samuel. More Pricks than Kicks London, England: Calder and Boyars, 1970.
Beckett, Samuel. Murphy. New York, NY: Grove, 1957.
Beckett, Samuel. Our Exagmination Round His Factification for Incamination of Work in Progress. London, England: Faber, 1972.
Beckett, Samuel. Proust. London, England: Calder and Boyars, 1965.
Beckett, Samuel. Samuel Beckett: The Complete Dramatic Works. London, England: Faber and Faber, 1986.
Beckett, Samuel. Texts for Nothing. London, England: Calder and Boyars, 1974.
Beckett, Samuel. The Unnamable. London, England: Calder and Boyars, 1975.
Beckett, Samuel. Waiting for Godot. London, England: Faber and Faber, 1965.
Beckett, Samuel. Watt. London, England: John Calder, 1976.
Brater, Enoch. Why Beckett? London, England: Thames and Hudson, 1989.
Coetzee, John M. "The Comedy of Point of View of Beckett's Murphy." Critique: Studies in Modern Fiction 12.2 (1970): 19-27.
Cohn, Ruby. "A Comic Complex and a Complex Comic." Samuel Beckett: The Comic Gamut. New Brunswick, NJ: Rutgers Univ Press, 1962, 283-300.
Cormier, Ramona, and Janis L. Pallister. "En attendant Godot: Tragedy or Comedy?" L'Esprit Créateur 11.3 (1971): 44-54.
Deane, Seamus. "Joyce and Beckett." Celtic Revivals: Essays in Modern Irish Literature-- Joyce, Yeats, O'Casey, Kinsella, Montague, Friel, Mahon, Heaney, Beckett, Synge. Winston-Salem, NC: Wake Forest University Press, 1985, 123-134.
Henkle, Roger B. "Beckett and the Comedy of Bourgeois Experience." Thalia 3.1 (1980): 35-39.
Kenner, Hugh. Flaubert, Joyce, and Beckett: The Stoic Comedians. Boston, MA: Beacon Press, 1962.
Kern, Edith. "Beckett and the Spirit of the Commedia dell'Arte." Modern Drama 9 (1966):

260-267.

Mercier, Vivian. The Irish Comic Tradition. Oxford, England: Clarendon, 1962.

Orr, John. "Samuel Beckett: Imprisoned Persona and Irish Amnesia." Tragicomedy and Contemporary Culture: Play and Performance from Beckett to Shepard. Ann Arbor, MI: University of Michigan Press, 1991, 47-71.

Reid, Alec. "Comedy in Synge and Beckett." Yeats Studies 2 (1972): 80-90.

Smith, Frederik N. "Beckett's Verbal Slapstick." Modern Fiction Studies 29 (1983): 43-55.

States, Bert O. The Shape of Paradox: An Essay on "Waiting for Godot." Berkeley, CA: University of California Press, 1978.

Topsfield, Valerie. The Humour of Samuel Beckett. Basingstoke, England: Macmillan, 1988.

Waters, Maureen. "Samuel Beckett's Murphy." The Comic Irishman. Albany, NY: State Univ of New York Press, 1984, 110-122.

Watson, David. Paradox and Desire in Samuel Beckett's Fiction. Basingstoke, England: Macmillan, 1991.

Flann O'Brien (Myles na Gopaleen)(né Brian O'Nolan) (1911-1966) IRELAND

A great deal of O'Brien's satire comes from a lifelong feud O'Brien had with James Joyce. Whereas Joyce was an "artist-priest transmuting ordinary experience into the 'radiant body of everlasting life,' " O'Brien "posits a writer who is in full flight from ordinary experience" (Waters 127). Joyce's portrait of Dublin was largely realistic; however, according to Ann Clissman, O'Brien's portrait of Dublin was merely a "satire of its worst tendencies, considerably enlivened by the author's zany and malicious humor." O'Brien maintained that Irish art was an elaborate ruse to escape the boredom of Irish life (Waters 128). "O'Brien parodies Joyce, but the comedy grows more and more corrosive as it turns inward, revealing the self-doubting anguish which is its driving force" (Waters 130).

While O'Brien's wrath at his own predicament is evident in the savagery of his wit, his response is often broadly comic or farcical. His own brilliant verbal resources are a source of much pleasure, which mitigates the harsher elements in his satire. At one point, for example, Finn complains about his treatment in Ulysses: "Who but a book-poet would dishonour the God-big Finn for the sake of a gap-worded story?" Who indeed? (Waters 131)
O'Brien also extends his parody of Joyce's "The Cyclops."

O'Brien's satire is schizophrenic in that the Irishman is constantly shown to be the "victim of his own brilliant heritage." The Irishman is enclosed in a myth of his own making. He can't resist "doing the witty Celtic act, even though the gap between word and reality continues to enlarge" (Waters 135). José Lanters refers to the "fantasy," to the "glorious craziness," to the "rigging up of alternate universes" of Flann O'Brien's writing (Lanters 161). Anthony Cronin compares the writing of Flann O'Brien with that of James Joyce and Samuel Beckett, saying that they were all three Irish realists rather than Irish romantics. Like Joyce and Beckett, O'Brien was also first and foremost a humorist. Cronin considers O'Brien to be "one of the funniest writers to use the English language in this century." He goes on to say that he believes that "everything he wrote was intended to be funny and that most of it succeeded." Furthermore, O'Brien was a humorous writer with a fierce sense of propriety. He was a master at colloquial idiomatic language; but at the same time he sometimes wrote English as if it were a dead language, a language which had to be written with great precision. Because of this he is extremely scornful of other people's errors and mistakes. Cronin states, "the fact that he is a humorous writer with such a strong undertow of belief in rightness and order is one of the things that accounts for the widespread appeal of his work" (Cronin x). Maureen Waters says that At-Swim-Two-Birds, An Béal Bocht, The Third Policeman, and The Dalkey Archive establish Flann O'Brien as "one of the finest modern satirists." It is ironic to note that "while Joyce satirized the leaders of the Revival in order to define his own position, O'Brien satirized Joyce for much the same reason" (Waters 123). As a student at University College in Dublin, O'Brien developed the reputation as a "funny man," and as he wrote he began to see his mission as similar to that of Jonathan Swift, that of "chastising the folly and hypocrisy of contemporary Ireland" (Waters 126).

The tone of At Swim-Two-Birds (1939) rapidly shifts from ordinary conversation to fantasy, to poetry, to folk tale, to western yarn, "mimicking and mocking the conventions of speech and literature and none more effectively that the Irish epic tale" (Waters 127). Maureen Waters considers At Swim-Two-Birds to be a "comic masterpiece" (Waters 123). The student narrator of At Swim-Two-Birds is a pimpled, corpulent, student-author, who spends most of his time in bed. His name is Demot Trellis. "In a literal application of the ancient technique of Irish satire, in which words alone are used to inflict harm, Trellis is torn to pieces. Every bone in his body is broken again and again, and the torture continues all the while he is being interrogated by a panel of fictional characters, most of them his own" (Waters 129). Trellis's agonies seem to be beyond the range of endurance--they are so overstated as to make Trellis a mock hero. His tormentor is the Pooka MacPhellimey, described as "a courtly member of the devil class" (Waters 130).

The narrator of At Swim-Two-Birds resembles James Joyce's Stephen Dedalus. He is a student who escapes the stultifying climate of contemporary Dublin not by going into exile, but by retreating into a world of fantasy, which is peopled by various figures from legend, myth, romance, and popular fiction. "At the center of this increasingly bizarre, but brilliantly and mordantly comic tale, is the isolated artist maddened by his efforts to make poetry out of modern Ireland" (Waters 91).

Because the framing narrative of At Swim-Two-Birds is essentially realistic, this is not an experimental novel. However, because the story the student works on becomes increasingly surreal, it is a realistic novel about the writing of an experimental novel (Devlin 97-98). The name of the novel is derived from "Snámh dá Én" ("Swim Two Birds"), a church far from Dublin in the West of Ireland. "Snámh dá Én" is in fact one of the resting places of mad Sweeny early in the novel (Devlin 98). Orlick describes his father as a grotesque:

> Trellis, wind-quick, eye-mad, with innumerable boils upon his back and upon various parts of his person, flew out in his sweat-wet night-shirt and day-drawers, out through the glass of the window till he fell with a crap on the cobbles of the street. A burst eye-ball, a crushed ear and bone-breaks two in number, these were the agonies that were his lot as a result of his accidental fall. The Pooka, a master of the science of rat-flight, fluttered down through the air. (O'Brien At Swim-Two-Birds 254)

At Trellis's trial, the judges, the jury, and the witnesses are all Trellis's characters. "The case before them does not seem particularly important either and they play cards and ignore the testimony being given. The defendant is offered the services of two lawyers, neither of whom speaks English." These entire proceedings are unnecessary, for it is obvious to all that Trellis is guilty (Devlin 99). This is the kind of humor that Bakhtin talks about when he says that "humor arises from carnivalesque inversions of everyday relations" (Devlin 103).

At Swim-Two-Birds is a series of intellectual jokes which depend for their effect on some knowledge of what the Irish Literary Revival was all about, and which also depend for their effect on the part which James Joyce played in superseding it or making it look ridiculous (Cronin viii).   At Swim-Two-Birds is deliberately nihilistic in its approach, and can be accurately described as "metafiction," a "self-reflexive novel," or even an "anti-novel" (Lanters 162).   "One beginning and one ending for a book was a thing I did not agree with. A good book may have three openings entirely dissimilar and inter-related only in the prescience of the author, or for that matter one hundred times as many endings" (O'Brien At Swim-Two-Birds 9).   But the novel is more complicated even than this, because the narrator's own book includes various other writers and story-tellers, and their stories include still other writers and story-tellers.   "Throughout the novel the narrator interrupts his various storylines, which he refers to as 'extracts,' at random points to take up other plots" (Lanters 168).   Infinity of repetition and endless circularity are also important comic devices in O'Brien's early novels.   At Swim-Two-Birds is a novel within a novel within a novel, and it opens with the fascinating perspective of "embedding or nesting an infinite number of novels." The writers in this novel are constantly borrowing each others plots, and the fact that they come to resemble each other also adds to the sense of infinity (Lanters 171).

There is some strange logic in At Swim-Two-Birds. It is strange for a novel to have a synopsis, for example. It is provided as a "summary of what has gone before, for the benefit of new readers," suggesting that some of the readers are showing up late, or that some readers will arbitrarily begin reading on page two hundred. Another logical infelicity involves the birth of Dermot Trellis's son. Sheila Lamont, the child's mother, is one of Trellis's fictional characters; therefore the son, Orlick, will be only half human.

> I had carefully considered giving an outward indication of the son's semi-humanity by furnishing him with only the half of a body. Here I encountered further difficulties. If given the upper half only, it would be necessary to provide a sedan-chair or litter with at least two runners or scullion-boys to operate it . . . . On the other hand, to provide merely the lower half . . . would be to narrow unduly the validity of the son and confine his activities virtually to walking, running, kneeling and kicking football. For that reason I decided ultimately to make no outward distinction and thus avoided any charge that my work was somewhat far-fetched. (O'Brien At Swim-Two-Birds 207)

Of course the narrator fails to mention that Trellis is himself a fictional character, and that the offspring of Sheila Lamont and Dermot Trellis should therefore have no body at all (Devlin 96).

Much of the macabre humor of At Swim-Two-Birds is associated with Sweeny, a mad poet who is lacerated by thorns and racked by cold and rain in quatrain after quatrain of writing "in praise of nature." But the more he suffers, the more eloquently he sings. In selecting his detail, O'Brien emphasizes the ludicrous rather than the poignant aspects of this legend called in Irish the "Buile Suibne" (Waters 132). "The tale provides O'Brien with an excellent opportunity for a satiric thrust at the clergy who were so generous in cursing anyone who interrupted their prayers" (Waters 133).

> The final view of Sweeny is linked to the short-lived reconciliation between the student-narrator and his uncle, a scene which parodies the episode between Bloom and Dedalus at Eccles Street. But while Dedalus's link to ordinary humanity has been confirmed by the night's ordeal, O'Brien's narrator is flung back into the labyrinth of the imagination. (Waters 136)

Sweeny is a man who thinks he has a glass bottom and will not sit for fear of breaking. The book ends in a flurry of self-mocking images of lunacy and suicide: art turned in upon itself, feeding upon itself, brought to a terrible impasse (Waters 136).

In At Swim-Two-Birds the characters battle against the author for their own autonomy.

> The novel, in the hands of an unscrupulous writer, could be despotic . . . .
> It was undemocratic to compel characters to be uniformly good or bad or
> poor or rich. Each should be allowed a private life, self-determination and
> a decent standard of living. This would make for self-respect, contentment
> and better service. It would be incorrect to say that it would lead to chaos.
> (O'Brien At Swim-Two-Birds 33)

If Dermot Trellis, the would-be novelist in the novel, failed to observe the above rules, the
result would be chaos (Devlin 92). Trellis creates a twenty-five-year-old character named
John Furriskey, as the main character and villain in Trellis's sleazy melodrama. Furriskey's
voice has an accent and intonation that are usually associated with the Dublin lower or
working classes. Furriskey's friends, Paul Shanahan, and Antony Lamont are in the same
social class as is Furriskey. In At Swim-Two-Birds, Trellis is brought to trial by these
characters, and all of the testimony focuses on the conditions of employment for the various
characters (Devlin 93). The characters claim to suffer from malnutrition and to be
inadequately clothed. Their inadequate play, and their ten-minute limit to eat their lunches,
don't give the characters an opportunity for a nourishing meal. Two of the characters
involved in the labor-management dispute are Pooka MacPhellimey and the Good Fairy.
The Pooka MacPhellimey is an advocate for the working class, while the Good Fairy is an
advocate for the upper classes (Devlin 94). When the group runs across the injured
Sweeny, the Good Fairy suggests, "Maybe he is drunk. I don't believe in wasting my
sympathy on sots, do you?" And when Sweeny begins to recite poetry, the Good Fairy is
even more convinced that he is drunk, and that they should leave him alone. The Pooka
suggests that they use moss to stop the flow of blood from Sweeny's wounds, while the
Good Fairy wants to stop the flow of poetry from Sweeny's mouth. Much of the irony
here is that Pookas are usually evil, and Good Fairies are usually good; here, however, the
evil Pooka is promoting the interests of the working class, and is displaying kindness and
amicability, while the Good Fairy is promoting the interests of property and is querulous
and unpleasant. This is, therefore, an inversion of the accepted notions of good and evil
(Devlin 95).

The Pooka and the Good Fairy have a long discussion about numerology. Since
truth is an odd number, the Good Fairy has the number three. And since the Pooka is a
devil, he has the even number two (Devlin 104). The novel ends with a ludicrously bloody
image that demonstrates the dissatisfaction of the victory of "goodness" over "evil."

> Well-known, alas, is the case of the poor German who was very fond of
> three and who made each aspect of his life a thing of triads. He went home
> one evening and drank three cups of tea with three lumps of sugar in each
> cup, cut his jugular with a razor three times and scrawled with a dying hand
> on a picture of his wife good-bye, good-bye, good-bye. (O'Brien At Swim-
> Two-Birds 316)

Under the pen name of Myles na Gopaleen, Brian O'Nolan wrote the "Cruiskeen
Lawn" ("little full jug") columns which appeared between 1940 and 1966 in the Irish
Times. The earlier pieces were more autonomous and self-contained. In an important way,
they created their own context (Lanters 179). These early pieces relied very heavily on
such surface humor as arbitrariness, wordplay, repetition, and reversals. Even the
potentially serious critical articles during this early period would often reverted to these
surface devices (Lanters 181). The later pieces were much more related to criticism and
debate concerning Irish politics, Irish art, Irish society, and so forth. (Lanters 179). The
later pieces contained much more significant and sustained types of humor, with "lapses"
less likely to occur in these later pieces. The sarcastic, pedantic voice was consistently
sustained, and the criticism was directed at realistic targets (Lanters 181).

Both the earlier and the later columns tended to take a denigrating perspective, and they were filled with acerbic wit and brilliance (Cronin vii). Many of the stories in this column begin, and are then interrupted or abandoned without reaching a satisfactory conclusion. A lot of the pieces which are about "The Brother" follow this pattern, and most of them, in fact, make no real point, but are amusing nevertheless because of the incongruity between the pointlessness of the story, and the elaborate and emphatic style of the narrator, who often abruptly ends the story by stepping onto a passing bus (Lanters 166). In 1934 Brian O'Nolan wrote a bit of nonsense verse entitled "A Word to Our Daughters" in Blather, his University College magazine. The poem was written in doggerel verse, and was a nonsense poem in the tradition of Lewis Carroll or Edward Lear. It talked about trying to oil a vehicle with "trehicle." It also talked about smearing syrup on your styrup, and it concluded by talking about the expense and the wear and tear on the body of such an undertaking finally rhymingg "do so" with "troso." (O'Nolan "Word" 27).

O'Nolan also played with the relationships between the English and Gaelic languages, by sometimes spelling English words according to Gaelic spelling conventions. Thus, instead of writing "Everybody here is under arrest," he would write "Éabharaighbodaigh thiar ios undar airéist." O'Nolan's most sophisticated word play, however, is to be found in the puns which form the anti-climax of a story carefully developed to lead the readers up the garden path. The story exists only to develop the terrible pun that comes at the end. In the old days,

> Keats and Chapman spent several months in the county Wicklow prospecting for ochre deposits. That was before the days of (your) modern devices for geological devination. With Keats and Chapman it was literally a question of smelling the stuff out . . . . [Chapman] had nosed away in the direction of Newtonmountkennedy . . . . He implored Keats to come and confirm his nasal diagnosis. Keats agreed. He accompanied Chapman to the site and lay down in the dirt to do his sniffing. Then he rose. "Great mines stink alike," he said. (O'Nolan Best 182-183)

Immanuel Kant has described the reason we laugh at this type of story as "the sudden transfiguration of a strained expectation into nothing" (Lanters 172). As a postscript, it should be noted that Chapman has a pigeon named Homer (Waters 126).

The literal interpretation of metaphors is yet another comic device which O'Nolan uses in "The Cruiskeen Lawn" column. Myles na Gopaleen is challenged by his hated landlord to "drink him under the table," and Myles accepts the challenge. First, he murders the landlord, and then he dissolves the landlord's body in a bath of acid.

> When I returned to London, I went up to the bedroom with some curiosity. There was nothing to be seen save the bath of acid. I carried the bath down to the sitting room and got a glass. I filled the glass with what was in the bath, crept in under the table and swallowed the burning liquid. Glass after glass I swallowed till all was gone. It was with grim joy that I accomplished my threat that I would drink this plumber under the table. (O'Nolan Best 336)

The Hard Life: An Exegesis of Squalor (1961) is a comedy of humors (Power 95). Annie is controlled by her withdrawal; Mrs. Crotty is controlled by her gruffness; Mr. Collopy is controlled by his ceremoniousness; and Manus is controlled by his rebellion and his imitation (Power 95-96). The Hard Life is also filled with verbal wit. Mr. Collopy, and Manus, and Finbarr, and Father Fahrt all have great facility with words. Mary Power considers the linguistic humor in this novel to be both conventional and predictable. Collopy can be counted on to use florid sentimental clichés and colorful oaths. Father Fahrt recites what the Church teaches. Manus undermines the gullible with misleading scientific and scholarly jargon. And Finbarr describes very complex situations with very simple language (Power 96). The plot of The Hard Life is also conventional, taken directly from the tradition of New Comedy in which the old society is in conflict with the new society, and the humorous and potentially heroic contend with each other. According to tradition, the older generation simply disintegrates. Mrs. Crotty and Mr. Collopy die and Father Fahrt stays in Rome (Power 97). The Hard Life ends with the demise of the old order and the scattering of the new (Power 102).

In The Hard Life, O'Brien turned comic nonsense into comic grotesque (Lanters 175). O'Brien himself described this novel as "a volume which contains a treatise on piss and vomit," and indeed much of the novel is concerned with squalor, cruelty, and disease. Myles says, "I AM, of course, intensely interested in education. I have every reason to be because I was disabled for life at the age of fifteen by a zealous master (although I had the laugh on him afterwards, when I came back from hospital with my two hands amputated)." In a letter to Mark Hamilton, O'Brien remarks, "One suggestion was that Father Fahrt was not objectionable enough and that he should have some disease. I absolutely turned down TB, which is never funny, but there is a lot to be said for some scaly skin disease (psoriasis?) which need not appear on the face but be conveyed by itching and scratching" (Lanters 177).

The Hard Life is about the life of a particularly strange family, the Collopys, at the turn of the century. The parents of Finbarr and his brother Manus die, and they are sent to Dublin to grow up in the house of their half-uncle, Mr. Collopy. Mr. Collopy is a jovial eccentric who is able to create a verbal façade to hide his personal faults. Mr. Collopy and Father Fahrt are both attracted to Church History, "the way some watch prize fights, bullfights, or cockfights" (Power 93). Mr. Collopy bears a close resemblance to Sir Toby in Shakespeare's Twelfth Night, which like The Hard Life is a "comedy of excess." Both Mr. Collopy and Sir Toby Belch rely on drink and good fellowship to keep them in good spirits. Toby's speech is filled with foreign phrases and legal jargon, while Collopy's is rich in derogatory Irish epithets and Dublin slang, like "gorawars," "pishrogues," "thooleramawns," "crawthumpers," and "bowsies" (Power 97).

Annie is always found with food either in her hands or on her mind. "She wins her male relatives' regard as only a well-meaning, singularly inarticulate, drudge, for her answer to any question is 'seemingly.' There is just a chance that this reply puts her in the ranks of the arch-skeptics" (Power 94). Annie is a prostitute, but manages to keep her profession a secret.

> By placing Annie's secret life beside her domestic life, O'Brien suggests that her drudgery in the household is as much prostitution as standing on Wilton Place. Accepting charitable sums, large and small, from male relatives is as degrading as payment for sex. At the end of the novel, Finbarr sees the parallel while drinking with Manus, and it makes him vomit. (Power 95)

The names of Manus and Finbarr are of some interest. "Manus" is Latin for "hand," but is also a corruption of "magnus" meaning "great." And "Finbarr" is Irish for "fair-headed." They therefore represent head and hand, since Manus is active, while Finbarr is contemplative (Power 87). Finbarr's appeal as narrator of the story is a result of his disarming honesty. His style is "numb, brusque, and self-effacing." The novel is an example of Roman (Juvenalian) satire, but this type of satire has English and Irish precedents as well. The novel itself also takes place in Dublin, London, and Rome, the three major cities that are part of Mr. Collopy's final pilgrimage (Power 88). Mary Power feels that the most significant object of O'Brien's satire is James Joyce. The Hard Life is specifically anti-Joycean, in that it demonstrates that mythic readings of Irish life are impossible and absurd. Power feels that O'Brien is relentless in his demythologizing of Joyce, as he describes Irish life without idealization of any kind. "Along with the River Liffey, O'Brien spurns such Joycean haunts as Sandymount, Glasnevin Cemetery, Howth and Jesuit Schools and substitutes Clontarf, Dean's Grange Cemetery and Christian Brothers

Schools" (Power 89). Power feels that the tightrope-walking incident is crucial to the understanding of the character Manus.   Finbarr views Manus's tightrope walking performance and blesses himself because he thinks he has observed a miracle. Manus is so flushed with pride by his success that he decides to write an instructional pamphlet on tightrope walking (Power 92). Manus's idol is Eugene Blondin, a French acrobat who successfully traversed Niagara Falls in a barrel.

> As an argument for the safety of his own stunts, the brother mentions that Blondin appeared in Belfast and died in bed of natural causes. Manus does not mention Blondin's catastrophic appearance in Dublin when, during his aerial act, two of his assistants plunged to their deaths. By calling Manus the Blondin of Dublin, O'Brien both acknowledges his familiarity with the incident and plays him no compliment. The comic and grotesque exist side by side in the brother's character, just as they do in the circus. (Power 93)

The Dalkey Archive (1964) is filled with in-jokes about Catholicism, predestination, and James Joyce (Cronin ix). The Dalkey Archive is written within a realistic framework. In a letter to Timothy O'Keeffe, O'Brien says that he wanted this novel to be above all "bitterly funny," and he achieved this tone by evoking feelings of revulsion and horror at the unacceptable behaviour of the characters, who are all presented as obnoxious, particularly to Mick, the narrator (Lanters 177). Much of the eccentricity of Sergeant Fottrell lies in his manner of speaking, and in his fantastic stories. One of these stories is "an almost verbatim version of the bicyclosis or 'mollycule' theory also put forward in The Third Policeman"(Lanters 178).   The Dalkey Archive is a blend of comedy, parody, nonsense, and grotesque, but it is serious as well. O'Brien himself called it "a mass of portentous material that looks unmanageable" (Lanters 179).

An Béal Bocht (The Poor Mouth) (1964) was originally written as a satirical in-joke which only Irish-language enthusiasts could understand (Cronin vii); it was translated into English in 1973. In this novel, O'Brien is skeptical of the way that the Gaelic language is often linked to an archaic and impoverished life style. "As a master of 'smooth learned Gaelic,' O'Brien made fun of contemporary autobiographical accounts of life in the Gaeltacht, those remote regions of the west which preserve what remains of the native culture." Waters warns, however, that because it is a parody, and because of the fact that some of the humor depends on linguistic puns and allusions, no translation can be entirely satisfactory (Waters 124).

In Corkadora the people are grim and melancholy. Here the sun never shines, and there is so much rain that the fishermen net an occasional pig as they make their way through the fields. Bonaparte O'Coonassa, the main character in The Poor Mouth, understands the world mainly from folklore, gossip, and the musings of "the old grey fellow" who "hunts" in order to provide them both with meat for their potatoes. But his "hunting," is merely a euphemism for stealing from the neighbors. Bonaparte is wrongly accused of a crime, and in a court where only English is spoken, and where the proceedings are consequently totally incomprehensible to him, he is sentenced to twenty-nine years of imprisonment. "On his way to the jail, he meets a feeble old pauper, who turns out to be his father, returning home after serving a similar sentence under similar circumstances" (Waters 125).

In The Poor Mouth, O'Brien makes an ironic negative correlation between how pure the language of the Irish peasants is, and how rich they are in worldly goods. The lives of the Corcadorans are filled with poverty and calamity; and they therefore speak the finest Gaelic. O'Brien is using satire to point out that the Irish peasants have been so much the subject of myth that their actual history has been trivialized and obscured. As Maureen Waters notes, "O'Brien observes rather acidly that the people themselves have begun to emulate literary patterns to act according to the prescriptions set down by anthropologists, historians, folklorists, writers of fiction and poetry" (Waters 124-125).

The parish of The Third Policeman (1967) does not exist in the middle dimension, the dimension of Newtonian physics. Rather, it exists in the dimension of both quantum mechanics and relativity (Tigges 212). The novel begins with a kind of tragi-comic tone. The first sentence of the novel reads, "Not everybody knows how I killed old Phillip Mathers, smashing his jaw in with my spade," but then he continues, "but first it is better to speak of my friendship with John Divney" (O'Brien The Third Policeman 7). Death is treated with irreverence in The Third Policeman. The old man Mathers is murdered for his black cash-box, and when he is struck down, the narrator remarks, "As he collapsed full-length in the mud he did not cry out. Instead I heard him say something softly in a conversational tone--something like 'I do not care for celery' or 'I left my glasses in the scullery' " (O'Brien The Third Policeman 16).   In a book entitled, An Anatomy of Literary Nonsense, Wim Tigges suggests that Flann O'Brien uses nonsense devices such as work-play in many of his satirical pieces. He furthermore suggests that The Third Policeman is O'Brien's only novel that can be considered a "truly nonsensical work." Although The Third Policeman was published posthumously in 1967, it was written as early as 1940. In this novel, "the norm of fantasy is tinged with the grotesque." This novel also has an affinity with Drama of the Absurd, and is a forerunner of the metafiction genre, the genre which is "fiction about fiction." Since The Third Policeman combines elements of fantasy, grotesque, absurd, metafiction, and humor, it is classified as "nonsense" by Tigges (Tigges 205).

Brian O'Nolan describes The Third Policeman as "the world of the dead--and the damned--where none of the rules and laws (not even the law of gravity) holds good" (Cronin viii). The novel contains a great deal of unconventional logic. The novel is paradoxical in that the narrator is dead, but he is nevertheless capable of telling his story. In The Third Policeman the concepts of circularity and serialization are fully exploited. The book is circular in that it ends where it began thereby suggesting that the events described will go on repeating themselves forever. The underground "hell" described in the book is also circular. Whatever direction a person walks in, he always returns to his original position. There is also infinity in Policeman MacCruiskeen's series of chests (Chinese boxes), "each containing an identical, smaller chest, the smallest of which are invisible" (Lanters 171). O'Brien also uses a rhetorical device which José Lanters describes as "relentless logic" in At The Third Policeman. This can be illustrated by the reasoning of de Selby, the mad scientist of the novel. The piece entitled "Sufferers Helped" is designed to help ballet dancers who are distressed by being required to perform difficult high jumps. De Selby's solution is to have the dancers wear the "Myles Patent Ballet Pumps" which have been fitted with miniature land mines. "If you give a little hop and take care to land on one mine, the mine will go off and you will be sent flying through the air with the greatest of ease." But the logic doesn't stop here: "But I am afraid the stage will be full of holes. I have for disposal a limited number of cork bungs suitable for stopping up the holes, price four shillings per dozen while they last. Bungs, pumps and all in a presentation casket with a suitable greeting card, twenty-eight bob, post free" (O'Brien The Third Policeman 50). Wim Tigges suggests that the "relentless logic" in this novel places it firmly in the Carrollian tradition (Tigges 206).

Another type of strange logic in The Third Policeman is the comic syllogism. By referring to the "atomic or mollycule theory," and by using syllogistic reasoning, Sergeant Pluck is able to explain how people can change into bicycles, and vice versa (Lanters 165). At one point in the novel, when a Police Inspector leans with one elbow on the counter, Pluck interprets this as a sign of "a sizeable bicycle component in a man." Later, there is an account of a bicycle being hanged, and still later Sergeant Pluck tells about having suffered from "a slow puncture, not of his tyre but of his own person" (Tigges 208). When

Sergeant Pluck interrupts de Selby's explanation of Atomic by saying, "you would be surprised at the number of people in these parts who nearly are half people and half bicycles," the narrator reacts with "I let go a gasp of astonishment that made a sound in the air like a bad puncture" (Tigges 211). Sergeant Pluck is responsible for much of the wordplay and false logic of The Third Policeman, and the result is often what is called an "Irish Bull." When the narrator asks Sergeant Pluck what time he is to be hanged, the Sergeant replies: "Tomorrow morning if we have the scaffold up in time and unless it is raining. You would not believe how slippery the rain can make a new scaffold. You could slip and break your neck" (Tigges 211).

Chapter V of The Third Policeman is filled with logical infelicities of various kinds, such as invisible sharpness, boxes within boxes receding to nothing, and inaudible music. In Chapter VII the reader is told how light can be "mangled into sound." just by "stretching the length of the waves (Tigges 208). De Selby, the mad scientist provides much of the humorous logic of The Third Policeman. De Selby has strange and illogical theories about houses (19), night (28), roads (33-34), names (35-367), journeys (44-45), time and eternity (567-57), life and the shape of the earth (80-83), night and sleep (101-103), air and water (125-128), and the sexes (144-145). Concerning time, for example, de Selby proposes that when a person looks in a mirror, it takes a small amount of time for the image to reach his eyes. It follows, then, that if he were to place an arrangement of parallel mirrors, each reflecting diminishing images of an interposed object indefinitely, in the last mirror he would see not what was there, but what used to be there some time ago. He performs such an experiment. "What he states to have seen through this glass is astonishing. He claims to have noticed a growing youthfulness in the reflection of his face according as they receded, the most distant of them--too tiny to be visible to the naked eye--being the face of a beardless boy of twelve" (Tigges 207). Wim Tigges feels that O'Brien displays just enough playfulness in The Third Policeman to keep it from crossing over into absurdity, but enough inconsistency to prevent it from becoming fantasy. Tigges feels that the novel thus borders on the edges of nonsense (Tigges 216).

The humor of both Myles na Gopaleen, and his alter ego, Flann O'Brien, tended to mature with time, as it moved away from the elements of nonsense to forms of humor which were more deeply rooted in reality (Lanters 181).

Flann O'Brien (Myles na Gopaleen)(né Brian O'Nolan) Bibliography

Cronin, Anthony. No Laughing Matter: The Life and Times of Flann O'Brien. London, England: Grafton, 1989.

Devlin, Joseph. "The Politics of Comedy in At Swim-Two-Birds." Éire-Ireland 27.4 (1992): 91-105.

Ingersoll, Earl G. "Irish Jokes: A Lacanian Reading of Short Stories by James Joyce, Flann O'Brien, and Bryan MacMahon." Studies in Short Fiction 2 (Spring, 1990): 237-245.

Lanters, José. " 'Still Life' Versus Real Life: The English Writings of Brian O'Nolan." Explorations in the Field of Nonsense. Ed. Wim Tigges. Amsterdam, Holland: Rodopi, 1987 161-181.

O'Brien, Flann. At Swim-Two-Birds. New York, NY: Penguin, 1967.

O'Brien, Flann. The Third Policeman New York, NY: New American Library, 1976.

O'Nolan, Brian. "A Word to Our Daughters." Blather 1.2 (1934): 27.

O'Nolan, Kevin. The Best of Myles: A Selection from "Cruiskeen Lawn". London, England, 1977.

Power, Mary. "Flann O'Brien and Classical Satire: An Exegesis of the Hard Life." Éire-Ireland 13.1 (1978): 87-102.

Tigges, Wim. "Flann O'Brien." An Anatomy of Literary Nonsense. Amsterdam, Holland:
    Rodopi, 1988, 205-216.
Waters, Maureen. "Flann O'Brien and Mad Sweeny." The Comic Irishman. Albany, NY:
    State Univ of New York Press, 1984, 123-136.

Mary Lavin (1912-) IRELAND

Ann Weekes alluded to the "sheer beauty and poetic allusiveness" of Mary Lavin's
prose, adding that this wins a place for her among the writers who are "disturbingly
different." Lavin is one of the earliest Irish writers to examine the "mundane areas of
women's existence," and in doing so she had a poet's eye for "the unusual, the beautiful,
and the universal in the ordinary." Lavin places the most delicate nuances of human
emotions into revealing cosmic patterns (Weekes 22).

Mary Lavin wrote such collections of short stories as the following: Tales from
Bective Bridge (1942), The Long Ago and Other Stories (1944), The Becker Wives (1946),
At Sallygap (1947), A Single Lady and Other Stories (1951), The Patriot Son and Other
Stories (1956), Selected Stories (1959), The Great Wave and Other Stories (1961), The
Stories of Mary Lavin (1964), In the Middle of the Fields and Other Stories (1967),
Happiness and Other Stories (1969), Collected Stories (1972), A Memory and Other Stories
(1972), The Stories of Mary Lavin, Volume 2 (1974), The Shrine and Other Stories (1977),
and A Family Likeness and Other Stories (1985).

Mary Lavin Bibliography

Weekes, Ann Owens. "Mary Lavin: Textual Gardens." Irish Women Writers: An Uncharted
    Tradition. Lexington, KY: University Press of Kentucky, 1990, 133-154.

Benedict Kiely (1919-) IRELAND

Proxopera: A Tale of Modern Ireland (1986) is a superb story in which the clown
takes the form of a modern gunman. Binchley is a retired schoolmaster being forced to
drive a car full of explosives into the streets of his town; thus the images of gaiety and
innocence in this context are perverted. A laughing boy becomes a madman, and a song
about a drunken adventure becomes a grotesque counterpoint to actual acts of violence
(Waters 179).

Benedict Kiely Bibliography

Waters, Maureen. The Comic Irishman. Albany, NY: State Univ of New York Press, 1984.

Brendan Behan (1923-1964) IRELAND

Brendan Behan was very popular, and he enjoyed this popularity, and in fact was
gradually consumed by it. "He became the proverbial comic Irishman, boisterous, hard
drinking, witty, a public performer, lionized in the pubs, and conspicuously avoided by the
'respectable' Irish at home and in America" (Waters 94). Behan satirized such aspects of
Irish life as the language movement, the temperance movement, the religion, the upper
classes, James Joyce, the Gaelic tradition, and Eamon de Valera. Maureen Waters says that

Behan's wit is more genial than is that of Sean O'Casey. It is also more dependent on such irreverent one liners as the following quote from The Hostage:

> PAT: . . . Your real trouble when you go to prison as a patriot, do you know what it will be?
> OFFICER: The loss of liberty.
> PAT: No, the other Irish patriots, in along with you.

As Walter Sorell says, "Behan loves rough and low comedy, be it in The Quare Fellow or The Hostage. He can transform the gallows humor of prisoners into wanton jocularity, even while they are digging the murderer's grave" (Sorell 301).

The Quare Fellow: A Comedy Drama (1956) takes place inside of a Dublin prison. Regan, one of the characters in the novel says that the quare fellow is a scapegoat, being executed by a crowd of bloody ruffians like himself; Maureen Waters suggests that the quare fellow is a Christ figure. Extending the Christ image, Regan believes that "those in power, particularly the judges, are more guilty of vice than the prisoners, whom he regards as condemned to do penance for the rest of mankind." The Quare Fellow is filled with humor, mirth, and melancholy that are also qualities of the old fashioned Irish wake. The novel also contains a great deal of burlesque, "ranging from the con games played by the old alcoholics, Dunlavin and Neighbor, to the posturing of the guards. Even the hangman is a figure of fun--a British bartender who sings a sentimental ballad, 'The Rose of Tralee,' unintentionally punning on the 'pure crystal fountain' ('poor Christian fountain')" (Waters 162). Behan also uses dialect as a source of humor and vitality. Behan's dialect humor is typically needling, aggressive, and epigramatic (Waters 163).

Borstal Boy (1959) is an autobiographical account of Behan's own experiences as a political prisoner in England. It is widely held among Irish critics that the most compelling character that Brendan Behan ever created was Brendan Behan himself. Even before Borstal Boy was published, Behan had attracted a great deal of public attention with his witty and rambunctious behavior (Waters 166). When Behan was remanded to the Borstal detention center for juveniles at Hollesley Bay, he was drawn into a new role--that of "Paddy, the comic Irishman." Behan "becomes a genial performer sought after by the other prisoners whom he regales with Irish songs and obscene limericks and jokes. His memoir amply attests to his craving for companionship and his use of comedy to break out of isolation and surround himself with an admiring throng of friends" (Waters 169). It is ironic that Behan's exploits so closely parallel the historical experience of the Irish people in general during the nineteenth century. During this time, the Irish were abused and ridiculed because of their cultural differences; but they were also applauded when these differences began to be amusing. They were viewed through the "distorted prism of a stereotype," and in order to survive, they often conformed to that stereotype (Waters 169).

Because of his reputation as a "wild Irishman," newsmen would follow Behan around taking down samples of his famous Irish wit. He was able to delight a vast audience, especially in England and America.

> He was evidently quick to seize opportunities to bring himself to the attention of the media, frequently turning mischance--a drunken brawl or a night in jail--into a comic interlude. He created a legend by his escapades and by his superb gift as a story teller and mime, able to captivate listeners for hours at a time. He had a fine tenor voice and an excellent repertoire as well as a talent for parody and for composing limericks extemporaneously. (Waters 170)

But Behan had mixed feelings, for he felt that he was betraying his deepest roots by ridiculing Irish nationalism and by turning his political past into "grist for the publicity mill." Behan represented the rebel as comedian. He was also an archetypal stage Irishman in real life. He had a tragic and early death from the combined ravages of diabetes and

alcoholism.
          The general consensus is that he first created and then was trapped by his
public image, by the expectations of the crowd. Toward the end of his life,
the amiable witty surface cracked open under the pressure of what must
have been extraordinary inner violence. He wrote less and less as his fame
increased and he deteriorated physically, collapsing into drunken diabetic
comas. (Waters 172)
          Walter Sorell considers The Hostage (1964)to be a savagely funny play in the style
of the commedia dell-arte. It is literary vaudeville in which song and speech alternate in
a mock-heroic tone. Behan had the ability to change a tragic lot like the kidnapping of a
Cockney soldier, and the threatening of this soldier with death--into a raucous comedy
(Sorell 301). An Giall: The Hostage is a play originally written in Irish. Behan believed
he could express certain moods in Gaelic that he couldn't express in English. Behan
explained that "Irish is more direct than English, more bitter." The bitterness of Gaelic is
also charged with comic energy as melancholy and mirth "flash together." The Hostage is
rapidly paced, and is interlaced with witty dialogue and wildly burlesque antics of the
various characters. Because of the force of death in the play, there is also much gallows
humor, not the "humor noir" of Beckett's Watt, (the laugh that laughs at "that which is
unhappy"). The gallows humor of The Hostage is spirited and "alive to the pleasures of
resistance." In The Hostage, Behan develops the "buck lepper" version of the stage
Irishman in the form of a mad patriot who parades around in kilts, plays the bagpipes, and
thinks that he is in the thick of the revolution (Waters 164). Behan also satirizes the
Anglo-Irish with his character Monsewer (a corruption of French "Monsieur"). These
Anglo-Irish ally themselves to the Republican cause and become "more Irish than the Irish
in behalf of the cultural revival." Waters suggests that most of the characters in The
Hostage are social outcasts. They are "a scruffy, belligerent lot." The most outspoken of
these social outcasts is Pat, an old witty and cynical IRA man. He ridicules the younger
militants, saying that they are "mechanical fools, completely devoid of humor or common
sense" (Waters 165). Behan is following stage Irish traditions in making his characters
boisterous drinkers and talkers who sing, joke, and dance in order to provide comic relief,
but this nevertheless leads up to the nightmarish scene in which Leslie is killed (Waters
166).

Brendan Behan Bibliography

McCann, Sean, Ed. The Wit of Brendan Behan. London, England: Frewin, 1968.
Sorell, Walter. Facets of Comedy. New York, NY: Grosset and Dunlap, 1972.
Waters, Maureen. "Flann O'Brien and Mad Sweeny." The Comic Irishman. Albany, NY:
          State Univ of New York Press, 1984, 123-136.

Thomas James Bonner Flanagan (1923-) IRELAND

          John Skow discusses Flanagan's trilogy, saying that while Year of the French (1979)
deals with an incident in 1798, and Tenants of Time (1988) begins with the uprisings in
the 1860s, the foreknowledge of history only colors these two works with an "agreeable
wash of irony." The End of the Hunt (1994), seems more tragic because the political
failures it describes lead directly to the bloody decades which follow, a time when ballad-
makers have given up, but the bomb-makers are still at work (Skow). The End of the Hunt
deals with a period of shaky nerves when men in overcoats are lurking about Dublin with
revolvers. There is "a notorious whispering gallery of rumor, malice, speculation, spiced

always and made palatable, such was the claim, by wit and vivacity" (Skow).

Thomas James Bonner Flanagan Bibliography

Skow, John. "Ballads' End: Thomas Flanagan Brings His Irish Trilogy to a Rueful Close."
Time May 23, 1994.

Flannery O'Connor (1925-1964) IRELAND

As a child, Flannery O'Connor used Pathé newsreels to train a bantam chicken to walk backwards. In 1938 while she was enrolled at Peabody High School in Milledgeville, Georgia, she confused her home economics teacher by dressing another bantam hen in a white piqué coat and striped pants, which she had sewn to specification. Up to the time of her death, at the age of thirty-nine, O'Connor retained a fondness for domestic fowl, especially the eccentric varieties. Her favorite was a chicken with one green eye and the other one orange, but she also liked those with overlong necks, or those with crooked combs (Muller 97). In college O'Connor served as an editor and a contributor to her college literary magazine. She also did cartoons and commentary with the sardonic humor that her readers have come to recognize as characteristic (Shloss 4).

In the two novels and thirty-one stories which Flannery O'Connor wrote during her lifetime, there are a number of rhetorical techniques which keep reappearing, namely: "hyperbole, distortion, allusion, analogy, the dramatization of extreme religious experience, the manipulation of judgment through narrative voice, and direct address to the reader" (Shloss 8). O'Connor was a Christian writing to an audience she perceived to be mainly non-Christian, an audience she considered to be "stunted and deformed." As a writer she was constantly trying to second-guess her "monstrous reader" (Shloss 103).

O'Connor's writing was like the Bible in that it contained many "epiphanies." There are significant epiphanies, for example in "Greenleaf," in "Good Country People," in "A Circle in the Fire," in "Parker's Back," and in "A View of the Woods." In all of these epiphanies "the protagonist is taken to the point of profound insight and then is killed or simply abandoned by an author who apparently fears that denouement will lessen the impact of undeniably dramatic events" (Shloss 104). Unlike James Joyce's secular epiphanies, O'Connor's epiphanies are supernatural. In Stephen Hero, Joyce defined epiphany as "a sudden spiritual manifestation, whether in the vulgarity of speech or of gesture in a memorable phrase of the mind itself. He believed that it was for the man of letters to record these epiphanies, with extreme care, seeing that they themselves are the most delicate and evanescent of moments" (Shloss 105). In contrast, Flannery O'Connor felt more of an affinity with the ancient concept of epiphany, one which tended to emphasize a divine intervention, one in which the recipients received some "great and even unsought knowledge." O'Connor's characters have decisive life experiences thrust upon them. A bull rams one; a Negress smashes another; another is captured and shot by a criminal. In all cases the human is passive and impotent, and it is an external force which provides the epiphany. In all cases, the passivity is seen to be a virtue, and the epiphany is more of a response, than an insight or an action (Shloss 107).

Flannery O'Connor was very skeptical of literary criticism, and after she had read Frederic Crews's The Pooh Perplex, she referred to the act of criticism as "the perplex business." O'Connor had a special ability to shock the reader into acknowledging the spiritual aspects of her fiction by creating some of the most outrageous protagonists and some of the most improbable action in contemporary fiction in what Gilbert Muller has termed the "Catholic Grotesque" (Muller vii). In 1950, O'Connor was on a train going home for Christmas vacation when she became terribly ill. She had developed disseminated lupus, the blood disease that had killed her father earlier (Shloss 5). With the exception of the six stories that she wrote as part of her master's thesis, and the beginnings of her first novel, Wise Blood, all of her published work was written in Georgia between the onset of her illness and her death (Shloss 7).

Flannery O'Connor was born in Georgia; however, her Irishness is evident both in her supreme ability as a story teller, and in her deep religious convictions. Her Wise Blood (1952) is a Gothic novel about a young religious fanatic from the Georgia mountains who attempts to establish a "Church Without Christ." Her The Violent Bear It Away (1960) is a macabre gothic story set in the backwoods of Georgia; it is about a fanatical boy intent on baptizing a still younger boy. Her A Good Man is Hard to Find (1955) and her Everything That Rises Must Converge (1965) are collections of grotesque short stories all set in the South.

There is little conventional Christian piety in O'Connor's work. Whenever Christian piety does occur, it is an object of "chilling satire and travesty." Christian piety is transformed into a comic and absurd world view, as when Ruby Turpin in "Revelation" considers her position in God's world, and expresses her gratitude to the Lord for not making her a Negro or poor white trash. For O'Conner, it is the sinner who is at the heart of Christianity, "for no one knows as much about Christianity as the sinner . . . . There are no saints in O'Connor fiction, but there is an incredible legion of sinners, because in her stories she presents the Catholic universe of evil" (Muller 101). O'Connor justifies the grotesqueness of her writing by saying, "My own feeling is that writers who see by the light of Christian faith will have in these times, the sharpest eye for the grotesque, for the perverse, and for the unacceptable." For O'Connor, violence, madness, and the inexplicable are there because such notions require a divine solution. "O'Connor's absurd tricksters and grotesque Christ figures take on the sins of the world . . . , for the gallows humor which permeates her fiction has its more serious side" (Muller 102). O'Connor is struck both by man's roguish capacity for sin, and by his capacity for salvation (Muller 112).

In an article entitled "The Comic Vision of Flannery O'Connor's A Good Man is Hard to Find," Alfred Castle notes that O'Connor's humor is based on various kinds of incongruity. O'Connor has a remarkable ability to blend the comic and the serious into a single view of reality, and this dual perspective has "led some to label her a comic genius" (Sullivan 339). Many critics have noted O'Connor's creative use of humorous descriptions of character, and her use of comic exaggeration; however, Alfred Castle notes that her real contribution is in her use of comic elements to support her "specific sacramental outlook." O'Connor's humor is the humor of incongruity, or more specifically, the humor of "disjointed, ill-suited pairings of ideas or situations that are divergent from habitual customs" (Castle 1). O'Connor's humor occurs when "the conscious is unawares transferred from great things to small--when there is a descending incongruity" (Spenser 463). But O'Connor's humor also involves "ascending incongruity, as when an insignificant entity develops unexpectedly into something great which more likely leads to the emotion of wonder or awe. O'Connor was clearly aware of the difference and used both brilliantly to achieve the desired emotions" (Castle 2). Castle notes a number of these disjointed pairings of perceptions vs. rigid ideas, such as the grandmother's inability to judge the Misfit of Red Sam correctly in A Good Man Is Hard To Find, Mr. Head's inability to reconcile his idea of the city with his perceptions of it in "The Artificial Nigger," Mrs. Cope's reluctant acceptance of the reality of evil despite her naive optimism about her independence and invulnerability in "A Circle in the Fire," and Hulga's awareness of the inadequacy of her conceptual categories in the face of radical evil. These are all "poignant examples of Schopenhauer's refinement of comic incongruity" (Castle 4).

Elizabeth Archer indicates that O'Connor's early critics classified her as a Gothic writer who exaggerates her characters into symbols of narcissistic love that causes the characters' families to disintegrate; however, more recent critics consider her to be in the Grotesque rather than the Gothic tradition, since an important feature of O'Connor's style is the blending of humor and horror in her development of secular characters in naturalistic environments. These later critics suggest that O'Connor is especially indebted to the Southwest Humorists, and to Nathanael West. O'Connor is also in the tradition of Southern novelists best exemplified by William Faulkner. Five of O'Connor's short stories have been produced as films, each one running an hour or less. These are "The Life You Save May Be Your Own," "The Comforts of Home," "A Circle in the Fire," "Good Country People," and "The Displaced Person." Typically, O'Connor's stories begin in a calm and pastoral Southern setting; then the rapid development of conflict and strong visual imagery culminates in a violent clash of characters, setting, symbolism, and theme. This clash usually highlights the conflicts that result from male-female struggles but with the added complication of an outsider who provides a sexual challenge. The resulting confrontations are often comic in tone (Archer 52-65). As O'Connor herself phrases it, "It's not necessary to point out that the book of this fiction is going to be wild, that it is almost of necessity going to be violent and comic, because of the discrepancies that it seeks to combine" (qtd. in Shloss 118).

Ruby, in "A Stroke of Good Fortune" (1953) is humorous because she is static and unchanging. Ruby represents Bergson's idea of humorous incongruity as "something mechanical encrusted on the living." Ruby reasons that childbearing is of little worth or merit for an aspiring suburbanite. Despite her precautions, Ruby becomes pregnant, nevertheless, so ironically, "she cannot escape her role as participant in the universal process of creation."

Mr. Shiftlet in "The Life You Save May Be Your Own" (1953) promises to marry the retarded Lucynell, but only in order to obtain a free car and some money. As Mr. Shiftlet is fleeing the scene in his "stolen" automobile he picks up a young hitch-hiker and in a self-righteous tone he lectures the boy on the virtues of revering one's mother: "It's nothing so sweet as a boy's mother. She taught him his first prayers at her knee, she gave him love when no other would, she told him what was right and what wasn't, and she seen that he done the right thing. Son, I never rued a day in my life like the one I rued when I left that old mother of mine" (O'Connor 67). At this point in the story, to make the situation even more ironic, the hitch-hiker swears at Mr. Shiftlet, flings open the car door, and jumps into the ditch with his suitcase (Castle 3).

"The Displaced Person" (1954) is a profound example of the quick descent from the sacred and theological to the profane. At one point in the story, a priest is sitting with Mrs. Shortley on a porch, and the priest slightly bows his head and says, "For when God sent his Only Begotten Son, Jesus Christ Our Lord as a Redeemer to mankind, He . . ." At this point, Mrs. Shortley interrupts the priest, saying, "I want to talk to you about something serious." The priest's right eye flinches, and Mrs. Shortley continues, "As far as I'm concerned, Christ was just another Displaced Person." This incongruity "serves O'Connor's general purpose of delineating character and of limning the dimensions of theological and moral impoverishment" (Castle 6).

"The Temple of the Holy Ghost" (1954) is a story told from the point of view of a precocious twelve-year-old girl who is contemptuous of her "less mature" friends in the convent school. But then this girl goes to a circus, and sees a hermaphrodite who lifts his dress to the public, and the hermaphrodite says, "God made me thisaway and if you laugh, God may strike you the same way." This story confounds the girl, and she starts thinking about God and about his creations, and at the end of the story there "was a huge red ball like an elevated Host drenched in blood and when it sank out of sight, it left a line in the sky like a red clay road hanging over the trees" (O'Connor 101). "Temple of the Holy

Ghost" satirizes such targets as the romantic illusions of teenage girls, sibling rivalry, education, individual follies and the blatant opportunism of people who exploit the handicapped or the unfortunate. O'Connor develops the satire by allowing the reader to see the world through the eyes of a child. This is an effective device, since the child blurts out whatever she thinks. There are no pretensions or constraints as the child expresses her emotions as she feels them. This lack of pretension also contrasts markedly with the pretensions and constraints of the other characters of the short story (Becker 9-13). O'Connor likes to blend the grotesque and the holy at the most unexpected moments. The hermaphrodite in "The Temple of the Holy Ghost" is an object who radiates mystery, for he connects his grotesque agonies with a deeper spiritual consciousness. O'Connor confronts such dark apocalyptic images of pain in order to force the reader to acknowledge both the Satanic nature of the world and the necessity of using divine intervention in order to radically transform the world (Muller 111).

Mr. Head, in "The Artificial Nigger" (1955) has taken his grandson, Nelson, to the evil city, and they soon become lost in this Dante's Inferno of a city. Mr. Head and his grandson, Nelson, become separated, and when Nelson returns to his grandfather he is being chased by a woman who claims that Nelson has broken her ankle, and that she is going to sue them both. Mr. Head, however, denies that he has ever seen Nelson before. "The women dropped back, staring at him with horror, as if they were so repulsed by a man who would deny his own image and likeness that they could not bear to lay hands on him." At the end of the story Nelson and his grandfather run into a grotesque plastic figure of a Negro "sitting bent over a low yellow brick fence that curved around a wide lawn." On encountering the figure, Mr. Head exclaims, "They ain't got enough real ones here. They got to have an artificial one" (qtd. in Shloss 122). The figure was old and weathered and had been vandalized. Its eyes were completely white. Alfred Castle suggests that the statue represented the crucified Christ, and he further suggests that Mr. Head's denial of his son was symbolic of the earlier denial of Christ (Castle 13-14). Mr. Head and his grandson finally emerge from Hell, and this story can then be classified as comedy, because it represents the full cycle: decay, death, and rebirth (Castle 15).

Thomas Gosset proposes that the humor of O'Connor's fiction ranges from introspective and ironic to extroverted and uproarious. Hulga Hopewell in "Good Country People" (1955) is a Ph.D. with a wooden leg. She entices a Bible salesman up into the hay loft for a roll in the hay with the added titillation in her mind that she is seducing a religious and innocent gentleman. Hulga's mother had told her how fine this Bible salesman was; he was admired as being in the class of "good country people." Hulga on the other hand is an existentialist, who says that she believes in nothing. But during the seduction, Hulga is surprised to discover that the Bible salesman is more worldly than she had thought. And he also wasn't all that religious, as he exclaims, "You ain't so smart. I been believing in nothing ever since I was born!" O'Connor is playing on the irony that an intelligent Ph.D. is so ignorant in this particular situation. O'Connor is a firm believer in the Christian faith, and much of her fiction exposes the follies and misunderstandings of very intelligent and educated people, as she considered these follies to be highly ironic. There are many twentieth century American authors who concentrate on wit, satire, and irony in their writings. Unlike most of these other writers, however, O'Connor's humor comes not from her skepticism but from her faith (Gosset 174-180).

Isidore Becker considers O'Connor's fiction to be permeated with comic insights developed by O'Connor's effective use of wit, satire, and irony. The two O'Connor short stories which best exemplify this comic spirit are "Greenleaf" and "Temple of the Holy Ghost." Mrs. May in "Greenleaf" (1956) is a self-righteous, egotistical neighbor of the Greenleafs. When the Greenleaf's bull starts chewing on Mrs. May's hedge, she rises against the Greenleafs in righteous indignation because she considers the beauty of her hedge to be a symbol of her righteous living. The real reason for Mrs. May's attack, however is that the Greenleafs are prospering and Mrs. May is not, even though Mrs. May considers herself to be a much better person than they are. This satire attacks the pride, prejudice, folly, ignorance, and hypocrisy of the supercilious Mrs. May (Becker 9-13).

In "Revelation" (1964), a Wellesley student with acne whispers to Ruby Turpin "Go back to hell where you come from, you old wart hog!" Ruby Turpin has difficulty understanding this accusation. "How am I a hog and me both? How am I saved and from hell too?" As she ponders this enigma, she has a vision which is stark and funny, and which gives her an epiphinal insight. It was a vision of a streak, a vast swinging bridge that extended "upward from earth through a field of living fire" (Shloss 109).

> Upon it a vast horde of souls were rumbling toward heaven. There were whole companies of black niggers in white robes, and battalions of freaks and lunatics shouting and clapping and leaping like frogs. And bringing up the end of the procession was a tribe of people whom she recognized at once as those who, like herself and Claud, had always had a little of everything and the God given wit to use it right. (Muller 112-113)

As Carol Shloss notes, "Ruby envisions herself to be last in line; this time in procession behind the white-trash, Negroes, and lunatics, and it is this image that completes the message of ill-founded self-esteem" (Shloss 112). Muller notes that this passage shows that O'Connor had a tolerance toward all humanity. "Flannery O'Connor was a visionary-- admittedly a comic one--whose powers of perception made both secular and religious experience more meaningful" (Muller 113).

There are several epiphanies in "Parker's Back" (1965). One of them takes place as O. E. Parker absentmindedly drives a tractor into a huge tree. He shouts "God above!" as he is hurled from the tractor, and he watches the tractor, the tree, and his own shoes burn as if the whole thing were a single burning bush. O'Connor writes, "he could feel the hot breath of the burning tree on his face." Parker jumps into his truck and flees from this scene to the city, realizing that there had been a great change in his life. Carol Shloss notes that Parker's epiphany happens to a person who is passive, and that the epiphany is both unanticipated and unwanted. Parker is so disturbed by the incident that he decides to get another tatoo. He has a flashback of a circus performer displaying his tatoos, and "flexing his muscles so that the arabesque of men and beasts and flowers on his skin appeared to have a subtle emotion, lifted up." This was also an epiphany for Parker. "Until he saw the man at the fair, it did not enter his head that there was anything out of the ordinary about the fact that he existed . . . [it was] as if a blind boy had been turned so gently in a different direction that he did not know his destination had been changed" (qtd. in Shloss 114-115). In something of a moral imperative Parker has the image of Christ tattooed on his back as a way of resolving his anxiety about the accident, and also hoping to please his wife Sarah Ruth, a religious fundamentalist, and he felt that "the eyes that were forever on his back were eyes to be obeyed" (Shloss 115). But when Parker returns home, Parker finds that Sarah has locked him out of his house. "The sky had lightened slightly and there were two or three streaks of yellow floating above the horizon. Then as he stood there, a tree of light burst over the skyline. Parker fell back against the door as if he had been pinned there by a lance" (qtd. in Shloss 116). Shloss notes that this tree of light completes the insight which had begun with the burning tree in the farm accident. "Parker recognizes himself as an Obadiah and, with this, receives the assurance that his choice is correct" (Shloss 116). O'Connor was writing about Parker's "getting religion," both in the religious, and in the literal sense. O. E. Parker had "met his God" (Shloss 117).

In an article entitled "Flannery O'Connor and the Problem of Modern Satire," Mark Edelstein notes the dearth of satire in contemporary fiction, and further suggests that

O'Connor's short fiction offers a biting satirical portrait of contemporary humankind. O'Connor creates her own satiric world of the grotesque and the exaggerated. She saw people as grotesques, because they were working so hard to escape their own salvations. Like Swift, O'Connor used satire to challenge the reader's beliefs, and like Swift, O'Connor was also using satire in attempt to convert these beliefs to a higher level of consciousness (Edelstein 139-144).

O'Connor saw herself as a Christian writing largely for a non-Christian audience, and she realized the value of using shock and the grotesque, to dissolve the pretensions of her profane characters who had chosen to insulate themselves from Christ. O'Connor wrote:

> My own feeling is that writers who see by the light of their Christian faith will have, in these times, the sharpest eyes for the grotesque, for the perverse, and for the unacceptable . . . . The novelist with Christian concerns will find in modern life distortions which are repugnant to him, and his problem will be to make these appear as distortions to an audience which is used to seeing them as natural; and he may well be forced to take over more violent means to get his vision across to this hostile audience. When you can assume that your audience holds the same beliefs you do, you can relax a little and use more normal means of talking to it; when you have to assume that it does not, then you have to make your vision apparent by shock--to the hard of hearing you shout, and for the almost blind, you draw large and startling figures. (Fitzgerald 34).

In 1964, as Flannery O'Connor lay dying in the Milledgeville hospital, she had with her a notebook which she kept under her pillow. In this notebook she was writing her final story, "Parker's Back." The doctor, she wryly remarked, had advised her that writing was an "acceptable pastime." But for O'Connor, writing was more than just an "acceptable pastime." In uncovering the mysterious workings and compulsions of the human soul, she also succeeded in telling a good story (Muller 114).

Flannery O'Connor Bibliography

Archer, Jane Elizabeth. " 'This is my Place': The Short Films Made from Flannery O'Connor's Short Fiction." Studies in American Humor NS1.1 (June 1982): 52-65.

Becker, Isidore H. "Flannery O'Connor's Satiric Humor." Selected Essays: International Conference on Wit and Humor Ed. Dorothy M. Joiner. Carrollton, GA: West Georgia College, 1988 9-13.

Castle, Alfred L. "The Comic Vision of Flannery O'Connor's A Good Man is Hard to Find." Unpublished Paper. Honolulu, HI: Hawaii Pacific College, 1989.

Cheney, Bernard. "Miss O'Connor Creates Humor Out of Ordinary Sin." Sewanee Review 71 (Autumn, 1963): 644-652.

Crews, Frederick C. The Pooh Perplex. New York, NY: E. P. Dutton, 1963.

Edelstein, Mark G. "Flannery O'Connor and the Problem of Modern Satire." Studies in Short Fiction 12 (Spring, 19075): 139-144.

Fitzgerald, Sally, and Robert Fitzgerald, eds. Mystery and Manners. New York, NY: Straus and Giroux, 1969.

Gosset, Thomas F. "Flannery O'Connor's Humor with a Serious Purpose." Studies in American Humor 3.3 (January 1977): 174-80.

Johansen, Ruthmann Knechel. The Narrative Secret of Flannery O'Connor: The Trickster as Interpreter. Tuscaloosa, AL: University of Alabama Press, 1994.

May, John R. The Pruning Word: The Parables of Flannery O'Connor. Notre Dame, IN: University of Notre Dame Press, 1976.

Muller, Gilbert H. Nightmares and Visions: Flannery O'Connor and the Catholic
    Grotesque. Athens, GA: University of Georgia Press, 1972.
O'Connor, Flannery. A Good Man is Hard To Find. New York, NY: Harcourt, Brace, and
    Co., 1955.
Sewell, Elizabeth. "Is Flannery O'Connor a Nonsense Writer?" Explorations in the Field
    of Nonsense. Ed. Wim Tigges. Amsterdam, Netherlands: Rodopi, 1987.
Shloss, Carol. Flannery O'Connor's Dark Comedies: The Limits of Inference. Baton
    Rouge, LA: Louisiana State University Press, 1980.
Spenser, Herbert. The Physiology of Laughter. New York, NY: Appleton, 1913.
Sullivan, Walter. "Southerners in the City: O'Connor and Percy." The Comic Imagination
    in American Literature. Ed. Louis I. Rubin (New Brunswick, NJ: Rutgers University
    Press, 1973): 339-348.

Mary Beckett (1926-) IRELAND

Mary Beckett's humorous writing can be seen in such works as Give Them Stones
(1987), and A Literary Woman (1990).

Mary Beckett Bibliography

Beckett, Mary. Give Them Stones. London, England: Bloomsbury, 1987.
Beckett, Mary. A Literary Woman. London, England: Bloomsbury, 1990.

James Patrick Donleavy (1926-) IRELAND

Although J. P. Donleavy was born in America, his father was an Irish immigrant,
he has lived in Ireland for many years, and most of his novels are set in Ireland. Donleavy
was moved by what he had learned by reading about Ireland, and he was moved by his
mother's stories about Dublin, so after World War II, he went to Dublin to attend Trinity
College (Moseley 131). Donleavy has been an Irish resident since 1953, and an Irish
citizen since 1967 (Moseley 132). Alan Pratt says that Donleavy became an Irish citizen
because of his distaste for American culture. Donleavy claims that many of the
misanthropic and picaresque features of his novels are autobiographical (Pratt 352).

About writing, Donleavy said, "Writing is turning one's worst moments into money.
And money is one of the motives for becoming a writer. The others are leisure and money,
women and money, fame and money, and sometimes just money all alone by itself"
(Moseley 133). Donleavy's perspective as an author is the interior monologue, though in
his earlier works he sometimes shifted to a limited third-person perspective to give a more
objective picture of the protagonist. To give a feeling of spontaneity and to replicate the
mental processes of his protagonists, Donleavy's writing also contains many sentence
fragments. Donleavy's central characters are lonely and sad. They are treated unjustly, and
they have to deal with the absurdities of the events they experience. Death is always an
important part of their consciousness (Masinton 52).

Donleavy's fiction relies heavily on the subjective lives of his protagonists.
Donleavy deals with their fears, their anxieties, and their sorrows, but he also deals with
their joys, their satisfactions, and their longings (Masinton 2). Donleavy is best known as
a comic writer, and Charles Masinton considers his comic abilities to be his "chief asset as
a writer" (Masinton 3). Donleavy's novels are loosely organized, and there is a reason for
this. If Donleavy had written the well-made, realistic novel, then plausibility and logical

progression of events would have been required, making the comic sequences and characters of Donleavy's novels extraneous because they don't contribute directly to the development and resolution of the plot (Masinton 32).

One comic rhetorical device which Donleavy uses is the alter ego, or double. In A Singular Man, Bonniface is George's double, and represents the "shadow" side of George's personality. He is George's intimate friend, and in fact George and Bonniface seem to be two halves of a single personality. They are friends during their school days and they share many of the same aims, desires, and fundamental values. But in Donleavy's writing, the double often fails in some way that the protagonist does not fail. Bonniface is saintly but poor; in contrast, George is stingy and rich. The same mutually-exclusive relationship holds for Sebastian and Kenneth. Unlike Sebastian in The Ginger Man, Kenneth fails to satisfy his sexual urges, and he also lacks Sebastian's brazen wit which he uses to make his way in Dublin and on the Continent. In The Beastly Beatitudes of Balthazar B, Beefy, Balthazar's Double, is bold, randy, and irreverent, and he loses his inheritance; in contrast, Balthazar is shy and withdrawn, and he keeps his fortune (Masinton 39).

Another theme that runs through Donleavy's novels is the lusty, earthy, sexually aggressive female. In The Ginger Man this is Mary, "the girl who surprises even Sebastian with her incessant demands for sex." In The Saddest Summer of Samuel S it is Abigail. In The Beastly Beatitudes of Balthazar B it is Sally Tomson, and Breda. In The Onion Eaters it is Rose and Charlene. None of these lusty females is the traditional "nice girl" because all of them are utterly frank concerning sex. They are straightforward and often risqué in their talk, and they all make their sexual desires known to the protagonist. They are enthusiastically sexual, and there isn't a tone of depravity or immorality when they openly acknowledge that they want to give themselves to the protagonist. "In fact, Mary, Sally, Breda, and Charlene are quite natural and tender in their expressions of love. Abigail and Rosa, while not exactly affectionate, are nevertheless sincerely passionate. These girls are all far superior to the more limited, self-centered types that Donleavy gives his protagonists for wives--Marian, Shirl, or Millicent" (Masinton 49).

In 1952 Donleavy submitted the manuscript of The Ginger Man (1955) to Scribner's and then to Random House. Although both publishers recognized the merits, they both rejected it because of its obscenity. When Donleavy had the manuscript accepted by Olympia Press, he was unaware that it was going to be published as part of the "Traveler's Companion" series, a collection of pornographic novels. The Ginger Man therefore spent a number of years as an underground classic, read mainly by the young, before it emerged to the broader reading public (Moseley 132). Patrick Shaw suggests that The Ginger Man is actually a picaresque treatment of the Christian myths, inverted for satiric effect. The virgin Mary becomes Mary the nymphomaniac, who longs for Sebastian to "give me a baby on Christmas Day." The "real virgin" is one-eyed Kenneth O'Keefe who is incapable either of seducing or of being seduced. "The resurrected Christ becomes one Percy Clocklan, who fakes suicide but is later 'reborn' for Sebastian as a mysteriously rich character who surfaces in England with 'a round face flowering angelically' " (Shaw 22).

As a picaresque novel, The Ginger Man (1955) is episodic in structure, and is dominated by a rogue-hero who rushes from one adventure to the next thereby maximizing the comic qualities of the novel. As a picaresque novel, The Ginger Man is also humorous and satiric (Shaw 22). Sebastian Dangerfield may be knavish and unprincipled, but he also displays so much vitality, humor, and love of life that he is clearly a sympathetic character. His great suffering also keeps us from judging him too harshly. Charles Masinton feels that Sebastian holds a prominent position among the outstanding fictional figures of Donleavy's literary generation--Saul Bellow's Herzog, Ralph Ellison's Invisible Man, Joseph Heller's Yossarian, and John Updike's Rabbit (Masinton 25).

As a picaro and a rogue, Sebastian Dangerfield has many repellent qualities. He is an inveterate sponger and a lazy dreamer. He is a bad student, and he cheats. He is a bad husband and a bad father. He beats his wife when she is pregnant, and has neglected his child so badly that she has rickets. The only time he pays attention to his wife is when he abuses her, or charms her into bed, or cadges money or shelter from her. He steals the milk money to spend on drink, and he pawns their pram. He destroys the plumbing in his house, and showers his family with excrement. Nevertheless, Sebastian Dangerfield is presented as a sympathetic character because of his humor, his resourcefulness, and his occasional generosity, but mostly because he is presented as a victim. The title, "The Ginger Man" suggests the theme of a man running from death, and Sebastian sees himself as a victim in a cruel and dangerous world. He says poignantly, "I may be just a bit younger than Christ when they tacked him up but they've had me outstretched a few times already" (Moseley 133). Sebastian lives in Dublin very close to Grangegorman, the insane asylum, and because of his paranoia, he walks with what he calls the "spider walk," a walk that "enables one to turn around without stopping and go in the opposite direction." This is only emblematic of the fact that Sebastian is indeed a character without direction. Sebastian howls; he screams; he kicks; he wallows in self-pity, but all of these protestations are merely echoes from Grangegorman (Shaw 24).

Sebastian is a powerful picaro, and his episodes are exciting. Donleavy uses elliptical grammar, sentence fragments, and shifting point of view, as the narrative shifts fluidly from first person to third person, "dramatizing Sebastian's intermittent attempts to objectify himself" (Moseley 133). Another rhetorical device which Donleavy uses is the "little verse," such as:

> In
> Algeria
> There is a town
> Called
> Tit.

Sebastian lives by his wits. At the beginning of the novel, for example, Sebastian receives credit for food and liquor at a local shop by wearing as a scarf a piece of blue blanket that is the same color as that worn by Trinity College's prestigious rowing team. Sebastian's knowledge of upper class behavior, and his upper class accent, allow him to bring home from the store all of the food that he can carry (Masinton 11). Using his high-born style, Sebastian is also able to deceive Miss Frost. "Like the rogue-heroes in other picaresque novels, he must survive by his wit; and he is clever enough to see that in mastering the characteristic gestures of the refined classes and adopting the mannerisms of English speech lie his best defense against poverty, humiliation, and even sexual frustration" (Masinton 12). Because Sebastian is playful in his employment of understatement, irony, and whimsy, he has an ability to view himself with some amount of detachment. Through his keen-witted speech, he is able to avoid thinking about himself and he is able to remove himself from his worries and enjoy his life fully (Masinton 13).

Donleavy's protagonists are all guided by their feelings and desires. That is why Sebastian Dangerfield in The Ginger Man, a mischievous and energetic character ruled by the pleasure principle, is such a vital and interesting character, while the other characters, who tend to be morose and withdrawn, tend also to be dull and lifeless by comparison. Sebastian Dangerfield is a truly original and comic character (Masinton 2). The Ginger Man contains many types of vital comedy. There is bawdy humor; there is the sly and evasive irony of Dangerfield's speech; and there are Dangerfield's roguish adventures. The end result is that this is "one of the most entertaining works of fiction in the last quarter-century or so" (Masinton 3). Dangerfield may suffer many anxieties and depressions, but he also has a vital will to live. He is a multi-faceted and well-rounded character, and that is one of the things that makes him such an arresting figure (Masinton 4).

Sebastian Dangerfield is developed as an engaging anti-hero. Patrick Shaw suggests that in Donleavy's satire the heroes are not heroes at all, but "merely another face in a very disillusioned mass of humanity" (Shaw 25). It is the time of World War II, and Sebastian is in the American Navy when he meets his Scottish girlfriend Marion. Soon after he is discharged, he marries Marion, and begins to study law at Trinity College, using the G.I. Bill to support his studies. Sebastian is expecting to inherit his rich father's money when the old man dies, but in the meantime Sebastian and Marion live with their daughter Felicity in a state of squalor and poverty. Because they have little money, Sebastian is forced to live by his wits. Being quite shrewd and engaging, he always manages to stay a step ahead of those who would force him to conform to society's dictates, although he does have some very narrow escapes. He flees from his responsibilities as a husband, as a father and as a responsible citizen. Some of the funniest episodes in the book are descriptions of Sebastian's eluding Egbert Skully, the landlord who chases him all over Dublin in order to collect unpaid rent on a run-down house that the Dangerfields had rented (Masinton 6).

Sebastian Dangerfield, like the Little Gingerbread Boy in the children's folk tale, is pursued by death, but he always manages to outwit his pursuer by freeing himself from the grasp of others (Masinton 8). Sebastian identifies himself with his patron saint, St. Sebastian, who was shot full of arrows and beaten with rods for converting people to Christianity (Masinton 9). In Chapter 10, when Sebastian gets on a train to go home, he forgets to button the fly on his pants, and what is even more embarrassing is that he also forgets to put his penis back into his pants when he hurries from the men's room to catch the train. Sebastian is very embarrassed when he finally realizes why people are staring at him (Masinton 10).

There are many comic scenes and episodes in The Ginger Man, scenes which show the absurdities of the world and the lighter side of outrageous conduct. One of the most amusing comic incidents in the novel is the drunken supper scene shared by Sebastian and his friend Kenneth O'Keefe who has two obsessions--sex and money. This supper scene occurs the evening before Marion returns from visiting her parents. It is the evening after Sebastian had forgotten to button up his fly, and just after he had made a clever escape from Skully. Sebastian had barricaded himself in his house against the prowling Skully, and he slammed the front door to make his former landlord think that he was escaping through it, but then he sneaked out of the back door unobserved (Masinton 17-18).

Donleavy has an uncanny ability to mix comedy, violence, and absurdity in The Ginger Man to produce what has come to be called "Black Humor." Some incidents in the novel demonstrate a biting and anxious sort of humor, such as the scene in which the plumbing breaks while Sebastian is using the toilet, and the burst pipes spray Marion and Felicity with excrement. This event may disturb and degrade Sebastian and Marion, but it strikes the reader as funny because it is so preposterous and surprising. Sebastian's constant fear of death is a burden to him, and it is darkly humorous when Donleavy tells about Sebastian's morbid habit of watching funeral processions from his window and then of joining these processions on his bicycle which he has appropriately painted black (Masinton 19).

Patrick Shaw considers the satire of The Ginger Man to be multifaceted. Donleavy's satire targets the church, sex, materialism, and misdirected idealism. "Donleavy shows that the old values are dead and that modern society in its lust and greed offers nothing to replace them" (Shaw 26). The Ginger Man is a satire against most of the traditional social values and activities. From one perspective, it is a satire against religion in general, but from another perspective it is a satire of the hypocrisy of the Christian society in particular, as epitomized by Miss Frost, the Catholic who refuses intercourse but consents to sodomy, because "it's so much less of a sin." (Shaw 24).

J. P. Donleavy's The Ginger Man is filled with a spirit of vigor; however, this vigor was replaced by a spirit of gloom in his later works (Masinton 4). Also, in the novels written after The Ginger Man, Donleavy increasingly tends to give the minor characters the funny lines to speak (Masinton 16). Each Donleavy character after Sebastian Dangerfield carries a heavier burden of sadness than the one before. The progression goes to George Smith, to Samuel S, and to Balthazar B. These characters are progressively less aggressive and confident, and each is a bit more sealed off from contact with other characters (Masinton 58). Merritt Moseley says that Donleavy's novels after The Ginger Man tend to be funny and sad. They are often set in Dublin, and when they are not, there is nevertheless an Irish aspect to the characters. The people in Donleavy's novels have funny names, and the titles are often alliterative: The Beastly Beatitudes of Balthazar B, The Saddest Summer of Samuel S, Meet My Maker the Mad Molecule, and The Destinies of Darcy Dancer, Gentleman (Moseley 134). A Singular Man (1963) is a very funny work. It contains the same types of farcical episodes, bawdy humor, and comic dialogue as The Ginger Man, but there is a growing mood of melancholy that will eventually overshadow the humor. In The Ginger Man, the sadness is subordinated to the bawdiness, and the explosively funny comic scenes, the brisk, humorous dialogue, and the roguish and unyielding protagonist. In contrast, A Singular Man contains much less comic dialogue. George Smith, the hero of A Singular Man is glum and he lacks vitality. In A Singular Man death is always peeking out from behind the humor (Moseley 134).

At the beginning of A Singular Man the reader is told that George Smith had traveled to the Old World--probably Ireland. As the novel opens, George is a clever businessman, a millionaire, and a witty letter writer (Masinton 4). Nevertheless, in his private life, George is a failure. He and his wife have separated; he doesn't enjoy his children; his affairs with his secretaries, Miss Martin and Sally Tomson, leave him with a great sense of loss and loneliness. Although he finds real love and affection in his relationship with Sally, he is already married, and has no hope for any permanent arrangement with her. In addition, she finally dies in an auto accident thus leaving George desolate and crushed. And in view of George Smith's depressing life, it is especially sad to have to note that his very common name is a clue that is he not "a singular man" at all, but in fact represents all of us in some sense (Masinton 27). As "a singular man," George has to contend with a number of absurdities; first are his unregenerate eccentricities (his "singularities"); second is the isolation from normal human relations caused by his drive for success; third is the separation from his family; and fourth is his inability to come to terms with the madness and malice he perceives all around him (Masinton 38).

Ironically, George lives in "Merry Mansions." He goes to work in his little office at 33 Golf Street; he belongs to the Game Club and takes fencing lessons. He later moves to Dynamo House on Owl Street, but even there he receives threatening letters (Masinton 28). These letters are hilarious in their pretensions. There is a letter from "Sun Shine and Son," the legal counsel of Harry Halitoid of Fartbrook who is suing Smith for knocking him onto the subway tracks and injuring him. "On Wednesday the 19th ultimo, at 3:34 P.M. (approx.) o'clock at Battery Station of the Rapid Transit system of this city you made an unprovoked and savage attack upon our client, Mr. Harry Halitoid which resulted in a knockment into the tracks of the said system where there was a sustainment of considerable head and body injury." Among other things they require George's "making good the suit of clothes which suffered spoilment in the tracks." This is a parody of legal language which is similar to the parody of legal language in George's will, which he calls his "last will and testicle" (Masinton 34).

This story makes very good newspaper copy, and one newspaper reports it as follows:

A summons was issued today against Mr. George Smith formerly of 33 Golf
Street and removed to Dynamo House, Owl Street where he was traced.
The victim Mr. H. Halitoid of Fartbrook claims he was the innocent
recipient of a right hook to the jaw in the rapid transit while his attention
was distracted with other passengers watching a rat gambol down the tracks.
As he and other spectators on the Battery platform (uptown side) waited for
the rodent to be electrocuted, Mr. Halitoid alleged a fist encased in a
knuckle duster thundered out of space and (according to his doctors) landed
on his lower mandible scattering bicuspids everywhere. (Masinton 36)

There is an incongruous story within a story in this newspaper account, as the attention
shifts to the rat. The plodding formula writing of newspaper style is satirized, and much
slang is intermixed with the more formal language. Thus we have such slang terms as
"knuckle duster," and "right hook to the jaw," and such unsuccessful pretensions at elevated
diction as "mandible," "bicuspids," and "gambol." These juxtapositions are jarring, and add
to the burlesque tone of Donleavy's writing (Masinton 36).

    Donleavy also parodies and ridicules business communication. George receives a
letter from J.J.J.Jr. responding to a letter which George had written earlier. "To hand your
letter of 'Turdsday' so unseemly spelled, in which you threaten us with the words 'Watch
out' and the postscript that you are blessed with two headlamps to focus on our medical
history. We now require by telegram that you send us something to salve the outrage
caused by these recent remarks to this office." According to Masinton, this is a
"masterpiece of irrelevance," because it is merely a "communication of threats and insults
to the competition." These letters provide lively entertainment for the reader, but the actual
purpose in the novel is to "constitute a satiric commentary on the letter writing style often
associated with the business community." Although the parody letters are written in a
serious, legal, even pretentious tone, they address themselves to trivial and unlikely or
grotesque events (Masinton 35).

    The reader never learns exactly what business George is in, but we do know that
he has made a fortune at it, and is an independent operator. His answers to the disturbing
letters he receives are always a high point in the comic relief of the novel. Although
George is shy and fearful, he always manages to be flip and insulting to J.J.J. George's
alter ego, Bonniface, reminds George that he has become hard and cold in order to make
money. Success in business has not brought George happiness or friendship. At one time
he was poor and well liked, but he learned to stifle his warm-hearted nature in order to rise
financially in the world (Masinton 28).

    Masinton states that there are many hilarious scenes and comic characters in A
Singular Man, but this comedy is created in the face of sorrow, loss, and the ever-present
fear of death (Masinton 29). One comic scene involves George's sad but funny sex life.
On his way to bring Christmas presents to Shirl and his children, Shirl insults him, so he
returns to the little rural hotel where he is staying, "The Goose Goes Inn." Shirl follows
him there and entreats him to make love to her, but love making is difficult for George
because of the long underwear he is wearing. He is also bothered by Shirl's request that
he hurry up, because she has friends waiting downstairs to take her to a party. Another
comic sex episode is when George takes his secretary Miss Martin to his cabin in the
woods to escape the newspaper reporters who are following him. When they get ready for
bed, Smith chooses the couch in the living room and tells Miss Martin to take the bedroom,
realizing that she will soon be frightened by one of the large spiders that live in the cabin.
During the night, she does see the spider and runs to George for protection, and once they
are in each others arms--both naked--they start making love with each other. Although the
night was a blissful one, George doesn't allow Miss Martin to call him by his first name,
saying that a tender exchange of caresses is alright, but a proper relationship must be

maintained between a boss and his secretary. George insists that there is no reason why she should address him familiarly (Masinton 30).

George is stunned by the idea of his own mortality and he is also so lonely, afraid, and abused that he decides to build a large and expensive tomb to house his remains. There is a strange juxtaposition here of that which terrifies the reader (death), and that which amuses the reader (George's ostentatious mausoleum), and the result is gallows humor (Masinton 38). George builds his mausoleum in the Renoun Memorial Cemetery under the name of Doctor Fear so that people will not be able to trace the building to him, but they trace it to him anyway (Masinton 20). George is persistent in his building of this tomb and near the end of the novel he sends out invitations for a reception celebrating its completion (Masinton 29). It is ironic that the reception never happens because of bad weather, and because Sally dies in a car accident and George has to attend her funeral instead (Masinton 29).

As the title suggests, The Saddest Summer of Samuel S (1966) is a sad tale, and is in fact the culmination of an extremely depressing life (Masinton 47). Samuel S in the novella possesses the wisdom of middle age, although he is a failure (Masinton 4). Samuel is miserably poor, and he is also middle-aged and without prospects for a bright future. He is an American living in Vienna, and his main income is an occasional gift from his rich friends in Amsterdam who send him money whenever he asks them for it. Samuel doesn't like Vienna. The clerks cheat him. He sees eyes peering at him from doorways and windows as he walks down the street, and he considers the people to be in the main unfriendly (Masinton 45).

Much of the humor of The Saddest Summer of Samuel S is provided by the robustness and honesty of the earthy females (Masinton 49). Abigail is fascinated with Samuel's aloofness and eccentricity, so she comes to his apartment and offers to go to bed with him. Samuel is lonely, and he would very much like to make love to her, but he thinks that for her the episode would only be a sort of exotic adventure, and he resents being thought of as a sex object. Nevertheless, Abigail does entice him into bed, but she says she will not marry him, and he in return refuses to satisfy her. After a while Samuel falls asleep, and Abigail gets revenge by unexpectedly biting him on the thigh and causing him to bleed (Masinton 46).

Another very humorous episode in The Saddest Summer of Samuel S is when Herr Doktor announces that he will no longer treat Samuel:

> "Hold it, something's wrong Doc."
> "Yes Herr patient."
> "Maybe you heard I'm organising a union of patients for lower fees. He he."
> "What I'm going to tell you Herr patient is something I do not want you to misunderstand. You are an extremely intelligent man and I do not think you will."
> "I am listening Herr Doc. What's your problem."
> "Herr S you are driving me nuts."
> "Whoa."
> "A sign that you are well and truly cured." (Saddest Summer 89)

In this dialogue the roles of the doctor and the patient are humorously reversed. Here as throughout the novel, the humor is closely tied to the pathos of Samuel's wretched situation (Masinton 51).

Charles Masinton says that The Beastly Beatitudes of Balthazar B (1968) is Donleavy's most romantic and lyrical work. It is a love story of Balthazar and Elizabeth Fitzdare, a girl he meets at Trinity College in Dublin and plans to marry. Balthazar and Elizabeth are rich, elegant, young people who enjoy each other's company. Everyone eagerly looks forward to their wedding, and their marriage promises to be an ideal one. But the wedding never takes place, because Miss Fitzdare falls from her horse and sustains a grave injury she never recovers from. Miss Fitzdare's death completely shatters Balthazar (Masinton 55).

At school, Balthazar meets Beefy, a puckish boy whose given name is also Balthazar. Beefy, is Balthazar's double and is one of Donleavy's most witty and laugh-provoking characters; Beefy has a witty command of language and a delightfully mischievous manner (Masinton 50). The active, picaresque role played by Sebastian in The Ginger Man is played by Beefy in The Beastly Beatitudes of Balthazar B. Although Beefy is often peripheral to the plot, he is a fun character (Moseley 134). Unlike Balthazar, Beefy is a brilliant student, a bold companion who is not afraid of the cruel pranks of other students, or the strict discipline of the school masters. Beefy calls himself the "magnificent masturbator," and he often leads his quiet, timid friend into trouble. Both are sent down from school and have to go their own ways (Masinton 55). At Trinity College, Balthazar meets Beefy again. Beefy is a Dionysian archetype who pursues every imaginable pleasure of the flesh, and when they meet again at Trinity College, Beefy again acts as a kind of guide to the Apollonian Balthazar, just as he had when they attended public school together (Masinton 55).

Donleavy makes a point of contrasting Beefy's "diabolical" urges with Balthazar's "saintly" qualities, so the reader gets the idea that it is only together that they make a whole. One scene which Masinton considers very funny in Beastly Beatitudes involves Balthazar's getting lost in Donnybrook after a date with Miss Fitzdare, and he drunkenly tries to find his way on a dark night from her uncle's house back to the College. In Donnybrook a sex-obsessed harridan accuses Balthazar of being an Arab who has come to her home at night in order to rape her. The publishing of an article about this event in the newspaper causes Balthazar much embarrassment at Trinity. Another hilarious comic episode involves Beefy's abortive attempt to smuggle girls into his college room to spend the night with him and Balthazar (Masinton 54). As Beefy is getting it on with Rebecca, Balthazar and Breda look on in astonishment (Masinton 56). Balthazer and Beefy are sent down from Trinity College as a result of their caper with Rebecca and Breda, thus repeating the pattern they established earlier at public school (Masinton 57). Masinton feels that these two stories "constitute the principal counterweights to the gloom that permeates the novel" (Masinton 56).

The Onion Eaters (1971) is filled with Rabelaisian humor (Moseley 135). Clayton Claw Cleaver Clementine is a young American protagonist who inherits Charnel Castle (which means house of death) from his great aunt located in a remote spot on the western coast of Ireland. But Clementine is not alone at this secluded Castle, since strange, eccentric, visitors keep showing up from time to time. So that by the end of the novel this unruly group has not only bankrupted Clementine, but has burned down much of the Castle as well (Masinton 59). The Castle is depicted as an absurd world of comic chaos ruled over by Clementine, who like his namesake, "Clementine of the Three Glands," has three testicles (Moseley 134). Clementine is somewhat sane and sensible even though most of the other characters he encounters are freakish or grotesque in some way. Econwald and his colleagues are mad scientists. Franz Decibel Pickle is an expert on putrefaction. George Putlog Roulette is a physicist; one of Roulette's progenitors invented the scaffold. Erconwald himself specializes in the gathering of data that relates to unnatural forms of sexuality and, along with Franz, is interested in the development of aphrodisiacs. All three men are vegetarians, and the title of the novel comes from the fact that they grow and eat their own raw onions (Masinton 60).

Another eccentric in The Onion Eaters is Lead Kindly Light. He is a surly and self-righteous madman who decides to blow up the group at dinner time. He uses a vial of nitroglycerin to destroy a large section of the dining hall, at the same time inflicting injuries on many of the guests (Masinton 61). Shortly after this scene there is another funny scene which involves a character named Bloodmourn fighting with Clementine's bull named Toro with an umbrella and a coat. Lead Kindly Light, dressed in armor and carrying a lance, joins Bloodmourn in the fight. Another humorous scene involves a testicle-squeezing contest between Lead Kindly Light and Bligh, conducted in the dark and dank tunnels below the Castle. Another comic scene involves Clementine and Trudy trying to make love; they are interrupted when Bligh's boat, filled with singing children, is washed out to sea, and has to be rescued. Clementine and a rag-tag crew set out to save them in Clementine's yacht, Noeena, but finally have to be towed back to the shore. There is still another comic scene when a couple named the "Utahs" and a girl named Gloria arrive at the Castle; Gloria is constantly having orgasms. At this point, Clementine decides he has had enough, and decides to go away for a few days. Later, although Clementine is strongly in debt and unable to repair the Castle, he nevertheless decides to throw an elaborate party for everyone in the neighborhood, including the soldiers from the army who have surrounded the Castle. The party is a madcap affair that of course ends in a riot (Masinton 62).

Later in the novel there is a terrible fire in the Castle when Erconwald decides to give Lead Kindly Light a hotfoot, as part of a scientific experiment designed to measure pain thresholds. Nails and Trudy Macfugger are the nearest neighbors to the Castle. Nails is a boisterous Anglo-Irishman who is responsible for much of the humor in the novel with his blustery talk. Victoria is a guest of the MacFuggers, and is attracted to the much younger Clementine. Victoria is so lascivious that she keeps a photo album of pictures she takes of men's penises, and as soon as she sees Clementine, she immediately wants to examine his genitals. On the first night of their stay, Victoria roller skates into Clementine's room with a parasol in her hand (Masinton 61).

The Unexpurgated Code: A Complete Manual of Survival and Manners (1975) is a nonfiction book designed to explain how to achieve undeserved social success, and how to survive in spite of being out of one's element. If for example, a person needs to announce that he doesn't have long to live, it is best to make this announcement in cowboy language reminiscent of the rough out of doors "in deference to the fighting spirit they think you want them to think you have." There is also advice on nose-picking, and on the clap, and the reader is even told what to do when his spit accidently lands on another person. The book is a parody of etiquette books, and is organized as such. After the reader has reached the top, Donleavy suggests that you climb to a high balcony overlooking a huge crowd and "commence peeing. If no one tries to rush the hell out of the way of your pissing all over them, you have reached the top" (Moseley 135).

A Fairy Tale of New York (1973) presents four episodes in the life of Cornelius Christian. Act IV is in a restaurant where the waiters refuse to serve Cornelius and his date, Charlotte Graves, because of the ugly peach-colored shoes he is wearing. The hoity-toity waiters assume that a refined person would not be wearing such gaudy shoes. Charlotte is embarrassed, and she and Christian begin to quarrel. He finally storms out of the door, but later reappears dressed in formal evening attire and looking like a member of some exotic royal family. On his feet he is wearing nothing except for a couple of diamonds on his toes. He and Charlotte are now served by the very attentive waiters, and Christian has his moment of triumph (Masinton 63).

Christian also has a relationship with Miss Musk, during which they make love in a room where corpses are treated. They are sitting near one of the corpses, and as a joke, Christian places the hand of the corpse on Miss Musk's shoulder; she faints from fright. There is also black humor in the remarks that Christian hears from Mr. Vine about the dignified nature of the funeral business, in Christian's posing as a corpse in a casket for a publicity photo, and in the description Christian's preparation of his first corpse for burial. He overdoes the make-up on the face of the corpse, and is sued by the dead man's widow for "making her husband too good-looking." The court scenes following this event are also funny and laugh provoking, though most of the rest of the book tends to be morbid, bitter, and sullen (Masinton 64-65).

In discussing Donleavy's novels, Patrick Shaw says that the picaresque tradition is very often associated both with humor and with satire. Donleavy's stories are filled with wild episodes and bawdy humor, but the fun is superficial. Donleavy's satire is actually more serious than it is humorous, so his novels are often not as funny as they first appear (Shaw 22, 26). Merritt Moseley says in summary that James Patrick Donleavy takes the style of Henry Miller, and Franz Kafka, and reproduces this style in the rollicking Irish tradition (Moseley 135).

James Patrick Donleavy Bibliography

Masinton, Charles G. J. P. Donleavy: The Style of His Sadness and Humor. Bowling Green, OH: Bowling Green Univ Popular Press, 1975.

Moseley, Merritt. "James Patrick Donleavy." Encyclopedia of American Humorists. Ed. Steven H. Gale. New York, NY: Garland, 1988 131-136.

Nilsen, Don L. F. "James Patrick Donleavy." Humor in American Literature: A Selected Annotated Bibliography. New York, NY: Garland, 1992, 356-358.

Pratt, Alan R. "J. P. Donleavy (1926-)." Black Humor: Critical Essays. New York, NY: Garland, 1993. 352.

Shaw, Patrick W. "The Satire of J. P. Donleavy's Ginger Man." Studies in Contemporary Satire 1.2 (1975): 9-16; Studies in Contemporary Satire 12 (1985): 22-26.

Vintner, Maurice. "The Artist as Clown: The Fiction of J. P. Donleavy." Meanjin Quarterly 29 (1970): 108-114.

Brian Friel (1929-) IRELAND

Brian Friel writes intimate stories about a closed community named Ballybeg in County Donegal. Brian Friel's plays are often about a gifted outsider with an antic intelligence. There is often a drastic revelation which leads to violence. Because the plays exhibit an eloquence and a wit, they "become articulators of a problem to such a degree that the problem becomes insoluble, so perfectly etched are all its numbing complexities" (Deane 166). Each of his plays develops an Irish theme, and these themes can be monastic as in The Enemy Within (1962); psychological, as in Philadelphia, Here I Come! (1964); sexual-familial, as in The Gentle Island (1971), or Living Quarters (1977); or political, as in The Freedom of the City (1973), or Volunteers (1975) (Deane 166). "The plays all work as parables in which the development of a particular action contributes to the representation of a general condition" (Deane 172).

Friel's characters are constantly aware of the paradox of Ireland. The Irish repudiate Ireland, but this repudiation gives them a sense of guilt, a sense of betrayal. "But equally, to give in to the place is a form of suicide." Ireland is a metaphor here as well as a place. It is the country of the young, a country of hope, it is a blending of fact and desire. But it is also the country of disillusionment, where everything is out of joint, violent, and broken (Deane 170). On the one hand, Ireland is viewed as a paradise; on the other hand Ireland is viewed as a ruin. "The result is a discrepancy in our language; words are askew, they are out of line with fact. Violence has fantasy and wordiness as one of its most persistent after-effects" (Deane 171). The Communication Cord (1982) reveals more obviously than his other plays just how strictly organized his plays are (Deane 167). The secret story in <u>Volunteers</u> concerns the ironically named Smiley, who has been reduced to idiocy by the brutal beatings he has received at the hands of the police (Deane 167).

Brian Friel's <u>Dancing at Lughnasa</u> (1990) dominated the 1992 Tony awards, and in the 1994 season was the most produced play in the United States, having at least sixteen major regional productions. <u>Dancing at Lughnasa</u> portrays in poignant detail the hard times of the five Mundy sisters in rural Ireland in 1937. The dominant memory left by the play was the explosive eruption into revelry mentioned in the title. Although the women had many reasons to be sorrowful, they nevertheless were able to hold onto their joy (Henry 89).

Brian Friel Bibliography

Deane, Seamus. "Brian Friel: the Double Stage." <u>Celtic Revivals: Essays in Modern Irish Literature--Joyce, Yeats, O'Casey, Kinsella, Montague, Friel, Mahon, Heaney, Beckett, Synge</u>. Winston-Salem, NC: Wake Forest University Press, 1985, 166-173.
Henry, William A., III. "Not Dancing But Drowning: The Same Themes Do Not Make This Bleak Work a <u>Lughnasa</u>." <u>Time</u> November 8, 1993, 89.

John Patrick Montague (1929-) IRELAND

In Sean O'Faolain's <u>The Bell</u> (1951), John Montague stated that what the Irish cause needed to clear the apathy from the air was a bit more of caustic Swiftian satire (Deane 146). Although Montague was born in New York, he was raised in his family home in Tyrone in Northern Ireland. He was educated in Dublin, and he spent long periods of time in the United States and France before returning to Ireland. Montague therefore knows from experience when he refers to Patrick Kavanagh's style as the "baffled fury of a man flailing between two faded worlds, the country he had left, and the literary Dublin he never found." Montague is able to articulate the feelings of an exile who returns to Ireland to find his home "incomprehensibly the same and yet, because of that, suddenly anachronistic, fossilized" (Deane 147).

John Montague Bibliography

Deane, Seamus. "John Montague: The Kingdom of the Dead." <u>Celtic Revivals: Essays in Modern Irish Literature--Joyce, Yeats, O'Casey, Kinsella, Montague, Friel, Mahon, Heaney, Beckett, Synge</u>. Winston-Salem, NC: Wake Forest University Press, 1985, 146-155.

Jennifer Johnston (1930-) IRELAND

Jennifer Johnston comes directly out of the Anglo-Irish tradition. Her mother was named Shelah Richards, and was an actress at the Abbey Theatre in Dublin. Her father, Denis Johnston, was a playwright, who had a play rejected by Lady Gregory, and who later renamed this play <u>The Old Lady Says No</u>. Johnston's first seven novels are about Johnston's own personal journey and the personal journeys of many other contemporary women into selfhood (Weekes 23). Johnston wrote such pieces as <u>The Captains and the Kings</u> (1972), <u>The Gates</u> (1973), <u>How Many Miles to Babylon?</u> (1974), <u>Shadows on Our Skin</u> (1978), <u>The Old Jest</u> (1979), <u>The Christmas Tree</u> (1981), <u>The Railway Station Man</u>

(1984), Fool's Sanctuary (1987), and Invisible Worm (1991).

Jennifer Johnston Bibliography

Weekes, Ann Owens. "Jennifer Johnston: From Gortnaree to Knappogue." Irish Women
Writers: An Uncharted Tradition. Lexington, KY: University Press of Kentucky,
1990, 191-211.

Stephen Frears (1936-) IRELAND

Stephen Frears's The Snapper (1993) is packed with lively characters, lively
language, and unpremeditated activities.   The effect is a kind of "lifelike untidiness,
fractiousness and believable goofiness that American movie comedy, with its stress on
easily summarizable concepts and subteen gag writing can only dream about" (Schickel 89).

Stephen Frears Bibliography

Schickel, Richard. "The Chaos of Life, Irish-Style." Time December 6, 1993, 89.

Christy Brown (1932-1981) IRELAND

My Left Foot, as demonstrated by the title, is filled with wry offbeat humor. It is
the autobiography of Christy Brown, as told to Shane Connaughton and Jim Sheridan.

Christy Brown Bibliography

Connaughton, Shane. My Left Foot. Boston, MA: Faber, 1989.

Julia O'Faolain (1932-) IRELAND

Both of Julia O'Faolain's parents were writers. Her father was so enthusiastic about
the new Irish state that he changed his name from the English Whelan to the Irish
O'Faolain. He spoke Gaelic in his home; he joined the Irish Republican Army, and he
wrote about traditional Irish subjects (Weekes 22). However, he became as disillusioned
with the Irish republicans as he had earlier been disillusioned with the British empire.
O'Faolain writes about Irish myths and Irish history which may not be totally familiar to
many of her readers (Weekes 23). Julia O'Faolain wrote such collections of short stories
as We Might See Sights (1968), Man in the Cellar (1974), and Daughters of Passion
(1982).

Julia O'Faolain Bibliography

Weekes, Ann Owens. "Julia O'Faolain: The Imaginative Crucible." Irish Women Writers:
An Uncharted Tradition. Lexington, KY: University Press of Kentucky, 1990, 174-
190.

Derek Mahon (1941-) IRELAND

Derek Mahon writes witty and sophisticated poetry about the urbanity of Belfast, a bleak and ruined city. His poetry is "haunted by intimations of collapse, pogrom, apocalypse. Mahon can be ironical at the expense of the barbarous when it is banal" (Deane 156). In Mahon's first two books, Night-Crossing (1968) and Lives (1972), there is a spirit of "bohemian camaraderie," and of "slightly raffish stylishness." There is also a certain intelligence that underlies the humor and the pace of such poems as "Beyond Howth Head," a poem which Seamus Deane describes as "a bright, chatty epistle which just manages to keep its decorum in the face of disaster and crisis" (157-158).

Derek Mahon Bibliography

Deane, Seamus. "Derek Mahon: Freedom from History." Celtic Revivals: Essays in Modern Irish Literature--Joyce, Yeats, O'Casey, Kinsella, Montague, Friel, Mahon, Heaney, Beckett, Synge. Winston-Salem, NC: Wake Forest University Press, 1985, 156-166.

Eric Cross (1942-) IRELAND

In The Tailor and Antsy, Eric Cross stages a wake for the benefit of visitors who are completely taken in by the sham until the "corpse" discovers that he hasn't been given his fair share of the whiskey (Waters 177).

Eric Cross Bibliography

Waters, Maureen. The Comic Irishman. Albany, NY: State Univ of New York Press, 1984.

Carson Ciaran (1948-) IRELAND

Carson Ciaran's comic poetry can be found in such volumes as The Irish for No (1987), The New Estate: and Other Poems (1988), and First Language 1993).

Carson Ciaran Bibliography

Ciaran, Carson. The Irish for No. Winston-Salem, NC: Wake Forest University Press, 1987.
Ciaran, Carson. First Language. Loughcrew, Oldcastle, Ireland: Gallery Press, 1993.
Ciaran, Carson. The New Estate: And Other Poems. Oldcastle, Meath, Ireland: Gallery Press, 1988.

Bryan Thomas MacMahon (1950-) IRELAND

Earl Ingersoll talks about the Irish short story as an elaborated joke, and compares Bryan MacMahon's "The Exile's Return" with James Joyce's "The Gallants" and Flann O'Brien's "The Martyr's Crown." All three stories are told in an Irish pub, and they all begin with two friends walking along an Irish street engaged in conversation. MacMahon's characters are named Timothy Hannigan and Paddy Kinsella. They are all told from the male's point of view, and all involve role reversal where the women in the stories have a masculine-type lust for sex. The women are targets in these stories, but so are the men, and of course the archetype of the exile is especially powerful in Irish culture because of the rich features associated with this archetype (Ingersoll 244).

Bryan MacMahon Bibliography

Ingersoll, Earl G. "Irish Jokes: A Lacanian Reading of Short Stories by James Joyce, Flann O'Brien, and Bryan MacMahon." Studies in Short Fiction 2 (Spring, 1990): 237-245.

Ellis Ni Dhuibhe-Almquist (1954-) IRELAND

Ellis Ni Dhuibhe-Almquist's humor can be seen in such works as Blood and Water (1988), The Bray House (1990), and Eating Women is Not Recommended (1991).

Ellis Ni Dhuibhe-Almquist Bibliography

Dhuibhe-Almquist, Ellis Ni. Blood and Water. Dublin, Ireland, Attic Press, 1988.
Dhuibhe-Almquist, Ellis Ni. The Bray House. Dublin, Ireland: Attic Press, 1990.
Dhuibhe-Almquist, Ellis Ni. Eating Women is Not Recommended. Dublin, Ireland: Attic Press, 1991.

Maura O'Halloran (1955-1982) IRELAND

Philip Zaleski wrote a positive review of Pure Heart, Enlightened Mind: The Zen Journal, and Letters (1994) in the New York Times Book Review. He said that "fun" is a word which comes immediately to mind in describing this book, since O'Halloran's protagonist, who might be called a spiritual masochist, is described by Zaleski as a balance of a spiritual masochist and "a healthy exuberance that amounts at times to sheer girlish high spirits." She laughs, jokes, and teases her fellow monks who are themselves "lovely, like great big kids, full of fun." She interrupts her meditations to drink in a bar, or to enjoy someone's Elvis impressions, or to attend a wedding and gush over the bride. Sometimes she could be described as silly, as when she reports on various psychic events ranging from telepathy to epiphany (10-11).

Maura O'Halloran Bibliography

Zaleski, Philip. "A Buddhist from Dublin: Review of Pure Heart, Enlightened Mind." New York Times Book Review July 24, 1994, 10-11.

Paul Muldoon (1956-) IRELAND

Paul Muldoon's great comic verses can be found in such volumes as New Weather (1973). These poems have such enigmatic titles as "The Electric Orchard," "Blowing Eggs," "Kate Whiskey," "Thinking of the Goldfish," "The Cure for Warts," "The Radio Horse," "Seanchas," and "The Indians on Alcatraz" (Muldoon 9).

Paul Muldoon Bibliography

Muldoon, Paul. New Weather. London, England: Faber and Faber, 1973.

Roddy Doyle (1958-) IRELAND

   Roddy Doyle's <u>Commitments</u> is a bittersweet story about Irish working-class kids forming a soul band in Dublin, and is a hot seller throughout the English-speaking world. Doyle's <u>Paddy Clarke Ha Ha Ha</u> (1993) is a novel written from the point of view of a ten-year-old boy who witnesses the collapse of his parents' marriage. It begins as follows "We were coming down our road." Paul Gray compares this to the opening of James Joyce's <u>A Portrait of the Artist as a Young Man</u>--"Once upon a time and a very good time it was there was a moocow coming down along the road." Gray suggests that Doyle's opening sentence was paying tribute to the fact that no Irish writer is going to be able to improve on Joyce. In October of 1993, <u>Paddy Clarke Ha Ha Ha</u> won Britain's prestigious Booker Prize. The book is intermittently funny, fresh, and engaging; it is also frustrating. The book is about some teenagers who spend a great deal of energy planning strategies for annoying their schoolmasters. When the supervisors' backs are turned, the boys make rude noises, and during the Friday showings of movies, they project hand images onto the screen. Paddy notes that "That was the easy part. The hard bit was getting back to your seat before they turned the lights back on. Everyone would try to stop you, to keep you trapped in the aisle." The conventional wisdom of Paddy and his friends is that "When you were doing a funny face or pretending you had a stammer and the wind changed or someone thumped your back you stayed that way forever." This novel is filled with such juvenile humor. Another example is the following joke: "Did you hear about the leper cowboy? He threw his leg over his horse" (Gray 82).

Roddy Doyle Bibliography

Gray, Paul. "Making Mischief in Dublin." <u>Time</u> December 6, 1993, 82.

APPENDIX

Important Irish Journals and Organizations

Canadian Journal of Irish Studies: Ron Marken, Editor; English Department; University of Saskatchewan; Saskatoon, Saskatchewan, Canada S7N OWO. This journal is sponsored by the Canadian Association for Irish Studies and publishes articles on Irish literature, history, and culture.

Colby Library Quarterly: Douglas Archibald, Editor; English Department; Colby College; Waterville, ME 04901. This journal takes a special interest in W. B. Yeats, James Joyce, and Irish writers from 1880 to the present.

Éire-Ireland: A Journal of Irish Studies: James Blake, Editor; Mail 5026; College of St. Thomas; St. Paul, MN 55105. This journal is sponsored by the Irish American Cultural Institute, and publishes articles related to any aspect of Irish culture in Ireland, or abroad.

The Flannery O'Connor Bulletin: Sarah Gordon, Editor; English Department; Box 44; Georgia College; Milledgeville, GA 31061. This journal publishes critical articles on the fiction of Flannery O'Connor.

The Independent Shavian: Richard Nickson, and Douglas Laurie, Editors; Box 1373; Grand Central Station; New York, NY 10163. This journal is sponsored by the Bernard Shaw Society, and publishes articles on George Bernard Shaw and items related to his life and works.

Irish Arts Series: Carroll F. Terrell, Editor; National Poetry Foundation; 302 Neville Hall; University of Maine; Orono, ME 04469. This series publishes monograph studies about Irish poets and writers.

Irish Bull Society: Des MacHale, President; Math Department; University College; Cork, Ireland. This organization is devoted to the study and promotion of Irish humour. The Boule Library at Cork University has the largest collection of primary and critical works on Irish humour in the world.

Irish Studies: Richard Fallis, Editor; Syracuse University Press; 1600 Jamesville Avenue;

Syracuse, NY 13244-1170. This press publishes monographs on scholarship and criticism of Anglo-Irish literature and Irish history and culture.

James Joyce Quarterly: Robert Spoo and Mary O'Toole, Editors; University of Tulsa; 600 South College Avenue; Tulsa, OK 74104-3189. This journal is interested in all aspects of James Joyce and his milieu. They are looking for comparative studies, research-oriented scholarship, bibliographical and biographical articles, and collectors' notes.

Journal of Beckett Studies: S. E. Gontarski, Editor; English Department; Florida State University; Tallahassee, FL 32306. This journal publishes scholarship and criticism on Samuel Beckett and his circle, as well as theatrical reviews and photographs of productions.

Journal of Irish Literature: Robert Hogan, Gordon Henderson, and Kate Danaher, Editors; Proscenium Press; P.O. Box 361; Newark, DE 19715. This journal publishes poetry, drama, fiction, criticism, book reviews, and bibliographies of Irish interest.

The Scriblerian and the Kit Cats: A Newsjournal Devoted to Pope, Swift, and Their Circle. Peter A. Tasch, Arthur J. Weitzman, and Roy S. Wolper, Editors; English Department; Temple University; Philadelphia, PA 19122. This journal publishes notes, queries, illustrations, and ephemera on the Scriblerians and Kit-Cats and their acquaintances.

Shaw: The Annual of Bernard Shaw Studies: Fred D. Crawford, Editor; English Department; Central Michigan University; Mt. Pleasant, MI 48859. This journal publishes articles on George Bernard Shaw and his milieu.

Workshop Library on World Humor: Herb J. Cummings, President; P.O. Box 23334; Washington, D.C. 20026. This group supports studies relating to Irish humor, and one of their affiliates is called the Irish Bull Society, and is located in Cork, Ireland.

Yeats: An Annual of Critical and Textual Studies: Richard J. Finneran, and Mary FitzGerald, Editors; English Department; University of Tennessee; Knoxville, TN 37996. This journal publishes Yeats scholarship in the form of articles, notes, editions, and an annual bibliography of criticism.

Yeats Eliot Review: A Journal of Criticism and Scholarship: Russell Elliot Murphy, Editor; English Department; University of Arkansas; Little Rock, AR 72204. This journal is interested in research-based papers and notes on all aspects of Yeats and Eliot studies, including bibliographical updates, book reviews, and review articles.

Index

About the Author

DON L. F. NILSEN is Professor of English at Arizona State University and Executive Secretary of the International Society of Humor Studies. His previous publications include *Humor Scholarship: A Research Bibliography* (Greenwood Press, 1993).

ISBN 0-313-29551-4

HARDCOVER BAR CODE